Praise for *Financial Risk Management*

"This book is the best combination of detailed descriptions of financial products and math and practical knowledge of what risk management is all about that I have seen. Anyone intending to make a career in risk management would benefit greatly from this book. (As a risk manager, I'd also like to make it required reading for traders.)"
—**John Breit,**
Managing Director, Head of Market Risk Management, Merrill Lynch

"Risk is a multi-faceted hydra of infinite complexity. In taming this beast, this book deftly combines the wisdom of the ages with modern approaches such as static hedging. Anyone concerned with coping with calamity is advised to act."
—**Dr. Peter Carr,**
Courant Institute

"*Financial Risk Management* is an accessible compendium of the key concepts of risk management. I hated to put down the book, with its pleasant and compelling prose. The conceptual coverage runs from asset-backed bonds to zero rates, including definitions of all the key types of risk and ideas for managing them. The book is as up-to-date as the unfortunate disclosures at Allied Irish Bank in 2002. Not only senior risk managers who have arrived recently from other parts of the bank, but also the green, quantitatively adept staffers who deal daily with the bits and bytes of risk management, would find that Allen's book provides them the big picture of risk management, as well as terms and concepts that could take them years to encounter in the normal course of business."
—**William Margrabe,**
President, The William Margrabe Group, Inc., and also known as the Internet's "Dr. Risk"

Financial Risk
management

Copyright © 2003 by Steven Allen. All rights reserved.

Published by John Wiley & Sons, Inc., Hoboken, New Jersey.
Published simultaneously in Canada.

For general information on our other products and services, or technical support, please contact our Customer Care Department within the United States at 800-762-2974, outside the United States at 317-572-3993 or fax 317-572-4002.

Wiley also publishes its books in a variety of electronic formats. Some content that appears in print may not be available in electronic books.

For more information about Wiley products, visit our web site at www.wiley.com.

Designations used by companies to distinguish their products are often claimed as trademarks. In all instances where John Wiley & Sons, Inc. is aware of a claim, the product names appear in initial capital or all capital letters. Readers, however, should contact the appropriate companies for more complete information regarding trademarks and registration.

Library of Congress Cataloging-in-Publication Data:

Allen, Steven, 1945–
    Financial risk management: a practitioner's guide to managing market
and credit risk (with CD-ROM) / Steven Allen.
        p. cm.
Includes bibliographical references and index.
    ISBN 0-471-21977-0 (acid-free)
    1. Risk management. 2. Finance. I. Title
    HD61 .A43 2003
    658.15'5—dc21

                                                    2002014900

Printed in the United States of America.

10 9 8 7 6 5 4 3 2 1

Financial Risk management

A Practitioner's Guide to Managing Market and Credit Risk

STEVEN ALLEN

WILEY

John Wiley & Sons, Inc.

To Caroline
For all the ways she has helped bring
this project to fruition
And for much, much more

contents

foreword

I suspect that you, the reader, have experienced the nuances of financial risk management hands on. Are you a student, perhaps planning a trip abroad, who needs foreign currency yet can't decide between traveler's checks and credit cards? A professional trader who thrives on the adrenaline rush of making trading decisions in the face of unknowable consequences? Someone in senior management wrestling with complex financial matters and wishing for greater clarity in your decision process? You share the human drive to make the best decision possible despite your discomfort with its imprecise implications.

Perhaps because the potential rewards have been so great, great advances in financial risk management have been made in the last 30 years. Much of what has been written, however, leads to a vague feeling of dissatisfaction for the reader. Academic literature has been a rich source for understanding the risks in financial products and their interplay in portfolios, but much of this work is accessible only to the rarefied reader who is steeped in math. Practitioners have enhanced this work through more pragmatic approaches that take into account the complexity of human motivations and the crudeness of market mechanisms. But until this book, you would have been hard-pressed to find a voice that speaks for both.

You will find that this book gives you the opportunity to discover how the best and brightest think about, and execute on, risk. It covers a wide-ranging treatment of the evolution of thought about risk management. Unlike other works, though, this book provides a genuine window into sound risk management practices. And it covers it all, including:

- *Market risk*, from how to decompose a single complex deal to how to ensure your decisions are rational when confronted with a portfolio of exposures. Drawing on anecdotes, mathematical models, and understandable logic, the principles of measurement and control are laid out in a rigorous and appealing way.
- *Credit risk*, including how the growing acceptance of a risk/return-based pricing mechanism can dovetail with the most advanced risk mitiga-

tion techniques. This builds on more rudimentary credit approaches and moves toward more active portfolio management without compromising the importance of fundamental credit analysis.

■ *Operational risk management*, a playing field where the most cutting-edge innovators will gain a meaningful competitive edge in the future. This book helps explain how to drive practical improvements in your business processes.

Whether you read this book as a text for the student looking for insight based on the real world or as a guidebook for the perplexed professional in need of a real-time solution, your thinking will be richer. Drawing on three decades of experience, Steve Allen gives you an insider's view of how risk is managed. He also gives you a fascinating explanation of some of the greatest crises that Wall Street has faced during the last 30 years. He is, simply put, one of the most respected thinkers and doers in risk management today, the person who gets the call when his friends in the industry need advice.

Lesley Daniels Webster
Executive Vice President
Head of Market Risk Management
and Fiduciary Risk Management
JPMorgan Chase

preface

This book offers a detailed introduction to the field of risk management as performed at large investment and commercial banks, with an emphasis on the practices of specialist market risk and credit risk departments as well as trading desks. A large portion of these practices is also applicable to smaller institutions that engage in trading or asset management.

I designed this book to fill a gap I perceived in the available texts when I began teaching risk management. Several excellent books that cover the fundamentals of mathematical finance have been written, but they only briefly touch on the risk-management aspects of this topic, such as Hull (2002) and Jarrow and Turnbull (1999). The available texts devoted to risk management, such as Jorion (2001) and Crouhy, Galai, and Mark (2001), place almost all their attention on statistical techniques such as value at risk (VaR) and portfolio credit management, which, although important, represent only a small portion of risk management activities. One book that does an excellent job of looking at how mathematical finance is used in managing trading risk, Taleb (1997), focuses exclusively on the viewpoint of a trading desk and does not give any coverage to the activities of specialist risk-management departments.

My aim in this book is to be comprehensive in looking at the activities of risk-management specialists as well as trading desks, at the realm of mathematical finance as well as that of the statistical techniques, and, most importantly, at how these different approaches interact in an integrated risk-management process.

This book is designed to be used either as a text for a course in risk management or a resource for self-study or reference for people working in the financial industry. To make the material accessible to as broad an audience as possible, I have tried everywhere to supplement mathematical theory with concrete examples and have supplied spreadsheets on the accompanying CD-ROM to illustrate these calculations. At the same time, I have tried to make sure that all the mathematical theory that gets used in risk-management practice is addressed. For those readers who find the theory heavy going, I'll point out that the theoretical developments are confined almost wholly to Chapters 8 through 12. For other readers who want to pursue the theoretical developments at greater length, a full set of references has been provided.

Although many readers may already have a background in the instruments—bonds, stocks, futures, and options—used in the financial markets, I have supplied definitions every time I introduce a term. Terms are italicized in the text at the point they are defined, and these definitions are highlighted as bold in the index. Any reader feeling the need for a more thorough introduction to market terminology should find the first seven chapters of Hull (2002) adequate preparation for understanding the material in this book.

My presentation of the material is based both on theory and how concepts are utilized in industry practice. I have tried to provide many concrete instances of either personal experience or reports I have heard from industry colleagues to illustrate these practices. Where incidents have received sufficient previous public scrutiny or occurred long enough ago that issues of confidentiality are not a concern, I have provided concrete details. In other cases, I have had to preserve the anonymity of my sources by remaining vague about particulars. My preservation of anonymity extends to a liberal degree of randomness in references to gender.

I maintain a Web page at www.math.nyu.edu/fellows_fin_math/allen/book where readers may exchange opinions, have questions answered, find electronic links to all articles referenced in this book that can be found on the Web (and others of interest that may appear in the future), and receive downloads of updated or new spreadsheets as they become available.

acknowledgments

The views expressed in this book are my own, but have been shaped by my experiences in the financial industry. Many of my conclusions about what constitutes best practice in risk management have been based on my observation of and participation in the development of the risk management structure at JPMorgan Chase and its Chemical Bank and Chase Manhattan Bank predecessors.

The greatest influence on my overall view of how financial risk management should be conducted and on many of the specific approaches I advocate has been Lesley Daniels Webster. My close collaboration with Lesley has now been going on for close to 20 years, and in the past 7 years, I have reported to her in her position as director of market risk management. I wish to express my appreciation of Lesley's leadership, along with that of Marc Shapiro, Suzanne Hammett, and Andy Threadgold, for having established the standards of integrity, openness, thoroughness, and intellectual rigor that have been the hallmarks of this risk management structure.

Throughout most of the period in which I have been involved in these pursuits, Don Layton was the head of trading activities with which we interacted. His recognition of the importance of the risk management function and strong support for a close partnership between risk management and trading and the freedom of communication and information sharing were vital to the development of these best practices.

Through the years, my ideas have benefited from my colleagues at Chemical, Chase, and JPMorgan Chase. I would particularly like to note the strong contributions that dialogues with Bob Benjamin, Paul Bowmar, Fawaz Habel, Jeff Katz, Bobby Magee, Mike Rabin, and Barry Schachter have played in the development of the concepts utilized here. Many of the traders I have interacted with through the years have also had a major influence on my views of how risk management should impact decision making on the trading desk and the proper conduct of relationships between traders and risk management specialists. I particularly want to thank Andy Hollings, Simon Lack, Jeff Larsen, Dinsa Mehta, Fraser Partridge, and Don Wilson for providing me with prototypes for how the risk management of trading should be properly conducted and their generosity in sharing their knowledge and insight. I also wish to thank those traders, who shall remain anonymous here, who have provided me equally valuable lessons in risk management practices to avoid.

This book grew out of the risk management course I have now taught for five years as part of the Masters in Financial Mathematics program at New York University's Courant Institute of Mathematical Sciences. For giving me the opportunity to teach and providing an outstanding institutional setting in which to do it, I want to thank the administration and faculty of Courant, particularly Neil Chriss, director of the Masters in Financial Mathematics program, who recruited me into the Courant community. I have gained many insights that have found their way into this book by attending other courses in the program taught by Marco Avellaneda, Jim Gatheral, Bob Kohn, and Nassim Taleb. The students in my risk management course have helped clarify many of the concepts in this book through their probing questions. I particularly want to thank Otello Padovani, who began as my student and became my collaborator on research into static hedging techniques. Mike Fisher has provided greatly appreciated support as my graduate assistant in helping to clarify class assignments that have evolved into exercises in this book.

The detailed comments and suggestions I have received from Neil Chriss on large portions of this manuscript far exceed the norms of either friendship or collegiality. In numerous instances, his efforts have sharpened both the ideas being presented and the clarity of their expression. I also wish to thank Mich Araten, Peter Carr, Bobby Magee, Barry Schachter, Nassim Taleb, and Bruce Tuckman for reading the text and offering helpful comments.

I also wish to extend my thanks to Chuck Epstein for his help in finding a publisher for this book. Bill Falloon, my editor at Wiley, has offered very useful suggestions at every stage of the editing. At MacAllister Publishing Services, Andy Stone has been very helpful as production manager and Jeanne Henning has been a thorough and incisive copy editor. I also wish to thank RiskMetrics Group for generously making available five years of daily historical data, which has allowed me to create more realistic exercises.

The individual to whom both I and this book owe the greatest debt is my wife Caroline Thompson. The number of ways in which her beneficial influence has been felt surpass my ability to enumerate, but I at least need to attempt a brief sample. It was Caroline who introduced me to Neil Chriss and first planted the idea of my teaching at Courant. She has been a colleague of Neil's, Jonathan Goodman's, and mine in the continued development of the Courant Masters in Mathematical Finance program. From the start, she was the strongest voice in favor of basing a book on my risk management course. At frequent bottlenecks, when I have been daunted by an obstacle to my progress that seemed insurmountable, it was Caroline who suggested the approach, organized the material, or suggested the joint effort that overcame the difficulty. She has managed all aspects of the production, format, and style of the book, including efforts from such distant ports as Laos, Vietnam, and Holland.

CHAPTER 1

Introduction

1.1 THE CONTENTS OF THIS BOOK

In the television series *Seinfeld*, the character George Costanza gets an assignment from his boss to read a book titled *Risk Management* and then give a report on this topic to other business executives. Costanza finds the book and topic so boring that his only solution is to convince someone else to read it for him and prepare notes. One sign that the book is boring is that it begins with the question, "What is risk management?"

I have hopefully avoided beginning this book in as trite a fashion, but still need to say something about what this book will cover. Risk management at a financial firm is primarily concerned with financial risks—taking action to reduce the impact of an unfavorable move in market prices or avoiding a financial disaster like the simultaneous bankruptcy of a significant subset of a firm's outstanding loans. This is in sharp contrast to risk management for an industrial firm, which generally focuses on issues of physical risk—insuring against the risk that a machine will fail or avoiding a physical disaster such as an accident that pollutes the environment.

During the 1990s, an increased focus on the new technology being developed to measure and control financial risk has resulted in the growth of corporate staff areas manned by risk management professionals. However, this does not imply that financial firms did not manage risks prior to 1990 or that currently all risk management is performed in staff areas. Senior line managers such as trading desk and portfolio managers have always performed a substantial risk management function and continue to do so. In fact, confusion can be caused by the tradition of using the term *risk manager* as a synonym for a senior trader or portfolio manager and as a designation for members of corporate staff areas dealing with risk. Although this book will cover risk management techniques that are useful to both line trading managers and corporate staff acting on behalf of the firm's senior management, the needs of these individuals do not completely overlap. I will try to

1

always make a clear distinction between information that is useful to a trading desk and information that is needed by corporate risk managers, and explain how they might intersect.

Books and articles on financial risk management have tended to focus on statistical techniques embodied in measures such as value at risk (VaR). As a result, risk management has been accused of representing a very narrow specialty with limited value, a view that has been colorfully expressed by Nassim Taleb. "There has been growth in the number of 'risk management advisors,' an industry sometimes populated by people with an amateurish knowledge of risk. Using some form of shallow technical skills, these advisors emit pronouncements on such matters as 'risk management' without a true understanding of the distribution. Such inexperience and weakness become more apparent with the value-at-risk fad or the outpouring of books on risk management by authors who never traded a contract." (See Taleb [1997, p. 4].)

In this book, I will give a more balanced account of risk management. Less than 20 percent of the material looks at statistical techniques such as VaR. The bulk of the book examines issues such as the proper mark-to-market valuation of trading positions, the determination of necessary reserves against valuation uncertainty, the structuring of limits to control risk taking, and the review of mathematical models and determination of how they can contribute to risk control. This allocation of material mirrors the allocation of effort in the corporate risk management staff areas with which I am familiar. This is reflected in the staffing of these departments. More personnel is drawn from those with experience and expertise in trading and building models to support trading decisions than is drawn from a statistical or academic finance background.

The focus of this book will be on the management of those risks that a financial firm faces that can be successfully quantified. These risks come in primarily two types: market risk and credit risk. *Market risk* can be defined as the potential that changes in the market prices of an institution's holding may have an adverse effect on its financial condition. *Credit risk* is the risk of economic loss from the failure of an obligor to perform according to the terms and conditions of a contract or agreement. This failure can be due to its financial inability and/or unwillingness to perform.

A financial firm faces many other risks that are generally grouped together under the category of *operational risk*. These risks include operations risk, legal risk, reputational risk, accounting risk, funding liquidity risk, and enterprise risk.

I do not believe that a risk is less important because it is difficult to quantify, but my area of expertise and the intended audience for this book limit the amount of time that can usefully be spent on these topics. Still, the management of risk often intertwines these different categories of risk. Therefore,

I have devoted one chapter to a broad discussion of operational risk and how to manage it. Throughout the book, I will touch on operational risk considerations when they arise in connection with market or credit risk.

This book is divided into three parts: a general background to financial risk management, the details of market risk management, and the statistical techniques for managing portfolio risk for both market and credit risk.

- The general background section (Chapters 2 through 5) gives an institutional framework for understanding how risk arises in financial firms and how it is managed. Without understanding the different roles and motivations of traders, marketers, senior firm managers, corporate risk managers, bondholders, stockholders, and regulators, it is impossible to obtain a full grasp of the reasoning behind much of the machinery of risk management or even why it is necessary to manage risk. In this part, you will encounter key concepts risk managers have borrowed from the theory of insurance (such as moral hazard and adverse selection), decision analysis (such as the winner's curse), finance theory (such as the arbitrage principle), and in one instance even the criminal courts (the Ponzi scheme). A summary will be provided of some of the most prominent financial disasters of the past 25 years. These serve as case studies of failures in risk management and will be referenced throughout the book. This part also contains a chapter on operational risk.
- The part on market risk management (Chapters 5 through 10), by far the longest part of the book, gives a general introduction to methodology and then discusses its application to spot risk, forward risk, vanilla options risk, and exotic options risk. As each risk type is discussed, a detailed analysis of the models used to price these risks and how these models can be used to measure and control risk will be presented. Given the heavy reliance of all quantitative risk management on models, Chapter 6 is devoted to the concept of model risk and how to manage it.
- The part on managing portfolio risk (Chapters 11 and 12) will focus on VaR, stress testing, and the management of portfolio credit risk.

1.2 THE USE OF MATHEMATICS IN THIS BOOK

A thorough discussion of how mathematical models are used to measure and control risks must make heavy reference to the mathematics used in creating these models. Since excellent expositions of the mathematics exist, I do not propose to enter into extensive derivations of results that can readily be found elsewhere. Instead, I will concentrate on how these results are used in risk management and how the approximations to reality inevitable in any mathematical abstraction are dealt with in practice. I will provide references to the derivation of results. Wherever possible, I have used Hull (2002) as a reference, since it is the one work that can be found on the shelf of nearly every practitioner in the field of finance.

Although the material for this book was originally developed for a course taught within a mathematics department, I believe that virtually all of its material will be understandable to students in finance programs and business schools and practitioners with a comparable educational background. A key reason for this is that whereas derivatives mathematics often emphasizes the use of more mathematically sophisticated continuous time models, discrete time models are usually more relevant to risk management, since risk management is often concerned with the limits that real market conditions place on mathematical theory.

1.3   OVERVIEW

Since about 1975, a new field of financial mathematics has grown that has fundamentally transformed the pricing of derivative instruments. Closely linked with this development, a new theory for managing the risk of these derivative instruments has also grown—for example, techniques for managing uncertainty about the future by measuring the range of possible financial outcomes that can result from investor strategies involving derivatives and for developing strategies to achieve desired outcomes. These new techniques for risk management have broadened from their original application to derivatives to become general risk management techniques for all financial instruments, including stocks, bonds, loans, deposits, and foreign exchange (FX) contracts.

The bulk of this work has taken place in and been applied to the field of investment banking (along with the investment banking affiliates of large commercial banks), although large contributions have also come from the academic community. The acknowledged success this work has achieved has resulted in its application to investors, such as hedge funds, pension funds, and insurance companies, and the financial decisions of nonfinancial firms. Recent attempts have even been made to apply this theory to nonfinancial decisions—for example, whether or not to build a manufacturing plant through the development of a theory of *real options*. An introduction to the theory of real options can be found in Dixit and Pindyck (1994).

The theory and practice of financial risk management has its roots in the broader and older field of *decision analysis*, a structured way of approaching decision making that forms a subdiscipline of statistics, operations research, economics, and psychology. Raiffa (1970) is the classic introduction to this field, and Clemen (1996) provides a good, recent overview.

Is financial risk management just the application of these broader decision-analysis principles to the specific domain of decisions that financial firms face, such as banks, investment banks, and asset management firms? In some ways, this appears to be the case. Certainly, we can recognize many of the standard paradigms of decision analysis in financial risk management, such as the discussion of expected value, risk aversion, and risk reduction through diversification. However, financial risk management has one primary characteristic that distinguishes it from the broader field—its heavy reliance on using the market prices of various risks as a focal point.

Why is this characteristic so important? We'll go into more detail in a minute, but the short answer is that traditional decision analysis often bogs down due to the difficulties in correctly assessing the probabilities and measures of risk aversion it requires to arrive at a recommended decision. This makes it difficult for an individual to apply the theory and even harder for a group of individuals to utilize the theory to resolve different viewpoints. The great success of the theory of financial risk management has been its capability to substitute market prices that can be objectively determined for some (but not all) of the probabilities and risk aversion measures needed for decision analysis. This has enabled financial risk management to achieve far more precise results than traditional decision analysis and has opened a career path to quantitative analysts whose skills lend themselves to extracting precise consequences from such prices.

Let's look in more detail at why having market prices readily available makes such a large difference in how decision analysis is performed. To keep our analysis somewhat concrete, we will focus on a particular case—how a financial firm will decide whether or not to invest in a complex instrument. We will see how the nature of analyzing this decision changed with a heavier utilization of market prices in the analysis.

Let's start in the 1960s, before market prices were significantly used. The analysis, to the extent it was formalized at all, would have utilized classical decision-analysis techniques. Different possible future scenarios would be identified, with probabilities assigned to each scenario, P_S, such that $\sum_S P_S = 1$. For each scenario, a set of cash flows $F_{T,S}$ would be determined, which the investment would provide at future time T given scenario S. Given a set of discount factors, D_T, for known (risk-free) cash flows at time T, the value of the investment to the firm would be:

$$\sum_S U\left\{ \sum_T (F_{T,S} D_T P_S) \right\} \tag{1.1}$$

where U is the firm's utility function, representing its degree of risk aversion.

How does classical decision theory say we are supposed to determine these probabilities, the P_Ss? Historically, the dominant theories were to either assign equal probabilities to a set of cases that were considered equally probable on intuitive grounds (for example, assigning one-sixth probability to each side of a seemingly fair die) or assigning probabilities based on long-run observations of frequencies. However, the first of these two methods is obviously only applicable to a quite limited number of situations and the second of the two methods raises questions of how to determine which is the relevant series of observations to use in a particular case. Should you base your frequencies for the price movements of a particular stock on just the history of that stock or on the history of stocks within the same industry or country? Should price observations from 100 years ago be excluded as no longer relevant? The lack of clear standards for answering such questions has led most practitioners of decision analysis to favor a personalist or subjective approach to probabilities, in which probabilities are taken to represent a particular individual's betting odds. (A clear discussion of these competing theories can be found in French [1986], Sections 6.3– 6.6.)

Techniques for extracting senior managers' betting odds and utility functions are major components of classical decision analysis. In practice, it has generally been found that managers are quite uncomfortable with these procedures and find it difficult to pin down values that are sufficiently precise to enable decisions to be made. Exacerbating the problem is that risk aversion raises very small probabilities to great importance. A rare economic occurrence, such as a disastrous sequence of terrible weather conditions leading to severe shortages of some commodity, which would make very little contribution to an expected value calculation, might be an event that threatens a firm with bankruptcy and receives significant weight from a risk-averse utility function. However, experiments have shown that almost all individuals perform extremely poorly at estimating probabilities for rare events, since the very rarity of the event implies that they seldom get feedback that enables them to correct errors.

Traditional decision analysis, which focuses on a single individual's decision-making process, faces its greatest challenges in dealing with the lack of coherence people often show in reaching decisions. Considerable machinery needs to be invented to try to impose some minimum standards of consistency on an individual's judgments, without which no genuine analytical theory would be possible. For example, an individual's decisions need to be consistent with a subjective probability measure that obeys the standard probability axioms, so that the well-developed mathematical machinery of probability and statistics can be utilized when analyzing these decisions. However, it is notoriously hard to get people to make decisions that are consistent with a subjective probability measure. (See, for example, discussions in Dawes [1988, pp. 165–167], concerning the Ellsberg paradox.) To deal with this problem, traditional decision analysis tries to get a person to modify some of his judgments by showing how the unmodified judgments can lead to the undesirable situation of allowing arbitrage, which can permit a return with no risk to someone who bets against the person in question (these are known as *Dutch book* or *money pump* arguments; see, for example, Lindley [1985, pp. 50–51] or French [1986, pp. 223–224]).

However, people often find it difficult to modify strongly held inconsistent judgments, even when faced with such arguments. This has led to a substantial literature on behavioral decision analysis. (See, for example, Kagel and Roth [1995], Thaler [1992], and Thaler [1993].) Daniel Kahneman and Vernon Smith won the Nobel Prize in economics in 2002 for work in behavioral decision theory.

To illustrate how frustrating attempts to apply traditional decision analysis can sometimes be, let me draw on a personal example. Several years ago, when I worked at Chase Manhattan, there was a manager whose job it was to quote the interest rates at which departments within the firm making loans would be charged for the use of money and at which departments within the firm taking deposits would be credited for the supply of money. He had been performing this job well for many years. Faced with a new product—deposits that had a forward-starting date—he very naturally quoted rates based on his best economic forecast of what rates would prevail in the market at that future time. However, often these quotes would be out of line with the rates that a theory based on financial arbitrage would arrive at by decomposing the forward-starting deposit into a standard deposit to the end date of the forward-starting deposit and a standard loan to the start date of the forward-starting deposit. This was proving frustrating to some of the firm's business managers, so I was dispatched to try to persuade the gentleman in question to bring his views into line with financial theory.

Armed with a background in traditional decision analysis, I was confident I could utilize a Dutch book argument to do the persuading. I carefully illustrated how the quotes he was giving for standard loan and deposit products in conjunction with the quotes he was giving at the same time for forward deposits would enable a department to place a 5-year loan and receive a 2-year deposit and a 3-year forward deposit starting in 2 years, a combination that would not require any net use or supply of money, and make a net profit based on his price quotations. They could just do as much of this business as they liked and make an unlimited amount of profit based on this inconsistency in pricing. Faced with what I thought to be an irresistible argument, his reply was simply, "I wouldn't let them do that."

The actual decision-making process in a large firm will often quickly degenerate into a highly politicized process. In the absence of precise guidelines for determining probabilities and utility functions, the temptation is strong (and seldom resisted) for proponents of a particular action to tweak probabilities and utilities until they find values that support their point of view. For example, a team that has been working on putting together the structure of a complex investment has strong psychological and financial motivation to find arguments to support the desirability of going ahead with the investment. If an initial study shows that the investment is undesirable, a bit of sensitivity analysis can determine how much probability assumptions and utility measures need to be altered to support approval of the investment. It is easy for a motivated team to convince itself of the rightness of their new assumptions. The persuasion of other decision makers may then hinge on internal political power.

The revolution in analysis that transformed the financial markets in the 1970s and early 1980s was the replacement of much of the subjective judgment about probabilities and utilities with actual market prices at which contingent cash flows (scenario-dependent cash flows) could be purchased and sold. This revolution, which we'll study in more detail in Chapters 8, 9, and 10, consisted of two mutually reinforcing trends: the growth of publicly traded markets in contingent claims such as options and the development of arbitrage-based analytic techniques for determining combinations of publicly traded contingent claims that could come close to reproducing complex scenario-dependent instruments. These two components were mutually reinforcing because the advances in analysis led to a greater demand for publicly traded contingent claims, as more users of complex instruments were motivated to use them for reducing uncertainty, while the availability of more publicly traded hedging instruments widened the scope of the building blocks available for arbitrage analysis. Although the development of arbitrage-based analytic techniques did not begin or end with the Black-Scholes model of 1974, this did represent a watershed event. It introduced dynamic hedging with publicly traded instruments as a technique for replicating the payoff profiles of complex instruments that are not publicly traded.

The use of publicly traded instruments to create close replications of complex instruments greatly reduced the need for subjective probability estimates and utility functions, which were now needed only to cover the remaining gaps left by imperfect replication. This significantly reduced the scope for the political manipulation of results and expanded the influence of mathematically trained personnel who could provide the relatively objective arbitrage analysis that was required.

Arbitrage analysis can be represented in many different but mutually consistent ways. One way, which is emphasized by the risk-neutral valuation approach (see, for example, Hull [2002, Section 12.7]), is to analyze the value of a complex scenario-dependent transaction by the equation:

$$\sum_S \sum_T (F_{T,S} D_T P_S) \qquad (1.2)$$

Note that Equation 1.2 is the same as Equation 1.1, except for two differences: the utility function U has now been dropped since the use of replication has to some degree of approximation eliminated uncertainty, and the P_Ss are now probabilities that reproduce the values of publicly traded instruments. As is often emphasized, these are not true probabilities in the sense of representing anybody's views of the future, not even an average view of market participants (see, for example, Baxter and Rennie [1996, p. 16]). Rather they are pseudo-probabilities (weights that add up to one and reproduce values that can be achieved by hedging in the publicly traded market). As such, the argument for using these values as probabilities is only as strong as the extent that hedging with these publicly traded instruments is truly an available alternative.

Of course, it is only an approximation to view instruments as being publicly traded or not. The volume of instruments available for trading differs widely by size and readiness of availability. This constitutes the depth of liquidity of a given market. Often a firm will be faced with a choice between the risks of replicating positions more exactly with less liquid instruments or less exactly with more liquid instruments.

A dominant theme of this book will be the trade-off between liquidity risk and basis risk. *Liquidity risk* is the risk that the price at which you buy (or sell) something may be significantly higher (lower) than the price you could have achieved under more ideal conditions. *Basis risk* is the risk that occurs when you buy one product and sell another closely related one, and the two prices behave differently. Let's look at an example. Suppose you are holding a large portfolio of stocks that do not trade that frequently and your outlook for stock prices leads to a desire to quickly terminate the position. If you try selling the whole basket quickly, you face significant liquidity risk since your selling may depress the prices at which the stocks trade. An alternative would be to take an offsetting position in a heavily traded stock futures contract, such as the futures contract tied to the Standards and Poor's (S&P) stock index. This lowers the liquidity risk, but increases the basis risk since changes in the price of your particular stock basket will probably differ from the price changes in the stock index. Often the only way in which liquidity risk can be reduced is to increase basis risk, and the only way in which basis risk can be reduced is to increase liquidity risk.

A useful categorization to make in risk management techniques, following Gumerlock (1999), is to distinguish between risk management through risk aggregation and risk management through risk decomposition. *Risk aggregation* attempts to reduce risk by creating portfolios of less than completely correlated risk, thereby achieving risk reduction through diversification. *Risk decomposition* attempts to reduce risk by analyzing a risk that cannot directly be priced in the market into subcomponents, all or some of which can be priced in the market. This book studies both of these types of risk management techniques—risk decomposition is discussed primarily in Chapters 5 through 10 and risk aggregation is discussed primarily in Chapters 11 and 12. However, although much of the recent focus in the risk management literature has been on risk aggregation approaches such as VaR and risk-adjusted return on capital (RAROC), more space in this book will be devoted to risk decomposition, which I believe is the more fundamental of the two approaches for the following two reasons:

- Since I have argued that the fundamental advantage of financial risk management over more general risk management is that it can utilize market prices in place of subjective probabilities and risk aversion measures, risk decomposition, by extending the use of market prices to a wider class of risks, significantly broadens the scope of this fundamental advantage.
- Risk aggregation measures are critically dependent on the ability to obtain market prices for the risks to be aggregated. For example, VaR measures must be built up from historical observations of correlated movements in market prices. If the prices used only represent subjective judgments of the value of instruments rather than actual prices in the market at which risks can be extinguished, then a measure of the risk of price change over a 1-day, 1-week, or 1-month time period really doesn't give much information. If the valuation at the end of the period is just as subjective as the valuation at the beginning of the period, how beneficial is it to know the amount by which this valuation can change? It's the knowledge that senior managers (or outside decision makers such as lenders or boards of directors) can insist on the liquidation of risk at known prices at the end of a period that gives real meaning to the risk that this value will change during a period in which traders have been ceded control over the portfolio. Risk decomposition broadens the range of instruments for which market pricing can be obtained and therefore effectively be addressed in risk aggregation.

Historically, risk decomposition has achieved significant results in two primary areas. The first is the pricing of forward commitments for definite payments, the realm of interest rate valuation. The second is the pricing of contingent commitments, the realm of option pricing. In both cases, the large number of contracts that are traded, with payments due on numerous different dates, products consisting of combinations of many different payments, and options written for a wide combination of dates and strike prices, makes it virtually impossible to obtain direct market quotes for more than a small fraction of the instruments in a given firm's portfolio. Risk decomposition techniques must be used to derive market prices for the full portfolio from the market prices available for select instruments. We will examine these techniques in detail in Chapters 8, 9, and 10, which discuss managing forward risk, vanilla options risk, and exotic options risk, respectively.

CHAPTER 2

Institutional Background

A financial firm is, among other things, an institution that employs the talents of a variety of different people, each with her own individual set of talents and motivations. As the size of an institution grows, it becomes more difficult to organize these talents and motivations to permit the achievement of common goals. Even small financial firms, which minimize the complexity of interaction of individuals within the firm, must arrange relationships with lenders, regulators, stockholders, and other stakeholders in the firm's results.

Since financial risk occurs in the context of this interaction between individuals with conflicting agendas, it should not be surprising that corporate risk managers spend a good deal of time thinking about organizational behavior or that their discussions about mathematical models used to control risk often focus on the organizational implications of these models. Indeed, if you take a random sample of the conversations of senior risk managers within a financial firm, you will find as many references to *moral hazard*, *adverse selection*, and *Ponzi scheme* (terms dealing primarily with issues of organizational conflict) as you will find references to *delta*, *standard deviation*, and *stochastic volatility*.

For an understanding of the institutional realities that constitute the framework in which risk is managed, it is best to start with the concept of moral hazard, which lies at the heart of these conflicts.

2.1 MORAL HAZARD—INSIDERS AND OUTSIDERS

The following is a definition of *moral hazard* taken from Kotowitz (1989):

> *Moral hazard may be defined as actions of economic agents in maximizing their own utility to the detriment of others, in situations where they do not bear the full consequences or, equivalently, do not enjoy the full benefits of their actions **due to uncertainty and incomplete or restricted contracts** which prevent the assignment of **full** damages (benefits) to the agent responsible. . . . Agents may possess informational*

advantages of hidden actions or hidden information or there may be excessive costs in writing detailed contingent contracts. . . . Commonly analyzed examples of hidden actions are workers' efforts, which cannot be costlessly monitored by employers, and precautions taken by the insured to reduce the probability of accidents and damages due to them, which cannot be costlessly monitored by insurers. . . . Examples of hidden information are expert services—such as physicians, lawyers, repairmen, managers, and politicians.

In the context of financial firm risk, moral hazard most often refers to the conflict between insiders and outsiders based on a double-edged asymmetry. Information is asymmetrical—the insiders possess superior knowledge and experience. The incentives are also asymmetrical—the insiders have a narrower set of incentives than the outsiders have. This theme repeats itself at many levels of the firm.

Let's begin at the most basic level. For any particular group of financial instruments that a firm wants to deal in, whether it consists of stocks, bonds, loans, forwards, or options, the firm needs to employ a group of experts who specialize in this group of instruments. These experts will need to have a thorough knowledge of the instrument that can rival the expertise of the firm's competitors in this segment of the market. Inevitably, their knowledge of the sector will exceed that of other employees of the firm. Even if it didn't start that way, the experience gained by day-to-day dealings in this group of instruments will result in information asymmetry relative to the rest of the firm. This information asymmetry becomes even more pronounced when you consider information relative to the particular positions in those instruments into which the firm has entered. The firm's experts have contracted for these positions and will certainly possess a far more intimate knowledge of them than anyone else inside or outside the firm. A generic name used within financial firms for this group of experts is the *front office*. A large front office may be divided among groups of specialists: those who negotiate transactions with clients of the firm, who are known as *salespeople, marketers*, or *structurers*; those who manage the positions resulting from these negotiated transactions, who are known as *traders, position managers*, or *risk managers*; and those who produce research, models, or systems supporting the process of decision making, who are known as *researchers* or *technologists*.

However, this group of experts still requires the backing of the rest of the firm in order to be able to generate revenue. Some of this dependence may be a need to use the firm's offices and equipment; specialists in areas like tax, accounting, law, and transactions processing; and access to the firm's client base. However, these are services that can always be contracted for. The vital need for backing is the firm's ability to absorb potential losses that would result if the transactions do not perform as expected.

A forceful recent illustration of this dependence is the case of Enron, which in 2001 was a dominant force in trading natural gas and electricity, being a party to about 25 percent of all trades executed in these markets. Enron's experts in trading these products and the Web-enabled computer system they had built to allow clients to trade online were widely admired throughout the industry. However, when Enron was forced to declare bankruptcy by a series of financing and accounting improprieties that were largely unrelated to natural gas and electricity trading, their dominance in these markets was lost overnight.

Why? The traders and systems that were so widely admired were still in place. Their reputation may have been damaged somewhat based on speculation that the company's reporting was not honest and their trading operation was perhaps not as successful as had been reported. However, this would hardly be enough to produce such a large effect. What happened was an unwillingness of trading clients to deal with a counterparty that might not be able to meet its future contractual obligations. Without the backing of the parent firm's balance sheet, its stockholder equity, and its ability to borrow, the trading operation could not continue.

So now we have the incentive asymmetry to set off the information asymmetry. The wider firm, which is less knowledgeable in this set of instruments than the group of front-office experts, must bear the full financial loss if the front office's positions perform badly. The moral hazard consists of the possibility that the front office may be more willing to risk the possibility of large losses in which it will not have to fully share in order to create the possibility of large gains in which it will have a full share. And the rest of the firm may not have sufficient knowledge of the front office's positions, due to the information asymmetry, to be sure that this has not occurred.

What are some possible solutions? Could a firm just purchase an insurance contract against trading losses? This is highly unlikely. An insurance firm would have even greater concerns about moral hazard because they would not have as much access to information as those who are at least within the same firm, even if they are less expert. Could the firm decide to structure the pay of the front office so that it will be the same no matter what profits are made on their transactions, removing the temptation to take excessive risk to generate potential large gains? They could, but experience in financial firms strongly suggests the need for upside participation as an incentive to call forth the efforts needed to succeed in a highly competitive environment.

Inevitably, the solution seems to be an ongoing struggle to balance the proper incentive with the proper controls. This is the very heart of the design of a risk-management regime. If the firm exercises too little control, the opportunities for moral hazard may prove too great. If it exercises too much control, it may pass up good profit opportunities if those who do not have as much knowledge as the front office make the decisions. To try to achieve the best balance, the firm will employ experts in risk-management disciplines such as market risk, credit risk, legal risk, and operations risk. It will set up independent support staff to process the trades and maintain the records of positions and payments (the *back office*); report positions against limits, calculate the daily profit and loss (P&L), and analyze the sources of P&L and risk (the *middle office*); and take responsibility for the accuracy of the firm's books and records (the *finance* function). However, the two-sided asymmetry of information and incentive will always exist as the personnel in these control and support functions will lack the specialized knowledge that the front office possesses in their set of instruments.

The two-sided asymmetry that exists at this basic level can be replicated at other levels of the organization, depending on the size and complexity of the firm. The informational disadvantage of the manager of fixed income products relative to the front office for European bonds will be mirrored by the informational disadvantage of the manager of all trading products relative to the manager of fixed income products and the firm's CEO relative to the manger of all trading products.

Certainly, the two-sided asymmetry will be replicated in the relationship between the management of the firm and those who monitor the firm from the outside. Outside monitors primarily represent three groups—the firm's creditors (lenders and bondholders), the firm's shareholders, and governments. All three of these groups have incentives that differ from the firm's management as they are exposed to losses based on the firm's performance in which the management will not fully share.

The existence of incentive asymmetry for creditors is reasonably obvious. If the firm does well, the creditors get their money back, but have no further participation in how well the firm performs; if the firm does very badly and goes bankrupt, the creditors have substantial, possibly even total, loss of the amount lent. By contrast, the firm's shareholders and management have full participation when the firm performs well, but liability in bankruptcy is limited to the amount originally invested. When we examine credit risk in Section 12.2.3, this will be formally modeled as the creditors selling a put option on the value of the firm to the shareholders. Since all options create nonlinear (hence asymmetric) payoffs, we have a clear source of incentive asymmetry for creditors.

It is less clear whether incentive asymmetry exists for shareholders. In principle, their interests are supposed to be exactly aligned with those of the firm's management, and stock-value-based incentives for management are used to strengthen this alignment. In practice, it is always possible that management will take more risk than shareholders would be completely comfortable with in the hope of collecting incentive-based compensation in good performance years that does not have to be returned in bad performance years. Kotowitz (1989) quotes Adam Smith from *Wealth of Nations*: "The directors of such companies, however, being managers rather of other peoples' money than of their own, it cannot well be expected, that they should watch over it with the same anxious vigilance with which the partners in a private company frequently watch over their own."

Government involvement arises from the asymmetric dangers posed to the health of the overall economy by the failure of a financial firm. If an implicit government guarantee is given to rescue large financial firms from bankruptcy (the notion of "too big to fail"), then moral hazard is created through management's knowledge that they can try to create profit opportunities, in which the government has only limited participation through taxes, by taking risks of losses that will need to be fully absorbed by the government. If the government is not willing to prevent the failure of large financial firms, then it will want to place restrictions on the externalities that those firms can create by not having to bear their share of the cost to the overall economy of the firm's potential bankruptcy.

In all three cases of moral hazard involving outside monitors, the information asymmetry is even more severe than when the information asymmetry takes place wholly inside the firm. Senior management and its risk monitors are at least on the premises, involved in day-to-day business with more junior managers, and can utilize informal measures, such as the rotation of managers through different segments of the firm, to attempt to diffuse both incentives and knowledge. Outside monitors will have only occasional contact with the firm and must rely mostly on formal requirements to obtain cooperation.

Let us look at some of the outside monitors that creditors, shareholders, and governments rely on:

- In addition to their own credit officers, creditors rely on rating agencies such as Moody's and Standard & Poor's (S&P) to obtain information about and make judgment on the creditworthiness of borrowers.
- Shareholders and creditors rely on investment analysts working for investment bankers and brokerage firms to obtain information about and make judgments on the future earnings prospects and share value of firms. Although neither ratings agencies nor investment analysts have any official standing with which to force cooperation from the firms they analyze, their influence with lenders and investors in bonds and stocks gives them the leverage to obtain cooperation and access to information.

- Governments can use their regulatory powers to require access to information from financial firms and employ large staffs to conduct examinations of the firms. For example, for the U.S. government, the Federal Reserve System and the Comptroller of the Currency conduct examinations of commercial banks. A similar function is performed by the Securities and Exchange Commission (SEC) for investment banks.
- Creditors, shareholders, and governments all rely on independent accounting firms to conduct audits of the reliability of the financial information disclosures that are required of all publicly held firms.

Over the years, many critical questions have been raised about how truly independent the judgment of these outside monitors really is:

- Credit rating agencies have been accused of being too slow to downgrade ratings in response to adverse changes in a firm's financial condition because their source of revenue comes from the firms whose debt they rate.
- Similarly, independent auditors have been suspected of being too deferential to the firms they monitor since these firms are the ones who pay their audit fees and hire them for consulting services. The fear is that the desire for more revenue will blunt objections to companies choosing accounting methods that cast their results in a favorable light.
- Investment banks have a built-in conflict of interest from competing for the business of the firms whose performance their investment analysts are monitoring. It has long been noted that analysts' buy recommendations far outnumber sell recommendations.
- Accusations have been leveled that government regulatory agencies are more concerned with protecting the interests of the firms being monitored than with protecting the public interest. These charges have particular force when personnel flow freely between employment in the regulatory agencies and in the firms they regulate.

All of these criticisms seem to be coming to a head in 2002, amid the scandals involving the now defunct auditing firm of Arthur Anderson, Enron's declaration of bankruptcy only a week after being rated investment grade, and the massive declines in the stock values of technology firms highly touted by investment analysts. Some useful reforms will no doubt be undertaken, such as forbidding auditing firms to sell consulting services to a firm they audit and not allowing the bonuses of investment analysts to be tied to investment banking fees collected from clients whose stocks they cover. However, the basic sources of conflict of interest remain, and investors and lenders will continue to need to employ a skeptical filter when utilizing input from outside monitors.

Although the conflicts between insiders and outsiders due to the two-sided asymmetry of moral hazard cannot be eliminated, a frank understanding by both sides can lead to a cooperative relationship. In a cooperative relationship, insiders will acknowledge the need to have outsiders exercise controls and will voluntarily share information and knowledge with outsiders. In a cooperative relationship, outsiders will acknowledge their need to learn from the insiders and will ease controls in response to a track record of openness, although both must recognize the need to always have some level of controls (the ancient folk wisdom states that "I trust my grandmother, but I still cut the cards when she deals").

A lack of understanding of moral hazard can lead to an uncooperative relationship fueled by mutual resentments between an insider, such as a trader or structurer, with an outsider, such as a corporate risk manager or regulator. An insider who does not understand the purely situational need to have someone less knowledgeable "look over my shoulder" will attribute it to an insulting lack of personal trust, an arrogant assumption of more knowledge than the outsider possesses, or a simple desire by the outsider to create a job or grab power (which is not to say that some of these motivations do not exist in reality, mixed in with the need to control moral hazard). The insider's response will then probably be to withhold information, obfuscate, and mislead, which will drive the outsider to even closer scrutiny and more rigid controls, which is clearly a prescription for a vicious circle of escalation. An outsider who lacks an understanding of the situation may defensively try to pretend to have more knowledge than he has or denigrate the knowledge of the insider, which will only exacerbate any suspicions of the process the insider has.

Moral hazard has long been a key concept in the analysis of insurance risks. A typical example would be an insurance company's concern that an individual who has purchased insurance against auto theft will not exercise as much care in guarding against theft (for example, parking in a garage rather than on the street) as one who has not purchased insurance. If the insurance company could distinguish between individuals who exercise extra care and those who don't, it could sell separate contracts to the two types of individuals and price the extra losses into just the type sold to those exercising less care. However, the information advantage of an individual monitoring his own degree of care relative to the insurance company's ability to monitor it makes this prohibitively expensive. So the insurance company needs to settle for cruder measures, such as establishing a deductible loss that the insured person must pay in the event of theft, thereby aligning the interests of the insured more closely with the insurer.

It has become increasingly common for moral hazard to be cited in analyses of the economics of firms in general, particularly in connection with the impact of the limited liability of shareholders willing to take larger gambles. The shareholders know that if the gamble succeeds, they will avoid bankruptcy and share in the profits, but will suffer no greater loss in a large bankruptcy than in a smaller one. To quote W. S. Gilbert:

You can't embark on trading too tremendous,
It's strictly fair and based on common sense,
If you succeed, your profits are stupendous,
And if you fail, pop goes your eighteenpence.
(from Gilbert & Sullivan's Utopia, Limited*)*

A firm's creditors can exercise some control over their actions and might be able to forbid such gambles, assuming they have sufficient knowledge of the nature of the firm's investments. This is where the informational advantage of the managers over the creditors with respect to the firm's investments comes in.

What sort of actions can we expect from a trader based on the concept of moral hazard? We can certainly expect that the trader may have a different degree of risk aversion than the firm's management, since her participation in favorable results exceeds her participation in downside results. Taleb (1997, p. 66) refers to this as the trader "owning an option on his profits" and states that in such circumstances "it is always optimal to take as much risk as possible. An option is worth the most when volatility is highest." This will probably become even more noticeable if the trader has been having a poor year. Knowing that she is headed toward a minimal bonus and possible dismissal may incline the trader to "swing for the fences" and take a large risk. The trader knows that if the risk turns out favorably, it might be enough to reverse previous losses and earn a bonus. If it turns out poorly, then "you can't get less than a zero bonus" and "you can't get fired twice." (You can damage your reputation in the industry, but sharing information about a trader's track record between competitor firms cannot be done that efficiently—more information asymmetry.) For this reason, firms may severely cut the trading limits of a trader having a poor year.

Beyond the differences in risk aversion, moral hazard can even result in the perverse behavior (for the firm) of having a trader willing to increase risk exposure when faced with a lower expected return. Consider the following advice to traders from Taleb (1997, p. 65):

How aggressive a trader needs to be depends highly on his edge, or expected return from the game:

- *When the edge is positive (the trader has a positive expected return from the game, as is the case with most market makers), it is always best to take the minimum amount of risk and let central limit slowly push the position into profitability. This is the recommended method for market makers to progressively increase the stakes, in proportion to the accumulated profits. In probability terms, it is better to mini-mize the volatility to cash-in on the drift.*

- *When the edge is negative, it is best to be exposed as little as possible to the negative drift. The operator should optimize by taking as much risk as possible. Betting small would ensure a slow and certain death by letting central limit catch up on him.*

The mathematics and economic incentives that this advice is based on are certainly sound. It is advice (which ought to be) known to every gambler and is well founded in statistical theory. When the odds are in your favor, place many small bets; when the odds are against you, place one large bet. Essentially, when the odds are against you, you are attempting to minimize the length of time you are playing against the house since you are paying a tax, in the form of a expected loss, for the privilege of playing.

However, although this makes perfect economic sense from the view-point of the individual trader, it is hardly the strategy the firm employing the trader would want to see her follow. The firm, whose P&L will be the sum of the results of many traders, would like to see traders with a negative expected return not take any positions at all rather than have these be the traders taking on the most risk. To the extent the firm's management can fig-ure out which traders have a negative edge, they will restrict their risk tak-ing through limits and the replacement of personnel. However, the individual trader has the information advantage in knowing more than the firm about her expected return. The trader also has the asymmetrical incentive to take larger risks in this case, even though it will probably hurt the firm. The trader will not derive much benefit from the firm doing well if she does not con-tribute to that result, but the trader will benefit if she does increase her risk and wins against the odds.

Moral hazard helps to explain the valuation that investors place on the earnings volatility of financial firms. You could argue that firms should just worry about the expected value and not about volatility, since the market should only place a risk premium on risk that it cannot hedge away (if an investor wants less risk, he will just take the highest expected return stock and diversify by mixing with government bonds). However, empirical evi-dence shows that the market places a stiff discount on variable trading earn-ings. The reason may be information asymmetry. It is hard for outsiders to tell whether a firm is taking sound gambles to maximize expected value or is maximizing its insiders' option on one-way bets. Perold (1998) states that:

I view financial intermediaries as being special in several ways: First, these firms are in credit-sensitive businesses, meaning that their cus-tomers are strongly risk-averse with respect to issuer default on con-tractually promised payoffs. (For example, policyholders are averse to

*having their insurance claims be subject to the economic performance of
the issuing firm, and strictly prefer to do business with a highly rated
insurer.) The creditworthiness of the intermediary is crucial to its ability
to write many types of contracts, and contract guarantees feature importantly in its capital structure.*

*Second, financial firms are opaque to outsiders. They tend to be in busi-
nesses that depend vitally on proprietary financial technology and that
cannot be operated transparently. In addition, the balance sheets of
financial firms tend to be very liquid, and are subject to rapid change.
Financial firms, thus, are difficult to monitor, and bear significant dead-
weight costs of capital. Guarantors face costs related to adverse selection and moral hazard . . .*

*Third, financial firms are also internally opaque. Information tends to
be private at the business unit level, or even at the level of individual
employees such as traders. Efficient management of these firms thus
involves significant use of performance-related compensation to mitigate
against monitoring difficulty.*

Moral hazard can create a battleground over information between insiders and outsiders. Insiders are fearful that any information obtained by outsiders will be used as a tool to tighten controls over insiders' actions. Insiders
can be expected to have an inherent bias against tighter controls, partly
because narrowing the range of actions available leads to suboptimal solutions and partly because incentive asymmetry makes riskier action more
rewarding to insiders than outsiders. One of the most common ways in
which insiders can mislead outsiders about the need for controls is termed a
Ponzi scheme.

2.2 PONZI SCHEMES

In its original meaning, a *Ponzi scheme* is a criminal enterprise in which
investors are tricked into believing that they will receive very high returns on
their investments by having early investors paid out at high rates of return
with payment coming from the cash invested by later investors. The illusion
of high return can be pretty convincing. After all, you can actually see the
early investors receiving their high return in cash, and the con men running
the scheme can produce very plausible lies about the purported source of the
returns. As a result, the pace of new investment can be intense, enabling the
illusion of profit to be maintained over a fairly long time period. It's a vicious
cycle—the eagerness of new investors to place money in the scheme leads to
the heightened ability to make investments appear highly profitable, which
leads to even greater eagerness of new investors. However, ultimately, any

Ponzi scheme must collapse as there is no ultimate source of investment return (in fact, investment return is quite negative, as the flow of new investment must also be partially diverted to the criminals profiting from it). Ponzi schemes are also sometimes called *pyramid schemes* and bear a close resemblance to chain letter frauds.

The original meaning of Ponzi schemes has been broadened by risk managers to include situations in which firms are misled as to the profitability of a business line by the inadequate segregation of profits on newly acquired assets and returns on older assets.

Let's consider a typical example. Suppose a trading desk has entered into marketing a new type of path-dependent option. The desk expects substantially more customer demand for buying these options than for selling them. They intend to manage the resulting risk with dynamic hedging using forwards and more standard options. As we will see when discussing path-dependent options in Section 10.3, it is very difficult to try to estimate in advance how successful a dynamic hedging strategy for path-dependent options will be.

In such circumstances, the pricing of the option to the client must be based on an estimate of the future cost of the dynamic hedging, applying some conservatism to try to cover the uncertainty. Let's assume that a typical trade has a 7-year maturity, and that the customer pays $8 million and the firm pays $5 million to purchase the initial hedge. Of the remaining $3 million, we'll assume that the desk is estimating dynamic hedging costs of $1 million over the 2 years, but the uncertainty of these costs leads to setting up a $2 million initial allowance (or reserve) to cover the hedging costs, leaving $1 million to be booked as up-front profit.

Suppose the trading desk has made a serious error in predicting the hedging costs and hedging costs actually end up around $5 million, leading to a net loss of $2 million on every transaction booked. You may not be able to do anything about deals already contracted, but you would at least hope to get feedback from the losses encountered on these deals in time to stop booking new deals or else raise your price to a more sustainable level. This should happen if P&L reporting is adequately detailed, so that you can see the losses mounting up on the hedging of these trades (this is called *hedge slippage*).

However, it is often difficult to keep track of exactly how to allocate a day's trading gains and losses to the book of deals being hedged. You want to at least know that trading losses are occurring so that you can investigate the causes. The most severe problem would be if you didn't realize that trades were losing money. How could this happen? If P&L reporting is not adequately differentiated between the existing business and new business, then the overall trading operation can continue to look profitable by just doing enough new business. Every time a new deal is booked, $1 million goes immediately into P&L. Of course, the more deals that are booked, the larger the hedging losses that must be overcome, so even more new trades are needed to swamp the hedging losses. The resemblance to a Ponzi scheme should now be obvious.

One key difference is that in its original meaning, the Ponzi scheme is a deliberate scam. The financial situation described is far more likely to arise without any deliberate intent. However, the front office, based on its close knowledge of the trading book, will often suspect that this situation exists before any outsiders do, but may not want to upset the apple cart. They would be jeopardizing bonuses that can be collected up front on presumed earnings. They may also be willing to take the risk that they can find a way to turn the situation around based on their greater participation in future upside than future downside. They may choose to hide the situation from outsiders who they suspect would not give them the latitude to take such risks. So moral hazard can turn an accidentally originated Ponzi scheme into one that is very close to deliberate.

As an historical footnote, the Ponzi scheme derives its name from Charles Ponzi, a Boston-based swindler of the 1920s. The following account is drawn from Sifakis (1982):*

> [Ponzi] discovered he could buy up international postal-union reply coupons at depressed prices and sell them in the United States at a profit up to 50 percent. It was, in fact, a classic get-rich-slowly operation, and as such, it bored Ponzi. So he figured out a better gimmick. He simply told everyone he was making the money and said he needed a lot of capital to make a lot of money. For the use of the funds, he offered investors a 50 percent profit in three months. It was an offer they couldn't refuse, and the funds just came rolling into Ponzi's Boston office. In a short time, he had to open offices in neighboring states.
>
> When Ponzi actually started paying out interest, a deluge followed. On one monumental day in 1920, Ponzi's offices took in an incredible $2 million from America's newest gamblers, the little people who squeezed money out of bank accounts, mattresses, piggy banks, and cookie jars. There were days when Ponzi's office looked like a hurricane had hit it. Incoming cash had to be stuffed in closets, desk drawers and even wastebaskets. Of course, the more that came in, the more Ponzi paid out. . . .
>
> As long as investors kept pouring in new funds, Ponzi could afford to pay interest on the old funds. . . . But Ponzi's bubble had to burst. The

*Source: From *The Encyclopedia of American Crimes* by Carl Sifakis. Copyright © 1982 by Facts on File, Inc. Reprinted by permission of Facts on File, Inc.

Boston Post *dug up his past record, which showed he had spent time in prison . . . It was enough to make large numbers of eager investors hesitate to put in more money; the moment had happened, Ponzi's fragile scheme collapsed, since it required an unending flow of cash. His books, such as they were, showed a deficit of somewhere between $5 and $10 million, or perhaps even more. No one ever knew for sure.*

2.3 ADVERSE SELECTION

Let's return to the situation we described previously. Suppose our accounting is good enough to catch the hedge slippage before it does too much damage. We stop booking new deals of this type, but we may find we have booked a disturbingly large number of these deals before the cutoff. If our customers have figured out the degree to which we are underpricing the structure before we do, then they may try to complete as many deals as they can before we wise up. This pattern has frequently been seen in the financial markets. For example, the last firms that figured out how to correctly price volatility skew into barrier options found that their customers had loaded up on trades that the less correct models were underpricing. A common convention is to label this situation as *adverse selection* as a parallel to a similar concern among insurance firms who worry that those customers with failing health will be more eager to purchase insurance than those with better health, taking advantage of the fact that a person knows more about his own health than an insurance company can learn (Wilson 1989). So adverse selection is like moral hazard since it is based on information asymmetry; the difference is that moral hazard is concerned with the degree of risk that might be taken based on this asymmetry, whereas adverse selection is concerned with a difference in purchasing behavior. In 2001, George Ackerlof, Michael Spence, and Joseph Stiglitz won the Nobel Prize in economics for their work on adverse selection and its application to a broad class of economic issues.

Concern about the risk from adverse selection motivates risk managers' concern about the composition of a trading desk's customer base. The key question is what proportion of trades are with counterparties who are likely to possess an informational advantage relative to the firm's traders. As a general rule, you prefer to see a higher proportion of trades with individuals and nonfinancial corporations who are likely trading to meet hedging or investment needs rather than seeking to exploit informational advantage. Alarm is raised when an overwhelming proportion of trades are with other professional traders, particularly ones who are likely to see greater deal flow or have a greater proportion of trades with individuals and nonfinancial corporations than your firm's traders. Seeing greater deal flow can give a firm an informational advantage by having a more accurate sense of supply-and-demand pressures on the market. A greater proportion of customers who are not professional traders yields two further potential informational advantages:

- At times, you work with such customers over a long period of time to structure a large transaction. This gives the traders advance knowledge of supply and demand that has not been seen in the market yet.
- Working on complex structures with customers gives traders a more intimate knowledge of the structure's risks. They can choose to retain those risks that this knowledge shows them are more easily manageable and attempt to pass less manageable risks onto other traders.

A trader may tend to underestimate the degree to which her profitability is due to customer deal flow and overestimate the degree to which it is due to anticipating market movements. This can be dangerous if it encourages the trader to aggressively take risks in markets in which she does not possess this customer flow advantage. A striking example I once observed was a foreign exchange (FX) trader who had a phenomenally successful track record of producing profits at a large market-making firm. Convinced of his prowess in predicting market movements, he accepted a lucrative offer to move to a far smaller firm. He was back at his old job in less than year, confessing he simply had not realized how much of his success was due to the advantages of customer flow.

A pithy, if inelegant, statement of this principle was attributed to the head of mortgage-backed trading at Kidder Peabody: "We don't want to make money trading against smart traders; we want to make money selling to stupid customers." Of course, *stupid* needs to be understood here as macho Wall Street lingo for *informationally disadvantaged*. It's the sort of talk that is only meant to be heard in locker rooms and on trading floors. An unfriendly leak resulted in his quote appearing on the front page of the *Wall Street Journal*. It is delightful to imagine the dialogue of some of his subsequent conversations with the firm's customers.

2.4 THE WINNER'S CURSE

In response to the risks of adverse selection, a trader may exhibit confidence that this is not something she needs to worry about. After all, adverse selection only impacts those with less knowledge than the market. It is a rare trader who is not convinced that she possesses far more knowledge than the rest of the market—belief in one's judgment is virtually a necessity for succeeding in this demanding profession. Whether the firm's management shares the trader's confidence may be another story. However, even if it does, the trader must still overcome another hurdle—the *winner's curse*, the economic anomaly that says that in an auction, even those possessing (insider) knowledge tend to overpay.

The winner's curse was first identified in conjunction with bidding for oil leases, but has since been applied to many other situations, such as corporate takeovers. My favorite explanation of the mechanism that leads to the winner's curse comes from Thaler (1992):

> *Next time you find yourself a little short of cash for a night on the town, try the following experiment in your neighborhood tavern. Take a jar and fill it with coins, noting the total value of the coins. Now auction off the jar to the assembled masses at the bar (offering to pay the winning bidder in bills to control for penny aversion). Chances are very high that the following results will be obtained:*
>
> 1. *The average bid will be significantly less than the value of the coins. (Bidders are risk averse).*
> 2. *The winning bid will exceed the value of the jar.*
>
> *In conducting this demonstration, you will have simultaneously obtained the funding necessary for your evening's entertainment and enlightened the patrons of the tavern about the perils of the* winner's curse.

When applied to trading, the winner's curse is most often seen in market making for less liquid products, where opinions on the true value of a transaction may vary more widely. Market makers are in competition with one another in pricing these products. The firm that evaluates a particular product as having a higher value than its competition is most likely to be winning the lion's share of these deals. Consider a market for options on stock baskets. As we will discuss in Section 10.4, a liquid market rarely exists for these instruments, so pricing depends on different estimates of correlation between stocks in a basket. The firm that has the lowest estimate for correlation between technology stocks will wind up with the most aggressive bids for baskets of technology stocks and will book a large share of these deals. Another firm that has the lowest estimate for correlation between financial industry stocks will book the largest share of those deals.

An anecdotal illustration comes from Neil Chriss. When Chriss was trading volatility swaps at Goldman Sachs, they would line up five or six dealers to give them quotes and always hit the highest bid or lift the lowest offer. The dealers knew they were doing this and were very uneasy about it, limiting the size of trades they would accommodate. One dealer, on winning a bid, told Chriss, "I am always uncomfortable when I win a trade with you as I know I was the best bid on top of five other smart guys. What did I do wrong?"

Adverse selection can be controlled by gaining expertise and increasing the proportion of business done with ultimate users rather than other market makers. However, the winner's curse can only be controlled by either avoiding auction environments or adequately factoring in a further pricing conservatism beyond risk aversion. It provides a powerful motivation for conservatism in pricing and recognizing profits for those situations such as one-way markets (see Section 5.1.1) in which it is difficult to find prices at which risks can be exited.

We will demonstrate the mechanism of the winner's curse with a simple numerical example involving a market with only three firms, two buyers, and one seller. The results are shown in Table 2.1.

We will consider two different situations. In the first, direct negotiation occurs on the price between the seller and a single buyer. In the second, both buyers participate in an auction.

There are 10 transactions that the seller might sell to the buyers. Neither the buyers nor the seller is certain of the true value of these transactions (for example, they might depend on future dynamic hedging costs, which depend on the evolution of future prices, which different firms estimate using different probability distributions). After the fact, we know the true realized

TABLE 2.1   The Winner's Curse

Deal	Actual Value	Seller's Offer	Buyer 1 Bid	Buyer 1 P&L	Buyer 2 Bid	Buyer 2 P&L	Auction P&L Buyer 1	Auction P&L Buyer 2
1	1.56	2.10	2.00	0.00	2.40	−0.69	0.00	−0.84
2	2.66	1.40	1.50	1.21	1.80	1.06	0.00	0.86
3	3.16	3.20	2.10	0.00	3.10	0.00	0.00	0.06
4	1.96	3.40	1.60	0.00	2.20	0.00	0.00	−0.24
5	1.36	1.90	1.70	0.00	1.20	0.00	−0.34	0.00
6	4.46	4.30	4.80	−0.09	3.00	0.00	−0.34	0.00
7	3.16	2.60	3.50	0.11	2.90	0.41	−0.34	0.00
8	1.96	1.80	1.40	0.00	2.10	0.01	0.00	−0.14
9	1.56	2.70	1.40	0.00	1.10	0.00	0.16	0.00
10	2.16	2.10	2.50	−0.14	2.70	−0.24	0.00	−0.54
Average	2.40	2.55	2.25		2.25			
Total				1.09		0.55	−0.86	−0.84
Correlation with actual value		63.2%	83.3%		72.2%			

Column 2 shows what the deals are really worth; column 3 is the asking price of a seller of deals.

Columns 4 and 6 are the bid price of buyers of deals.

The seller is posting conservative asking prices (higher by .15 on average than true prices).

The buyers are posting conservative bids (lower by .15 on average than true prices).

Columns 5 and 7 are the buyers' profits if they negotiate to the average of the seller's asked and buyer's bid.

Columns 8 and 9 show the profits of the buyers in an auction.

value of each transaction, as shown in column 2 of the table. Buyer 1 has superior knowledge of this market to buyer 2, and both have superior knowledge to the seller. This can be seen by the correlations between realized value and each party's estimate of transaction value (83.3 percent for buyer 1, 72.2 percent for buyer 2, and 63.2 percent for the seller). The consequences of this informational advantage is that both buyer 1 and buyer 2 make a profit at the expense of the seller in direct negotiations, and that buyer 1's profit in this situation is higher than buyer 2's profit.

In the direct negotiation situation, we assume that the buyer, being risk averse, has successfully biased his bids down to be on average lower than the realized value, and the seller, being risk averse, has successfully biased his asked prices up to be on average higher than realized value. We assume no transaction takes place if the buyer's bid is lower than the seller's asked. If the buyer's bid exceeds the seller's asked, we assume the transaction takes place at the average price between these two prices. As a result, buyer 1 has a total P&L of +1.09, and buyer 2 has a total P&L of +0.55.

Now consider what happens in the auction when the buyers have to compete for the seller's business, a situation very typical for market-making firms that must offer competitive price quotations to try to win customer business from other market makers. The seller no longer relies on his own estimate of value, but simply does business at the better bid price between the two firms. Even though both firms continue to successfully bias their bids down on average from realized values, both wind up losing money in total, with buyer 1 having a P&L of −.86 and buyer 2 having a P&L of −.84. This is because they no longer have gains on trades that they seriously undervalued to balance out losses on trades that they seriously overvalued, since they tend to lose trades that they undervalue to the other bidder. This illustrates the winner's curse.

The spreadsheet **WinnersCurse** on the accompanying CD-ROM shows the consequences of changing some of the assumptions in this example.

2.5 MARKET MAKING VERSUS POSITION TAKING

An important institutional distinction between participants in the financial markets that we will refer to on several occasions throughout this book is between *market making* and *position taking*:

- Market making (also called *book running* or the *sell side*) consists of making two-way markets by engaging in (nearly) simultaneous buying and selling the same instruments, attempting to keep position holdings to a minimum and to profit primarily through the difference between (nearly) simultaneous buy and sell prices.

■ Position taking (also called *market using, price taking, speculation,* or the *buy side*) consists of deliberately taking positions on one side or the other of a market, hoping to profit by the market moving in your favor between the time of purchase and the time of sale. Positions may be taken on behalf of a firm (in which case it is often labeled *proprietary trading*) or on behalf of an individual client, or group of clients, such as a mutual fund, hedge fund, or managed investment account.

Some time lag nearly always occurs between the purchase and sale involved in market making. Depending on the length of time and degree of deliberate choice of the resulting positions, these may be labeled position-taking aspects of market making. Market making almost always involves risk because you cannot often buy and sell exactly simultaneously. The market maker makes a guess on market direction by its posted price, but bid-ask spread can outweigh even a persistent error in directional guess as long as the error is small. (In Exercise 7.1, you'll be asked to build a simulation to test out the degree to which this is true.) The experience and information gained from seeing so much flow means you most likely will develop the ability to be right on direction on average. However, the position taker has the advantage over the market maker of not needing to be in the market every day. Therefore, the position taker can stay away from the market except when possessed of a strong opinion. The market maker cannot do this; staying away from the market would jeopardize the franchise.

The different objectives of market makers and position takers tend to be reflected in different attitudes toward the use of models and valuation techniques. A position taker generally uses models as forecasting tools to arrive at a best estimate of what a position will be worth at the conclusion of a time period tied to an anticipated event. He will pay attention to the market price of the position during that time period to determine the best time to exit the position and check whether new information is coming into the market. However, a position taker will generally not be overly concerned by prices moving against his position. Since he is usually waiting for an event to occur, price movements prior to the time the event is expected are not that relevant. A frequently heard statement among position takers is "If I liked the position at the price I bought it, I like it even better at a lower price."

By contrast, a market maker generally uses models to perform risk decomposition in order to evaluate alternative current prices at which a position can be exited. She will pay close attention to current market prices as the key indicator of how quickly inventory can be reduced. The direction in which prices will move over the longer term is of little concern compared to determining what price will currently balance supply and demand.

An amusing analogy can be made to gambling on sports. Position takers correspond to the gamblers who place their bets based on an analysis of which team is going to win and by what margin. Market makers correspond to the bookmakers whose sole concern is to move the odds quoted to a point that will even out the amount bet on each side. The bookmaker's concern is not over which team wins or loses, but over the evenness of the amounts wagered. Close to even amounts let the bookmakers come out ahead based on the spread or *vigorish* in the odds, regardless of the outcome of the game. Uneven amounts turn the bookmaker into just another gambler who will win or lose depending on the outcome of the game.

As indicated in Chapter 1, much of this book is devoted to the techniques of risk decomposition and the use of current market prices to reduce the subjectivity of risk management. This view is much more closely aligned with market making than with position taking. In fact, the arbitrage-based models that are so prominent in mathematical finance have been developed largely to support market making. Position takers tend more toward the use of econometric forecasting models. In Section 5.1.5, we will further discuss the issue of the extent to which position takers should adopt the risk-management discipline that has been developed for market makers.

Some authors distinguish a third type of financial market participant besides market makers and position takers—the *arbitrageurs*. I believe it is more useful to classify arbitrage trading as a subcategory of position taking. Pure arbitrage, in its original meaning of taking offsetting positions in closely related markets that generate a riskless profit, is rarely encountered in current financial markets, given the speed and efficiency with which liquid prices are disseminated. What is now labeled arbitrage is almost always a trade that offers a low but relatively certain return. The motivation and use of models by those seeking to benefit from such positions is usually closely aligned with other position takers.

A good example is *merger arbitrage* (sometimes misleadingly called *risk arbitrage*). Suppose that company A and company B have announced a forthcoming merger in which two shares of A's stock will be traded for one share of B's stock. If the current forward prices of these stocks to the announced merger date are $50 for A and $102 for B, an arbitrage position would consist of a forward purchase of two shares of A for $100 and a forward sale of one share of B for $102. On the merger date, the two shares of A purchased will be traded for one share of B, which will be delivered into the forward sale. This nets a sure $2, but only if the merger goes through as announced. If the merger fails, this trade could show a substantial loss. Merger arbitrageurs are position takers who evaluate the probability of mergers breaking apart and study the size of loss that might result. They are prototypical forecasters of events with generally little concern for market price swings prior to the occurrence of the event.

CHAPTER 3

Operational Risk

Operational risk is usually defined in the negative—it includes all of the risks that are not categorized as either market or credit risk. The industry does not yet have consensus on this terminology. Some firms use the term operational risk to cover a subset of the risks other than market and credit risk. For further discussion, see Jameson (1998A). Broadly speaking, these risks are the most difficult to quantify.

One attempt at a more positive definition that has been gaining some currency, has been made by the Basel Committee on Banking Supervision: "the risk of direct or indirect loss resulting from inadequate or failed internal processes, people, or systems, or from external events." Another attempt would be to break apart risk into three pieces. View a financial firm as the sum total of all the contracts it enters into. The firm can suffer losses on the contracts in one of three ways:

- Obligations in contracts may be performed exactly as expected, but changes in economic conditions might make the sum of all contracted actions an undesired outcome. This is market risk.
- The other parties to some of the contracts may fail to perform as specified. This is credit risk.
- The firm may be misled about what the contracted actions are or the consequences of these actions. This is operational risk.

Operational risk can be subdivided into the following categories:

Operations risk.   The risk that deficiencies in information systems or internal controls will result in unexpected loss. Operations risk can be further subdivided into the risk of fraud, risk of nondeliberate incorrect information, disaster risk, and personnel risk.

Legal risk.   The risk that the terms or conditions of a contract or agreement will prove unenforceable due to legal defects in the contract or in related documentation and procedures. Legal risk includes regulatory risk.

Reputational risk. The risk that the enforcement of contract provisions will prove too costly in terms of damage to the firm's reputation as a desirable firm for customers to do future business with.

Accounting risk. The risk that an error in accounting practice will necessitate a restatement of earnings, which adversely affects the investors' or customers' perception of the firm.

Funding liquidity risk. The risk that an institution will have to pay higher than prevailing market rates for its funding due to either the investors' perception that the credit quality of the institution is impaired, possibly due to earnings problems or capital structure problems, or the overly heavy use of particular funding sources within a given time period, with the large size of transactions impacting funding cost.

Enterprise risk. The risk of loss due to change in the overall business climate, such as the needs of customers, actions of competitors, and pace of technological innovation.

This chapter briefly discusses each of these risks and possible controls, and then presents an overview of how these risks can be identified and the extent to which they can be quantified.

A valuable source of ideas on operational risk and control procedures is the *Trading and Capital-Markets Activities Manual* of the Federal Reserve System. I have used it as a foundation for several of the points in this chapter and recommend that readers interested in this topic look closely at the following sections: 2050.1 and 2060.1 (Operations and Systems Risk), 2070.1 (Legal Risk), 2150.1 (Ethics), 2030.1 (the subsection on Funding Liquidity Risk), and 2040.1 (the subsection on New Products).

3.1 OPERATIONS RISK

Operations risk can be further subdivided into the risk of fraud, risk of nondeliberate incorrect information, disaster risk, and personnel risk.

3.1.1 The Risk of Fraud

The actual diversion of cash can take the form of creating unauthorized payments, conducting transactions at prices that are not the best available in return for bribes, or utilizing one's position to engage in profitable personal trading at the expense of the firm's profits.

Deception about earnings, in order to generate unearned bonuses or further one's career (or simply avoid being fired), can take the form of recording trades at incorrect prices or misreporting the current value of positions. We'll encounter examples of such deceptions that occurred at Kidder Peabody, Barings, and Allied Irish Bank (AIB) in Section 4.1.

Deception about positions, in order to appear to be operating within limits when an individual is actually outside them or mislead management about the size of positions being taken, is done in order to preserve freedom of action—avoiding requirements to close down positions. This can be because a trader has a different belief about market movements than management or a different view toward risk than management (the moral hazard issue discussed in Section 2.1). Deception about positions can entail the outright misreporting of positions through the failure to enter transactions (*tickets in the drawer*) or manipulation of management reporting, or hiding positions by arranging for them to be temporarily held by another party with an unrecorded promise to take the position back (*parking*).

The most fundamental control for preventing fraud is by separating the responsibilities between the front office and support staff (middle office, back office, and controllers), making sure that all entries of transactions and management reporting systems are under the complete control of the support staff. To make this separation of responsibilities work, the support staff must have a separate line of reporting from the front-office staff and compensation that is reasonably independent of the reported earnings of the business area being supported. As much as possible, the reporting lines and compensation structure should align support staff interests with those of management rather than with those of the front office. However, even the best designed structures of this type are subject to pressures in the direction of alignment of support staff interests with front-office interests. Constant vigilance is required to fight against this. These pressures include:

- Support staff compensation cannot be completely independent from trading performance. At a minimum, unsuccessful results for trading may lead to the shrinking or elimination of a trading operation along with associated support staff positions. Since trading profits are the ultimate source from which expenses get paid, it is difficult to avoid some linkage between the trading performance and level of compensation. Section 4.1.4 presents a vivid example of how this pressure was felt in practice at AIB.
- Front-office personnel almost always command higher compensation and prestige than members of the support staff, usually considerably higher. Often, support staff are hoping to eventually move into front-office positions. Front-office staff can afford to offer informal incentives to the support staff for cooperation such as helping them seek front-office jobs, giving access to perks such as lavish meals and free tickets to otherwise unavailable sports events, and even offering outright cash bribes. The higher prestige of front-office positions and the reality of the greater market experience of front-office personnel relative to support personnel can be utilized to place tremendous pressure on the support staff to adopt front-office views.

- Since support staff has responsibilities for supporting the front office as well as for supporting management, their ratings for job performance are often heavily dependent on the views of front-office personnel, who are likely to be working far more closely with them than management personnel.

In addition to the separation of responsibilities, controls include:

- Support staff procedures should be thoroughly documented. Making these as unambiguous as possible lessens the scope for front-office influence.
- Trader lines should be taped to create a potential source for spotting evidence of collusion with brokers or traders at other firms.
- Make sure that trades are entered into the firm's systems as close to execution time as possible. The farther away from execution time you get, the greater the possibility that subsequent market movements will create a temptation to hide or otherwise misrepresent the transaction.
- Review all trades to look for prices that appear off-market and perform a thorough investigation of any trades identified as such.
- Make sure that all market quotes used to value positions come into support staff, not front-office personnel, and are polled from as large a universe of sources as possible.
- Provide daily explanations of profit and loss (P&L) change and cash needs produced by the support staff. Incorrect reporting of positions can often be identified by the inability to explain P&L and cash movements based on the reported positions.
- Every customer confirmation of a new trade or a payment required by a previous trade should be reviewed by the support staff for consistency with transactions and positions being reported. All customer complaints should be reviewed by the support staff, not just front-office personnel. The confirmation process should only be conducted with support personnel at other firms, not with front-office personnel at other firms.
- Personal trading of both front-office and support personnel should be closely monitored.
- Tight controls should be placed on after-hours and off-premises trading to ensure that transactions cannot be omitted from the firm's records.
- Broker usage should be monitored for suspicious patterns—undue concentrations of business that might be compensation for supplying off-market quotes or direct bribery.

- Firms should insist on performing thorough background checks of a potential customer's creditworthiness and business reputation before entering into transactions. In other words, they should refuse to deal with customers they do not know, even on a fully collateralized basis. Unknown customers could be in collusion with the firm's personnel for off-market trading or parking.
- Systems security measures should be in place to ensure that no one other than authorized support personnel can make entries or changes to management information systems. In particular, no front-office personnel should have such access.
- The firm's auditors should perform a periodic review of all operating procedures.

3.1.2 The Risk of Nondeliberate Incorrect Information

It is far more common to have incorrect P&L and position information due to human or systems error than incorrect P&L and position information due to fraud. Many of the controls for nondeliberate incorrect information are similar to the controls for fraud. The separation of responsibilities is effective in having several sets of eyes looking at the entry of a trade, reducing the chance that a single individual's error will impact positions. Checking confirmations and payment instructions against position entries, P&L and cash reconciliation, and the investigation of off-market trades are just as effective in spotting inadvertent errors as they are in spotting fraudulent entries. Equally close attention needs to be paid to making sure customers have posted collateral required by contracts to avoid inadvertently taking unauthorized credit risk. (For a further discussion of the role of collateral in managing credit risk, see Sections 4.2.1, 8.1.4, and 12.4.)

It is every bit as important to have front-office personnel involved in reconciliation (to take advantage of their superior market knowledge and intuitive feel for the size of their P&L and positions) as it is to have support personnel involved (to take advantage of their independence). Front-office personnel must be held responsible for the accuracy of the records of their P&L and positions, and cannot be allowed to place all the blame for incorrect reports on support personnel in order to ensure that they will place sufficient importance on this reconciliation. Front offices should be required to produce daily projections of closing positions and P&L moves based on their own informal records, prior to seeing the official reports of positions and P&L, and should reconcile significant differences between the two.

To prevent incorrect P&L and position information, it is important to ensure that adequate support personnel and system resources are available, both in quantity and quality, relative to the size and complexity of trading. Careful attention needs to be paid to planning staff and system upgrades to anticipate growth in trading volume. Management needs to be ready to resist premature approval of a new business if support resources cannot keep pace with front-office development.

Should model risk be regarded as an operations risk issue? The viewpoint of this book is that model risk is primarily a market risk issue, since the proper selection and calibration to market prices of models and the provision for adequate reserves against model uncertainty are best dealt with by the market risk discipline. Chapter 6 will elucidate this view. However, the proper implementation of models and the assurance that system changes are undertaken with the proper controls is best dealt with by the operations risk discipline. An area independent of model and system developers and the front office should be established to perform quality assurance testing of system implementation and modifications, and to review the adequacy of system documentation.

3.1.3 Disaster Risk

The adequacy of support personnel and system resources for reporting P&L and positions must also be ensured in the event of a physical disaster. Examples of such disasters would include a power failure, fire, or explosion that closes down a trading facility and/or its supporting systems. Another example would be a computer system problem, such as a virus or error with consequences far-reaching enough to jeopardize the entire support structure (the most famous example is the Y2K crisis). Resource adequacy cannot be limited to just the ability to keep track of existing positions. It is also necessary to allow continued trading in a sufficiently controlled environment, at least at a level that will permit the on-going management of existing positions.

The steps to deal with disaster risk begin with the development of a detailed contingency plan, which includes plans for backup computer systems, frequently updated backup data sets, backup power sources, and a backup trading floor. The adequacy of contingency plans must be judged against the likelihood that both the primary and backup facilities will be impacted by the same event. This concern was sharpened by the tragic events of September 11, 2001, when Bank of New York had both its primary and secondary trading systems, which were located in separate but nearby buildings, knocked out at the same time. This has caused many financial firms to rethink the degree of geographic separation that should be required between alternative sites.

Widespread computer errors that cut across all systems of the firm (backup as well as primary) are particularly worrisome. For example, the only way around the Y2K bug was to get a complete fix in place and thoroughly tested prior to the onset of the potential problem.

3.1.4 Personnel Risk

Investment banking firms have a history of raiding a competitor's personnel and hiring, en masse, an entire group of traders along with key support staff. This can have the same impact on the raided firm as a physical disaster, but it has a longer recovery time, since replacement personnel must be identified, hired, and trained. Protective steps are to utilize cross-training and occasional backup duties as widely as possible to ensure that personnel are available to at least temporarily take over the duties of departed personnel. The requirements for thorough documentation of systems and procedures are also important.

3.2 LEGAL RISK

The legal risk that the terms or conditions of a contract will prove unenforceable due to legal defects can prove a more serious problem than the credit risk that a counterparty does not have the financial capacity to perform on a contract. If a contract is found to be unenforceable, it may simultaneously impact a large number of contracts and have exactly the same impact on a trading firm as if a large number of counterparties defaulted simultaneously. A classic case of this was the finding by British courts that derivative contracts with British municipalities were *ultra vires*—that is, they were not contracts that the municipalities were legally authorized to enter into. This simultaneously cancelled all outstanding derivatives contracts that financial firms had with British municipalities. For more detail, see Malcolm et al. (1999, pp. 149–150). Another reason why legal risk can be more serious than credit risk is that it suffers more from adverse selection. Counterparty default is generally unrelated to whether the counterparty owes money or is owed money. However, lawsuits only occur when counterparties owe money.

The major mitigants to legal risk are:

- Thoroughly reviewing contract terms by experienced lawyers to ensure that language is properly drafted and that the contracted activities are authorized for the contracting parties
- Thoroughly documenting what terms have been agreed to
- Restricting dealings to reputable counterparties (know your customer)
- Placing limits on exposure to legal interpretations
- Ensuring that contracts specify that legal jurisdiction reside with court systems that have experience in dealing with the particular issues involved and have previously demonstrated fairness in dealing with such cases

A thorough review of contract terms may require lawyers with specialized legal knowledge of particular subject areas of law and legal jurisdiction (such as laws of particular countries, states, and districts), including knowledge of how courts and juries in a jurisdiction tend to interpret the law as well as applicable precedents. This often requires that legal work be contracted to outside counsel who specialize in certain areas and jurisdictions. However, care must be exercised to prevent front-office areas, which have a vested interest in seeing that a transaction gets done, from using this process to legal opinion shop, hiring a legal firm that can be counted on to provide a favorable opinion. The process of outside contracting legal opinions must be controlled by an in-house legal department or a single trusted outside legal firm that can be counted on to offer independent judgments in the interest of the trading firm when this conflicts with the interest of individual front-office areas within the firm.

Adequate and clear legal language may prove useless if sufficient documentation has not been obtained showing customer agreement to the language. The most important measure in this regard is a strong commitment to following up verbal trade agreements with well-documented confirmations and signed legal agreements. This requires adequate documentation staff within trade support functions and the discipline to turn down potentially profitable business from counterparties that do not follow through on the required documentation. The enforcement of these rules is often placed with the credit risk function. Documentation should include written confirmation that a counterparty's board of directors and senior management have knowledge of the activities being contracted and have authorized the officers of the counterparty firm with which the trading firm is dealing to enter into such contracts on behalf of the counterparty firm. It is also useful to tape all conversations between the counterparties and trading firm personnel so that disputes as to what terms were verbally agreed to can be settled equitably, without resorting to costly legal proceedings.

Firms have started to worry about what may be termed *legal-basis risk*. This arises when a firm treats transactions with two different customers as offsetting and hence without market risk (although not without credit risk). However, it may turn out that slightly different wording in the two contracts means that they are not truly offsetting in all circumstances. Although carefully vetting contractual language is a necessary countermeasure, an even better preventative is to use standardized contractual language as much as possible to make it easier to spot differences. The International Swaps and Derivatives Association (ISDA) has been working to develop standardized language that can be used in derivatives contracts. See Section 8.1.8 for more details.

In addition to enforcing documentation rules, the credit risk function also needs to restrict the extension of credit to reputable counterparties. It is necessary to recognize that the willingness of a counterparty to meet contractual obligations is every bit as important as its financial ability to meet those obligations. A counterparty that does not have a good business reputation to protect may feel free to look for the slightest pretext to enter a legal challenge to meet its contractual obligations. Even if a firm has legal right strongly on its side, dealing with such a client may be very costly due to the expense of litigation and the threat of using a lawsuit as an excuse for a fishing expedition discovery process designed to uncover internal corporate information that can cause public embarrassment. The threat of such costs may incline a firm to settle for less than the full amount contractually owed, which serves as an incentive for unscrupulous firms to delay the settlement of legitimate claims. By contrast, a firm or individual whose reputation for ethical business dealings is one of its assets will actually lean in the direction of making payments that meet its understanding of its obligations, even when the formal contract has been imperfectly drawn.

Because it is extremely difficult to quantify legal risk, firms may overlook the usefulness of quantitative limits to control exposure. Consider an example of a particular legal interpretation that has the potential to void all contracts of a specific type. The firm's legal consultants can issue opinions on the degree of likelihood that such an interpretation will be issued in the future by a court or regulatory body. Ultimately, business management must make a judgment on whether the economic benefits of the contract, relative to alternative ways of achieving the desired financial result, outweigh this risk. On a single deal, this is a binary decision—you either enter into the contract or you don't. There are few circumstances under which protection against an unfavorable contract interpretation can be purchased, making legal risk very different from market or credit risk. However, this is all the more reason to place a quantitative limit on the total size of contracts subject to all being voided by a single interpretation, where the size of the contract can be quantified by the potential loss from being voided. Quantitative limits place a control on risk, can be sized based on the degree of economic benefit relative to the perceived degree of legal uncertainty, and provide a framework for ensuring that individual deal approval is limited to those with the greatest potential benefit relative to potential loss.

One particular issue of legal risk that often causes concern is how bankruptcy courts will treat contractual obligations. When a counterparty goes into default, the counterparty's reputation and desire to deal fairly no longer serve as a bulwark against litigation risk. In bankruptcy, all of the bankrupt firm's creditors become competitors in legal actions to gain as much of a share of remaining assets as possible. Even when legal documents have been well drawn to provide specific collateral against an obligation or specific netting arrangements between derivative contracts on which the bankrupt firms owes and is owed money, other creditors may try to convince bankruptcy courts

page

that it is only fair that they receive a share of the collateral or derivatives on which the bankrupt firm is owed money. Bankruptcy courts have been known to issue some very surprising rulings in these circumstances.

Contractual intention can be voided not only by courts, but also by regulatory authorities or legislatures, which may issue rules that make certain contractual provisions unenforceable. Financial institutions can and do mount lobbying campaigns against such changes, but other parties may be as or more effective in lobbying on the other side. Financial firms often need to analyze what they believe is the prospect for future regulatory actions in order to determine whether certain current business will prove to be worthwhile.

3.3 REPUTATIONAL RISK

Firms need to be sure that contract provisions are not only legally enforceable, but also that the process of enforcing their legal rights will not damage their business reputation. Even if a contract is strictly legal and enforceable, if its terms seem palpably unfair or can be portrayed as taking advantage of a client, the enforcement of the legal claims may be as or more damaging to the firm than the inability to enforce the claims would have been. All transactions need to be reviewed by business managers from the viewpoint of whether the transaction is one that the client fully understands and can reasonably be interpreted as a sensible action for the client to take. Ever since the Banker's Trust (BT) fiasco with Proctor & Gamble (P&G) and Gibson Greetings, described in Section 4.3.1, all firms have placed increased emphasis on processes to ensure that transactions are appropriate or suitable for the client. The following processes are included:

- Conduct a careful review of all marketing material to make sure that transactions have been fully explained, no misleading claims have been made, and no ambiguity exists as to whether the financial firm is simply acting as deal structurer or is also acting as an advisor to the client with fiduciary responsibility for the soundness of its advice. A full explanation of transactions may need to include simulations of possible outcomes, including stress situations.
- Make certain that any request from a client for a mark-to-market valuation of an existing transaction is supplied by support personnel using objective standards and not by marketing personnel who may have motivations to mislead the client as to the true performance of the transaction. Further, all valuations supplied need to be clearly labeled as to whether they are actual prices at which the trading firm is prepared to deal or simply indications of the general market level.
- Rank clients by their degree of financial sophistication and transactions by their degree of complexity and ensure that a proper fit exists between the two. In cases where complex transactions are negotiated

with less sophisticated clients, extra care needs to be taken to ensure that any advice given to the client by marketing personnel is consistent with its knowledge of the client's needs.

■ Verify that clients fully understand the nature of the transactions they are undertaking, including written confirmation of such assurances from senior managers in some cases, based on the size and complexity of deals. These steps to ensure appropriateness/suitability are important not only to guard a trading firm's reputation, but, in extreme cases, they may also serve as protection against litigation. Note that the need to ensure the suitability of transactions to clients and the need to provide clients with evaluations that the trading firm can certify as reliable limit a trading firm's ability to simply serve as a credit intermediary between two counterparties using back-to-back derivatives.

3.4 ACCOUNTING RISK

Accounting risk can be viewed as a form of reputational risk. When a firm makes serious accounting errors, requiring the restatement of past earnings, it does not lead to any net loss of cash to the firm, as in cases of fraud, operations errors, or incorrectly drawn contracts. However, it can damage investor, creditor, and regulator confidence in the accuracy of information that the firm supplies about its financial health. This loss of confidence can be so severe that it threatens the firm's continued existence, as the Kidder Peabody financial disaster discussed in Section 4.1.2, illustrates.

Measures to control accounting risk are similar in nature to those needed to control legal risk. Instead of needing knowledge of legal issues and precedents and how courts tend to interpret the law, knowledge of generally accepted accounting principles (GAAP) and how accounting boards of standards and regulatory authorities tend to interpret these principles is needed. The need for specialized knowledge by accounting jurisdiction is similar to the need for specialized knowledge by legal jurisdiction. The need to obtain independent accounting opinions and avoid opinion shopping parallels those considerations for legal risk. The need for thorough documentation showing that accounting rules are being followed parallels the need for thorough documentation of contractual understandings. The need for limits on exposure to accounting policies open to interpretation parallels the need for limits on exposure to legal interpretation.

3.5 FUNDING LIQUIDITY RISK

Funding liquidity risk should be clearly differentiated from the liquidity risk we discuss as part of market risk (see Section 1.3), which is sometimes called *asset liquidity risk*.

Funding liquidity risk has two fundamental components:

- The risk that investors' perception of the firm's credit quality will become impaired, thereby raising the firm's funding costs relative to that of competitors across all funding sources utilized
- The overly heavy use of a particular funding source in a given time period, raising the firm's funding cost relative to that of competitors for that particular funding source only

Controlling the cost of the firm's liabilities by managing investors' perception of the firm's credit quality is the flip side of the coin of credit risk's management of the credit quality of the firm's assets. Crises in investor confidence are usually triggered by problems with earnings or the inadequacy of capital. As a result, they are functions of the overall management of the firm's business. The Chief Financial Officer of the firm has particular responsibility for controlling funding liquidity risk by explaining the earnings situation to financial analysts and ratings agencies and ensuring that capital levels are maintained to meet both regulatory guidelines and the expectations of financial analysts and rating agencies. Specific funding liquidity responsibilities of the Treasury function of the firm include ensuring that any such crisis is not exacerbated by having to raise too much funding from the market at a time of crisis. Preferably, the firm should be able to reduce to a bare minimum its funding during a crisis period to gain time for the firm to improve its fundamental financial condition and tell its side of the story effectively to financial analysts, ratings agencies, and individual investors.

The ability to avoid too much market funding in these circumstances requires:

- Long-term plans to get more funding from stable sources less sensitive to a firm's credit rating (such as retail deposits and transaction balances), lengthen the maturity of market funding, create cushions of market funding to tap in emergencies by raising less than the full amount of potential funds available, and arrange backup lines of credit.
- Information systems to project periods of large funding needs in order to spread out the period of time over which such funding is raised. Of particular importance is the use of funding needs projections to avoid having funding requirements over a short period being so heavy that they trigger a crisis of investor confidence.
- Well-developed contingency plans for handling a funding crisis, which could include steps such as selling liquid assets, unwinding liquid derivatives positions that tie up collateral, and utilizing untapped cushions of funding and backup lines of credit.

The Treasury function's management of particular funding sources to avoid overuse is also tied to information systems that can project future funding needs. It may be necessary to restrict particular types of investment or derivative transactions that depend on access to particular funding sources to be profitable. For example, some transactions are only profitable if off-balance sheet commercial paper funding can be obtained, bypassing the need for capital to be held against on-balance sheet assets. However, the Treasury function may need to limit the total amount of commercial paper being rolled over in any particular period to reduce the risk of having to pay a premium for such funding.

3.6 ENTERPRISE RISK

Enterprise risk can be tied to the fixed nature of many of the costs of engaging in a particular line of business. Even heavily personnel-intensive businesses, such as trading, still have fixed cost components such as buildings, computer and communications equipment, and some base level of employee compensation below which a firm loses its ability to remain in the business line through downturns in activity. However, these fixed costs entail the risk of losses to the extent that the amount of business that can be attracted in a downturn cannot cover the fixed costs.

By its nature, the management of enterprise risk belongs more naturally to individual business managers than to a corporate-wide risk function. Usually, the corporate-wide operational risk function will restrict itself to attempting to include some measurement of enterprise risk in the risk-adjusted return on capital (RAROC) or shareholder value added (SVA) measures.

3.7 THE IDENTIFICATION OF RISKS

In Damon Runyon's short story on which the musical *Guys and Dolls* is based, a gambler named Sky Masterson relates the following advice he received from his father:

> *Son, no matter how far you travel or how smart you get, always remember this: Some day, somewhere, a guy is going to come to you and show you a nice brand-new deck of cards on which the seal is never broken, and this guy is going to offer to bet you that the jack of spades will jump out of the deck and squirt cider in your ear. But, son, do not bet him, for as sure as you do you are going to get an ear full of cider.*

The equivalent of this story for a risk manager is the trader or marketer who informs you that "There is absolutely no risk of loss on this product."

As my experience with markets has grown, I have come to recognize this assertion as a sure harbinger of painful losses to come, either sooner or later. However, my first encounter with the statement came well before I was involved with the financial side of banking, when I was working in Chase Manhattan's Operations Research Department on projects like the simulation of the truck routes that delivered checks from branches to the head office and the sorting machines that then processed the checks.

One day on the subway, I ran into someone I had worked with on these simulations, but had not seen in a few years. He told me about the wonderful new job he had heading up a unit of the bank that matched firms that wanted to borrow securities with those that wanted to lend them. The bank received a nice fee for the service and he was aggressively growing the business. The key to profitability was operational efficiency, at which he was an expert. He told me that since the bank was not a principal to any of these transactions, there was absolutely no risk of loss on the product.

The losses came a few years later. When Drysdale Securities, a large borrower of government securities, could not repay its borrowings, it turned out that considerable ambiguity existed about whether the lenders of the securities understood they were being borrowed by Chase or Drysdale, with Chase merely arranging the borrowing. The legal contracts under which the transactions had been executed were open to the interpretation that Chase was the principal. Chase lost $285 million in settling these claims (see Section 4.1.1 for a more detailed discussion). My acquaintance, needless to say, lost his job.

Before a risk can be controlled, it must first be recognized. Often, the management team that is involved with the introduction of a new product may lack the experience to perceive a possibility of risk and as a result may fail to call in the expertise needed to control the risk. For example, if a new legal risk is not recognized, the firm's legal experts may never thoroughly review the existing contracts. This is why it has become the accepted best practice in the financial industry to establish a new product review process in which more experienced business managers and experts in risk disciplines (such as market risk, credit risk, legal, finance, and audit) vet proposals for products to make sure risks are identified and controls are instituted.

3.8 OPERATIONAL RISK CAPITAL

We started this chapter by stating that operational risks are the most difficult to quantify. This is not to say that quantitative measures cannot be developed for operational risk. The primary impetus for developing quantitative measures of operational risk has been a desire to develop a methodology for operational risk capital to complement the measures of capital allocated for market risk and credit risk. In particular, the push by the Basel Committee on Banking Supervision to promulgate international standards requiring all banks to allocate capital against operational risk has spurred much work on how to quantify this capital requirement. However, unlike market risk and credit risk, where quantification plays an important role in designing methods to reduce risk, the quantification of operational risk is almost wholly confined to capital allocation.

Operational risk capital can be approached in two ways—bottom up and top down. The bottom-up approach emphasizes quantitative measures of factors that contribute to operational risk. Some possibilities are:

- Audit scores as a measure of operations risk
- Counts of unreconciled items or error rates as a measure of operations risk
- Measures of delay in obtaining signed confirmations as a measure of legal risk

Although these measures provide good incentives, tying reduction in capital to desirable improvements in controls, it is very difficult to establish links between these measures and the possible sizes of losses. Some firms are pursuing research on this, but supporting data is scarce.

The top-down approach emphasizes the historical volatility of earnings. This measure provides a direct link to the size of losses and can include all operational risks, even enterprise risk. But what incentive does this measure provide to reducing operational risk? No credit is given to a program that clears up back-office problems or places new controls on suitability.

Neither of these approaches bears much resemblance to the use of actual market prices for reduction of risk, which we discussed in Chapter 1 as the hallmark of modern financial risk management. The absence of liquid markets in operational risks marks them as far more difficult to quantify than either market or credit risks. To the extent market prices are available for some operational risks, it would come from the insurance market, since it is possible to purchase insurance against some types of risk of fraud, operations errors, disasters, loss of personnel, legal liability, and accounting errors.

Much more information on methodological approaches to quantifying operational risk capital and the regulatory background of the Basel Committee initiatives can be found in books by Hoffman (2002), King (2001), and Cruz (2002).

CHAPTER 4

Financial Disasters

One of the fundamental goals of financial risk management is to avoid the type of disasters that can threaten the viability of a firm. So we should expect that a study of such events that have occurred in the past will prove instructive. A complete catalog of all such incidents is beyond the scope of this book, but I have tried to include the most enlightening examples that relate to the operation of financial markets, as this is the primary focus of this manuscript.

A broad categorization of financial disasters would involve a three-part division:

- Cases in which the firm or its investors and lenders were seriously misled about the size and nature of the positions it had
- Cases in which the firm and its investors and lenders had reasonable knowledge of its positions, but had losses result from unexpectedly large market moves
- Cases in which losses did not result from positions held by the firm, but instead resulted from fiduciary or reputational exposure to positions held by the firm's customers

4.1 DISASTERS DUE TO MISLEADING REPORTING

A striking feature of all the financial disasters we will study involving cases in which a firm or its investors and lenders have been misled about the size and nature of its positions is that they all involve a significant degree of deliberation on the part of some individuals to create or exploit incorrect information. This is not to say situations do not exist in which firms are misled without any deliberation on the part of any individual. Everyone who has been in the financial industry for some time knows of many instances when everyone at the firm was misled about the nature of positions because a ticket was entered into a system incorrectly. Most typically, this will represent a purchase entered as a sale, or vice versa. However, although the size of such errors and the time it takes to detect them can sometimes lead to substantial losses, I am not aware of any such incident that has resulted in losses that were large enough to threaten the viability of a firm.

An error in legal interpretation can also seriously mislead a firm about its positions without any deliberate exploitation of the situation. However, such cases, although they can result in large losses, tend to be spread across many firms rather than concentrated at a single firm, perhaps because lawyers tend to check potentially controversial legal opinions with one another. The best known case of this type was when derivatives contracted by British municipalities were voided. See Section 3.2.

If we accept that all cases of financial disaster due to firms being misled about their positions involve some degree of complicity on the part of some individuals, we cannot regard them completely as cases of incorrectly reported positions. Some of the individuals involved know the correct positions, at least approximately, whereas others are thoroughly misinformed. Understanding such cases therefore requires examining two different questions:

- Why does the first group persist in taking large positions they know can lead to large losses for the firm despite their knowledge of the positions?
- How do they succeed in keeping this knowledge from the second group, who we can presume would put a stop to the position taking if they were fully informed?

I will suggest that the answer to the first question tends to be fairly uniform across disasters, while the answer to the second question varies.

The willingness to take large risky positions is driven by moral hazard. As we saw in our discussion of moral hazard in Section 2.1, it represents an asymmetry in reward structure and asymmetry in information—in other words, the group with the best information on the nature of the risk of a position has a greater participation in potential upside than potential downside. This often leads insiders to desire large risky positions that offer them commensurately large potential gains. The idea is that a trader owns an option on his profits; therefore, the trader will gain from increasing volatility, as we discussed in Section 2.1. The normal counterweights against this are the attempts to place controls on the amount of risk taken by representatives of senior management, stockholders, creditors, and government regulators, who all own a larger share of the potential downside than the traders. However, when those who could exercise this control substantially lack knowledge of the positions, the temptation exists for traders to exploit the control weakness to run inflated positions. This action often leads to another motivation spurring the growth of risky positions—the Ponzi scheme, as discussed in Section 2.2.

Some traders who take risky positions that are unauthorized but disguised by a control weakness will make profits on these positions. These positions are then possibly closed down without anyone being the wiser. However, some unauthorized positions will lead to losses and traders will be strongly tempted to take on even larger, riskier positions in an attempt to cover up unauthorized losses. This is where the Ponzi scheme comes in. I think it helps to explain how losses from unauthorized positions can grow to be so overwhelmingly large. Stigum (1989) quotes an "astute trader" with regard to the losses in the Chase/Drysdale financial disaster: "I find it puzzling that Drysdale could lose so much so fast. If you charged me to lose one-fourth of a billion, I think it would be hard to do; I would probably end up making money some of the time because I would buy something going down and it would go up. They must have been extraordinarily good at losing money." I would suggest that the reason traders whose positions are unauthorized can be so "extraordinarily good at losing money" is that normal constraints that force them to justify positions to outsiders are lacking and small unauthorized losses already put a trader at risk of her job and reputation. With no significant downside left, truly reckless positions are undertaken in an attempt to make enough money to cover the previous losses. This is closely related to double-or-nothing betting strategies, which can start with very small stakes and quickly mushroom to extraordinary levels in an effort to get back to even.

This snowballing pattern can be seen in many financial disasters. Nick Leeson's losses on behalf of Barings were just $21 million in 1993, $185 million in 1994, and $619 million in just the first 2 months of 1995 (Chew [1996], Table 10.2). John Rusnak's unauthorized trading at Allied Irish Bank (AIB) accumulated losses of $90 million in its first 5 years through 1999, $210 million in 2000, and $374 million in 2001 (Ludwig [2002], Section H). Joseph Jett's phantom trades at Kidder Peabody started off small and ended with booked trades in excess of the quantity of all bonds the U.S. Treasury had issued.

The key to preventing financial disasters based on misrepresented positions is therefore the ability to spot unauthorized position taking in a timely enough fashion to prevent this explosive growth in position size. The lessons we can learn from these cases primarily center on why it took so long for knowledge of the misreported positions to spread from an insider group to the firm's management. We will examine each case by providing a brief summary of how the unauthorized position arose, how it failed to come to management's attention, and what lessons can be learned. In each instance, I will provide references for those seeking more detailed knowledge of the case.

4.1.1   Chase Manhattan Bank/Drysdale Securities

4.1.1.1   Incident   In 3 months of 1976, Drysdale Government Securities, a newly founded subsidiary of an established firm, succeeded in obtaining unsecured borrowing of about $300 million by exploiting a flaw in the market practices for computing the value of U.S. government bond collateral. This unsecured borrowing exceeded any amount they would have been approved for, given that the firm had only $20 million in capital. Drysdale used the borrowed money to take outright positions in bond markets. When they lost money on the positions they put on, they lacked cash with which to pay back their borrowings. Drysdale went bankrupt, losing virtually all of the $300 million in unsecured borrowings. Chase Manhattan absorbed almost all of these losses because they had brokered most of Drysdale's securities borrowings. Although Chase employees believed they were only acting as agents on these transactions and were not taking any direct risk on behalf of Chase, the legal documentation of the securities borrowings did not support their claim.

4.1.1.2   Result   Chase's financial viability was not threatened by losses of this size, but they were large enough to severely damage its reputation and stock valuation for several years.

4.1.1.3   How the Unauthorized Positions Arose   Misrepresentation in obtaining loans is unfortunately not that uncommon in bank lending. A classic example would be Anthony De Angelis, "The Salad Oil King," who, in 1963, obtained $175 million in loans supposedly secured by large salad oil holdings, which turned out to be vast drums filled with water with a thin layer of salad oil floating on top. Lending officers who came to check on their collateral were bamboozled into only looking at a sample from the top of each tank.

The following are some reasons for featuring the Drysdale shenanigans in this section rather than any number of other cases of misrepresentation:

- Drysdale utilized a weakness in trading markets to obtain its funds.
- Drysdale lost the borrowed money in the financial markets.
- It is highly unusual for a single firm to bear this large a proportion of this large a borrowing sting.

There is not much question as to how Drysdale managed to obtain the unsecured funds. They took systematic advantage of a computational shortcut in determining the value of borrowed securities. To save time and effort, borrowed securities were routinely valued as collateral without accounting for accrued coupon interest. By seeking to borrow large amounts of securities with high coupons and a short time left until the next coupon date, Drysdale could take maximum advantage of the difference in the amount of cash the borrowed security could be sold for (which included accrued interest) and the amount of cash collateral that needed to be posted against the borrowed security (which did not include accrued interest).

4.1.1.4 How the Unauthorized Positions Failed to Be Detected Chase Manhattan allowed such a sizable position to be built up largely because they believed that the firm's capital was not at risk. The relatively inexperienced managers running the securities borrowing and lending operation were convinced they were simply acting as middlemen between Drysdale and a large group of bond lenders. Through their inexperience, they both failed to realize that the wording in the borrowing agreements would most likely be found by a court to indicate that Chase was taking full responsibility for payments due against the securities borrowings or to realize the need for experienced legal counsel to review the contracts.

4.1.1.5 How the Unauthorized Positions Were Eventually Detected There was some limit to the size of bond positions Drysdale could borrow, even given the assumption that the borrowings were fully collateralized. At some point, the size of their losses exceeded the amount of unauthorized borrowings they could raise and they had to declare bankruptcy.

4.1.1.6 Lessons Learned The securities industry as a whole learned that it needed to make its methods for computing collateral value on bond borrowings more precise. Chase, and other firms who may have had similar control deficiencies, learned the need for a process that forced areas contemplating new product offerings to receive prior approval from representatives of the principal risk control functions within the firm (see Section 3.7).

4.1.1.7 Further Reading Chapter 14 of Stigum (1989) gives a detailed description of the Chase/Drysdale incident, some prior misadventures in bond borrowing collateralization, and the subsequent market reforms.

4.1.2 Kidder Peabody

4.1.2.1 Incident Between 1992 and 1994, Joseph Jett, head of the government bond trading desk, entered into a series of trades that were incorrectly reported in the firm's accounting system, artificially inflating reported profits. When this was ultimately corrected in April 1994, $350 million in previously reported gains had to be reversed.

4.1.2.2 Result   Although Jett's trades had not resulted in any actual loss of cash for Kidder, the announcement of such a massive misreporting of earnings triggered a substantial loss of confidence in the competence of the firm's management by customers and General Electric, which owned Kidder. In October 1994, General Electric sold Kidder to Paine Webber, which dismantled the firm.

4.1.2.3 How the Unauthorized Positions Arose   A flaw in accounting for forward transactions in the computer system for government bond trading failed to take into account the present valuing of the forward. This enabled a trader purchasing a cash bond and delivering it at a forward price to book an instant profit. Over the period between booking and delivery, the profit would inevitably dissipate, since the cash position had a financing cost that was unmatched by any financing gain on the forward position.

Had the computer system been used as it was originally intended (for a handful of forward trades with only a few days to forward delivery), the size of error would have been small. However, the system permitted entry not only of contracted forward trades, but also of intended forward delivery of bonds to the U.S. Treasury, which did not actually need to be acted on, but could be rolled forward into further intentions to deliver in the future. Both the size of the forward positions and the length of the forward delivery period were constantly increased to magnify the accounting error. This permitted a classic Ponzi scheme of ever mounting hypothetical profits covering the fact that previously promised profits never materialized.

Although it has never been completely clear how thoroughly Jett understood the full mechanics of the illusion, he had certainly worked out the link between his entry of forward trades and the recording of profit, and increasingly exploited the opportunity.

4.1.2.4 How the Unauthorized Positions Failed to Be Detected   Suspicions regarding the source of Jett's extraordinary profit performance were widespread throughout the episode. It was broadly perceived that no plausible account was being offered of a successful trading strategy that would explain the size of reported earnings. On several occasions, accusations were made that spelled out exactly the mechanism behind the inflated reporting. Jett seemed to have had a talent for developing explanations that succeeded in totally confusing everyone (including, perhaps, himself) as to what was going on. However, he was clearly aided and abetted by a management satisfied enough not to take too close a look at what seemed like a magical source of profits.

4.1.2.5 How the Unauthorized Positions Were Eventually Detected   Large increases in the size of his reported positions and earnings eventually triggered a more thorough investigation of Jett's operation.

4.1.2.6 Lessons to Be Learned Two lessons can be drawn from this: Always investigate a stream of large unexpected profits thoroughly and make sure you completely understand the source. Periodically review models and systems to see if changes in the way they are being used require changes in simplifying assumptions (see Section 6.2.2).

4.1.2.7 Further Reading Jett has written a detailed account of the whole affair (see Jett [1999]). However, his talent for obscurity remains and it is not possible to tell from his account just what he believes generated either his large profits or subsequent losses. For an account of the mechanics of the deception, one must rely on the investigation conducted by Gary Lynch on behalf of Kidder. Summaries of this investigation can be found in Hansell (1997), Mayer (1995), and Weiss (1994).

4.1.3 Barings

4.1.3.1 Incident The incident involved the loss of roughly $1.25 billion due to the unauthorized trading activities during 1993 to 1995 of a single, relatively junior trader named Nick Leeson.

4.1.3.2 Result The size of the losses relative to Barings' capital along with potential additional losses on outstanding trades forced Barings into bankruptcy in February 1995.

4.1.3.3 How the Unauthorized Positions Arose Leeson, who was supposed to be running a low-risk, limited return arbitrage business for Barings in Singapore, was actually taking increasingly large speculative positions in Japanese stocks and interest rate futures and options. He disguised his speculative position taking by reporting that he was taking the positions on behalf of fictitious customers. By booking the losses to these nonexistent customer accounts, he was able to manufacture fairly substantial reported profits for his own accounts, enabling him to earn a $720,000 bonus in 1994.

4.1.3.4 How the Unauthorized Positions Failed to Be Detected A certain amount of credit must be given to Leeson's industriousness in perpetrating a deliberate fraud. He worked hard at creating false accounts and was able to exploit his knowledge of weaknesses in the firm's controls. However, anyone reading an account of the incident will have to give primary credit to the stupendous incompetence on the part of Barings' management, which ignored every known control rule and failed to act on myriad obvious indications of something being wrong. What is particularly amazing is that all those trades were carried out in exchange-traded markets that require immediate cash settlement of all positions, thereby severely limiting the ability to hide positions (although Leeson did even manage to get some false reporting past the futures exchange to reduce the amount of cash required).

The most blatant of management failures was an attempt to save money by allowing Leeson to function as head of trading and the back office at an isolated branch. Even when auditors' reports warned about the danger of allowing Leeson to settle his own trades, thereby depriving the firm of an independent check on his activities, Barings' management persisted in their folly. Equally damning was management's failure to inquire how a low-risk trading strategy was supposedly generating such a large profit. Even when covering these supposed customer losses on the exchanges required Barings to send massive amounts of cash to the Singapore branch, no inquires were launched as to the cause. A large part of this failure can be attributed to the very poor structuring of management information so that different risk control areas could be looking at reports that did not tie together. The funding area would see a report indicating that cash was required to cover losses of a customer, not the firm, thereby avoiding alarm bells about the trading losses. A logical consequence is that credit exposure to customers must be large since the supposed covering of customer losses would entail a loan from Barings to the customer. However, information provided to the credit risk area was not integrated with information provided to funding and showed no such credit extension.

4.1.3.5 How the Unauthorized Positions Were Eventually Detected The size of losses Leeson was trying to cover up eventually got too overwhelming and he took flight, leaving behind an admission of irregularities.

4.1.3.6 Lessons to Be Learned One might be tempted to say that the primary lesson is that there are limits to how incompetent you can be and still hope to manage a major financial firm. However, to try to take away something positive, the major lessons would be the absolute necessity of an independent trading back office, the need to make thorough inquiries about unexpected sources of profit (or loss), and the need to make thorough inquiries about any large unanticipated movement of cash.

4.1.3.7 Further Readings A concise and excellent summary of the Barings case constitutes Chapter 10 of Chew (1996). Chapter 11 of Mayer (1997) contains less insight on the causes, but is strong on the financial and political maneuvers required to avoid serious damage to the financial system from the Barings failure. Leeson has written a full-length book that appears to be reasonably honest as to how he evaded detection (Leeson 1996). Fay (1996) and Rawnsley (1995) are also full-length accounts.

4.1.4 Allied Irish Bank (AIB)

4.1.4.1 Incident John Rusnak, a currency option trader in charge of a very small trading book in AIB's Allfirst First Maryland Bancorp subsidiary, entered into massive unauthorized trades during the period 1997 through 2002, ultimately resulting in $691 million in losses.

4.1.4.2 Result This resulted in a major blow to AIB's reputation and stock price.

4.1.4.3 How the Unauthorized Positions Arose Rusnak was supposed to be running a small arbitrage between foreign exchange (FX) options and FX spot and forward markets. He was actually running large outright positions and disguising them from management.

4.1.4.4 How the Unauthorized Positions Failed to Be Detected To quote the investigating report, "Mr. Rusnak was unusually clever and devious." He invented imaginary trades that offset his real trades, making his trading positions appear small. He persuaded back-office personnel not to check these bogus trades. He obtained cash to cover his losses by selling deep-in-the-money options, which provided cash up front in exchange for a high probability of needing to pay out even more cash at a later date, and covered up his position by offsetting these real trades with further imaginary trades. He entered false positions into the firm's system for calculating value at risk (VaR) to mislead managers about the size of his positions.

In many ways, Rusnak's pattern of behavior was a close copy of Nick Leeson's at Barings, using similar imaginary transactions to cover up real ones. Rusnak operated without Leeson's advantage of running his own back office, but had the offsetting advantage that he was operating in an over-the-counter market in which there was not an immediate need to put up cash against losses. He also was extremely modest in the amount of false profit he claimed so he did not set off the warning flags of large unexplained profits from small operations, which Leeson and Jett at Kidder Peabody triggered in their desire to collect large bonuses.

Like Barings, AIB's management and risk control units demonstrated a fairly startling level of incompetence in failing to figure out that something was amiss. AIB at least has the excuse that Rusnak's business continued to look small and insignificant, so it never drew much management attention. However, the scope and length of time over which Rusnak's deception continued provided ample opportunity for even the most minimal level of controls to catch up with him.

The most egregious was the back office's failure to confirm all trades. Rusnak succeeded in convincing back-office personnel that not all of these trades needed to be confirmed. He relied partly on an argument that trades whose initial payments offset one another didn't really need to be checked since they did not give rise to net immediate cash flow, ignoring the fact that the purported trades had different terms and hence significant impact on future cash flows. He relied partly on booking imaginary trades with counterparties in the Asian time zone, making confirmation for U.S.-based back-office staff a potentially unpleasant task involving middle-of-the-night phone calls, perhaps making it easier to persuade them that this work was not really necessary. He also relied on arguments that costs should be cut by weakening or eliminating key controls.

Once this outside control was missing, the way was opened for the ongoing manipulation of trading records. Auditors could have caught this, but the spot audits performed used far too small a sample. Suspicious movements in cash balances, daily trading profit and loss (P&L), sizes of gross positions, and levels of daily turnover were all ignored by Rusnak's managers through a combination of inexperience in FX options and over-reliance on trust in Rusnak's supposedly excellent character as a substitute for vigilant supervision. His management was too willing to withhold information from control functions and too compliant with Rusnak's bullying of operations personnel as part of a general culture of hostility toward control staff. This is precisely the sort of front-office pressure that reduces support staff independence, which was referred to in Section 3.1.1.

4.1.4.5 How the Unauthorized Positions Were Eventually Detected In December 2001, a back-office supervisor noticed trade tickets that did not have confirmations attached. When informed that the back-office personnel did not believe all trades required confirmations, he insisted that confirmation be sought for existing unconfirmed trades. Although it took some time for the instructions to be carried out, when they finally were carried out in early February 2002, despite some efforts by Rusnak to forge written confirmations and bully the back office into not seeking verbal confirmations, his fraud was bought to light within a few days.

4.1.4.6 Lessons to Be Learned This incident does not provide many new lessons beyond the lessons that should already have been learned from Barings. This case does emphasize the need to avoid engaging in small ventures in which the firm lacks any depth of expertise—there is simply too much reliance on the knowledge and probity of a single individual.

On the positive side, the investigative report on this fraud has provided risk control units throughout the financial industry with a set of delicious quotes that are sure to be trotted out anytime they feel threatened by cost-cutting measures or front-office bullying and lack of cooperation. The following are a few choice samples from Ludwig (2002):

- When one risk control analyst questioned why a risk measurement system was taking market inputs from a front-office-controlled system rather than from an independent source, she was told that AIB "would not pay for a $10,000 data feed from Reuters to the back office."
- When questioned about confirmations, "Mr. Rusnak became angry. He said he was making money for the bank, and that if the back office continued to question everything he did, they would drive him to quit . . . Mr. Rusnak's supervisor warned that if Mr. Rusnak left the bank, the loss of his profitable trading would force job cuts in the back office."
- "When required, Mr. Rusnak was able to use a strong personality to bully those who questioned him, particularly in Operations." His supervisors "tolerated numerous instances of severe friction between Mr. Rusnak and the back-office staff."
- Rusnak's supervisor "discouraged outside control groups from gaining access to information in his area and reflexively supported Mr. Rusnak whenever questions about his trading arose."
- " . . . in response to general efforts to reduce expense and increase revenues, the Allfirst treasurer permitted the weakening or elimination of key controls for which he was responsible . . . Mr. Rusnak was able to manipulate this concern for additional cost cutting into his fraud."

4.1.4.7 Further Reading Since this is the newest of the disasters, not much has been written on it yet. I have relied heavily on the very prompt and thorough report issued by Ludwig (2002).

4.1.5 Union Bank of Switzerland (UBS)

4.1.5.1 Incident This incident involves losses of between $400 million and $700 million in equity derivatives during 1997, which appear to have been exacerbated by lack of internal controls. A loss of $700 million during 1998 was due to a large position in Long Term Capital Management (LTCM).

4.1.5.2 Result The 1997 losses forced UBS into a merger on unfavorable terms with Swiss Bank Corporation (SBC) at the end of 1997. The 1998 losses came after that merger.

4.1.5.3 Were the Positions Unauthorized? Less is known about the UBS disaster than the other incidents discussed in this chapter. Even the size of the losses has never been fully disclosed. Considerable controversy exists about whether the 1997 losses just reflected poor decision making or unlucky outcomes or whether an improper control structure led to positions that management would not have authorized. The 1998 losses were the result of a position that certainly had been approved by the UBS management, but evidence suggests that it failed to receive adequate scrutiny from the firm's risk controllers and that it was not adequately disclosed to the SBC management that took over the firm.

What seems uncontroversial is that the equity derivatives business was being run without the degree of management oversight that would be normally expected in a firm of the size and sophistication of UBS, but there is disagreement about how much this situation contributed to the losses. The equity derivatives department was given an unusual degree of independence within the firm with little oversight by, or sharing of information with, the corporate risk managers. The person with senior risk management authority for the department doubled as head of quantitative analytics. As head of analytics, he was both a contributor to the business decisions he was responsible for reviewing and had his compensation tied to trading results, which are both violations of the fundamental principles of independent oversight.

The equity derivative losses appear to have been primarily due to four factors:

- A change in British tax laws, which impacted the value of some long-dated stock options
- A large position in Japanese bank warrants, which was inadequately hedged against a significant drop in the underlying stocks (see the fuller description in Section 9.4)
- An overly aggressive valuation of long-dated options on equity baskets, utilizing correlation assumptions that were out of line with those used by competitors
- Losses on other long-dated basket options, which may have been due to modelling deficiencies

The first two transactions were ones where UBS had similar positions to many of its competitors so it would be difficult to accuse the firm of excessive risk taking, although its Japanese warrant positions appear to have been unreasonably large relative to competitors. The last two problems appear to have been more unique to UBS. Many competitors made accusations that their prices for trades were off the market.

The losses related to LTCM came as the result of a position personally approved by Mathis Cabiallavetta, the UBS CEO, so they were certainly authorized in one sense. However, accusations have been made that the trades were approved without adequate review by risk control areas and were never properly represented in the firm's risk management systems. Although about 40 percent of the exposure represented a direct investment in LTCM that had large potential profits to weigh against the risk, about 60 percent of the exposure was an option written on the value of LTCM shares. However, there was no effective way in which such an option could be risk managed given the illiquidity of LTCM shares and restrictions that LTCM placed on UBS delta hedging the position.

The imbalance in risk/reward trade-off for an option that was that difficult to risk manage had caused other investment banks to reject the proposed trade. UBS appears to have entered into the option because of its desire for a direct investment in LTCM, which LTCM tied to agreement to the option. Agreeing to this type of bundled transaction can certainly be a legitimate business decision, but it is unclear whether the full risk of the option had been analyzed by UBS or whether stress tests of the two positions taken together had been performed.

4.1.5.4 Lessons Learned This incident emphasizes the need for independent risk oversight.

4.1.5.5 Further Reading The fullest account of the equity derivative losses is contained in a book by Schutz (2000), which contains many lurid accusations about improper dealings between the equity derivatives department and senior management of the firm. Schutz has been accused of inaccuracy in some of these charges—see the October 1998 issue of *Derivatives Strategy* for details. There is also a good summary in the January 31, 1998 issue of the *Economist*.

A good account of the LTCM transaction is Shirreff (1998). Lowenstein (2000), an account of the LTCM collapse, also covers the UBS story in some detail.

4.1.6 Other Cases

Other disasters involving unauthorized positions will be covered more briefly, because they had less of an impact on the firm involved, because it is harder to uncover details on what occurred, or because they do not have any lessons to teach beyond those of the cases already discussed:

- Toshihida Iguchi of Daiwa Bank's New York office lost $1.1 billion trading Treasury bonds between 1984 and 1995. He hid his losses and made his operation appear to be quite profitable by forging trading slips, which enabled him to sell without authorization bonds held in customer accounts to produce funds he could claim were part of his trading profit. His fraud was aided by a situation similar to Nick Leeson's at Barings—Iguchi was head of trading and the back-office support function. In addition to the losses, Daiwa lost its license to trade in the United States, but this was primarily due to its failure to promptly disclose the fraud once senior executives of the firm learned of it. A more detailed account of this by Rob Jamesson of ERisk can be found on their Web site, www.erisk.com.

■ The Sumitomo Corporation of Japan lost $2.6 billion in a failed attempt by Yasuo Hamanaka, a senior trader, to corner the world's copper market—that is, to drive up prices by controlling a large portion of the available supply. Sumitomo management claimed that Hamanaka had employed fraudulent means in hiding the size of his positions from them. Hamanaka claimed that he had disclosed the positions to senior management. Hamanaka was sent to jail for his actions. The available details are sketchy, but some can be found in Dwyer (1996), *Asiaweek* (1996), Kooi (1996), and McKay (1999).

■ Askin Capital Management and Granite Capital, hedge funds that invested in mortgage securities, went bankrupt in 1994 with losses of $600 million. It was revealed that David Askin, the manager of the funds, was valuing positions with his own marks substituted for dealer quotes and using these position values in reports to investors in the funds and in marketing materials to attract new clients. For a brief discussion, see Mayer (1997).

■ Merrill Lynch reportedly lost $350 million in trading mortgage securities in 1987, due to risk reporting that used a 13-year duration for all securities created from a pool of 30-year mortgages. Although this duration is roughly correct for an undivided pool of 30-year mortgages, when the interest-only (IO) part is sold and the principal-only (PO) part is kept, as Merrill was doing, the correct duration is 30 years. See Crouhy, Galai, and Mark (2001).

■ National Westminster Bank in 1997 reported a loss on interest rate caps and swaptions of about $140 million. The losses were attributed to trades dating back to 1994 and had been masked by deliberate use by traders of incorrect volatility inputs for less liquid maturities. The loss of confidence in management caused by this incident may have contributed to NatWest's sale to the Royal Bank of Scotland. I have heard from market sources that the traders were taking advantage of the middle-office saving costs by checking only a sample of volatility marks against market sources, although it is unclear how the traders were able to determine in advance which quotes would be checked. A more detailed account by Eric Wolfe can be obtained on ERisk's Web site, www.erisk.com.

4.2 DISASTERS DUE TO LARGE MARKET MOVES

We will now look at financial disasters that were not caused by incorrect position information, but were caused by unanticipated market moves. The first question that should be asked is how is a disaster possible if positions are known. No matter what strategy is chosen, as losses start to mount beyond acceptable bounds, why aren't the positions closed out? The answer is lack of liquidity. We will focus on this aspect of these disasters.

4.2.1　Long Term Capital Management (LTCM)

The case we will consider at greatest length is that of the large hedge fund managed by LTCM, which came close to bankruptcy in 1998. In many ways, it represents an ideal example for this type of case since all of its positions were marked to a market value daily, the market values were supplied by the dealers on the other end of each trade, no accusations have been made of anyone at LTCM providing misleading information about positions taken, and the near failure came in the midst of some of the largest market moves in recent memory.

To review the facts, LTCM had been formed in 1994 by about a dozen partners. Many of these partners had previously worked together at Salomon Brothers in a highly successful proprietary trading group. Over the period from 1994 until early 1998, the LTCM fund produced quite spectacular returns for its investors. From the beginning, the partners made clear that they would be highly secretive about the particulars of their investment portfolio, even by the standard of other hedge funds. (Since hedge funds are only open to wealthy investors and cannot be publicly offered the way mutual funds are, they are not subject to legal requirements to disclose their holdings.)

Within the firm, however, the management style favored sharing information openly, and essentially every investment decision was made by all the partners acting together, an approach that virtually eliminates the possibility of a rogue trader making decisions based on information concealed from other members of the firm. Although it is true that outside investors in the fund did not have access to much information beyond the month-end valuation of its assets and the track record of its performance, it is equally true that the investors knew these rules prior to their decision to invest. Since the partners who managed the fund were such strong believers in the fund that they had invested most of their net worth in it (several even borrowed to invest more than their net worth), their incentives were closely aligned with investors (in other words, there was little room for moral hazard). If anything, the concentration of partner assets in the fund should have led to more risk-averse decision making than might have been optimal for outside investors, who invested only a small portion of their wealth in the fund, with the exception of UBS, discussed in Section 4.1.5.

In fact, even if investors had been given access to more information, there is little they could have done with it, since they were locked into their investments for extended time periods (generally, 3 years). This reflected the basic investment philosophy of LTCM, which was to locate trading opportunities

that represented what they believed were temporary disruptions in price relationships due to short-term market pressures, which were almost certain to
be reversed over longer time periods. To take advantage of such opportunities, they needed to know they had access to patient capital that would not
be withdrawn if markets seemed to be temporarily going against them. This
also helped to explain why LTCM was so secretive about its holdings. These
were not quick in-and-out trades, but long-term holdings, and they needed
to prevent other firms from learning the positions and trading against them.

The following are two examples of the type of positions the LTCM fund
was taking:

- LTCM was long U.S. interest rate swaps and short U.S. government
  bonds at a time when these spreads were at historically high levels.
  Over the life of the trade, this position will make money as long as
  the average spread between the London Interbank Offering Rates
  (LIBORs) at which swaps are reset (see Section 8.1.6) and the RP rates
  at which government bonds are funded (see Section 8.1.2) is not
  higher than the spread at which the trade was entered into. Over
  longer time periods, the range for the average of LIBOR-RP spreads
  is not that wide, but in the short run, swap spreads can show large
  swings based on relative investor demand for the safety of governments versus the higher yield of corporate bonds (with corporate bond
  issuers then demanding interest rate swaps to convert fixed debt to
  floating debt).
- LTCM sold equity options at historically high implied volatilities. Over
  the life of the trade, this position will make money if the actual volatility is lower than the implied, but in the short run, investor demand
  for protection against stock market crashes can raise implied volatilities to very high levels. Perold (1999A) presents further analysis of
  why LTCM viewed these trades as excellent long-term investments and
  presents several other examples of positions they entered into.

One additional element was needed to obtain the potential returns
LTCM was looking for. They needed to be able to finance positions for
longer terms in order to be able to ensure there was no pressure on them to
sell positions before they reached the price relationships LTCM was waiting for. However, the banks and investment banks who financed hedge fund
positions were the very competitors that they least wanted to share information on holdings with. How were they to persuade firms to take credit
risk without knowing much about the trading positions of the hedge fund?

To understand why the lenders were comfortable in doing this, we need
to digress a moment into how credit works in a futures exchange. A futures
exchange (see Section 8.1.4) represents the extreme of being willing to lend

without knowledge of the borrower. Someone who purchases, for example, a bond for future delivery, needs to deposit only a small percentage of the agreed purchase price as margin and does not need to disclose anything about her financial condition. The futures exchange is counting on the nature of the transaction itself to provide confidence that money will not be lost in the transaction. This is because any time the value of the bond falls, the purchaser is required to immediately provide added margin to fully cover the decline in value. If the purchaser does not do so, her position is closed out without delay. Loss is only possible if the price has declined so much since the last time the price fell and margin was added that the incremental price drop exceeds the amount of initial margin or if closing out the option results in a large price move. The probability of this occurring is kept low by setting initial margins high enough, restricting the size of position that can be taken by any one investor, and designing futures contract to cover sufficiently standardized products to ensure enough liquidity that the close-out of a trade will not cause a big price jump.

LTCM wanted to deal in over-the-counter markets as well as on futures exchanges partly because they wanted to deal in some contracts more individually tailored than those available on futures exchanges and partly because of the position size restrictions of exchanges. However, the mechanism used to assure lenders in over-the-counter markets is similar—the requirement to cover declines in market value by immediately putting up cash. If a firm fails to put up the cash, then positions are closed out. LTCM almost always negotiated terms that avoided posting the initial margin. Lenders were satisfied with the lack of initial margin based on the size of the LTCM fund's equity, the track record of their excellent returns, and their recognized investment management skills. Lenders retained the option of demanding initial margin if fund equity fell too much.

This dependence on short-term swings in valuation represented a potential Achilles' heel for LTCM's long-term focused investment strategy. Because they were seeking opportunities where market pressures were causing deviation from long-run relationships, a strong possibility always existed that these same market pressures would push the deviation even further. LTCM would then immediately need to come up with cash to fund the change in market valuation. This would not be a problem if some of their trades were moving in their favor at the same time as others were moving against them, since LTCM would receive cash on upswings in value to balance putting up cash on downswings (again, the same structure as exchange-traded futures). However, if many of their trades were to move against them in tandem, LTCM would need to raise cash quickly, either from investors or by cutting positions.

In the actual events of August and September 1998, this is exactly what led to LTCM's rapid downfall. The initial trigger was a combination of the

Russian debt default of August, which unsettled the markets, and the June 1998 decision by Salomon Brothers to liquidate proprietary positions it was holding, which were similar to many of those held by LTCM. The LTCM fund's equity began to decline precipitously, from $4.1 billion as of the end of July 1998, and it was very reluctant to cut positions in a turbulent market in which any large position sale could easily move the valuations even further against them. This left the option of seeking new equity from investors. LTCM pursued this path vigorously, but the very act of their doing so created two perverse effects. First, rumors of their predicament caused competitors to drive market prices even further against what they guessed were LTCM's positions, in anticipation of LTCM being forced to unload the positions at distressed prices. Second, to persuade potential investors to provide new money in the midst of volatile markets, LTCM was forced to disclose information about the actual positions they held. As competitors learned more about the actual positions, their pressure on market prices in the direction unfavorable to LTCM intensified.

As market valuations continued to move against LTCM and the lack of liquidity made it even more unlikely that reducing positions would be a viable plan, it became increasingly probable that in the absence of a truly large infusion of new equity, the LTCM fund would be bankrupt. Its creditors started to prepare to close out LTCM's positions, but quickly came to fear that they were so large and the markets were so illiquid that the creditors would suffer serious losses in the course of doing so. The lenders were also concerned that the impact of closing out these positions would depress values in the already fragile markets and thereby cause considerable damage to other positions held by the creditors and other investment firms they were financing.

Ultimately, 14 of the largest creditors, all major investment banks or commercial banks with large investment banking operations, contributed a fresh $3.65 billion in equity investment in the LTCM fund to permit the firm to keep operating and allow for a substantial time period in which to close out positions. In return, the creditors received substantial control over fund management. The existing investors had their investment valued at the then current market value of $400 million so they had only a 10 percent share in the positions of the fund. Although some of the partners remained employed to help wind down investments, it was the consortium of 14 creditors who now exercised control and insisted on winding down all positions.

As a result, the markets calmed down. By 2000, the fund had been wound down with the 14 creditors having recovered all of the equity they invested and avoided any losses on the LTCM positions they had held at the time of the bailout. This outcome lends support to two propositions: LTCM was largely right about the long-term values underlying its positions, and the creditors were right to see the primary problem as one of liquidity, which required patience to ride out.

Please note that the bailout was not primarily a rescue of LTCM's investors or management, but a rescue of LTCM's creditors by a concerted action of these creditors. Even recently, I continue to encounter the view that the bailout involved the use of U.S. government funds, helped the LTCM investors and management avoid the consequences of their mistakes, and therefore contributed to an attitude that some firms are "too big to fail" and so can afford to take extra risks because they can count on the government absorbing some of their losses.

I do not think evidence is available to support any of these claims. (An interested reader can form her own conclusions by looking at the detailed account of the negotiations on the rescue package in Lowenstein [2000]. An opposing viewpoint can be found in Shirreff [2000].) The only government involvement was some coordination by the Federal Reserve, acting out of legitimate concern for the potential impact on the financial markets. The LTCM creditors took a risk by investing money in the fund, but did so in their own self-interest, believing (correctly, as it turns out) that they were thereby lowering their total risk of loss. LTCM's investors and managers had little left to lose at the point of the bailout since they could not lose more than their initial investment. It is true that, without a rescue, the fund would have been liquidated, which would have almost certainly wiped out the remaining $400 million market value of the investors. However, in exchange for this rescue, they were able to retain only a 10 percent interest in the fund's positions, since the $3.65 billion in new investment was explicitly not being used to enable new trades, but only to wind down the existing positions.

LTCM management was certainly aware of the potential for short-term market movements to disrupt their fundamental trading strategy of focusing on longer-term relationships. They tried to limit this risk by insisting that their positions pass value at risk (VaR) tests based on whether potential losses over 1 month due to adverse market moves would reduce equity to unacceptable levels. Where they seem to have fallen short of best practices was a failure to supplement VaR measures with a full set of stress test scenarios (see Section 11.2). They did run stress versions of VaR based on a higher than historical level of correlations, but it is doubtful that this offers the same degree of conservatism as a set of fully worked through scenarios.

A lesson that all market participants have learned from the LTCM incident is that a stress scenario is needed to look at the impact of a competitor holding similar positions exiting the market, as when Salomon decided to cut back on proprietary trading. However, even by best practice standards of the time, LTCM should have constructed a stress test based on common economic factors that could cause impacts across their positions, such as a flight to quality by investors, which would widen all credit spreads, including swap spreads, and increase premiums on buying protection against stock market crashes, hence increasing option volatility.

Another point on which LTCM's risk management could be criticized is a failure to account for the illiquidity of its largest positions in its VaR or stress runs. LTCM knew that the position valuations it was receiving from dealers did not reflect the concentration of some of LTCM's positions, either because dealers were not taking liquidity into account in their marks or because each dealer only knew a small part of LTCM's total size in its largest positions.

Two other criticisms have been made of LTCM's management of risk with which I disagree. One is that a simple computation of leverage would have shown that LTCM's positions were too risky. However, as will be seen in Section 12.2.3, leverage by itself is not an adequate measure of risk of default. It must be multiplied by volatility of the firm's assets. But this just gets us back to testing through VaR or stress scenarios. The second criticism is that LTCM showed unreasonable faith in the outcome of models. I see no evidence to support this claim. Major positions LTCM entered into—U.S. swap spreads to narrow, equity volatilities to decline—were ones that many proprietary position takers had entered into. For example, the bias in equity implied volatilities due to demand for downside protection by shareholders had long been widely recognized as a fairly certain profit opportunity for investors with long enough time horizons. That some firms made more use of models to inform their trading judgement while others relied more on trader experience tells me nothing about the relative quality of their decision making.

Most of the focus of LTCM studies has been on the decision making of LTCM management and the losses of the investors. I believe this emphasis is misplaced. It is a fairly common occurrence, and to be expected, that investment funds will have severe drops in valuation. The bankruptcy of an investment fund does not ordinarily threaten the stability of the financial system the way the bankruptcy of a firm that makes markets or is a critical part of the payments system would. It just represents the losses of a small number of investors. Nor is there a major difference in consequences between bankruptcy and a large loss short of bankruptcy for an investment fund. It shouldn't matter to an investor whether a fund in which she has invested $10 million goes bankrupt or if a fund in which she has invested $30 million loses a third of its value. By contrast, losses short of bankruptcy only hurt the stockholders of a bank, while bankruptcy could hurt depositors and lead to loss of confidence in the banking system.

The reason that an LTCM failure came close to disrupting the financial markets and required a major rescue operation was its potential impact on the creditors to LTCM so we need to take a closer look at their role in the story. In retrospect, the creditors to LTCM believed they had been too lax in their credit standards and the incident triggered a major industry study of credit practices relating to trading counterparties (Counterparty Risk Management Policy Group [1999]).

Some suggestions for improved practices, many of which are extensively addressed in this study, have been:

- **A greater reluctance to allow trading without initial margin for counterparties whose principal business is investing and trading.** A counterparty that has other substantial business lines, for example, auto manufacturing or retail banking, is unlikely to have all of their economic resources threatened by a large move in financial markets. However, a firm that is primarily engaged in these markets is vulnerable to illiquidity spreading from one market to another as firms close out positions in one market to meet margin calls in another market. For such firms, initial margin is needed as a cushion against market volatility.
- **Factoring the potential costs of liquidating positions in an adverse market environment into estimates of the price at which trades can be unwound.** These estimates should be based on the size of positions as well as the general liquidity of the market (see Section 5.1.2). These potential liquidation costs should impact estimates of the amount of credit being extended and requirements for initial margin.
- **A push for greater disclosure by counterparties of their trading strategies and positions.** Reliance on historical records of return as an indicator of the volatility of a portfolio can be very misleading because it cannot capture the impact of changes in trading style (see Section 11.1). Increased allowance for liquidation costs of positions will be very inexact if the creditor only knows the positions that a counterparty holds with the creditor without knowing the impact of other positions held. To try to deal with counterparties' legitimate fears that disclosure of their positions will lead to taking advantage of this knowledge, creditors are implementing more stringent internal policies against the sharing of information between the firm's credit officers and the firm's traders.
- **Better use of stress tests in assessing credit risk.** To some extent, this involves using more extreme stresses than were previously used in measuring risk to reflect the increased market volatility that has been experienced in recent years. However, a major emphasis is also on more integration of market risk and credit risk stress testing to take into account overlap in risks. In the LTCM case, this would have required recognition by a creditor to LTCM that many of the largest positions being held by LTCM were also being held by other investment funds

to which the firm had counterparty credit exposure, as well as by the firm's own proprietary traders. A full stress test would then look at the losses that would be incurred by a large market move and subsequent decrease in liquidity across all of these similar positions.

A complete account of the LTCM case covering all aspects of the history of the fund and its managers, the involvement of creditors, and the negotiations over its rescue can be found in Lowenstein (2000). The Harvard Business School case studies of Perold (1999A) and Perold (1999B) are a detailed but concise analysis of the fund's investment strategy and the dilemma that it faced in August 1998.

4.2.2 Metallgesellschaft (MG)

The disaster at Metallgesellschaft (MG) reveals another aspect of liquidity management. In 1992, an American subsidiary of MG, Metallgesellachaft Refining and Marketing (MGRM), began a program of entering into long-term contracts to supply customers with gas and oil products at fixed costs and hedge these contracts with short-term gas and oil futures. Although some controversy exists about how effective this hedging strategy was from a P&L standpoint, as we'll discuss in just a moment, the fundamental consequence of this strategy for liquidity management is certain. The futures being used to hedge were exchange-traded instruments requiring daily cash settlement, as explained in Section 8.1.4. The long-term contracts with customers involved no such cash settlement. So no matter how effective the hedging strategy was, the consequence of a large downward move in gas and oil prices would be to require MGRM to pay cash against its futures positions that would be offset by money owed to MGRM by customers who would be paid in the future.

A properly designed hedge will reflect both the cash paid and the financing cost of that cash during the period until the customer payment is due and hence will be effective from a P&L standpoint. However, the funding must still be obtained, which can lead to funding liquidity risk (see Section 3.5). As we will discuss in Section 5.1.4, such cash needs must be planned in advance. Limits need to be set on positions based on the amount of cash shortfall that can be funded.

It appears that MGRM did not communicate to its parent company the possible need for such funding. In 1993, when a large decrease in gas and oil prices had resulted in funding needs of around $900 million, the MG parent responded by closing down the future positions, leaving unhedged exposure to gas and oil price increases through the customer contracts. Faced with this open exposure, MG negotiated unwinds of these contracts at unfavorable terms. It may be that MG, with lack of advance warning as to possible cash needs, responded to the demand for cash as a sign that the trading strategy was deeply flawed—if only Barings' management had reacted similarly.

As mentioned earlier, the MG incident spurred considerable debate as to whether MGRM's trading strategy was reasonable or fundamentally flawed. Most notably, Culp and Miller (1995A) wrote an article defending the reasonableness of the strategy, and Mello and Parsons (1995) wrote an article attacking the Culp and Miller conclusions, which were then defended by Culp and Miller (1995B). Although it is difficult to settle the factual arguments about the particular events in the MG case, I believe the following lessons can be drawn:

- It is often a key component of a market maker's business strategy to extend available liquidity in a market (see Section 8.2.2). This requires the use of shorter-term hedges against longer-term contracts. Experience shows that this can be successfully carried out when proper risk controls are applied.
- The uncertainty of roll cost is a key risk for strategies involving shorter-term hedges against longer-term risk. As explained in Section 8.2.2, this requires the use of valuation reserves based on conservative assumptions of future roll cost. MGRM does not appear to have utilized valuation reserves; it just based its valuation on the historical averages of roll costs.
- A firm running short-term hedges against longer-term risk requires the flexibility to choose the shorter-term hedge that offers the best trade-off between risk and reward. It may legitimately choose to follow a hedging strategy other than a theoretical minimum variance hedge, or choose not to hedge with the longest future available, based on liquidity considerations, or take into account the expectation of positive roll cost as part of potential return. It is not reasonable to conclude, as Mello and Parsons do, that these choices indicate that the firm is engaged in pure speculation rather than hedging. At the same time, regardless of a firm's conclusions about probable return, its assessment of risk should include valuation reserves, as in the previous point, and volume limits based on reasonable stress testing of assumptions.

4.3   DISASTERS DUE TO THE CONDUCT OF CUSTOMER BUSINESS

In this section, we focus on disasters that did not involve any direct financial loss to the firm, but were completely a matter of reputational risk due to the conduct of customer business.

4.3.1 Banker's Trust (BT)

The classic case of this type is the Banker's Trust (BT) incident of 1994, when BT was sued by Procter & Gamble (P&G) and Gibson Greetings. Both P&G and Gibson claimed that they had suffered large losses in derivatives trades they had entered into with BT due to being misled by BT as to the nature of the positions. These were trades on which BT had little market or credit risk, since they had hedged the market risk on them with other derivatives and there was no credit issue of P&G or Gibson being unable to pay the amount they owed. However, the evidence uncovered in the course of legal discovery for these lawsuits was severely damaging to BT's reputation for fair business dealing, led to the resignation of the firm's CEO, and ultimately had such negative consequences for their ability to do business that they were forced into an acquisition by Deutschebank, which essentially amounted to a dismemberment of the firm.

The exact terms of these derivative trades were quite complex and are not essential to understanding the incident. Interested readers are referred to Chew (1996, Chapter 2) for details. The key point is that the trades offered P&G and Gibson a reasonably probable but small reduction in funding expenses in exchange for a potentially large loss under some less probable circumstances. P&G and Gibson had been entering into such trades for several years prior to 1994 with good results. The derivatives were not tailored to any particular needs of P&G or Gibson in the sense that the circumstances under which the derivatives would lose them money were not designed to coincide with cases in which other P&G or Gibson positions would be making money. Their objective was just to reduce expected funding costs. Since the only way to reduce costs in some cases is to raise them in others, P&G and Gibson can be presumed to have understood that they could lose money under some economic circumstances. On what basis could they claim that BT had misled them?

One element that established some prima facie suspicion of BT was the sheer complexity of the structures. It was hard to believe that BT's clients started out with any particular belief about whether there was a small enough probability of loss of a structure to be comfortable entering into it. BT would have had to carefully explain all the intricacies of the payoffs to the clients for them to be fully informed.

Since it was quite clear that the exact nature of the structures hadn't been tailored to meet client needs, why had BT utilized so complex a design? The most probable reason was that they were designed to be complex enough to make it difficult for clients to comparison shop the pricing to competitor firms. However, this also made the clients highly dependent on BT on an ongoing basis. If they wanted to unwind the position, they couldn't count on getting a competitive quote from another firm.

BT claimed that they had adequately explained all the payoffs and risks to P&G and Gibson. But then came the discovery phase of the lawsuit. BT, like all trading firms, taped all phone lines of traders and marketers as a means of resolving disputes about verbal contracts (see Sections 3.1.1 and 3.2). However, this taping also picked up internal conversations between BT personnel. When subpoenaed, they produced evidence of BT staff boasting of how thoroughly they had fooled the clients as to the true value of the trades and how little the clients understood the true risks. Further, the internal BT tapes showed that price quotes to P&G and Gibson were being manipulated to mislead them. At first, they were given valuations of the trades that were much too high to mask the degree of profit BT was able to book up front. Later, they were given valuations that were too low because this was BT's bid at which to buy back the trade or swap it into a new trade offering even more profit to BT. For more details on what was revealed in the tapes, see Holland and Himelstein (1995).

The BT scandal caused all financial firms to tighten up their procedures for dealing with customers, both in better controls on matching the degree of complexity of trades to the degree of financial sophistication of customers and in providing for customers to obtain price quotes from an area independent of the front office. These measures were detailed in Section 3.3.

Another lesson that you would think would be learned is to be cautious about how you use any form of communication that can later be made public. BT's reputation was certainly hurt by the objective facts about their conduct, but it was even further damaged by the arrogant and insulting tone some of their employees used in referring to clients, which could be documented through recorded conversations. However, even with such an instructive example, we have seen Merrill Lynch's reputation being damaged in 2002 by remarks their stock analysts made in emails and tape-recorded conversations (see the article "Value of Trust" in the June 6, 2002 *Economist*) along with a number of similar incidents surrounding Wall Street's relations with Enron (see the article "Banks on Trial" in the July 25, 2002 *Economist*).

4.3.2 Other Cases

The following are some examples of other cases in which firms damaged their reputation by the manner in which they dealt with customers:

- Prudential-Bache Securities was found to have seriously misled thousands of customers concerning the risk of proposed investments in limited partnerships. In addition to damaging their reputation, Prudential-Bache had to pay more than $1 billion in fines and settlements. An account of this incident can be found in Eichenwald (1995).

- In 1995, a fund manager at Morgan Grenfell Asset Management directed mutual fund investments into highly speculative stocks, utilizing shell companies to evade legal restrictions on the percentage of a firm's stock that could be owned by a single fund. In addition to damage to their reputation, Morgan Grenfell had to pay roughly $600 million to compensate investors for resulting losses. A brief case study can be found on ERisk's Web site, www.erisk.com.
- JPMorgan's reputation was damaged by allegations that it misled a group of Korean corporate investors as to the risk in derivative trades that lost hundreds of millions of dollars based on the precipitous decline in the Thai bhat exchange rate against the dollar in 1997. An account of these trades and the ensuing lawsuits can be found in Gillen, Lee, and Austin (1999).

CHAPTER 5

Managing Market Risk

This is the first of six chapters devoted to the management of market risk. Specific risk-management techniques for spot risk, forward risk, vanilla options risk, and exotic options risk will be addressed in other chapters focusing on each risk type. In this chapter, we will look at some general principles that apply to all these risks.

The management of market risk can be divided into two parts—risk measurement and risk control. In general, the industry agrees more on how risk should be measured than how it should be controlled.

5.1   RISK MEASUREMENT

The critical components of risk measurement are mark-to-market valuation, the establishment of valuation reserves, the analysis of revenue to identify sources of risk, and the measurement of exposure to changes in market prices. We will discuss each in turn. Although most of the emphasis will be on the risk measurement of market makers, we will also address the question of how applicable these principles should be to position takers.

In the course of these discussions, we will sometimes refer to the recommendations for managing derivatives risk that were issued by the Group of Thirty (G-30) in July 1993. These recommendations have proved very influential not just for the management of derivatives risk, but also for all trading risk. The G-30 is a private, nonprofit organization that studies international economic and financial issues, and is headed by 30 senior representatives of the international business, regulatory, and academic communities. The following box shows the recommendations that relate most directly to the measurement of trading risk. The original numbering of the G-30 report was included.

GROUP OF 30 RECOMMENDATIONS RELATING TO THE MEASUREMENT OF TRADING RISK

Recommendation 2: Marking to Market

Dealers should mark their derivatives positions to market, on at least a daily basis, for risk management purposes.

Recommendation 3: Market Valuation Methods

Derivatives portfolios of dealers should be valued based on mid-market levels less specific adjustments, or on appropriate bid or offer levels. Mid-market valuation adjustments should allow for expected future costs such as unearned credit spread, close-out costs, investing and funding costs, and administrative costs.

Recommendation 4: Identifying Revenue Sources

Dealers should measure the components of revenue regularly and in sufficient detail to understand the sources of risk.

Recommendation 5: Measuring Market Risk

Dealers should use a consistent measure to calculate daily the market risk of their derivatives positions and compare it to market risk limits.

- Market risk is best measured as 'value at risk' using probability analysis based upon a common confidence interval (e.g., two standard deviations) and time horizon (e.g., a one-day exposure).
- Components of market risk that should be considered across the term structure include: absolute price or rate change (delta); convexity (gamma); volatility (vega); time decay (theta); basis or correlation; and discount rate (rho).

Recommendation 6: Stress Simulations

Dealers should regularly perform simulations to determine how their portfolios would perform under stress conditions.

Recommendation 7: Investing and Funding Forecasts

Dealers should periodically forecast the cash investing and funding requirements arising from their derivative portfolios.

Source: Group of 30, *Global Derivatives and Principles*, 1993.

5.1.1 Market Valuation

The policy of marking to market all trading positions, at least as often as the close of business each day, as per the G-30's Recommendation 2, constitutes the essential foundation for measuring trading risk because of three primary reasons. First, without a nearly continuous mark to market, it would be possible that ineffective hedging strategies would not be recognized until long after being put in place. Second, the analysis of revenue will only yield insight if the revenue figures being analyzed are tied to genuine changes in value. Third, in measuring the risk exposure to market moves, it is far easier to make good judgments about possible short-term moves than it is about longer-term moves. But if trades are not revalued frequently, it becomes necessary to measure risk exposure over longer periods.

When highly liquid external prices are available for marking a position to market, then the issues involved in performing the mark are largely operational. An example might be a position in spot foreign exchange (FX) for the dollar versus Japanese yen. This is a market for which quotations are readily available on trading screens, with market conventions that ensure that firms' posting prices are prepared to actually deal in reasonable size at these prices. Quotations for mark-to-market purposes can be captured electronically from trading screens or entered by hand and later checked against printouts from screens—the choice should be based on the operational cost versus error rate and the cost of correcting errors. Another example would be a position in a well-traded stock or exchange-traded futures option for which the last price at which an actual trade occurred is readily available from an exchange ticker.

For many positions, mark to market is not this straightforward. Either the market itself does not have this type of liquid quote available or the size of position held is so large that closing it out might impact the market. The price at which the position can be exited will be uncertain to some degree. In such cases, two interrelated questions must be asked:

- How should a most likely exit price be arrived at?
- Should some markdown of the price be used to account for the uncertainty and, if so, how should the amount of reserve be determined?

The most likely price can be established through two approaches. One is to use some type of model to create a mark based on more readily available prices of other instruments. Models can range from very simple computations, such as the interpolation of an illiquid $2\frac{1}{2}$-year bond from prices on more liquid 2- and 3-year bonds, to complex theoretical constructions. A discussion of how to use models in the marking process and how to establish reserves against the associated uncertainty can be found in Chapter 6.

The second approach to establishing the most likely price is to determine the price based on those quotes that can be obtained for the particular transaction in question.

In the latter case, price quotes are available, but are not sufficiently liquid for a readily agreed external valuation. This implies that deriving the most likely exit price from these quotes requires an understanding of the relative quality of available quotes. For each quote, questions like the following need to be answered: Is the quote one at which the firm or broker providing the quote is offering to do business, or is the quote just provided as a service to indicate where the market is believed to be today? If the quote is an offer to do business, how large of a transaction is it good for? What is the track record of the quotation provider in supplying reliable information? Are there possible motivations of providing misleading information to attempt to influence pricing to move in a direction that favors a quote provider's position? How frequently are quotes updated?

With such a multiplicity of information bearing on the issue, there is no doubt that traders of an instrument have the best judgment on determining this valuation. Their continuous contact with other firms' traders and brokers enables them to build the experience to make these judgments. The ability to make such judgments is a major factor in determining a trader's success, so traders who have built a successful earnings track record can make a strong claim of having the expertise to determine most likely exit prices.

Unfortunately, reliance on traders' judgment raises moral hazard concerns. As discussed in Section 2.1, traders are often tempted to mislead management about position exit prices, in order to inflate reported profits, or increase flexibility in the positions they are allowed to hold. Outsiders, from corporate risk management or corporate finance or middle office, need to be involved in making these judgments to preserve independence. However, designing mechanisms for resolving disputes between traders and control personnel raises many difficult issues:

- How can control personnel obtain a sufficient knowledge base to challenge trader judgments? At a minimum, traders should be required to make the information on which judgments are made public. This can be accomplished by insisting that quotes be sent to the firm in writing (whether through trading screens, email, or fax). Alternatively, control personnel should have the right to selectively listen in on phone conversations in which quotes are made.
- Ideally, control personnel should have a range of experience that enables them to arrive at independent conclusions regarding quotations, perhaps even prior trading experience.
- Records should be kept of prior experience with the reliability of a particular trader's valuations by tracking the path of internal marks

leading up to an actual purchase or sale price and noting suspicious patterns. Control personnel should adjust their deference to trader valuations by the degree of proven reliability.
■ A trader's ultimate weapon for bringing credibility to her valuation is to actually exit part of the position. A recorded price narrows disputes down to the single question of whether the size of the trade relative to the retained position is large enough to be a reliable indicator of the exit price for the remainder.

Despite best efforts to design dispute resolution processes that balance power between traders and control personnel, traders inevitably retain a strong advantage based on information asymmetry. They can utilize their knowledge of a wide variety of sources of price quotes to selectively present only those that are the most advantageous to their case. They sometimes use friendships and exchanges of favors to influence other market participants to provide quotes biased toward their valuations. Traders also often rely on aggressive personal style and internal political power based on their profitability to prevail through intimidation.

To remedy this power asymmetry, some firms prefer to rely on more objective computations for determining valuations, even where this reduces accuracy by lessening the role of judgment. A typical approach would be to average the quotes obtained from a set panel of other firms or brokers, perhaps discarding outliers before averaging (discarding outliers is a possible protection against a few quotes that have been biased by friendship or favor). Changes in panel membership should be difficult to make and require agreement between traders and control personnel.

A promising development toward more objective valuations for less liquid instrument is the TOTEM Valuation Services, which is affiliated with Price Waterhouse. This service is designed to share information between firms making markets in less liquid products. Firms can only obtain access to quotes on those products for which they are willing to provide quotes. Their access to quotes can be cut off if the quotes they provide are frequently outliers, indicating either a lack of expertise or an attempt to bias quotations. Although the extensive machinery of this process means it can only make quotes available once a month and with a lag of a few days, it still provides a valuable check on the valuations of a firm's traders.

The following are some pitfalls to be wary of when setting up a procedure for deriving valuations from less than fully liquid market quotes:

■ **Model-derived quotes.** Here is an illustration of a frequently encountered problem. You need a valuation for a particular bond and you have a choice: either use a model to compute the value based on observed prices of more liquid bonds with similar maturities and credit ratings or use price quotes for the particular bond obtained from brokers. Before choosing the latter, ask the following question: Are the brokers providing a quote specific to this bond or are they just providing the output of their own model based on prices of more liquid bonds? If your external source is model based, are you better using your own model? The following are some advantages to using a model-based external quote:

- You may be able to get model-based quotes from several sources with the hope that errors will average out.
- The external models are being tested by the use of the quotes by many different firms, so it is more likely that objections will be raised if the model is missing something.
- It is less likely that traders will influence the outcome when an external source is being used.
- The quotes may become so widely used as to be a good indicator of where the market is trading.

The primary disadvantage to using a model-based external quote is that you may not be able to obtain details of the model used, so it is harder to estimate potential error and build adequate reserves for uncertainty than when using your own model.

- **Revealing positions.** When quotes are not available on regularly displayed screens or reports, firms seeking quotes may need to make specific inquiries to obtain quotes. Their inquiries reveal information about the positions the firm holds that can be used to the firm's disadvantage by other market participants. This is particularly true if the conventions of the market require an indication of either buy or sell interest to obtain a quotation, as opposed to obtaining a bid-ask quote. Even when you do not need to reveal the direction of your interest, in some markets the direction of a firm's position is well known to other participants and the expression of interest in a particular instrument is highly revealing of holdings. It is always possible to disguise positions by requesting quotes for a range of instruments, which includes instruments held and not held. However, the quality of the response may suffer as efforts to provide quotes get diffused over too many instruments. Market conventions concerning the tolerated ratio of inquires to actual transactions also limit the amount of information that can be obtained. If trader reluctance to reveal positions limits the extent of the external quotes obtained, models may need to be relied on more heavily to infer valuations.
- **One-way markets.** You not only need to worry about the size of transaction for which an obtained quote is valid, but you must also worry about whether the quote is valid for your firm. Markets that tend to be one way, with customer demand strongly on one side and

market maker supply on the other, may lead to quotations that are good for customers only. A typical example would be an options market in which almost all customer interest in options beyond 5 years was to sell options, not buy them. A market maker, in such circumstances, might supply reasonably liquid quotes for the purchase of long-term options to customers, but be unwilling to buy on the same terms from other market makers. The principle is to reserve the limited capacity to take on risk to encourage customer relationships, not to help competitors for this customer business by allowing them to distribute some of their risk. This is not to say that market makers will never buy longer-term options from one another in such circumstances, but they may do so only on a negotiated basis, with no actionable quotes available, even through brokers.

A market maker may still succeed in finding out the prices that other market makers are paying customers for longer-term options, since customers often let them know what bids they are seeing from other firms. It will be a definite source of comfort to know that the firm's prices are in the same range as that of their competitors', since this is an indication that the firm's models and trading strategies are not suffering from some major error, such as overlooking a source of risk. Equivalently, a firm derives comfort from seeing that it wins its fair share of deals in a given category, neither too many nor too few.

Although this comfort is genuine, it should not be confused with obtaining a price at which the firm can exit its risk positions. In the absence of quoted prices at which the firm itself can transact, it is prudent to anticipate the need to hold risk longer and utilize models to estimate longer-term profit and loss (P&L) and reserves and limits to control the associated risk, as discussed in Section 6.2.3.

5.1.2 Valuation Reserves

The doubts that have been raised in the investment public's minds during 2001 and 2002 by scandals from companies such as Enron and WorldCom have called into question many accepted practices for reporting on the financial condition of a firm. One reaction has been to question the use of the estimated valuation of a future uncertainty in the current P&L. To select just one example to stand for many, Timothy Lucas, the director of research at the Financial Accounting Standards Board, the principal U.S. accounting rulemaker, was quoted as saying in connection with revelations concerning Enron's use of mark-to-market accounting for energy trades, that it had not occurred to him that anyone would use models to try to forecast prices for 10 years and then use these models to report profits (Norris and Eichenwald [2002]).

However, this leaves the question of how to value assets that lack liquid price quotations. The only alternative to placing an estimated value on future uncertainty is to utilize some form of accrual accounting in which only current income is recognized. Having worked in environments that have involved both accrual accounting and mark-to-market accounting, I am confident that any possible misrepresentation using mark-to-market pales in comparison to what can occur with accrual accounting. It is easy to structure transactions that provide good current cash flows in exchange for probable future losses. With accrual accounting, all that shows up are the current cash flows. By the time the future losses are due, you only need to book more of the same type of transactions to provide more of the high current cash flows to push the losses further into the future, a form of a Ponzi scheme.

My hope would be that the lesson learned from these reporting failures is that mark-to-market valuation *is* needed, but with a proper degree of conservatism in estimating future values that are uncertain. The conservatism can be provided by calculating a *valuation reserve* that can be subtracted from the most likely future value.

The issue of how large reserves should be for valuation uncertainty is probably the single issue that leads to the greatest conflicts between traders and corporate risk managers. Based on their experience and knowledge of the motivations of the creators of market quotes, traders tend to believe they know the price at which positions can be exited with a fair degree of certainty. With some justice, they will point out that the uncertainty is mostly on the part of the outsiders, such as corporate risk managers and the corporate finance function, who do not have the traders' access to information. Reserves lower the reported P&L, which is the ultimate scorecard for the traders, determining bonuses, promotions, the size of positions management will allow, and, ultimately, continued employment. Understandably, traders will push to minimize reserves. (The one universal exception to this tendency is a trader who inherits a book from another trader. Invariably, the new trader will want to increase reserves for the inherited positions. I call this the principle that no profit should fund only a single bonus.)

Occasionally, though, one encounters a trader who claims to be a proponent of large reserves. I came across one when a trading book of exotic options was being established for which I was to be responsible for the risk management. The head trader expounded on his philosophy of avoiding any appearance of claiming too much P&L before achieving certainty of the results. He wanted reserve levels to be generously high. Here, I thought, was someone I could get along with well. And so I did, through many months in which both P&L and reserve levels were high, with easy agreement between the two of us on the reserves.

Then came the unfortunate day when an operations error in booking a trade was discovered several months after the trade had been booked.

Rebooking the trade correctly would lead to a large loss, large enough that the trading desk would show its first negative P&L for a month. The head trader, although duly upset by the operations failure, was unfazed by the P&L consequence. Now, he informed me, was the time to release some of that reserve that had been accumulating—just enough to make P&L for the month come out positive. I protested. First of all, the reserves had been created for valuation uncertainty, not as a hedge against possible operating errors. Second, the amount of uncertainty in the valuation was exactly the same on the day after the error was discovered as it was on the day before it was discovered. So how could a lowering of reserves be justified? The era of good feelings had come to an abrupt end.

This experience illustrates why a great deal of suspicion exists around valuation reserves, which is often expressed by regulators, such as the Securities Exchange Commission (SEC) and auditors. Aren't reserves just a cushion to allow reported earnings of a trading book to be smoothed, creating an illusion of less uncertainty of return than what actually exists? To avoid this, a definite principle must be in place that reserves are strictly for uncertainty concerning current valuation and never for uncertainty concerning future market variation. As an example, take a position in a liquid instrument, such as the dollar versus Japanese yen spot FX we previously cited. The future movements of this highly volatile exchange rate (and hence the P&L) may be surrounded by great uncertainty, but there should be no reserve, since the position can be exited at short notice at a known price. A reserve should only be considered if the position reaches a size that places a limit on this freedom of exit and therefore calls into question the valuations of the current position.

To make sure that this principle of using reserves only for the uncertainty of current valuation and not for the uncertainty of future market variation is followed, clear independence of reserve determination from the control of insiders with a motivation to show smoothed earnings must be demonstrated. This requires the final decision authority to be with an independent business unit, such as corporate risk management or corporate finance, and relatively objective standards for determining reserves be utilized.

The uncertainty of current valuation could be due to the illiquidity of available price quotes or it could be due to reliance on a model to obtain a valuation. Section 6.2.3 discusses how to establish objective standards for reserves against model uncertainty. We now focus on how to establish objective standards for reserves against positions for which only illiquid price quotations are available.

The most direct method for reserving against an illiquid position is to estimate the degree to which exiting this position in the market might cause prices to move. This can accommodate fairly objective standards by using *haircut* tables on valuation. These have set percentage discounts tied to the size of the position held relative to some measure of the market size, such as the average amount of daily trades. This method takes proper account of both types of possible illiquidity, since this ratio could be high based on a small denominator, indicating an illiquid market, or based on a large numerator, indicating a big position in a liquid market. The downside to this method is that it may be difficult to establish reasonable haircut percentages to use. Rarely do firms keep good historical records of the impact of exiting large positions, and it will, in any case, be very difficult to sort out such impacts from other effects on market prices. This leaves the determination of haircut percentages to a subjective debate in which the traders' greater experience will be difficult for outsiders to question.

A method that lends itself to a more evenly matched debate is to first estimate the amount of time it will take to exit a position without substantially moving prices and then reserve against a possible market move over this time period. This exit time estimate will also be based on a ratio of size of position held to daily trading volume. It thus shares the previous method's advantages of taking proper account of both types of possible illiquidity and also the previous method's disadvantage of making it difficult for outsiders to debate trader judgment. However, the potential price move estimate allows for outsider objectivity, since it is very similar to the sort of calculation that goes into VaR. It also enables reserve levels to be calibrated to management-determined levels of uncertainty that should be reserved against. A uniform uncertainty level used for different trading desks can help to ensure the comparability of results across the firm.

For example, consider a $500 million position in a stock in which the amount that can be transacted in 1 day without adversely impacting prices is estimated to be $50 million. So $500 million/$50 million = 10 days of price moves should be reserved against, which implies that on average there will be 10/2 = 5 days of price moves prior to sale. If the daily standard deviation of price moves is 1.5 percent, and if management decides on a reserve to a 95 percent confidence level, which is equivalent in 1.65 standard deviations of a normal distribution, then the reserve level should be:

$$\$500 \text{ million} \times 1.65 \times 1.5\% \times \sqrt{10/2} = \$27.7 \text{ million} \quad (5.1)$$

It should be reiterated that despite the appearance of a term that is tied to the uncertainty of future market variation, this remains a reserve methodology based on current valuation uncertainty. Future market variation is only being reserved to the extent it is outside management control, due to the large position size preventing exit at a desired time.

A third method, which can be used as a complement to the other two, is to create a reserve against aged positions. This method establishes a formula that marks a position down by a certain percentage the longer it is held. This can only be used as a complement to one of the other two methods, since it will not establish any reserve against a large illiquid position recently entered into.

Why should there be uncertainty about position valuation just because a position has been held for a long time? It is based on the observation that traders may delay exiting a position when they suspect that it will cause a decline in value from the level they are currently marking it at. Although I have heard much anecdotal evidence supporting this observation, it would be intriguing to perform a statistical study on the correlation between the length that positions are held and the size and direction of the price move between the last mark and actual sale. An aging reserve policy can also be justified on the pragmatic grounds that it is providing traders with the right incentives—to realize profits and cut losses in a reasonably short time period.

As I stated at the beginning of this section, reserving against valuation uncertainty is probably the leading cause of the greatest conflicts between traders and corporate risk managers. The risk managers need to provide a degree of conservatism that will assure investors, lenders, and government regulators that P&L is not being overstated and provide a degree of independence to allay suspicions that reserves are being used as a means for smoothing earnings results. However, this leads traders to suspect that too much conservatism is being used to protect risk managers against any possibility of criticism. A reserve that is too conservative hurts not only the trader, but also the ultimate profitability of the firm by limiting the amount of business that can be transacted.

In my experience, traders often misunderstand the need for conservatism and independence. One argument I've frequently encountered when specifying the reserve I think needs to be placed on an illiquid position goes something like this: "If you want the firm to value the asset at that low a value, then you would be happy if I went massively short the asset at that price." However, this mistakes conservatism for a view on fair price—if the trader was to go short this illiquid asset, I would want reserves to establish a conservatively high value for the short position. In other words, reserves are used to establish a bid-ask spread on an illiquid position, and the greater the illiquidity, the wider the spread. I've also encountered the argument from traders that they have excellent inside information as to where a position will trade, but they don't currently want to enter into the trade at that price. I need to point out that unless they can find some means of translating inside information into something publicly verifiable, we cannot ask the firm's shareholders and depositors to bear the risk that they are wrong.

Of course, my dialogue with traders is far from a one-way street. Often it is a case of their educating me on sources of information or aspects of hedges that cause me to change my initial view. Over time, with almost all of the traders I've dealt with, we've come to an accommodation of mutual respect, but with a realization that our interests sometimes differ. However, I still wonder at times whether other risk managers have found better ways to avoid initial contentiousness. I was therefore a bit amused at some dialogue I recently heard.

I was meeting with the head of market risk at a major investment bank, one of the most respected individuals in the industry. Our conversation was interrupted by an urgent phone call from one of his staff. I only heard his side of the phone conversation, which went something like this: "Well, certainly you need to put a reserve on a trade like that . . . I don't care whether the trader likes it. If he doesn't, let him sell some of the position and show us where it should be priced . . . You can't accept a statement like that from him. The fact that the reserve you've calculated would make him book an up-front loss doesn't prove that your reserve is stupid. Tell him that your reserve calculation shows that his price is stupid."

5.1.3 Analysis of Revenue

The G-30 study states, in support of Recommendation 4 to identify revenue sources, that "measuring the components of profit helps participants to understand the profitability of various activities over time relative to the risk undertaken, as well as to gain insight into the performance of hedges." A basic justification of using mark-to-market valuation in the management of risk is that it will lead to an early identification of ineffective hedging strategies, which can trigger experimentation with alternative hedges or changes in the mix of products being offered. This can only happen if an effective and frequent analysis is made of what is causing changes in P&L. In particular:

- P&L must be segregated by product line to identify which products may be encountering hedging difficulties.
- P&L must be broken out into that part attributable to newly booked business versus that part attributable to hedging activity on existing business. This ensures that hedging problems will not be masked by the offset of profits from new business, leading to a Ponzi scheme, as discussed in Section 2.2. A persistent pattern of profitable new business offset by hedging losses is an indication that either traders have chosen to take positions that (at least temporarily) have had bad results or valuation reserves have been inadequate.
- To distinguish between these two cases, it is important to identify what portion of hedging profits is due to movements against specific risk factors, such as delta, gamma, vega, and theta. In this way, losses stemming from deliberately taken positions can be distinguished from

those that arise from risks such as correlation exposure, which the trader cannot completely hedge. This analysis is also important in confirming that risk positions are reported correctly. If daily P&L swings cannot be accounted for by the reported size of risk positions and the daily changes in market variables, it is a warning that the reported risk measurements may be incorrect. This should lead to investigations of whether some transactions have been misrepresented in the reporting systems or whether additional or more detailed risk measures are required. Particular attention should be paid to unexplained P&L swings that take place around a date on which a payment is made or determined. If a model is not properly valuing a payment that has already been determined or is very close to determination, the probability is very high that the trade has been misrepresented.

■ It is extremely important to highlight any P&L changes due to changes in those assumptions that cannot be directly tested against available market prices or changes in models. This eliminates the possibility that P&L due to such changes will mask the results of ineffective hedging strategies.

■ Significant differences between official P&L changes and the informal trading desk estimation of these changes should be investigated. These differences can be indicators of hedges that are not performing as expected.

5.1.4 Exposure to Changes in Market Prices

The need for measuring exposure to market changes is emphasized in G-30 Recommendations 5, 6, and 7. Proper daily mark-to-market valuation, as discussed in Section 5.1.1, is the key to properly measuring the exposure to changes in market prices. The correct daily valuation ensures that exposure is being evaluated from the correct starting point and also serves as a basis for translating changes in observable market prices into changes in portfolio valuation. Since the daily mark-to-market needs to relate valuation to some observable external prices, possibly through the use of models, this same relationship can be used to take a change in market price and convert it into a change in instrument value.

To take a concrete example, consider an option position on the Standard and Poor's (S&P) 500 index with an expiry in 5 months. When considering how to value it, decisions must be made about what model to use and what the inputs to the model should be. Let us say a Black-Scholes model is chosen, requiring input for the price of the underlying and an implied volatility. For the underlying price, we might decide to use an average of one-third of the closing 3-month S&P futures price and two-thirds of the closing 6-month S&P futures price. For the implied volatility, we might decide to use an average consisting of one-third of the implied volatility of the closing 3-month S&P option price and two-thirds of the implied volatility of the closing 6-month S&P option price. These choices will be made based on trade-offs between basis risk and liquidity risk and could include reserve adjustments for lack of liquidity. However, once the choices are made for valuation, they become simple recipes for translating changes in market prices of the 3-month S&P futures, 6-month S&P futures, 3-month S&P implied volatility, and 6-month S&P implied volatility into a change in the 5-month option price, utilizing the Black-Scholes model.

Once these pieces have been established, the remaining task is to decide on the market price shifts on which to calculate exposure. Three primary types of shifts are used:

- **Standard shifts such as a 1-basis-point interest rate move, a 1 percent stock price move, or a 1 percent implied volatility move.** The advantage of standard shifts is that they easily convey a precise meaning to a wide group of users. The main issue to be decided when using standard shifts is which market prices to group together—do you want to report exposure to each individual stock price moving, all stock prices moving together, a particular industry shifting relative to all others? These detailed decisions are best examined in the context of specific risks. We address these decisions more closely in subsequent chapters, particularly Chapter 7, Section 8.4, and Section 9.4.

- **Shifts based on the statistical analysis of the probability of the size of the change.** The advantage of statistically based shifts is that they make it easier to compare the size of exposures in different risk classes. For example, it's hard to say whether a $5 million loss for a 1 percent change in stock prices is more of a danger or less of a danger than a $2 million loss for a 1 percent change in implied interest rate volatilities. However, a $5 million loss for a stock price change that has a 5 percent probability of occurring is clearly more worrisome than a $2 million loss for an implied interest rate volatility change that has a 5 percent probability. Probability distributions also make it possible to combine shifts in unrelated asset classes into a single measure, such as the 95th percentile VaR, defined as the amount of loss that will be exceeded only 5 percent of the time, based on all of the positions within a portfolio. The difficult issue with statistically based measures of risk is how to determine the probability distributions. These measures and the means of deciding on distributions are discussed in Section 11.1.

- **Shifts based on scenarios determined by economic insight into the potential size of different shifts and the relation between them.** An example would be a stress scenario for the impact of the debt default of a particular large developing economy, which might be judged to result in, say, a 5 percent decline in all stock prices, a larger decline in the stock of companies with large investment in that economy, a 10 percent decline in all emerging market FX rates, a 15 percent increase in the credit spread of all emerging market debt, and so on. We study alternative approaches to defining such shifts in Section 11.2. Scenario analysis is needed for cash flow as well as for P&L to anticipate funding liquidity problems, which is consistent with the G-30 Recommendation 7, as discussed in Sections 3.5 and 4.2.2.

5.1.5 Risk Measurement for Position Taking

It can be argued that the G-30 recommendations should apply to the market-making function of trading with an emphasis on keeping position holdings to a minimum, but not to the position-taking function of trading, where positions may be held for very long time periods based on fundamental views of where market prices are headed (refer to Section 2.5 for the distinction between position taking and market making). Is it really important to measure short-term price fluctuations in positions being held for the long term? It is interesting to note that a recent SEC letter (December 8, 1999) has emphasized the obligation of mutual funds to value assets based on *fair value*, the amount an arm's length buyer would currently pay for a security. The SEC letter specifically states that fair value cannot be based on "what a buyer might pay at some later time, such as when the market ultimately recognizes the security's true value as currently perceived by the portfolio manager" or "prices that are not achievable on a current basis on the belief that the fund would not currently need to sell these securities." These views reflect the G-30 principles.

Arguments for applying current market valuation and short-term price exposure measures to positions being held for the long-term include:

■ The desire to hold positions long term may reflect the motivation of fund or proprietary position managers, but they may not be the only constituency for valuation information on the fund. Fund investors, lenders to the fund, senior managers of the firm of which the proprietary position managers are a part, and regulators may all have an interest in knowing prices at which the positions may be exited in the near future. Investors may want to exit the fund. Lenders may need assurance that margin calls can be met. Senior managers could decide that they want to reduce the amount of risk-taking authority being allocated to the position takers. Senior firm management will also want to view integrated risk reports for the entire firm, which will cover both market making and proprietary positioning functions.

Regulators may be seeking assurance that fund withdrawals can take place in an orderly manner. All these points were particularly emphasized by the Long Term Capital Management (LTCM) experience discussed in Section 4.2.1.

■ It is possible to find anecdotal evidence of successful fund managers and proprietary traders who do not desire any feedback from market price changes. They view themselves as investing for the long run, and they see short-term price changes as distracting noise that does not reflect changes in fundamental values, but only short-lived shifts caused by supply and demand imbalances. However, it is possible to counter this with anecdotal evidence of successful fund managers and proprietary traders who want to receive constant feedback from the market. Even though they are investing long term, they want to be constantly aware of the price at which risk positions can be unwound. They attempt to make money by having a few positions on which they are right and earn a large amount and avoid having any positions on which they lose a large amount. The constant feedback of market prices at which positions can be exited provides both a means to ensure that a limit is placed on the amount lost on any one position and a signal that markets are moving in ways they do not fully understand. In such circumstances, they seek to exit the market and wait until they can gain a better understanding before reentry.

5.2   RISK CONTROL

Once an adequate measurement of risk is available, the next logical question is how to control it. Two fundamental and complementary approaches are available. The first is for higher levels of management to place detailed limits on the amount and type of risk that lower levels of management can take—limits on VaR, position size, vega, gamma, and so on. The second is for higher levels of management to provide incentives to lower levels of management to optimize the trade-off between return and risk. The latter approach, based on incentives, gives lower levels of management, which are closer to the information required to make informed trade-off decisions, the flexibility to find combinations of risks that can maximize the return for a total risk level approved by senior management. However, the incentive approach can also lead to unacceptable risks in the aggregate, if too many traders decide to take a similar position, pointing toward a mixed use of both approaches. This is the pattern that can be found at almost all investment banks and will be the approach followed in this book for discussions of control techniques for specific risk classes.

The most extreme form of an incentive-based approach is to restrict controls to assigning to each trading desk a maximum amount of trading losses they will be allowed to take before their positions are closed out. This gives the trading desk maximum flexibility in deciding what positions to put on and gives complete freedom so long as unacceptable losses are avoided. Everyone concerned, the traders, senior managers, and risk managers, can agree on such *stop-loss* limits as a bare minimum for risk control. If all positions could be instantaneously liquidated at any time at the values reflected on the firm's books, it could be argued that this is an adequate limit structure. However, there have been too many instances where a trader has built up a large risk exposure that proved costly to exit when management decided to stop out losses. The time that traders exceed loss limits is often also the time when markets are moving wildly, decreasing liquidity and subjecting positions to large P&L moves even when closeout can be accomplished in the relatively short time of a day or two. At least some additional form of risk control is needed.

Historically, added risk controls have most often been quite detailed limits on the sizes of specific exposures that could be taken, with limit sizes closely tied to both the liquidity of exiting the exposure and the degree of management confidence in the trader.

When the VaR measure was first introduced, it was initially seen as a possible supplement for limiting risk. However, soon traders came to see it as a tool for gaining added flexibility, since it treats all risk as fungible in arriving at a single risk number. Since this risk number is a statistical estimate of the loss that could occur during the period in which a position is being closed down, an argument could then be made for using this as the only supplement to a stop loss limit, allowing control on the loss that can occur after management has decided to close out a risk position without the need to place detailed controls on particular exposures. This control can take the form of a limit on the total VaR exposure that a trading desk can take and/or a measure of risk in a calculation of return on risk or risk-adjusted return that can be used to compare the performance of different trading desks against targets and against one another to decide on compensation, promotion, and continued employment.

The following are arguments favoring an incentive approach, with senior management input reduced to broad measures such as stop-loss limits and VaR limits or risk-return targets, giving great flexibility in deciding on the risk-taking profile to the business:

- It enables trading desks to respond quickly to new opportunities without slowing down decision making by needing to make their case to senior management.
- By not restricting a given trading desk to positions in a particular asset class, it encourages broad thinking across asset classes, searching for interrelationships.

- When a trading desk is confined to a particular market, at a time when there is a shortage of good trading opportunities in that market, traders are often tempted to pursue riskier opportunities in that market as the only hope for earning a bonus. Giving trading desks the flexibility to trade in other markets when the one they specialize in is less promising is a way to avoid this temptation.
- It is less risky to have many traders with the ability to take positions in a given market than to restrict position taking to a single trading desk. In most circumstances, positions taken by one desk will be offset by positions taken by a desk with a different opinion. When enough desks all line up in the same direction to create a sizable net position, it is a good indication of particularly favorable return-on-risk circumstances.

The following are arguments favoring a more detailed limit approach:

- It enables management to restrict position taking in a particular market to only those trading desks possessing sufficient knowledge and expertise in the market to be able to make reasoned judgments.
- As a corollary to the previous argument, it forces trading desks to focus their attention on those areas in which they are expert without having this focus distracted by trying to find opportunities in other markets.
- The real danger is that a trading desk that does not have a successful strategy in its primary market can obscure management recognition of this fact by trying to build a profitable trading record in another market. This can be particularly harmful if it helps to perpetuate a Ponzi scheme in which the firm is delayed in recognizing the mispricing of a transaction with long-term consequences. If a desk is allowed to play in another market, it is important to make sure that P&L attribution firmly separates the results for different products for the same reason we have seen it is important to separate P&L in newly booked deals from that on management of existing deals. As a particular case, if an options trading desk is allowed to take substantial outright positions in the underlying, the P&L from underlying positions must be clearly separated from that on management of volatility and convexity risk. Likewise, if an exotic options trading desk is not forced to lay off the substantial part of the vanilla options risk it generates, then the P&L from vanilla options risk must be clearly separated from that on the residual exotic options risk.
- The last argument given in favor of more flexible position taking is actually quite misleading in two directions. First, it underestimates the degree to which opinions can be infectious and create bandwagon

effects, particularly among traders who are not experts in a particular market. The risk is that when the trading desk with the most expertise in a particular market puts on a position, other trading desks will pile on to get a piece of the action. As a result, the firm as a whole will wind up with a much larger position than the trading desk with the expertise would have thought prudent. Second, when situations with less certainty arise and trading desks put on offsetting positions, the firm as a whole winds up being arbitraged—it has flat P&L if the market moves in either direction, but must pay a bonus to the winning trading desk in either case. This points to the need for trading management to insist on trading desks utilizing diverse styles to avoid this form of arbitrage, and detailed limits can play an important role in enforcing the diversity of trading style.

■ Management may distrust the excessive reliance on statistical measures of risk. Statistics are based on history and may not reflect management judgment about risk. This may be particularly true in markets that tend toward infrequent but large jumps, such as pegged FX rates, which, due to government intervention, may show a long history of very little movement followed by one sharp break. When the government resources are no longer adequate to hold the desired peg, the tendency is for the resulting move to be very large to reflect the market pressures whose reflection in the price has been suppressed by government intervention. In a period when the peg still holds, historically based VaR will show very little risk, but this will not adequately reflect the possibility of a jump move. Instead of historical relationships, VaR can be based on implied volatilities, which reflect a market judgment of future uncertainty, or on management estimates of risk. A more direct approach is to explicitly limit exposures to management-designed stress scenarios.

The issue of whether to permit a trading desk to take positions in instruments outside its primary expertise is not just a question of whether a desk should be allowed to actively seek such positions. This issue also comes up as a question of whether a desk should be forced to close out positions that result as by-products of its primary product focus.

Consider an FX options market-making desk. Their primary expertise would be on issues such as the proper management of volatility risk. However, outright FX positions arise naturally in the course of its business, as changes in exchange rate levels lead to changing deltas on its option positions. Should the options desk be forced to close out these outright FX positions, leaving the firm's positioning of outright FX to the spot-and-forward FX market makers, the firm's experts at managing these positions? Or should the options desk be allowed to take its own view on these positions? The same arguments, pro and con, that we have presented previously apply here as well, with a particular emphasis on the second argument pro flexibility and the third argument against flexibility.

Those who favor flexibility point to the broader view of economics and the markets that will come from the trading desk looking at its options positions as a whole, rather than trying to break them apart into a position in the underlying and a position in volatility. They will point out that this encourages thinking about correlations between underlying prices and volatility levels that can best be taken advantage of by being able to manage positions in both the underlying and volatility. These are powerful arguments, as discussed in Chapter 9.

Those suspicious of the consequences of flexibility point to cases in which poor pricing of volatility risks and poor management of options positions were delayed in being recognized by profits that came from taking positions in the underlying (perhaps just by copying positions that the primary underlying desk was putting on). This certainly indicates the need to have, at a minimum, risk reporting that clearly breaks out P&L attributable to the underlying position from P&L attributable to volatility positions.

Even if management decides in favor of the less flexible approach with specific limits on options traders taking positions in the underlying, some degree of flexibility should be retained from a pure transactional efficiency viewpoint. For example, if an options trading desk is never allowed any position in underlying, it will need to spend too much of its time writing tickets to close out delta shifts arising from underlying price changes and will lose too much of its P&L in bid-ask spreads. (Even if these are only internal, and hence not lost to the firm, it will still be demotivating to the traders.)

The arguments we have presented here for options traders and their positions in the underlying apply equally to forward traders and their position in the spot, basis traders and their position in legs of the basis, and exotic options traders and their positions in vanilla options that can hedge part of the exotics risk.

This discussion on risk controls has important implications for the use of risk decomposition techniques throughout the second section of this book. It explains why I place such a strong emphasis on utilizing risk decomposition to break apart less liquid transactions into constituent parts—usually a more liquid piece and a less liquid residual. Identifying the more liquid constituents enables the separation of P&L attribution and encourages closing out positions with the desk that can create the maximum liquidity for the firm. It also avoids the booking of phantom P&L by having a different valuation technique used for the same position depending on whether it was created directly or created as part of a more complex transaction. Finally, it also avoids the firm's unknowingly building a large position in a particular product. For example, this motivates the use of a formula for vanilla options that does all the pricing and representation of risk in terms of forward prices derived from the trading desk that is the primary market maker in that product (see Chapter 9) and motivates the attempt to price and represent the risk of exotic options to the greatest extent possible as a combination of vanilla options prices derived from the trading desk that is the primary market maker in that product (see Chapter 10).

A closely related question is whether trading books that take positions in a product in which they are not a primary market maker should be forced to do all their transactions through the firm's primary market-making desk for the product. As a concrete example, consider a trading desk specializing in FX options, which will certainly need to transact hedges in underlying spot and forward FX. Should they be forced to transact all such hedges with the firm's spot and forward FX trading book or should they be given the choice of dealing directly in the market?

Note that this issue arises whether or not trading limits are used to force the options desk to restrict its outright FX positions to a small size. In either case, the desk will be transacting at least some hedges either internally or with the market.

The arguments for requiring internal hedging are powerful:

- It enables the desk with the greatest expertise and advantage in trading a product to be the one initiating all external transactions.
- It reduces the amount of transaction costs the firm must pay by encouraging trades in opposite directions to be closed out within the firm and enabling internal trades to be crossed with customer transactions. Nothing pleases a trader more than to be able to boast of the profits he has made by standing in the middle of trades in opposite directions put on by different desks of a rival firm. Even if positions are not completely offsetting or exactly simultaneous, funneling the trades through a single desk enables that desk to see the total flow of the firm's dealings in the product. This desk can build on observed patterns of usage to forecast and anticipate flows, and minimize transaction costs.
- The use of a common central trading desk forces all desks within the firm to value positions in the same product at a common price. This avoids phantom profits arising from the internal arbitrage that can occur if two desks value their positions in the same trade using different broker quotes or different models. Proper valuation discipline can eliminate this even if a policy of forcing all trades through a single desk is not employed, but this is the easiest mechanism for enforcing this rule.

The argument for permitting several desks to trade the same product directly with other firms is that competition for business will create enough efficiencies to overcome these strong advantages. The fear is that creating an internal monopoly in a product will permit the monopolist to try to collect monopoly rents from the other desks trading in the product—that is, to price at excessive bid-ask spreads that will increase profits of the central desk, but decrease the firm's overall profit by discouraging optimal use of the product by other desks. Avoiding this situation may require a difficult internal policing effort (it's not always easy to measure the size of the bid-ask spreads being used, since trades in different directions do not come in simultaneously).

CHAPTER **6**

Model Risk

Any book on the topic of financial risk management needs to address the subject of *model risk*—the risk that theoretical models used in pricing, trading, hedging, and estimating risk will turn out to produce misleading results. This book, which emphasizes quantitative reasoning in risk management, pays particularly close attention to how models can be used and misused in the risk-management process. Most of this discussion can be found throughout the book as related to particular models, but there are enough common themes to justify a short separate chapter on the subject. Readers with a particular interest in this topic may want to compare my analysis with those of Derman (2001), Rebonato (2001), Hull and Suo (2001), and Crouhy, Galai, and Mark (2001, Chapter 15).

6.1 THE ROLE OF MODELS IN MANAGING RISK

When examining model risk, one immediately encounters a very wide range of views on the role that models can play in controlling risk and creating new risks. These vary all the way from viewing model error as the primary cause of financial risk to viewing models as largely irrelevant to risk.

The view that models are largely irrelevant to risk can often be encountered among traders who view models as just convenient mathematical shorthand with no real meaning. All that really matters are the prices the shorthand stands for. A good example is the yield of bonds as calculated by Securities Industry Association standards. This includes many detailed calculations that have no theoretical justification, but can only be explained historically (for example, some parts of the calculation use linear approximations, which made sense before calculations were done on computers). No one would claim that this yield has a precise meaning—you don't necessarily prefer owning a bond yielding 7 percent to one yielding 6.90 percent. However, you can translate between yield and precise price given the industry standard rules. It is convenient shorthand to convey approximate values. The degree to which these calculations give misleading yields hurts intuitive understanding, but does not result in mispricing.

Those who view models as playing no real role in pricing and risk management view almost all models used in financial firms as playing a similar role to that of bond yield calculation. A typical claim would be that the Black-Scholes option model, probably the model most frequently used in the financial industry, is just a mathematical convenience that provides shorthand for quoting options prices as implied volatilities rather than as cash prices. In this view, implied volatilities are an attractive way of providing quotations, both because of common usage and because they provide more intuitive comparisons than a cash price, but they should not be regarded as having any meaning beyond representing the price that they translate to using the Black-Scholes formula.

If this viewpoint is correct, models would play an extremely minimal role in controlling risk and model testing would consist of little more than rote checking to see if industry-standard formulas had been properly implemented. However, this extreme a view cannot explain all the ways in which trading firms use models such as Black-Scholes. The valuation of unquoted options is derived by interpolating the implied volatilities of quoted options. The Black-Scholes model is used to translate prices to implied volatilities for the quoted options and implied volatilities to prices for the unquoted options. The risk reports of position exposures use the Black-Scholes model to compute the expected impact of changes in underlying prices on option prices. Scenario analyses presented to senior management quantify the impact of changes to the implied volatility surface. For more details, see Chapter 9 on managing vanilla options risk. This behavior is inconsistent with a claim that the model is being used purely to provide convenient terminology. By contrast, the industry standard bond yield formulas are not used in comparable calculations—interpolations and risk reports are based on a more sophisticated model of separately discounting the individual cash flows that constitute a bond, with a different yield applying to each cash flow. In this computation, none of the linear approximations of the industry standard formulas are utilized. For more details on these calculations, see Chapter 8 on managing forward risk.

A more plausible view of the claim that models play a minimal role is that the only role models play is to serve as interpolation tools from observable to unobservable prices. This no doubt provides valuable insight into why certain models have been able to achieve a high degree of acceptance in financial management. It is much easier to agree on an interpolation methodology than it is to agree on a fundamental method for pricing an instrument. The danger is that this view leads to unwarranted complacency, since model builders often regard interpolation as being a mathematically trivial or uninteresting task. The result can be uncritical acceptance of what seems a plausible interpolation method or a view that the choice of interpolation methods is somehow a matter of taste.

A closer examination will show that every choice of interpolation method entails significant financial assumptions. The interpolation of an unobservable price based on a set of observable prices amounts to the theory that the instrument with the unobservable price can be well hedged by the set of instruments with observable prices. As with any theory, this should be subjected to empirical testing and competition with alternative hedging proposals. Even the simplest sounding interpolation proposal (for example, calculating the $2^1/_2$-year rate as a 50–50 average of the 2- and 3-year rate) should be regarded as a model subject to the same tests as more mathematically complex models. We examine this in more detail in Section 8.2.1. Models rarely cost firms money because modelers have made an error in complex mathematics; they frequently cost firms money because they embody financial assumptions that are not borne out by future events.

The view that models are the primary cause of financial risk is often encountered in articles describing major trading losses, which are frequently ascribed to the firm having the wrong model. What is often unclear in these claims is whether "having the wrong model" just means making incorrect forecasts about the future direction of market prices or if it means misleading the firm's traders and managers about the nature of positions being taken. A good illustration is the discussion in Section 4.2.1 of whether Long Term Capital Management's (LTCM's) reliance on models should be viewed as a primary cause of the collapse of their fund.

Any firm engaged in making markets or investing assets must take positions whose profit or loss will depend on the correctness of forecasts of moves in market prices. Different strategies will be tied to different price relationships. Some depend on overall market direction, whereas others depend on the relative price of related assets; some depend on getting a long-term trend right, whereas others depend on correctly anticipating short-term moves. However, traders will always need to make judgments about an uncertain future, and firm managers in turn will always need to make judgments about how much of a risk of loss they will allow a trader to take in exchange for a possible gain. When making this judgment, management will be guided by evidence of prior accuracy of the trader's forecast.

Nothing in the last paragraph will be altered by whether a trader uses a model as a computational aid in forecasting, unless perhaps management is lulled into a false sense of security by believing that the use of a model lessens the chance of errors in trading judgment. However, if a model results, either purposely or inadvertently, in misleading traders and managers about the relationship between positions being taken and the size of possible losses, then the accusation that model error resulted in the loss is far more plausible.

These concepts can be clarified by distinguishing between three different ways a specific model can be used:

- The model is not used to value positions or measure risk; instead, it is used as part of a trader's decision-making process for quoting prices at which the firm will trade or for deciding which positions to buy or sell.
- The model is used to value trading positions as part of the firm's accounting process.
- Positions are valued directly from independent pricing sources, but the model is used to gauge the impact of changes in market variables on prices and therefore forms a part of the risk-measurement process.

Let's first consider a model that is not being used to value positions or measure risks, but is being used as part of a trader's decision-making process. For example, a spot foreign exchange (FX) trader could be using a very complex model when deciding which positions to take. This could even extend as far as program trading, in which a computer actually issues the buy and sell instructions based on model output. However, spot FX positions can easily be valued based on external quotes, and position size is extremely easy to understand without the aid of models (see the discussion in Chapter 7 on managing spot risk). So it is easy for management to see what the profit and loss (P&L) is every day and to cut the risk if P&L performance has been poor. Thus, the modeling does not have any of the dangers of hidden risk, such as Ponzi schemes (see Section 2.2). No FX trader would dream of asking to report more profits this year because he can "prove" that his model (or trading style) will work better next year than this year.

Models are ultimately tools for predicting the future. A strong trend in twentieth-century philosophy of science says that no rules can be laid down in advance for how to best predict the future. In this view, science cannot rely on a set of regulations for deciding what types of inquiry should be pursued. Rather, science must rely on keeping the debate open to as many points of view as possible and openly criticizing views that do not prove to be good predictors. The parallel idea for financial firms is that they must try to be open to as many trading ideas as possible and not dismiss ideas on the grounds that they do not line up with some approved theory (for example, rational expectations or market place efficiency). However, a culling process must also be available for measuring the success of trading ideas and eliminating those ideas that are not proving successful. In financial firms, this generally translates to giving traders the freedom to innovate, but cutting their limits, and eventually considering firing them, if they do not succeed.

The implication of this for models is to give as much freedom in structuring models as possible. Models need to take advantage of as much inside information, in the form of trader beliefs about the future, as possible. A corporate risk management area trying to audit a model used for decision making is no more sensible than one trying to audit a trader's thought process. (The trader, however, will probably want to ask for an independent review of his model, just to check that it is doing what she thinks. The trader's manager might very well want to review both the trader's thought process and model as part of deciding how much risk authority to grant the trader.) However, this must be controlled by making certain that profits are not booked and bonuses are not paid out until the forecasts of the models have proven correct. This means that to the greatest extent possible, models used for valuation must be linked to the price at which risk exposure can currently be sold in the market. Residual risk positions for which market prices cannot be obtained must be priced based on theory, but great caution should be employed to ensure that the theory relied on is adequately reviewed by outsiders who do not have the insiders' set of incentives to realize profits early, and that reserves and limits are kept against a reasonable statistical estimate that the theory is wrong.

The outside reviewers must be especially careful not to rely on historical proofs of correctness of the theory that have been prepared by insiders. It is notoriously easy to employ data-mining techniques to find statistical proofs of nearly any relationship by selecting the right historical data set. Statistical controls, such as careful discipline about segregating historical data into sample periods to fit parameters and out-of-sample periods to test results, are useful, but can still be defeated by sufficiently industrious data mining.

Insiders should be given latitude in the theories used in deciding how to trade, but not in the theories used in deciding when to recognize P&L. For the latter, it is better to rely on outsiders to avoid bias. You may lose accuracy by not having access to the insiders' market knowledge, but this will only result in delays in recognizing earnings, which is not as serious a problem as taking the wrong positions. Insiders may object that this delay in recognizing P&L will cause them to turn away good business, but they have two alternatives: Find others in the market who share their opinions and sell off the risk recognizing the profits, or if they are sufficiently confident, wait to recognize the P&L until after the risk position has matured.

How should the validity of models be judged? As already stated, models are tools for predicting the future so they must be judged on their success in doing so. Models used to mark trading positions to market or gauge the impact of market variables on prices tend to be models of relative processes, trying to predict how one set of prices will move relative to another set of prices. The relative nature of models used to gauge the impact of market variables on products should be obvious. The relative nature of models used to mark to market follows because they are interpolation tools for moving from observable prices to unobservable prices. They are trying to predict how well the instruments with observable prices will serve as hedges to the instrument with an unobservable price.

A model for a relative price process should naturally be tested on its ability to predict how relative movements in prices occur. For example, if a Black-Scholes model is being used to price an option at a 105 strike based on option prices at strikes of 100 and 110, the success of the model should not be judged on its capability to predict the future behavior of the price of the 105 strike option; rather, it should be judged on its capability to predict the behavior of a hedged package of a purchased 105 strike option and sold 100 and 110 strike options (in whatever proportion the model shows to be most effective as a hedge).

In assessing how well a model has predicted relative price movements, a sufficiently long time period must be employed to see how well the hedge is really performing. Over a short time period, almost any model chosen will appear to perform well by a type of circular reasoning: The instrument with unobservable prices will be valued using the model and the observable price inputs. Therefore, the movement of the unobservable prices relative to the observable prices will seem stable since the same model is being used for valuation throughout the time period.

The soundness of the model can only be judged over longer time periods, when longer-term unobservable prices transform into shorter-term observable prices, when there is enough time to observe the impact of required rehedges, or when trades reach maturity and require contractual payments. Since judgment on model adequacy is often required in a shorter time frame than can be accommodated by this need to withhold judgment, it is necessary to employ historical simulations to evaluate how well the model would have performed in the past. Chapters 8, 9, and 10 on managing forward risk, managing vanilla options risk, and managing exotic options risk, respectively, contain many examples of such simulations.

6.2 MODEL CONTROL

The analysis of the last section argues for the importance of performing a thorough and independent model validation for models being used for valuation or risk measurement, but not for models being used as part of a trader's decision-making process. Valuation models that fail to provide accurate assessments of the prices at which risks can be sold can delay the recognition of ineffectual hedging strategies, result in unwarranted bonuses being paid, and cause firms public embarrassment if previously recognized profits need to be reversed. Risk-measurement models that incorrectly forecast the impact of a change of market prices on position values can lead firms to take unintended and dangerous exposures.

I will classify the reasons for valuation and risk control model inaccuracy into three categories:

- The model is correct, but it has been implemented incorrectly, either through the incorrect derivation of equations or mistakes in programming.
- A key source of risk has not been included in the model or has been included in a way that obscures the relationship to market prices.
- The value of one or more of the input parameters cannot be determined based on liquid market prices for hedging instruments.

I will discuss each category and the steps that can be taken to control that source of inaccuracy.

6.2.1 Incorrect Implementation

This is by far the easiest of the categories to control so it only rarely leads to serious problems. All that is required is an insistence on adequate model documentation and thorough checking of implementation by competent analysts before the model is put into production. However, a few rules should be kept in mind to avoid the occasional error:

- The best check on an implementation is to perform an independent implementation and see if the results agree. It is tempting to cut costs by confining checking to having an independent analyst read through the documentation, equations, and code of the model builder and confirm that it is correct. However, it is much easier to miss an error when reading through someone else's equations or programming code; it is much more unlikely for two analysts working independently of one another to make the same error.
- Whenever possible, the independent implementation used as a check should employ a different solution methodology than the implementation being tested. For example, if the implementation being tested has used a Monte Carlo simulation, the test should be made solving backwards on a tree, where this is feasible. Using different implementation methodologies further reduces the chances that the two implementations will have the same flaw.
- Models should be tested on degenerate cases that have known solutions. For example, a down-and-out call with a barrier of zero is equivalent to a vanilla call, so setting the barrier to zero in a down-and-out

call model should produce the standard Black-Scholes result. Other examples would be always checking that put-call parity for European-style options is preserved for any model used to price options and always checking exotic option models against known analytic solutions for flat volatility surfaces (see the introduction to Section 10.1 and Section 10.3.1).

- Produce graphs of model output plotted against model inputs and explore any instances where they do not make intuitive sense.
- Be careful about the degree of complexity introduced into models. Is there sufficient gain in the accuracy to justify the reduction in intuitive understanding that results from added complexity? This can be illustrated by an example from my own experience:
  I had recently taken a new job and found that my most pressing problem was widespread user dissatisfaction with a model upgrade that had recently been introduced. The old model had been easy for traders and risk managers to understand. The new one was supposed to be more accurate, but could only be understood by the model development group. My initial examination showed that, on theoretical grounds, the difference between answers from the two models should be too small to make an actual difference in decision making, so I tried to persuade the model builder to switch back to the original, simpler model. Finding him adamant on the need for what he viewed as theoretical correctness, I examined the new model more closely and found a major implementation error—a factor of two had been dropped in the equation derivation. This is the sort of mechanical error that would certainly have been picked up as soon as a formal model review was performed. However, a similar error in a less complex model would have been caught long before by the people using it on a day-to-day basis.

6.2.2 Missing a Key Source of Risk

This is the most worrisome case of model error. In my experience, this type of error is rarely due to modelers and traders being unaware of the source of risk; it is almost always due to what seems a reasonable trade-off between model accuracy and the need for models to be efficient in their response time and use of computer resources.

Consider the Kidder Peabody disaster as an illustration, which was discussed in Section 4.1.2. No matter what your opinion about whether Joseph Jett was deliberately gaming the system, there is no doubt that the firm was ill served by having a model that computed the value of forward transactions without proper discounting. But Kidder Peabody was hardly the only firm in the industry using a model that omitted the discounting of forwards.

This is not due to a widespread ignorance of this fundamental principle of finance. What does often happen—and this is a pattern I have seen over and over again—is that a sensible decision is made at the time a model is built, but is not subjected to adequate review as circumstances change.

So a model might be set up for valuing forwards that at the time of implementation are being used to evaluate trades that are of moderate size and have short forward time periods. The added accuracy that comes from correct forward discounting might be quite small and thus easily justify a decision not to devote the added programming time and computational resources to include this factor. As the situation changes through time, at some point, the proper decision would be to change to a more accurate model. However, the decision to invest the resources needed to improve accuracy can be a difficult one, involving considerable expense, a diversion of resources from important new ventures, and perhaps a limitation on trading volume until the change is made. The environment may be changing gradually, so that no single point in time stands out as the time at which to switch.

This pattern suggests the following set of controls to ensure that key sources of risk are not missed:

- Model reviews should explicitly recognize the trade-offs between model accuracy and the investment of resources. All models are only approximations to reality and some factors will always be omitted. Models used in production must be sufficiently fast to produce answers within the time frame required for providing quotes to customers and risk analysis to the trading desk and senior management or they will prove useless. Their development cost must be reasonably related to the revenue that can be realized on the products they support. The time required for development must be consistent with the overall business plans.

- The inaccuracy of a production model must be evaluated in comparison to a more complete model that includes more risk sources. Since model testing needs to be performed on only a handful of examples and can be performed over a period of days or weeks, as compared to the minutes or seconds required of a production model, there is ample room to develop much more inclusive models in testing environments. A comparison of results to the production model will show just how much accuracy is being lost by the omission of risk factors. For example, an interest rate model driven by a single factor is often used in the valuation of Bermudan swaptions, but a multifactor rate model should be used to assess accuracy. See Section 10.5.2 for more details.

- If the test just referred to shows a significant loss of accuracy due to the omission of risk factors, recommended remedies can include, in addition to an upgrade of the production model, valuation reserves against inaccuracy, limits on the size of transactions or transaction types (for example, no transactions greater than 6 months to maturity) for which the model can be used, and periodic revaluations with a slower but more accurate model.

■ All model reviews must be updated at regular intervals. A typical regime could call for a review update annually but with a greater frequency to be triggered by large growth in the size and the number of transactions booked using the model. Updates should not be repeats of previous tests, which would be largely wasteful; instead, they should be an evaluation of changes that have taken place in the environment in which the model operates since the original review. This would obviously include growth in the size and number of transactions or characteristics of transactions, such as the lengthening of maturities, which might cause changes to previous evaluations of what constitutes a significant variance from a more complete model. However, it should also include new developments in theory, which might suggest new risk factors that should be considered or new developments in markets. For example, a risk factor that previously could not be priced based on market observation might now have liquid prices available, which would change previous conclusions about which model inputs need to be derived from market prices.

■ A clear distinction needs to be made between the number of risk factors needed to specify initial market conditions and the number of risk factors needed to specify the evolution of market conditions. This is a distinction that sometimes confuses novice model builders and novice model reviewers. In part, this is due to the complexity of the computation part of the trade-off, since accommodating just a single added factor for market evolution can be a computationally daunting task—for example, moving from a one-factor interest rate tree to a two-factor tree. By contrast, interest rate models can easily accommodate very complete specifications of the initial yield curve. However, the distinction also stems from considerations of accuracy. For example, as we will see in Section 10.5.2, a multifactor model for the evolution of interest rates does not offer much added accuracy over a single-factor model for the valuation of Bermudan swaptions. But an inaccurate specification of the shape of the initial yield curve can have a very significant impact on this valuation.

When evaluating whether all sources of risk have been modeled, it is necessary to also ask whether the model chosen makes adequate use of the available liquid market prices. This point can be most clearly made using a concrete example, which is discussed in more depth in Sections 10.4.2 and 10.4.4.

Consider an option written on a basket consisting of two stocks. You could choose two different ways to model this: Have a complete model of the price evolution of each of the two stocks individually and assume a correlation between them, or directly model the price evolution of the basket. We'll call these approaches the correlation model and the direct model, respectively. Assume that liquid market prices for options on the individual stocks are available, but no liquid market prices for options on the basket or on the correlation are available, which is a fairly standard situation.

It can be argued that either model is a reasonable choice. In either case, you will need input for a variable that cannot be observed in the market. In both cases, you have included all the sources of risk in your model.

However, as is shown in more detail in Section 10.4.2, if correlation is not expected to be too negative, the first model offers definite advantages in terms of making better use of liquid market prices. Options on the individual stocks will serve as effective partial hedges for the basket option, so utilizing the first model, which can be calibrated to current market quotes for these options, offers the following advantages over the second model:

- The correlation model permits representation on the basket trade in the exposure reports for the option positions on the two individual stocks. This encourages the use of liquid hedges.
- The correlation model requires valuation changes in the basket when changes are in the implied volatility of the two individual stock options. The direct model does not require such valuation changes so it can result in stale valuations not fully reflecting the cost of unwinding some of the risk in the trade.
- The correlation model exhibits significantly lower statistical uncertainty of results compared with the direct model. This should permit lower required reserve levels and larger limits than could be allowed if the direct model was used.
- If the direct model is used but the trading desk decides to hedge some of its volatility risk using options on the two individual stocks, trading desk P&L will show unwarranted volatility. When implied volatility quotes change on the individual stocks, the valuation of the hedges will change without any offsetting change in the valuation of the basket option.

Note that the advantages of the correlation model over the direct model are based on empirical findings, not theoretical ones. As can be seen in the more in-depth discussion, if correlation levels are expected to be very negative or if the product were structured differently (for example, an option on the difference between the stock prices rather than on the basket), the advantages of the first model over the second would diminish to the point of indifference between the models.

6.2.3 Uncertain Input Parameters

This category is unlike the other two in that we cannot hope that sufficient vigilance will eliminate this source of inaccuracy. So long as not all instruments have liquid markets, it will be necessary to utilize valuation models that require some inputs that cannot be extracted from liquid market prices.

Since we cannot hope to eliminate this source of uncertainty, we must find a way to try to control the possible impact it can have on trading profitability. One control was just mentioned in the last section—use models that maximize the dependence on liquid prices and minimize the dependence on nonliquid factors. The other controls can be pretty well divided into the categories of reserves and limits:

- By placing a reserve against the valuation of a product, an attempt is made to only recognize the portion of P&L that is almost certain to be realized.
- By placing limits on the amount of P&L that can be lost if nonliquid factors turn out to have values different from those assumed, an attempt is made to place an upper bound on future losses.

Both reserves and limits provide the correct motivation to traders and marketers. They are encouraged to design and market product variants that minimize dependence on nonliquid factors. They are also encouraged to structure and market trades that will reduce existing dependence, both to reduce reserves, and thereby recognize P&L, and free up limits to enable more business to be done.

It can be argued that both reserves and limits are needed for effective control. Reserves are required to avoid misleading investors and lenders by claiming P&L that must be reversed later. Reserves are also required to avoid paying out bonuses to traders and marketers who may no longer be with the firm when it is eventually recognized that profit potential was overstated. If reserves were taken down to the point that no loss from that level is possible, then limits would not also be necessary. However, this is rarely possible so limits are needed to keep eventual losses within bounds. If limits are tight enough, then reserves may not be needed, if the amount of possible P&L restatement is sufficiently small.

In order to effectively implement limits and reserves for particular positions, it is necessary to study the nonliquid parameters of the models used in putting on the positions. Specifically, it is necessary to produce an estimate of the distribution of these parameters in order to establish numerical bounds for the near-worst-case scenarios. No matter how much historical data is available to support these estimates, they remain projections of future behavior from past experience requiring theoretical assumptions, so they are subject to error and possess irreducible elements of subjectivity.

Some general rules for guidance in making a statistical estimate of the distribution are:

- As already argued in Section 6.1, it is better to have such estimates made by outsiders, such as controllers or corporate risk managers, whenever distributions are being used for control purposes such as reserves and limits. (Distributions used for making trading and pricing decisions are, correspondingly, best made by insiders such as traders and marketers.)

- For similar reasons, it is best to have automated formulas for when to take and release reserves, based on a particular assumption about the distribution of the parameter. For example, if it is decided to reserve to a 90th percentile degree of certainty, and if it is determined that the 90th percentile of a correlation parameter is −40 percent, then reserves should be computed based on a model calculation with −40 percent correlation as input. This reduces the temptation to use reserves as a way of smoothing P&L fluctuations, as described in Section 5.1.2. Any new trades that increase the firm's exposure to a decline in correlation automatically add to reserves, and reserves cannot be reduced except through trades maturing or being offset in the market.

- When more than one input to a model is nonliquid, care must be exercised to avoid creating reserves and limits that are too extreme. For example, if the desire is to reserve to a 90th percentile degree of certainty, using 90th percentile values of the distribution of two or more input parameters will likely result in a far greater than 90th percentile degree of certainty in the reserve. A good way to avoid this, where computationally feasible, is by taking the Monte Carlo approach in which many reruns of the valuation model are made based on sample points chosen randomly from the assumed distribution of each nonliquid variable and with explicitly assumed correlations between variables. The 90th percentile of model outputs can then be computed.

- Statistical assumptions used when determining distributions should not be constrained by any assumptions made within the valuation model. For example, the valuation model may assume a normal distribution of a factor because it is computationally simple and the increase in accuracy from using a different distribution might not be worth the added investment. This would not in any way justify

assuming that the corresponding input variable is normally distributed when calculating a reserve, since the computational trade-offs
motivating the model-building decision do not apply to the reserve-
setting calculation.

- It is important that statistical analysis of the distribution of parameters is based on actual market observations instead of derived values
since the derived values often themselves contain modeling assumptions subject to error. This is analogous to the point made at the end
of Section 6.1 about avoiding circular reasoning in model validation.

6.3 MARK TO MARKET VERSUS MARK TO MODEL

As a risk manager, I am sometimes asked the following question by regulators: "Are you marking this product to market or are you marking it to
model?" My somewhat flip answer is "We never mark products to model;
we always mark them to market, but in some cases we use models to help
us figure out where the market is." The serious content behind this remark
summarizes this chapter: For valuation purposes, models should not be used
to override observed market prices, and when no observed market price is
available, a model should make as much use as possible of observed prices
for hedging instruments.

If the disagreement between an observed market price and a model value
represents a clear difference between where a risk can be sold at the current
time and a theory as to the value of the asset over a longer period of time,
then no matter how sound the reasoning behind the theory, I would recommend holding to the mark-to-market principle. If a firm deviates from
this principle and values based on longer-term values that it believes can be
realized, rather than on prices at which risks can currently be exited, it is
turning short-term risks into much harder-to-evaluate long-term risks.

However, sometimes the difference between an observed market price
and a model value represents two different ways in which a risk can be sold
at the current time. Although this would seem to violate several important
axioms of finance theory—the *no-arbitrage principle* and the *law of one price*
—these are just models and cannot expect any absolute deference in the face
of empirical exceptions. However, there needs to be careful evaluation of
what lies behind an observed difference between a market price and a model
price before an intelligent decision can be made as to which is the best of
two different ways to represent the risk.

Let's focus on a concrete illustration. You have observable market
prices for a European call option, a European put option, and a forward to
the same expiry date, with the same underlying and, in the case of the put
and the call, the same strike price. The combined prices, however, do not

agree with put-call parity. This would imply, for example, that a position in the put that you have sold can be offset in two different ways—you could buy a put, or you could synthetically create a put by buying a call and entering into a forward. It also implies that the call-forward combination will offset the position at a cheaper price than the direct purchase of the put.

What should a risk manager recommend in such circumstances? Since the main argument behind a no-arbitrage principle such as a put-call parity is that the lack of parity will be quickly eliminated by profit-seekers taking advantage of a riskless opportunity to make money, any persistence of parity violation is suggestive of some liquidity difficulties preventing the opportunity from being exploited. We'll consider some possibilities:

- This is an arbitrage that very few market participants can take advantage of, but your firm is one that can. This could be because the market for the put is in some way restricted to only a few firms. It could be an arbitrage that is difficult to identify computationally and your firm has a computational advantage. It could be a diversified basket of assets that is difficult to accumulate and your firm has an advantage in its market access (see the discussion in Section 10.4.1). In such cases, it is right to base valuation on the model-derived price (in this instance, the call-forward combination), since this represents a liquid external price at which risk can actually be extinguished in the short term.
- One of the prices is less liquid than the others. For example, the amount of trading for that strike and date could be much more active in calls than in puts. This would be a strong indication of the desirability of using a model (put-call parity) to supply a price based on more liquid quotations rather than utilizing a less liquid price. The same reasoning would apply if the call and put markets are significantly more active than the forward market, in which case I would recommend replacing an illiquid forward price with a put-call parity-derived price based on liquid put and call prices.
- A timing difference exists in price quotations. Perhaps the options market posts closing prices at an earlier time of day than the forwards market. It is certainly legitimate to use a model to update both call and put quotes to adjust for changes in the forward since the time the options market closed.
- Some contract features make the model not completely applicable. Sometimes, on closer examination, contract provisions call into question the applicability of a model. In this case, it might be an allowance for early option exercise in certain circumstances, whereas put-call parity only applies to options without early exercise provisions.

This last type of case has led to a considerable number of disputes between risk managers and trading desks. One example that has arisen at several firms is traders' desire to unlock stock option values contained in convertible bonds. Option models applied to convertible bond prices frequently indicate implied volatilities that are quite low compared with the implied volatilities that can be derived from plain equity options on the same stock, leading traders to conclude that buying the convertible is a good value trade. Trading desks hungry to book immediate profits have pressed for overriding reasonably liquid convertible price quotes with a model-driven quote based on the implied volatility from the equity options market. But a convertible bond contains the option to exchange a bond obligation for a stock obligation rather than to exchange cash for a stock obligation so it cannot be completely reduced to the value of an equity option (see the discussion in Section 10.4.4). When turned down on their first attempt, some trading desks have shown good enterprise in marketing total return swaps on the bond portion of the convertible in an attempt to isolate the equity option portion. So long as the swap has been properly engineered to cover all contingencies, such as canceling the swap without penalty in the event that the bond is converted for equity, a complete decomposition can be achieved and it is legitimate to value the resulting position as an equity option. Risk managers have, however, been very careful to check that no uncovered contingencies are present before allowing this valuation change.

CHAPTER 7

Managing Spot Risk

Spot trades are trades that involve an immediate exchange. This includes trades such as purchases of stock, purchases of gold, and exchanges of one currency for another. It excludes trades that involve a promise to deliver at some future time. Most of our study of risk involves future promises to deliver—unconditional promises constitute *forward transactions,* and promises whose payments are predicated on some future condition constitute *options transactions.*

The mathematical modeling and risk management of forwards and options are far more complex than the corresponding elements of spot transactions, and far more space in this book is devoted to forwards and options than to spot positions. However, positions in spot trades often constitute the largest portion of a firm's risk. Spot transactions are also the fundamental building blocks for valuing and risk managing forward and option positions. We can find the present value equivalent of a set of forward cash flows or the delta equivalent of an options position, but we then need to be able to value and risk manage these resulting spot positions. So a brief survey of the management of spot risk is in order.

All instruments traded by financial firms are *commodities* in the sense of not being individually identifiable. (If I borrow—that is, rent—a house from you, you expect me to return that exact same house, so houses are not a commodity; this is not true for dollar bills, bars of gold, barrels of oil, shares of IBM stock, specified amounts of a given bond, and so on.) This commodity feature means that a trader is free to sell before he buys, since he can always borrow the instrument in order to make delivery. In this way, financial markets are more symmetrical than noncommodity markets such as houses, where you must build up an inventory by buying before you can sell.

Commodities can be divided into *physical commodities*, such as gold and oil, and *financial commodities*, such as stocks, bonds, and currencies. We do not study any trading in bonds in this chapter. Since bonds represent a fixed obligation to deliver an amount of currency, they are studied in

113

Chapter 8 on managing forward risk. A general convention in the market is to use the term *commodities* to mean physical commodities only. Financial commodities are now almost universally transferable from one location to another in electronic form so they have negligible transportation and storage costs per unit. Physical commodities have non-negligible transportation and storage costs, which will have consequences we will study shortly.

Let us begin by looking at the hedging activities of a market maker in the dollar versus yen spot foreign exchange (or to adopt the terminology of that market, USD–JPY FX). In terms of instruments used, this represents the simplest type of trading possible—it is completely one-dimensional. The trader's position at any point in time can be represented as either long or short a certain quantity of JPY (or, completely equivalently, short or long a certain quantity of USD). In a more complex spot market, such as the commodities market for wheat, a trader's position would need to reflect being long or short different grades of wheat. However, currencies do not have grades—$1 million is $1 million, whether it is made up of 1,000 $100 bills or 10,000 $10 bills or 100,000,000 pennies.

Our market maker will receive orders throughout the day from customers who are either looking to sell JPY and buy USD or looking to sell USD and buy JPY. Each customer will state the quantity of USD she wishes to sell and ask for a bid of the quantity of JPY that the market maker will exchange for it, or state the quantity of JPY she wishes to sell and ask for a bid of the quantity of USD the market maker will exchange for it. Trading screens are available at all times that show the best bids currently available from other market makers for selling JPY in exchange for USD and for selling USD in exchange for JPY. The market maker is constantly submitting his own bids for these two trades for the consideration of other market makers. When a customer's inquiry is for a small enough quantity, the market maker can guarantee a profit by quoting a bid just slightly higher than the best bid currently quoted on the trading screen—if the customer accepts the bid, the market maker will immediately be able to close out the position created by hitting the bid quoted on the trading screen and making the small differences between the two as profit.

The market maker is only required to decide how much of a margin to build into the quote to the customer. The higher the margin, the higher the profit, but the greater the chance that the customer will turn down the quote and seek a quote from another market maker. The size of margin quoted must depend on the market maker's knowledge of the customer—how likely is this customer to be polling a large number of market makers simultaneously rather than just coming to a single firm seeking a quote? In practice, the decision making at a firm will probably be divided up between a trader and salesperson. The salesperson, who has a close knowledge of and continuing relationship with the customer, will bear the primary responsibility for determining the size of margin quoted. The trader will only be credited, in the internal record keeping of the firm, with a small portion of this margin.

A trader who followed this risk-averse a strategy would be unlikely to retain a job for long. The firm would probably judge that the profit the trader was making for the firm was not worth the opportunity cost of the trading seat. Higher profits would likely come from giving the seat to a more aggressive trader who would choose to take some risk by not closing positions out immediately. It is true that the more aggressive trader is running the risk that prices will move against him, but, assuming that the firm sees a decent flow of customer orders, it is likely that a customer order will soon come in on the other side, and, on average, over time, the spread between the bid on each side of the market will be greater than losses from price movement through time.

When a large customer order comes in, then the market maker has no choice but to take some risk—the only choice is how to divide the risk between the liquidity risk of trying to offset the position immediately and the basis risk of offsetting the position over time. With a large order, the trader can no longer count on being able to close the position out at the price posted on the trading screen since this quote will only be for a reasonably small transaction. Of course, the customer will be charged a premium for the liquidity risk posed by the size of the order, which will provide some cushion to the trader against the risk that must be taken. The trader needs to make a judgment as to the relationship of this large customer order to overall market conditions. Is it an order that simply reflects the idiosyncratic circumstances of this customer, perhaps a payment that needs to be made in the customer's business? In this case, it is unlikely that a relationship exists between the order and any price trend in the market. Unless the trader has some other reason to believe that the market will be trending in a direction that will cause losses to this position, it will be better to close the position slowly, relying on customer orders and small trades with other market makers, minimizing liquidity risk. However, if the large customer order is likely to be part of a large movement, such as a customer wanting protection against the announcement of economic data that may impact the market, it may be better to close the position more quickly, bearing some liquidity cost in order to reduce the exposure to market trend.

Almgren and Chriss (2001) show how to calculate the efficient frontier of strategies that have the optimal trade-off between the liquidity costs of offsetting the position in large blocs and the volatility risk (which we call *basis risk*) that the price at which the offset occurs differs from the price at which the position was put on. In the absence of price drift, the strategy that minimizes liquidity cost is one in which position covering is spread out over as long a period of time as possible, minimizing transaction size, and the strategy that minimizes volatility risk is one in which the entire position is offset at once, with as little chance for prices to change as possible.

Thus far, we have pointed out two advantages of seeing good customer order flow to a market-making firm—the increased likelihood of closing out positions at the favorable side of the bid spread and knowledge about the motives behind large orders. There are other advantages as well. Working with customers closely enables a firm to anticipate a large order and allows positions to accumulate through customer flow to meet part of the order in advance, thereby further lowering liquidity risk. When a firm's traders have a market view and want to put on a position, customer order flow enables them to put positions on and close out the positions more cheaply than if all positioning had to be done by aggressively seeking bids from other market makers. All of these advantages of customer order flow and the trade-offs of liquidity versus basis risk are present in all market-making activities, but can be observed in their purest form in spot risk market making, where other complicating factors do not intrude.

Even for the simplest spot product, FX spot, positions can be closed over time in other possible ways. For example, another source of liquidity is to spread out the closing of the position between the spot FX market and forward FX markets. This introduces a new basis risk in the form of the risk of unfavorable interest rate movements between the time the forward position is put on and the time it is closed out, but lowers the time basis risk. The trader must judge which is the most favorable risk mix. A trader in the currency of a smaller economy, let us say one trading the Danish krone against the dollar, might choose to temporarily hedge some of a position by a euro-USD trade that will eventually be closed out by a krone-euro trade. Adding a leg to the trade adds transaction costs, but euro-USD has more liquidity than krone-dollar and the trader's judgment may be that the basis risk of a krone-euro position is considerably smaller than that of a krone-USD position, given the closer tie of the Danish economy to the economy of the euro bloc countries than to the U.S. economy. When we move to more complex spot products such as commodities or equities, the potential avenues for redirecting basis risk multiply enormously. A position in IBM stock could be temporarily hedged by a Standards and Poor's (S&P) index future, judging this basis risk to be smaller than an outright IBM stock position. A position in one grade of wheat could be temporarily hedged with a position in another grade of wheat that trades with greater liquidity.

Firm-level risk management for spot risk is relatively straightforward. The more liquid spot positions can be valued by directly obtaining market prices. As a result, it is not necessary to utilize models for valuation and establish reserves against possible model errors. Most spot markets are liquid enough that prices can be obtained from trading screens or closing prices on public exchanges, so it is not even necessary to arrange for a price collection from brokers. For market-making trading desks with reasonable customer order flow, positions should be marked to mid-market, since the presumption is that, on average, most positions can be unwound without needing to aggressively seek bids from other market makers. The only adjustment that might arise with any frequency is a reserve against liquidity risk if a spot position grows sufficiently large relative to the size of customer order flow that significant liquidity costs may arise in closing the position. For proprietary trading desks, positions should generally be marked to the side of the bid-ask spread that is least favorable for the position, since, in the absence of customer order flow, it should be presumed that position close-out will require aggressively seeking bids from market makers.

Less liquid spot markets may require some form of modeling for valuation purposes. For example, an over-the-counter stock that does not trade very often or a commodity grade that is thinly traded may not have readily available price quotes. A model may need to be established that relates this price to a price of a more liquid instrument. For example, the over-the-counter stock price could be priced in relationship to a stock index, or a less liquid commodity grade could be priced as a spread to a more liquid commodity grade. In this way, the valuation can be updated daily based on quotes for the more liquid instruments. The relationship can be reestimated less frequently, as reliable trading prices for the less liquid instrument are obtained. When models of this type are used, a reserve is needed against the statistical uncertainty of the relationship between liquid and less liquid prices being utilized.

The issues of nonstatistical limits and risk reporting to senior management for spot positions center completely on issues of which positions should be grouped together, since the position in any particular spot instrument is a single number. To illustrate this point, we'll confine ourselves to the example of FX spot risk. Certainly, a USD-based firm will want to limit and report to senior management its net FX spot exposure to USD. This firm will also want to have individual currency limits for FX spot exposure for every currency it trades. It will set limit sizes relative to the overall liquidity of the market for that currency and the firm's degree of customer order flow in that currency to ensure that traders have explicit management approval to build up positions that will require large time periods to reverse. However, senior management would probably need to be informed only of the largest individual currency positions. The remaining decision is determining which currency groupings are the best to use in setting net FX spot exposure limits and reporting to senior management. For example, does a grouping of all Asian currencies make sense? A grouping of all Asian currencies excluding the yen, Australian dollar, and New Zealand dollar? Should Asian currencies be divided into groupings based on national Gross Domestic Product (GDP) per head? Each firm will reach its own conclusions based on economic theory, trading experience, and, perhaps, statistical analysis of which currency movements tend to occur together.

Physical commodities are further complicated by the presence of transportation costs, which leads to different markets for the same commodity in different locations (for example, oil for delivery in Seattle is a different product from oil for delivery in El Paso). This plays a role in valuation, since delivery at a location where liquid prices are not available could be priced using a model based on a more liquid price for delivery at another location and estimated transportation cost between the two locations. It also plays a role in the design of limits and reporting. Locations that are reasonably closely related in price, by having low transportation costs between them, should have their positions summed into a net position for reporting and perhaps limits.

An interesting analogy can be made between location relationships based on transportation costs and relationships between forward prices for different time periods. In Section 8.3.2, we will see that some commodities have forward prices for different times tightly linked by the possibility of cash-and-carry arbitrage. It is instructive to think of this as a form of location relationship, with the storage and financing costs as the cost of "transporting" the commodity from one time period to a later one. Just as transportation can be so expensive between some locations that they virtually form independent markets, storage can be so expensive for some commodities, such as electricity, as to virtually eliminate the possibility of cash-and-carry arbitrage. However, although transportation costs are almost always symmetrical (it costs just as much to ship from A to B as from B to A), a commodity cannot be transported from a later period to a former period, so cash-and-carry arbitrage only works in the forward direction.

EXERCISES

7.1

A market maker in a spot market is operating under the constraint that she must close out her position by the end of each trading day. We want to see the impact of different possible trading limits on the size of position that can be built up.

Divide the trading day into 100 time segments. In each time segment, except the last, there is a 50 percent chance of receiving a customer order for 1 unit. A customer order has a 50 percent chance of being a buy and a 50 percent chance of being a sell.

Customers pay $0.10 per trade in transaction costs. So if the mid-market price is $100.00, a customer will purchase at $100.10 and sell at $99.90.

The market maker cannot close out a trade without waiting at least one period. Mid-market price changes from one period to the next are normally distributed with a standard deviation of $0.10 (assume a starting mid-market price of $100.00). The market maker must close out her open position by the last trading period. She pays $0.05 per trade in transaction costs to close positions with another market maker. So if mid-market is $100.00, she sells positions at $99.95 and purchases at $100.05.

It is to the market maker's advantage if she can wait until a customer order comes in to close out her position, since she will make a $0.10 transaction spread on each side of the trade, for a total of $0.20, rather than making only $0.10 minus $0.05, for a total of $0.05 in transaction spread by closing out with another market maker. However, the longer she waits for a customer order, the greater her risk of prices moving against her.

Simulate a set of trading rules to see the trade-off between expected return and risk. Use 1,000 paths for each simulation. The measure of expected return should be simply average over these paths. You can choose any reasonable measure of risk, such as the 95th percentile loss or the standard deviation. One trading rule should be to never close out until the last period. Another should be to always close out in the period immediately after the customer trade. Intermediate rules can be based on a limit of how large the absolute size of a position is allowed to grow—when the position gets larger than this limit, the excess must be closed out.

1. Determine the impact on the risk-return trade-off of a lower standard deviation of the mid-market price of $0.05 per period.
2. For a more extended exercise, you could experiment with more complex trading rules, such as having the transaction cost for closing a position be an increasing function of the absolute size of position to be closed, or allowing the market maker to influence the probability of customer trades being buys or sells by shifting her quoted mid-price away from the mid-market.

CHAPTER 8

Managing Forward Risk

Managing forward risk is considerably more complex than managing spot risk due to the large number of dates on which forward payments can take place. With some forward markets going out to 30 years and even beyond, even if we restrict deliveries to take place on the 250 business days of a year, it still leaves $30 \times 250 = 7,500$ days on which future flows can occur, which each require a mark-to-market valuation and risk measurement. It is clearly impractical to have liquid market quotations for each possible forward so modeling needs to be heavily relied upon.

Having a spot versus forward position is an interest rate differential position, not a price view. If I believe the market will get a surprise announcement that will raise the stock price, even if I think it will not come for 3 months, I don't want to be long the forward and short the spot. When the announcement comes, both will be roughly equally impacted. I want this position only if the announcement I expect is something like a one-shot dividend that will impact the relative value of the spot and forward. If I put on a long forward and short spot position, I'm taking a view on the interest rate.

Let me cite a real example. On June 24, 1998, a trader was holding a long forward position in Telecom stock against which he was short the stock. AT&T announced plans to purchase Telecom at a sizable premium, but the trader wound up with a sizable loss. Why? His outright position in Telecom stock was even, so he didn't gain from the rise in the stock price. Telecom had never paid a dividend, so the forward traded at a large premium to the cash. As soon as the market anticipated that the stock could be traded for a dividend-bearing AT&T stock, this forward to cash premium shrunk significantly since it was now less expensive to hold a cash position in the stock for delivery into a forward sale.

The difference between an outright position and a borrowing or lending position is the difference between wanting to hold an asset as a good investment (you expect it to gain value) versus wanting to make use of an asset. Consider a house. When you buy it, you get a combination of an investment and a place to live. You might want to split the two. If you like it as an investment but don't want to live there, you can buy it and lend it to someone (rent it out). If you want to live in it but don't like it as an investment, you should borrow it (rent it) rather than buy it.

Similarly, a firm that is in the business of milling wheat and is running short of wheat supply to keep its production process going but does not like wheat as an investment (does not believe it will go up in price) will seek to borrow wheat rather than buy it (although borrowing may take the form of buying spot wheat while selling forward wheat). Likewise, a firm that likes wheat as an investment but does not need it for any production process will buy wheat and then lend it out (possibly combining the two steps into one by buying forward wheat).

Although a clear distinction can be made between an outright spot position and a borrowing or lending position, they also share close relationships. As we saw in the discussion of spot risk management in Chapter 7, maintaining a spot risk position over a longer period than a single trading day requires some form of borrowing or lending. In some markets, the use of borrowing or lending to maintain outright spot risk positions becomes such a dominant force that it is the principal driver of interest rate movements in the market. In many trades, such as forward purchases and sales, spot and forward risk are bound together, so it will be necessary to study the interactions between these two risks to fully understand the dynamics of forward risk management. It is important for the risk-management function to clearly separate spot risk from forward risk in transactions in which they are bundled to ensure that all the firm's spot risk in a given asset is reported and managed in a unified fashion.

The borrowing and lending markets in currencies and gold started as a means for businesses and individuals to adjust the timing between when income is earned and when purchases are made. Borrowing and lending in other commodities started with users and suppliers of the commodity satisfying short-term needs, as in the previous milling example. Borrowing in stocks and bonds started with the need for short sellers, who want to act on the view that an asset will decline in value, needing to first borrow what they wanted to sell short. Borrowing to support short selling is also a feature of all the other borrowing markets.

Once borrowing and lending markets are established, they begin to attract investors, speculators, and hedgers who have views on the borrowing rate rather than on the asset price. So one trader who believes that a particular borrowing rate will soon decline will lend at that rate solely in hopes that he can match that lending with a borrowing at a lower rate when the rate declines. Another trader might believe that the borrowing rate for May 2003 is too high relative to the borrowing rate for April 2003 so she will borrow for April and lend for May, hoping to reverse the transactions when rates return to a more normal relationship. Another trader might believe that borrowing rates for a particular corporation will decline relative to those of another corporation or the government, so he will lend to the former by buying its bond and borrow to support a short sale of the latter's bond. A business firm worried about the possible impact of high borrowing costs on the financial health in 2005 will borrow funds now that do not become available until 2005.

The emphasis I am placing on borrowing and lending rates as the foundation of forward risk is somewhat nonstandard (but see Williams [1986] for an incisive economic analysis of forward, futures, and lending markets for commodities using this approach). A more conventional exposition, such as Hull (2002, Chapter 3), would focus on borrowing rates only for currencies and would analyze forward risk on commodities and securities through forward contracts that involve exchanging the commodity or security for currency. The borrowing rate on the commodity or security still comes into play as one of the inputs determining the price of the forward or implied by the price of the forward.

The two methods are mathematically equivalent, so choosing between them is a matter of deciding which is the most convenient and supplies the greatest financial insight. My choice of emphasis is based on the following considerations:

- Direct borrowing and lending markets exist for many assets—such as gold, stocks, and government bonds—that do not require any involvement with borrowing/lending risk on currencies. Let's look at an example. Suppose that the rate for borrowing gold for 3 months is 2 percent annualized. If I want to borrow 1,000 ounces of gold today, I must be prepared to return $1,000 \times (1 + 2\% \times 3/12) = 1,005$ ounces of gold in 3 months. No mention has been made of any currency—there is simply an equivalence of a certain amount of gold on one date and some other amount of gold on another date.
- A uniform approach to all underlying instruments makes for easier exposition of some concepts. For example, Section 8.2 on mathematical models for forward risk is built around a single discount curve that could represent borrowing costs for a currency, but could represent borrowing costs for a security or commodity equally as well.
- It is consistent with a risk-management viewpoint in which, for example, it is natural for a gold trader to be taking risk with regard to gold borrowing rates, but not with regard to dollar borrowing rates. Gold borrowing costs are primarily impacted by economic factors unique to the gold market, including the supply and demand for gold, so it would be a sound risk-management practice for the same trading desk to run risks in the gold spot and borrowing. However,

there is little linkage between gold and dollar borrowing rates. A gold trader running dollar borrowing risks through the vehicle of positions in gold/dollar forwards requires serious management scrutiny. At a minimum, dollar interest rate exposures taken in this way need to be reported and aggregated together with other dollar rate risks throughout the firm. Similar comments apply to borrowing risk on other commodities and securities.

The primary argument against a borrowing rate focus is that for some assets, such as oil, no borrowing market exists, requiring forward risk to be managed through forward contracts. Even for some assets for which a borrowing market does exist, the borrowing market has considerably less liquidity than the comparable forward contract. However, it is always possible to take spot and forward prices and currency interest rates and derive implied asset borrowing rates that can then be used just as if they had been obtained by a direct quote. Indeed, even in some currency markets, the most liquid source for rate quotes is to combine forward foreign exchange (FX) prices with dollar rates to derive interest rates for the currency. This is no bar to developing discount curves for the currency or combining directly obtained rates that are the most liquid price source for some maturity segments with implied rates for other maturity segments and using them to form a single discount curve.

Given the complexities of forward risk management, we will need to carefully organize our study into the following sections:

- **Section 8.1.** This is a study of the variety of instruments that entail forward risk and that can be used to manage forward risk. The large variety of structures in which spot and forward risk (and occasionally implicit options risk) are woven together means that an important part of risk analysis is often just making sure that all the risks of a particular trade have been properly identified. In addition to the market risks, slight variations in structure, which may result in virtually identical spot and forward risk, can have large differences in credit risk, legal risk, and funding liquidity risk.
- **Section 8.2.** This section provides a study of the mathematical models used to value and measure forward risks. Although these models have been used heavily for many years and a great deal of consensus has been built up around them, enough subtle issues remain to merit a careful understanding of the residual risks of model uncertainty.
- **Section 8.3.** This section takes a brief look at the factors that impact borrowing and lending costs. Although this is not primarily a book about economics, at least some familiarity with the determinants of

forward prices is necessary to properly understand the requirements for designing a risk-management structure for forward risks.

■ **Section 8.4.** This section provides a study of how to design a risk-management reporting system for forward risk.

8.1 INSTRUMENTS

The management of forward risk can involve a number of different instruments that can be used to take on the same market risk position. These instruments may differ in legal form, with different regulatory consequences and standing in bankruptcy proceedings, and have different implications for credit risk and funding liquidity risk. They also differ in the extent to which they bundle together spot and forward risk.

We consider each of the following categories:

■ Direct borrowing and lending
■ Repurchase agreements
■ Forwards
■ Futures
■ Forward rate agreements (FRAs)
■ Interest rate swaps
■ Total return swaps
■ Default swaps
■ Asset-backed securities

8.1.1 Direct Borrowing and Lending

Suppose a trader wants to sell a given asset short. In a number of asset markets—such as stocks, bonds, currencies, and gold—the asset can be borrowed directly in order to sell short. Other markets, such as most physical commodities, have not developed direct borrowing products.

One drawback to using borrowing as the means of obtaining an asset to short is that it creates a sizable credit risk and funding liquidity risk for the asset lender, who could lose the entire value of the asset if the borrower defaults and who has to finance the asset that has been lent. The borrower may be paying for credit usage that is not really needed, since the cash raised by selling the asset short is incidental to the original objective of selling the asset short to position for a price drop. One solution is to use the cash raised as collateral against the borrowing. This reduces the credit risk for the asset lender, who can hold onto the cash collateral in case of borrower default, and reduces the funding liquidity risk, since the cash collateral received by the asset lender can be used to fund the asset purchase.

Providing cash collateral to the asset lender creates credit risk for the asset borrower, even though this is mitigated by the value of the asset, which does not need to be returned if the recipient of the cash collateral defaults.

8.1.2 Repurchase Agreement

In the previous example, one party borrows the asset and provides cash collateral to the other party. An equivalent way of describing the same trade is to say that one party borrows the asset and lends cash, whereas the other party borrows cash and lends the asset. Yet another equivalent way of describing the same trade is a transaction in which the first party purchases the asset for cash and, at the same time, contracts to sell the asset back to the second party at an agreed forward date for an agreed cash price. Table 8.1 demonstrates that all three ways of describing this transaction are equivalent in terms of the flows of cash and asset.

The third description, which is known as a *repurchase agreement*, possesses some legal advantages in the event of default. If the party lending the asset defaults, the other party technically owns the asset, since it purchased it rather than just borrowing it, so it has fewer legal restrictions on its ability to use the asset. If the party borrowing the asset defaults, the party lending the asset, since it technically sold the asset and received cash as payment rather than just as collateral for the borrowing, has fewer legal restrictions in its ability to use the cash.

8.1.3 Forwards

A *forward contract* is an agreement to pay a fixed price on a set forward date for a specified amount of an asset. As such, it combines into a single transaction borrowing the asset and then selling the asset in the spot market. The seller of the forward needs to deliver the asset at a fixed forward date and price, exactly as a borrower of the asset must do. The seller of the forward is at risk for increases in the asset's price and will gain from decreases in the asset's price, just like a borrower of the asset who sells it in the spot market. The buyer of the forward is in the same position as a buyer of a spot who lends out the underlying asset, but does not need to fund the currency to purchase the asset. Since no cash will change hands until the forward date, it does not have the credit and funding liquidity risks that an uncollateralized borrowing of the asset would have. From a credit risk standpoint, a forward transaction is very similar to a borrowing of the security that has been collateralized by cash.

Credit risk on either a forward or a borrowing collateralized by cash starts close to zero, but can build up as the market price of the underlying asset goes up or down. Managing this counterparty credit risk can be quite

TABLE 8.1 Alternative Descriptions of an Asset Borrowing Collateralized by Cash

Description 1	
Today	A borrows $1 million par amount of a Treasury bond from B. A sells the bond in the market and receives $980,000. A places the $980,000 as collateral with B.
One month from today	A buys the $1 million par bond in the market and returns it to B. B returns the $980,000 collateral to A. A pays $1,000 in interest for borrowing the bond to B. B pays $5,000 in interest for the use of the cash to A.
Net effect	A delivers $1 million in par amount of the Treasury bond to A. B pays $980,000 + $5,000 − $1,000 = $984,000 in cash to A.

Description 2	
Today	A borrows $1 million par amount of a Treasury bond from B. B borrows $980,000 in cash from A.
One month from today	A repays the $1 million par Treasury bond loan to B plus $1,000 cash in interest on the loan. B repays the $980,000 in cash to A plus $5,000 in interest on the loan.
Net effect	A delivers $1 million par amount of the Treasury bond to A. B pays $980,000 + $5,000 − $1,000 = $984,000 in cash to A.

Description 3	
Today	A purchases $1 million par amount of a Treasury bond from B for $980,000 in cash.
One month from today	B buys the $1 million par amount of the Treasury bond from A at the prearranged price of $984,000.

complex, as the amount of credit exposure varies through time and is correlated with movements in a market price. We will not be fully prepared to address this issue until Section 12.4 on counterparty credit risk. For now, we will just note that a frequently used approach to mitigate this credit exposure is the collateral call, in which the borrower and lender agree in advance that upward moves in the asset price will require the asset borrower to increase the amount of collateral placed with the lender and downward moves in the asset price will require the asset lender to increase the amount of collateral placed with the borrower. This cross-collateralization agreement is an automatic feature of futures contracts, which are very closely related to forward transactions.

8.1.4 Futures Contracts

Future contracts are identical to forward contracts in their market price exposures. They also specify the payment of a fixed price on a set forward date for a specified amount of an asset. They differ from forward transactions in two primary dimensions: the management of counterparty credit risk and the degree to which they are tailored to trade-off basis risk versus liquidity risk. We will briefly discuss both aspects.

Unlike forward transactions, which are direct transactions between two firms or individuals, future contacts are always arranged to have a futures exchange as one of the counterparties to each contract. So if firm A agrees to sell 100,000 barrels of oil for delivery on June 15, 2005 to firm B in exchange for $3 million, it is technically broken up into an agreement for A to deliver 100,000 barrels of oil on June 15, 2005 to the futures exchange in exchange for $3 million and an agreement for B to pay $3 million to the futures exchange for the delivery of 100,000 barrels of oil on June 15, 2005. This greatly simplifies credit risk management for the firms, who do not need to worry about the creditworthiness of one another but only need to evaluate the creditworthiness of the futures exchange. This would involve enormous credit management problems for the futures exchange since it has credit exposure to every firm trading on the exchange, but it is managed by strict insistence on continuous cash payments to and from the futures exchange as the prices of the futures transactions rise and fall (details can be found, for example, in Hull [2002, Section 2.4]). This also requires sufficient initial collateral to reduce credit risk to a minimum. This has several significant implications.

Because of the continuous collateral calls, a firm using futures contracts will have constant inflows and outflows of cash as asset prices rise and fall. This has important consequences for both funding liquidity risk and market risk. The funding liquidity risk consequence is that if a firm is using futures contracts to offset transactions that do not have this cash settlement feature, it may lead to substantial funding needs. For details, refer back to the Metallgesellschaft (MG) case in Section 4.2.2. The market risk implication is that the constant cash payments create risk to the extent that payment amounts are correlated with the time value of the payments—see the discussion on convexity risk in Section 8.2.4.

This system of credit risk control requires that the terms of futures contracts be standardized with only a few possible delivery dates and assets that can be contracted for. This contrasts with forward transactions, which, as agreements between two firms, can be tailored to very specific forward dates and assets to be delivered. This freedom is permitted by the firms performing their own management of the credit considerations of the transaction. However, the futures exchange must have the ability to quickly close out any contract on which a counterparty cannot meet a collateral call. The ability to quickly close out contracts without a substantial risk of loss requires the liquidity derived from a few standardized contract terms.

The liquidity that results from this standardization can also be attractive to potential counterparties who may welcome the reduction in liquidity risk this offers. With only a few standardized contracts, it is easier to find good price valuations and close out positions that are no longer desired. The price of lower liquidity risk is, as always, heightened basis risk. A firm might desire to hedge flows on particular dates, but need to accept a hedge with nearby standardized dates. It may also desire to sell short a particular asset, say, a particular grade of wheat, but need to accept a hedge with a related standardized grade. The maintenance of necessary liquidity may require the provision that several possible grades be deliverable, which requires formulas for determining how much of each grade must be delivered. However, changes in actual market conditions will differ from any set formula, resulting in profit opportunities and basis risks that may need quite complex modeling. For an example, see the discussion of the modeling of delivery options on Treasury bond futures in Hull (2002, Section 5.10).

8.1.5 Forward Rate Agreements (FRAs)

A *forward rate agreement* (FRA, pronounced "fra") is a particular type of forward contract in which the asset to be delivered on the forward date is a borrowing with a specified maturity date, interest rate, and borrower. For example, it might be an agreement to deliver 2 years from today a $200 million 1-year deposit with Bank of America paying an interest rate of 6.50 percent. This means that in 2 years the buyer of the FRA will be able to deposit $200 million with Bank of America in exchange for receiving $213 million back at the end of the third year ($200 million $\times$ (1 + 6.50%) = $213 million).

The standard practice for FRAs is to *cash settle*, meaning that no actual deposit of cash with Bank of America is expected; instead, a cash amount equal to the value of the deposit will change hands. In our example, if Bank of America is offering 5.00% on 1-year deposits at the end of 2 years, the right to place a deposit at 6.50% is worth 1.50% $\times$ $200 million = $3 million. Therefore, the FRA seller owes $3 million to the FRA buyer, which will be paid at the end of the 1-year deposit period. (In most, but not all, cases, the payment will be made when the FRA settles, which is the beginning of the deposit period, not the end. However, the settlement price will be determined by the present value of the payment due, using the prevailing discount rates at the time of settlement. Economically, this is no different in value from receiving the payment at the end of the deposit period, but it has the beneficial effect of reducing credit exposure.) If Bank of America is offering 7.50% on 1-year deposits at the end of 2 years, the requirement to place a deposit at 6.50% has a cost of 1.00% × $200 million = $2 million. Therefore, the FRA buyer owes $2 million to the FRA seller, which will be paid at the end of the 1-year deposit period.

FRAs are valuable tools for managing forward risk since they can be used to lock in borrowing and lending costs for future time periods or take positions on rates rising or falling. They are almost wholly confined to rates offered on currency borrowings by very high-credit-grade banks, since they have developed primarily as tools for managing the cost of borrowing and lending currencies rather than tools for speculating on changes in credit quality. The most popular instruments are those tied to the deposit rates averaged over a panel of high-grade banks, such as the London Interbank Offering Rate (LIBOR), thereby reducing the link to credit quality even further. Some interest rate futures, such as LIBOR futures, are essentially FRAs contracted using futures rather than forward structuring.

8.1.6   Interest Rate Swaps

Standard *interest rate swaps* are equivalent to a package of FRAs. A very typical example would be a 5-year swap for $200 million settled quarterly with one party paying U.S. dollar LIBOR and the other party paying a fixed rate of 6.50 percent. This is equivalent to a package of 20 FRAs that are settled on each quarterly date for the next 5 years.

Interest rate swaps are extremely flexible instruments that can be tailored to specific customer needs. Although it is typical that the terms of each FRA that constitutes the package will be the same on all terms except the forward date, it is quite possible for customers to arrange swaps with rates, deposit lengths, and notional amounts that differ by period. It is also quite common to combine FRAs in different currencies into a single swap and combine FX forwards along with FRAs into a single swap. To better understand the customer motivation for these features, it is important to understand the relationship between bonds and interest rate swaps.

The primary initial demand for interest rate swaps, and much of the demand to this day, comes from issuers of and investors in corporate bonds. Most corporate bonds pay fixed coupons, as this represents the form popular with most investors. However, bond issuers may prefer to borrow at a floating interest rate rather than a fixed rate, either because they believe rates are likely to fall in the future or because they believe floating-rate borrowings are a better match to their overall asset-liability position. Some investors may prefer lending at a floating rate rather than at the fixed coupon on a bond, either because they believe rates are likely to rise or because they are primarily looking to take a position in the creditworthiness of the firm and don't want to combine this with a position on whether risk-free rates will rise or fall. For such clients, a fixed-for-floating single-currency interest rate swap, which is just a package of FRAs for a single currency, can transform a fixed-rate bond position into a floating-rate one.

Another instance of interest rate swap demand arising out of the corporate bond market occurs when the currency a firm would prefer to owe debt in is different than the currency that is preferred by a segment of investors in the firm's bonds. A typical example would be a European firm that wanted to tap into investor demand in the U.S. market. The firm might prefer to have all its debt in euros, but most U.S. investors prefer to invest in dollar-denominated bonds. One solution is to have the firm issue a dollar-denominated bond, but then enter into a cross-currency interest rate swap in which the firm receives fixed dollar payments equal to the coupon payments it owes on the dollar-denominated bond and pays fixed euro cash flows. The firm would probably also want to combine this with an FX forward contact to exchange the euro principal it wants to pay on the maturity date of the bond for the dollar principal that it owes on the dollar-denominated bond. This combination is a standard product, a cross-currency interest rate swap with the exchange of fixed principal. The firm might also want to make floating-rate euro coupon payments rather than fixed-rate euro coupon payments for the reasons given in the previous discussion on single currency swaps. Rather than execute two separate swaps, this can all be accomplished in a single fixed dollar for floating euro cross-currency swap. Cross-currency swaps can therefore be a combination of a bundle of FRAs and a bundle of FX forwards. As such, it combines the spot FX risk of FX forwards, the forward risk of FX forwards, and the forward risk of FRAs.

8.1.7 Total Return Swaps

We have already seen how a cross-currency swap can combine FRA and forward positions in a foreign currency asset. *Total return swaps* are instruments that generalize this approach to enable forward positions to be taken in any asset. Instead of having an agreement to exchange a fixed amount of euro for a fixed dollar price on an agreed forward date, as might be the case in a cross-currency swap, an agreement might be made to exchange a fixed amount of an asset such as a bond or stock for a fixed dollar price on an agreed forward date.

The most common form of total return swap calls for the following. Party A makes a series of intermediate payments to party B, usually tied to intermediate coupon payments or stock dividends. Party A delivers an asset to party B on a fixed date for a fixed price. Finally, Party B makes a series of intermediate payments to party A, usually tied to a funding index such as LIBOR. This form of total return swap is economically equivalent to a forward transaction. Like a forward, it combines into a single bundle the spot sale of an asset and the borrowing of that asset for a fixed term. However, although a forward bundles together the sale price and borrowing costs into a single final fixed price, the total return swap makes the intermediate borrowing costs more explicit.

One major contractual difference between total return swaps and forwards is that a total return swap can be used by a party that might otherwise find it difficult, for legal or institutional reasons, to invest in a particular asset class. Although the forward contract generally calls for the actual delivery of the asset on the specified forward date, the total return swap will often call for a cash settlement based on the value of the asset on the specified date. This can be a necessity for a party that cannot legally own the asset (for example, they may not have a subsidiary in the country in which the asset trades). This can still be a great convenience for a party that can legally own the asset but may not be well positioned to trade it. In effect, they are contracting out to the other party the actual sale, which makes sense if the other party is a major market player in this asset or if the asset is actually a participation in a portfolio of assets.

The downside of this arrangement is that it can lead to disputes as to what the actual settlement price should be in cases where there is not a publicly available and reliable pricing source. So although it may be easy to agree that the settlement of a basket of stocks traded on the New York Stock Exchange (NYSE) will end up at the published closing exchange prices for the day, it may be necessary to build elaborate legal processes for the settlement of a bond of limited liquidity. (For example, the processes could involve an appeal to a panel of other market makers or the right of the party receiving the value of the bond to take physical delivery in the event of failing to agree on a cash price.)

The primary initial impetus for the total return swap market came from parties wanting to purchase assets they would have difficulty holding. They were either assets they could not legally hold or would have difficulty trading, leading to the demand for a cash settlement discussed previously, or assets they would have difficulty funding. A firm wanting to purchase a bond with a higher credit grade than that of the firm could face the negative carry costs of having to fund at a higher credit spread than it can earn on the bond. To avoid this situation, one must find a way to borrow against the collateral of the security, as discussed previously in Sections 8.1.1 and 8.1.2. The total return swap offers the convenience of bundling purchases together with a locked-in borrowing cost for a fixed period. Collateralization is not required since the asset will not be delivered until the end of the borrowing period.

Another example of funding difficulty would be a firm with a sufficiently high credit grade that is under regulatory pressure to reduce the size of its balance sheet. If it can find another high-credit-grade firm that is not under similar regulatory pressure, it can "rent the balance sheet" of the other firm by entering into a total return swap, although it must expect to pay for the service.

Many of the suppliers of total return swaps to parties wanting to purchase assets they would have difficulty holding simply purchase the asset and hold it until the scheduled delivery or cash settlement. They are being paid to provide a service, as a market maker able to skillfully execute purchases and sales at good prices, an efficient provider of a desired portfolio of assets, a firm having the legal standing to hold assets of a desired country, or a firm with a higher credit standing and lower funding costs or more balance sheet room. However, as the market has evolved, many suppliers are also using this market as an efficient means of borrowing assets in which they want a short spot position. As with a forward, the total return swap provides convenient bundling of the asset borrowing and short sale into a single transaction. For example, a firm wanting to gain on a price decline of a specific bond, either because of a market view or because this offers a hedge against the credit exposure they have to the bond issuer, can enter into a total return swap in which they need to deliver the bond forward (or equivalently cash settle) and then simply *not* hold a cash bond against this forward obligation.

8.1.8 Default Swaps

As discussed previously, total return swaps can be an efficient vehicle for enabling firms with credit exposure to particular borrowers to purchase protection against that exposure from parties who are willing to invest in the bonds of that borrower. However, the protection purchased may not be an exact fit to the protection desired. Exposure may be mostly all or nothing —with loss if the borrower defaults and no loss otherwise. A total return swap on the borrower's bond offers protection against default, but bundles it with protection that may not be wanted—a gain when credit spreads widen —along with an exposure that may not be wanted—a loss when credit spread decreases.

To avoid this unwanted additional protection and exposure, you would need a total return swap with the same maturity date as the borrower's bond, so that default is the only reason for settlement not to be at par. However, a bond may not available in the market with a maturity date matching the period for which protection against default is desired. A more precisely tailored product to meet this need is a *default swap*, which pays off only when the borrower defaults. In a typical structure, the party purchasing protection would make periodic payments to the party selling protection, receiving nothing in return if default does not occur during the life of the swap and receiving a payment if default does occur.

The trade-off against the more precise tailoring of the product is that it offers greater difficulties in settlement. Whereas a total return swap's payments are completely defined by the price of a given bond on a given day, the default swap's payments depend on the definition of a default event. Does default mean any delay in a scheduled payment of the borrower or only one of a particular magnitude? Is a formal declaration of bankruptcy a necessity? What happens if the terms of the borrower's debt are voluntarily renegotiated with creditors (and how can you tell how voluntary it has been)? This only touches on how to define a default event.

Default swaps, more than any other derivative instrument, have led to the concept of *legal basis risk*. A market maker may believe its risk on a default swap is matched exactly by the protection purchased through another default swap, only to find it has to make a payment under the contractual language of the first swap but receives nothing under the slightly different language of the second swap.

The International Swaps and Derivatives Association (ISDA), the industry group that sets standards for derivatives contracts, has made several valiant attempts to remedy the situation by standardizing contract wording. The resulting checklist of possible contract terms is a daunting document. Even so, new disputes continue to arise. Any firm participating in this market needs to be thoroughly aware of all the relevant history of the disputes and needs to be certain it fully understands the terms of the risk it has taken on. A good synopsis of the ISDA standards and the motivation behind them can be found in Anson (1999, pp. 151–162). For further background on the issues, see Henderson (1998), Falloon (1998), Cass (2000), Bennett (2001), and the following articles from the *Economist*: "Is there money in misfortune?" (July 16, 1998), "Of devils, details, and default" (December 3, 1998), "Fixing the holes" (August 12, 1999), and "The swaps emperor's new clothes" (February 8, 2001).

When the default swap product was first offered, many default swaps were structured to offer protection against a specific bond. If the firm issuing the bond defaulted, the party that bought the protection would then be able to sell that bond at par to the party providing the protection. This achieved perfect protection for the specific bond on which the default swap was based, but had perverse effects when investors attempted to use the swap to hedge other credit risk to the same firm. For example, banks with loans outstanding to the firm purchased credit protection through default swaps tied to a bond. They anticipated that in the event of the firm's default, they could buy the bond at what would now be a severely depressed market price, sell it at par under the contractual terms of the default swap, and use the profit as an offset to their credit loss on the loan. When many banks pursued the same strategy, the demand after the default event to buy the specific bond needed for delivery into the default swap drove its price up in the market and reduced the profit achieved to far less than what was needed to offset the loan loss. (For more details, see the articles from the *Economist* in July 16, 1998 and December 3, 1998 referenced previously.)

As a result, market practice has shifted toward default swap contracts that enable virtually any credit instrument of the defaulting firm to be delivered for par. This provides the buyers of protection much greater assurance that their full exposure will be compensated. It also introduces a delivery option feature into the default swap. In the event of default, the buyer of default swap protection can search for the instrument issued by the defaulting firm that is selling at the lowest price in the market, buy it, and deliver it at par while selling the instrument actually held into the market. This delivery option needs to be evaluated and priced into the default swap, analogously to the delivery option on futures, which is referenced toward the end of Section 8.1.4. With the exception of the delivery option, default swaps can be valued as total return swaps on a bond with the same maturity date as the swap—that is, a bond with locked-in borrowing costs. For a more detailed discussion, see O'Kane and McAdie (2001).

Another solution to this problem is to have a default swap with a fixed payment in the event of default. This resolves the issue of how to determine payment, but may not be a good fit to the risk needs of a holder of a bond or loan. Suppose I am holding a $100 million bond issued by ABC. I can buy a standard default swap on $100 million notional. If the loss in the event of default turns out to be $20 million, it should pay roughly $20 million. If it turns out to be $80 million, it should pay roughly $80 million. However, if I buy a default swap with a fixed dollar payout, I must make a guess as to the loss in the event of default and run the risk that I have either purchased too little protection or paid for too much protection. Default swaps with fixed payoffs are also harder to value since this requires an estimate of the probability of default, whereas a standard bond price is based on the product of the probability of default and loss given default. See Section 12.1.

8.1.9 Asset-Backed Securities

In general, an *asset-backed security* can be viewed as an alternative instrument to total return swaps in taking on exposures to asset classes where the actual management of the exposure is desired to be left to another party. The reasons why this might be desirable could be copied almost verbatim from Section 8.1.7. The use of asset-backed securities rather than total return swaps in a particular situation is largely a matter of how documentation and collateralization of the swap agreement are handled.

When a particular total return exposure is expected to have a fairly broad appeal to a class of investors, it may be desirable to standardize the terms and offer the exposure through a security rather than a swap. This eliminates the need to individually negotiate swap terms since a single document covers the terms of the security, but the trade-off is a loss of flexibility in fitting terms to an individual investor. The use of a security structure forces investors to invest cash up front, a convenient solution to collateralization concerns, particularly when the number of investors is potentially too large to make the negotiation of individual credit coverage attractive. Of course, the disadvantage is that investors must tie up cash in the transaction, but in return they get a standardized security that can be sold or pledged as collateral. By contrast, it is hard to transfer ownership of a swap position since your counterparty on the swap, which did not place cash up front, may object to the creditworthiness of the new party to which you want to transfer ownership.

The cash nature of the investment protects the party managing the assets from credit concerns. Investors get credit protection by having the assets on which the exposure will be taken placed in some form of trust, thereby immunizing their payoff from default on the part of the party managing the assets. This leads to a potential problem in the flexibility of asset-backed securities in relation to total return swaps. If assets need to be walled off in a trust, then how can a market maker use this as a vehicle for taking a short sale position in the asset as we showed can be done with a total return swap. The solution is to have a total return swap as an asset placed with the trust and sufficiently collateralize or protect it by third-party insurance.

Asset-backed securities lend themselves to pooling positions in a large number of similar assets, such as mortgages, credit card outstandings, loans to businesses, or bonds. The standardized nature of the documentation is well suited to the sharing of exposure by a large number of investors in a large pool of assets, thereby decreasing the event risk of each investor owning a particular block of assets. However, this is more a matter of convenience than necessity, and virtually any financial position that can be achieved through an asset-backed security can also be achieved through a total return swap.

Table 8.2 summarizes the difference in risk between the different types of instruments through which forward risk can be taken. Spot risk refers to the underlying asset. Forward risk is always present for the underlying asset, but may or may not also involve forward risk in a currency (in the case where the underlying asset is a currency, the question is whether forward risk in a second currency is involved). Credit risk refers only to credit risk to the counterparty on the instrument, not to any credit risk embedded in the underlying asset. The distinction between the lender and borrower refers to their position relative to the underlying asset.

TABLE 8.2   Comparison of Risks in Forward Transactions

| Instrument | Primary Market Risk Exposure | | Credit Risk for Lender | Credit Risk for Borrower | Other Risks |
	Spot Risk	Currency Forward Risk			
Direct borrowing and lending—including loans, bonds, and deposits	No	No	Yes, but can be mitigated by collateral.	Only if collateral needs to be posted.	Funding liquidity risk for the lender, unless collateralized.
Repurchase agreement	No	Yes	Small, only to the extent collateral is inadequate.	Small, only to the extent collateral is in excess of borrowing.	
Forward contract	Yes	Yes	Starts at zero, but can build up if not mitigated by collateral.	Starts at zero, but can build up if not mitigated by collateral.	
Futures contract	Yes, except for some interest rate futures	Yes	Credit exposure is to the futures exchange and is small due to cash settlement.	Credit exposure is to the futures exchange and is small due to cash settlement.	May have delivery option. Convexity risk caused by cash settlement. Possible funding liquidity risk if hedging positions that do not have cash settlement.
FRAs	No	No	Starts at zero, but can build up if not mitigated by collateral.	Starts at zero, but can build up if not mitigated by collateral.	

(continued)

TABLE 8.2 Comparison of Risks in Forward Transactions (continued)

| Instrument | Primary Market Risk Exposure | | Credit Risk for Lender | Credit Risk for Borrower | Other Risks |
	Spot Risk	Currency Forward Risk			
Interest rate swaps:					
Single currency swaps	No	No	Starts at zero, but can build up if not mitigated by collateral.	Starts at zero, but can build up if not mitigated by collateral.	
Cross-currency swaps	Typically yes	Yes	Starts at zero, but can build up if not mitigated by collateral.	Starts at zero, but can build up if not mitigated by collateral.	
Total return swaps	Yes	Yes	Starts at zero, but can build up if not mitigated by collateral.	Starts at zero, but can build up if not mitigated by collateral.	
Default swaps	Yes	Yes	Very small, only for receipt of credit spread.	Yes.	
Asset-backed securities	Yes	Yes	Yes, but can be mitigated by collateral and by trust structure.	Typically no, fully collateralized.	May have delivery option. Legal basis risk.

8.2 MATHEMATICAL MODELS OF FORWARD RISKS

The most important fact about the mathematical models used to manage forward risk is that they rely on one very simple principle—a flow on a given date owed by a particular entity should be regarded as absolutely equivalent to any other flow of the same quantity on the same date owed by the same entity (the term *flow* is used rather than cash flow, since we want to consider more general cases than cash payments, such as an entity owing an amount of gold or oil).

At first glance, this may look like a tautology, a statement true by definition. And it is close to one, which helps to explain why practitioners agree so widely on the models used to manage forward risk. However, it is not quite a tautology—a reminder that mathematical finance deals with market realities, not theoretical abstractions. When the product a trader is dealing with is actually a complicated bundle of flows on a large number of different dates, it is not immediately clear that breaking the valuation apart into many different pieces, few of which can independently be priced in the market, is the best way to proceed. Indeed, a few decades ago, objections to this practice were still being raised along the lines that it would be very expensive in terms of transaction costs for a trader to actually hedge the instrument in this way. By now, everyone involved has come to appreciate that the principle, far from causing traders to try to aggressively rehedge each piece of a deal, is actually a powerful analytic tool that enables very complex transactions to be managed in a way that permits a maximum amount of netting of risks before resorting to aggressive hedging.

We need to examine where the complexities in this approach lie in order to see what residual risks still need to be managed. Before turning to the hard part, however, let's first take a few moments to appreciate some of the benefits entailed by the simplicity of this approach.

One benefit is the computational simplicity of the method. The actual bundles of forward transactions that trade in the market can have very complex structures. Our fundamental principle says to ignore all these complexities; just calculate the individual flows that have been bundled together, calculate the present value of each flow in isolation from the others, and then sum the present values. It is not necessary to devise special methods that apply to particular cases, a feature that hobbled many of the methods that were used before the fundamental principle was generally adopted.

A second benefit is the generality of the principle. The same computational method can be used for cash flows, commodity flows, bonds, swaps, forwards, futures, risk-free debt, risky debt, and obligations to deliver stock. (Please note carefully that this is not saying that this method can be used for valuing stocks since stocks involve unknown future obligations rather than known flows; what is being said is that an obligation to deliver a fixed number of shares of a stock in the future can be translated into an equivalent amount of shares of the stock to be delivered today.) The same computational method can be used to value individual transactions or portfolios of transactions, since each can be reduced to the summation of a set of individual flows, and therefore can also be used for valuing total return swaps or asset-backed securities tied to portfolios of transactions. One caveat exists —a slight correction is needed for risky debt, a topic that we will postpone until Section 12.1.

A third benefit is that when all transactions are completely reduced to their respective constituent obligations, you are free to describe transactions in whatever manner is most convenient in a given context. When discussing a physical commodity such as gold, it is often convenient just to think in terms of equivalent quantities—for example, you are willing to trade 100 ounces of gold for delivery today for 102 ounces of gold for delivery in 1 year. When discussing a currency, you might prefer to talk about the interest rate to be paid—say, 6 percent for 1 year. Although this is just a different way of saying that you are willing to trade $100 for delivery today for $106 for delivery in 1 year, the interest rate view is often easier to understand using economic theory. When doing computations, it is usually best just to think of discount factors to be multiplied by each flow and then summed to get a net present value equation. When checking the reasonableness of a given set of input parameters to the model, it is often most convenient to think in terms of interest rates that apply to distinct forward time periods—the rate that applies to a particular month, week, or day. Improbable inputs can be more easily spotted if you can see that they imply that a rate of 20 percent on one day will occur in between a 7 percent rate on the immediately preceding and following days.

Formulas for translating from discount factors to zero-coupon interest rates, par-coupon interest rates, or forward interest rates and back again are readily available, as should be expected from our general principle. You are probably already familiar with these formulas. If not, consult Hull (2002, Sections 5.2 to 5.5).

The **Rates** spreadsheet on the accompanying CD-ROM illustrates the techniques for valuing a portfolio of flows based on a given set of forward rates. The forward rates are translated into equivalent zero-coupon rates, par rates, and discount factors. Each set of flows, which might correspond to a forward, a swap, a bond, or any of the other instruments discussed, is broken up into its individual flows. For each individual flow, a discount factor is determined based on interpolation from the discount factors derived from the given forward rate. Each individual flow is then multiplied by its discount factor and these values are summed over the portfolio.

The interpolation methodology used in this spreadsheet for illustrative purposes is a simple linear interpolation. In practice, more complex interpolation methodologies are often used. Tuckman (2002, Chapter 4) presents a good introduction.

The same spreadsheet will be used elsewhere in this chapter to illustrate how to derive a set of forward rates that can match a given set of observed market prices and to demonstrate the calculation of risk statistics for a portfolio of flows.

Having postponed looking at complexities, it's time to face up to the task. Basically, this discussion can be divided into four topics:

- **Section 8.2.1.** Models are needed to perform interpolation from flows for which market prices are available to other flows.
- **Section 8.2.2.** Models are needed to extrapolate prices for longer-dated flows.
- **Section 8.2.3.** In some cases, going from flow prices to bundle prices is not as simple as the general approach. This is because some products involve flows representing a promised delivery that is actually a promise to deliver a future flow (for example, a forward purchase of a bond). Untangling these flows involves some complexities.
- **Section 8.2.4.** Although the method is designed to handle fixed obligations, it can be applied to a very important class of nonfixed obligations with just a bit of work—flows that will be determined by certain types of indices. However, this extension must be performed with care; otherwise, a significant source of risk can slip in unidentified.

8.2.1 Pricing Illiquid Flows by Interpolation

As was pointed out at the beginning of this chapter, the large number of days on which future flows can occur makes it almost certain that liquid quotations will only be available from the market for a small portion of possible flows. Creating price quotes for all possible flows will require some theory that enables the inference of prices of illiquid flows from prices of liquid flows. We will present two theories:

- The interpolation of the price of an illiquid flow from prices of liquid flows that are both earlier and later than it
- A stack-and-roll methodology for pricing flows that have longer maturities than any flows with liquid prices

The mathematics of interpolation is so simple that it can be easy to lose sight of the fact that interpolation is a financial model to the same degree as more complex options models. It shares the same characteristics of being a methodology for predicting future financial events, requiring well-thought-out assumptions about the financial markets as grounds for choosing one possible methodology over another, and being a source of potential earnings loss to the extent future events diverge from predictions.

When the modeling nature of interpolation is not kept clearly in mind, the choice of interpolation method can be made based on aesthetic criteria, as if it is just a matter of individual taste with no financial consequences. So let us be very specific about financial assumptions and the financial consequences of choices.

Consider the following example, which is typical of the circumstances in which interpolation needs to be employed in pricing forward flows. You need to price a forward flow occurring in $6\frac{1}{2}$ years in a market in which liquid prices can be obtained for 6- and 7-year flows, but nothing in between. Let us suppose you choose to price the $6\frac{1}{2}$-year flow as the average of the prices of the 6- and 7-year flow. If you put on a hedge that consists of 50 percent of the 6-year flow and 50 percent of the 7-year flow, you will be perfectly hedged in the short run, since at first changes in the daily mark of the $6\frac{1}{2}$-year flow will just reflect the average of changes in the daily mark of the 6- and 7-year flows. The same would be true of any other interpolation method chosen (for example, 25 percent of the 6-year flow and 75 percent of the 7-year flow) as long as you match the hedge to the chosen interpolation method.

The test of the hedge's effectiveness will come through time. How well will it hold up as flows come closer to maturity, encountering the denser price quotations that exist (in all forward markets) for nearby flows? If, in this example, liquid prices are available for 2-, $1\frac{1}{2}$-, and 1-year flows, then the hedge will prove effective to the extent that the $1\frac{1}{2}$-year flow is priced at the average of the 1- and 2-year flows at the time 5 years from today, when it will be possible to unwind the trade and its hedge at these liquid prices. To the extent the interpolated value differs from the actual value at unwind, an unexpected loss, or gain, will result. Note that the unwind values are determined by the relationship between 1-, $1\frac{1}{2}$-, and 2-year flow prices 5 years from now. The current relationship between 1-, $1\frac{1}{2}$-, and 2-year flow prices cannot be locked into and play no role other than serving as a historical observation to use in forecasting future relationships.

An interpolation methodology needs to be judged by the stability of the valuations it will lead to. Trading desks develop a feel over time for how stable the valuations produced by particular interpolation techniques are in a particular market. Historical simulation can be used as a quantitative check on these judgments. (Exercise 8.1 takes you through a test of some possible interpolation methods judged by their degree of instability around historical price quotes.) The potential valuation errors determined by simulation can be controlled through limits and reserves. The most important lessons to be drawn are:

- Interpolation, like any other model, represents a judgment about what is most likely to occur in the future. To the extent the judgment is wrong, unanticipated future losses and gains will result.
- The key event that needs to be projected by an interpolation model is determining the actual relations between prices for flows at a future date when more liquid unwinds are possible.
- Historical relationships between these liquid flows can be used as input to and tests of judgments about future relationships. Limits and reserves can be based on measured historical instability.

The preference usually shown for interpolations that produce smooth pricing curves can be explained by two complementary facts: Historical relationships between most liquid flows tend to show smooth pricing curves, and economic intuition about future events tends toward long-term trends without a belief that at some specific future date a sharp change in conditions will occur. However, these are only general trends, not rules. If some specific dates may be believed to have forecastable effects, you should expect to see patterns, such as seasonal patterns, reflected in the interpolations. For a discussion of the impact of seasonal patterns on different forwards markets, see Section 8.3.4.

The choice of which variables to interpolate, whether they are discount prices, zero rates, or forward rates, is in one sense arbitrary since we know that each way of representing prices of forward flows is mutually translatable. However, interpolation using one representation may turn out to be more natural than interpolation using a different representation based on the economic motivation supporting the interpolation method chosen.

One approach that would follow naturally from our discussion would be to choose an interpolated value that minimizes a selected smoothness measure for forward rates or zero-coupon rates. Methods that are utilized on many trading desks, such as cubic splines, have been justified on formal or informal arguments along these lines. Another approach that is fairly widely used is to interpolate the logarithm of the discount factor. Table 8.3 shows how this works, with the resulting zero-coupon rates and forward rates.

As shown in Table 8.3, the impact of this interpolation method is to use a constant forward rate in all subperiods of the period between two already determined discounts. This method is generally favored by traders with backgrounds in the forwards and futures markets who believe that "all you really know is the quoted forward." So if you have a forward rate agreement that runs from the end of month 9 to the end of month 12 of 7 percent and no other market observations in this vicinity, this method would assign forward rates of 7 percent to the subperiods from the end of month 9 to the end of

TABLE 8.3 Interpolation Based on the Logarithm of the Discount Factor

Time	Zero Rate	Discount Factor	Forward Rate
T_1	R_1	$e^{R_1 T_1}$	
T_2	R_2	$e^{R_2 T_2}$	$\dfrac{R_2 T_2 - R_1 T_1}{T_2 - T_1}$
$T_1 + K(T_2 - T_1)$		$e^{(1-K)R_1 T_1 + K R_2 T_2}$	$\dfrac{((1-K)R_1 T_1) + K R_2 T_2 - R_1 T_1}{K(T_2 - T_1)}$
			$= \dfrac{K R_2 T_2 - K R_1 T_1}{K(T_2 - T_1)}$
			$= \dfrac{R_2 T_2 - R_1 T_1}{T_2 - T_1}$

month 10, the end of month 10 to the end of month 11, and the end of month 11 to the end of month 12.

But what do you do if you have a 7 percent deposit maturing at the end of month 3 and 8 percent FRA from the end of month 3 to the end of month 6 and you are looking to price a FRA from the end of month 3 to the end of month 4? The methodology says use 8 percent, but most practitioners' economic intuition says the rate should be lower than 8 percent, since it seems as if the market is anticipating rising rates over the period. Most traders make some kind of exception when rates are changing this sharply, but an interpolation methodology tied to a smoothness measure has the advantage of building on this approach in a more general setting.

Computationally, it would be convenient if a definitive set of flows was available for which liquid prices could be obtained on the basis of which prices for all other flows could be interpolated. This is rarely true for two reasons:

■ Price liquidity is a matter of degree. Some instruments have prices that are less liquid than others but still show some liquidity. Therefore, these should be given less weight in determining the discount curve, but should not be completely ignored in setting the curve.
■ Prices are often not available for single flows, but are available for bundles of flows—for example, coupon-paying bonds and fixed-for-floating swaps. If enough liquid flow prices are available to interpo-

late prices for all but the last of the flows in a bundle, then the common technique of *bootstrapping* (see Hull [2002, Section 5.4]) can be used to first price all the flows except the last and then derive the price of the last flow from these prices and the price of the bundle. However, often not enough prices are available to value all but the last flow. For example, many bond markets have a liquid price for a 7- and 10-year bond, but have no liquid prices in between. To derive a value for the flows occurring in the eighth, ninth, and tenth years, it is necessary to combine interpolation and price fitting into a single step.

The **Rates** spreadsheet on the accompanying CD-ROM provides a sample discount curve-fitting methodology that is very general in allowing the optimization of a weighted mixture of the accuracy of fitting known liquid prices and determining a forward rate curve that fits closely to an expected smoothness criterion.

The optimization method simultaneously determines all the discount rates needed to match all of the market prices of instruments that can potentially be priced off a single discount curve. All these discount rates are taken as input variables in the optimization. The objective function of the optimization is a combination of two measures. The first is a measure of how closely the derived price comes to the market-quoted price for each instrument, and the second is a measure of how smooth the discount curve is.

The measure of closeness of fit of the derived price to market quote can take several forms. The spreadsheet uses a very simple measure, a summation of the square of the differences between the derived price and market quote summed over all instruments. Each is multiplied by a selected weight. Higher weights are assigned to more liquid prices and lower weights are assigned to less liquid prices. This places a greater premium on coming close to the more reliable prices while still giving some influence to prices that have some degree of reliability. Greater complexity can be introduced, such as placing a higher weight on differences that are outside the bid-ask spread. The most extreme form of this approach would be to introduce constraints that require that the fit be within the bid-ask spread (this is equivalent to placing an extremely high weight on differences outside the bid-ask spread). The desirability of putting such a high weight on the bid-ask depends on your opinion of the quotations you are obtaining, how prone they are to error, and whether you really can count on being able to get trades done within the bid-ask range.

The measure of the smoothness of forward rates used in the spreadsheet is also a very simple one: to minimize the squares of second differences of the forward rates. This measures smoothness based on how close the forward rates come to a straight line, since a straight line has second differences equal to zero. (For example, the sequence 7, 7.5, and 8, which forms a straight line, has first differences of $7.5 - 7 = .5$ and $8 - 7.5 = .5$, and therefore a second difference of $.5 - .5 = 0$. The sequence of 7, 7.25, and 8, which is not linear, has first differences of .25 and .75 and therefore a nonzero second difference of .5.) Practitioners may use more complex measures of smoothness, such as minimizing second derivatives.

Different weights can be specified for how important the closeness of price fit is relative to the smoothness of the discount curve. This is just one more appearance of the trade-off between basis risk and liquidity risk. The lower the weight put on smoothness and the more even the weight put on fitting each of the instruments, the greater the assurance that the discount curve produced matches exactly the observed market prices of all instruments. This minimizes basis risk, but increases liquidity risk. If it turns out that you really cannot close out one of these positions at the price obtained from the market, you could have significant losses, since the price you used for valuation was based only on the assumed market price, even if this differed a great deal from the price that could be obtained by hedging with more liquid instruments. Conversely, the higher the weight put on smoothness and the more weight put on more liquid instruments, the greater the assurance that you are pricing off hedges that are based on liquid, achievable prices. This minimizes liquidity risk, but increases basis risk, since you are now pricing off hedges that can be achieved with combinations of nearby instruments in the market.

The same guidance we have given for testing the financial impact of interpolation rules carries over to testing the financial impact of procedures for extracting a discount curve from a set of liquid prices. Historical simulation should be used to estimate the stability of valuations that will result from a candidate procedure. Figure 8.1 illustrates the degree to which greater smoothness of forward curves can be achieved with the optimization procedure just discussed than with a simple version of the bootstrapping technique. (This simple version is used in Hull [2002, Section 5.4] and is used on a number of trading desks; the **Bootstrap** spreadsheet gives details of this comparison.) To repeat, the degree of importance of the greater smoothness resulting from the optimization is not to be found in aesthetic pleasure, but should be measured quantitatively in financial impact.

We have been assuming that all the instrument prices can be completely be determined by discount prices. However, some instruments could have option features, such as callable bonds or futures, that have a nonlinear component to their price. This can be handled by subtracting the option component of the price leaving a pure nonoption portion that can be priced off the discounts. A complexity is that the option component price may depend in part on the discount curve. An iterative process might be needed. Option components based on a first approximation to discounts can be used to get

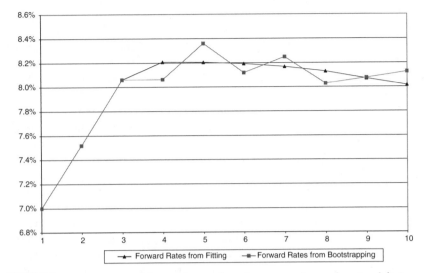

FIGURE 8.1   Comparison of forward rates from bootstrapping and optimal fitting.

the inputs to the optimization, which yields a discount curve. This is then used to reprice the option components. These can be used as inputs to a second round of optimization. This cycle can be repeated until the discount curves produced stabilize.

When developing discount factors, it is important to remember that every obligor will have its own set of factors—a promise to deliver a flow on a given date will be worth something different depending on how reliable the promise is. There even need to be multiple sets of discount factors for promises of the same obligor since some debts are senior to others and will more likely be paid in case of a default condition.

Before this multiplicity of sets of discount factors seems too overwhelming, let's introduce a note of simplification. It is rare that the type of flow owed plays any role in determining the probability of payment. If you can observe a set of discount factors for a firm relative to the discount factors for the assured delivery of one asset, you can infer the discount factors for that firm for delivery of any other asset. This rule has exceptions. If the government of Mexico owes you a debt denominated in its own currency, the peso, you would certainly apply a different discount factor than to its promise to pay a debt denominated in another currency. Mexico has control over the supply of its own currency and can create new currency to meet its payments. It has no such ability in another currency, and although it could create new pesos and exchange them for the currency owed, this might have a severe enough impact on the exchange rate between the currencies to call into question the country's willingness, and even its ability, to do so.

As the procedures for minimizing credit exposure to a counterparty become more complex, involving collateralization, netting, and margin calls, among other techniques, it becomes more difficult to represent the credit exposure in discounting procedures. Any oversimplification should definitely be avoided, such as discounting the flows owed by A to B on a swap at a discount rate appropriate for A's obligations and the flows owed by B to A on the same swap at a discount rate appropriate to B's obligations. This treats the gross amounts owed on the swap as if they were independent of one another, completely ignoring a primary motivation for structuring the transaction as a swap—the netting of obligations.

As credit exposure mitigation techniques grow in sophistication, they demand a parallel sophistication in valuation technology. This consists of initially treating all flows on a transaction to which credit exposure mitigation has been applied as if they were flows certain to be received. The actual credit exposure must then be calculated separately, taking into account the correlation between the net amount owed and the creditworthiness of the obligor. This methodology is more complex than we can tackle at this point in the book. We will return to this topic in Section 12.4.

8.2.2 Pricing Long-Dated Illiquid Flows by Stack and Roll

An issue that arises frequently for market-making firms is the need to provide value to customers by extending liquidity beyond the existing market. This need arises not only for bonds and single currency swaps and forwards, but also for FX forwards and commodity forwards. A concrete example would be a firm trying to meet customer demand for 40-year swaps in a market that only has liquidity for swaps out to 30 years.

To see the actual profit and loss (P&L) consequences of a methodology for pricing these longer-term flows, we need to consider a well-known trading strategy: the *stack-and-roll hedge*. In our example, a stack-and-roll hedge would call for putting on a 30-year swap in the liquid market as a hedge against a 40-year swap contracted with a customer. Then, at the end of 10 years, the 20-year swap to which the 30-year swap has evolved will be offset and a new 30-year swap in the liquid market will be put on, which will completely offset the original 40-year swap, which is, at this point, a 30-year swap.

This stack-and-roll strategy can be characterized as a quasistatic hedge in that it requires one future rehedge at the end of 10 years. The results of this rehedge cannot currently be known with certainty, either as to the transaction costs (that is, bid-ask spread) or the impact without transaction costs. However, the fact that only a single rehedge is required allows for great simplification in estimating the expected cost of the hedging strategy and its statistical uncertainty. These features recommend using the methodology to quantify the cost and risk of the longer-term position.

To carry out a numerical example, assume that today's 30-year yield is 6.25 percent. Since you are planning to roll at the end of 10 years from a 20- to 30-year yield, to the extent you expect yield curve shifts to be predominantly parallel, you should enter into a duration-weighted hedge of 1.192 30-year swaps for every 40-year swap you are trying to create. The number 1.192 is the ratio of a 30-year swap duration (13.40) to a 20-year swap duration (11.24), assuming a 6.25 percent annual par swap rate. To estimate the impact of the roll, you should look at the history of the relationship between 20- and 30-year swap rates. If 30-year swap rates tend to be 5 basis points higher on average than 20-year swap rates plus or minus a standard deviation of 7 basis points, and if you want to keep a reserve against a 2 standard deviation adverse move, you could mark the 40-year swap to a rate of 6.25% + .05% = 6.30% and set up a 14-basis-point reserve. If historical analysis shows that 30-year swap rates minus 105% of 20-year swap rates have a lower standard deviation (say, 5 basis points) than an unweighted spread, because 20-year rates are more volatile than 30-year rates, you could set up a hedge ratio of 1.192/1.05 = 1.135 and set up a 10-basis-point reserve.

The actual hedging practice on a trading desk might be to initiate a stack and roll, but it would probably be flexible as to the time at which the roll was actually carried out. The roll could take place at the end of 10 years, but the trading desk might, at that time, decide it was more favorable to defer the roll, since the roll could just as well be carried out at other times using equally liquid instruments—for example, roll at the end of 20 years from a 10-year swap into a 20-year swap. The trading desk might also decide, opportunistically, to roll into a less liquid instrument. For example, after 2 years, the opportunity might arise in which a bid is available for a 38-year swap that would close out the remaining term of the 40-year swap. In this case, the desk would also need to look for a 28-year swap to close out the remaining term of the 30-year swap it was using as a hedge.

Although a trading desk will want to retain flexibility in managing a stack-and-roll strategy once it is entered into, modelers and risk managers can best achieve their aims by assuming a fixed-roll strategy that involves liquid instruments. By considering a strategy that involves liquid instruments, it should be possible to get very reasonable data history that bears on the probable cost of the strategy. If 20- and 30-year swaps have liquid market quotes available, it may be possible to obtain several years' worth of daily data on the cost of rolling out of a 20-year swap into a 30-year swap. This data can be used not just to decide on an expected roll cost, but also to determine a probability distribution of roll costs. The probability distribution can give reasonable estimates of the uncertainty of results, which can serve as an objective basis for establishing limits and reserves.

The advantages of this method for risk management are:

■ Appropriate hedge ratios can be based on historical data since different possible hedge ratios can be judged based on the relative degree of historical uncertainty of roll cost.

■ The method makes a clear distinction between the portion of the expected cost of creating a long-term instrument that can be locked into at current market prices versus the portion that requires projections. In this example, the portion that can be locked into is the current 30-year rate and the portion that requires projection is the spread between the 30- and 20-year rates at the time of the roll (in 10 years).

■ This approach gives a solid financial foundation for what is often a loose intuitive argument along the following lines: "The current 20- to 30-year portion of the yield curve is flat to slightly upward sloping, so to price the 40-year swap at the same yield as the current 30-year swap is conservative relative to extrapolating the 20- to 30-year upward slope out to 40 years." This approach makes clear that what matters is not the current 20- to 30-year relationship, but the projected one, which can probably best be estimated based on a longer history of this relationship.

■ Estimates of uncertainty for establishing limits and reserves can be based on readily observable historical market data.

■ Future liquidity costs, such as the potential payment of the bid-ask spread, are confined to a single point in time.

Exercise 8.2 takes you through some sample calculations using the stack-and-roll methodology.

8.2.3 Flows Representing Promised Deliveries

Let us consider a typical example of a product involving a flow that represents a promised delivery of future flows. A market maker is asked to quote a price for a 3-year U.S. Treasury bond to be delivered in 7 years (let's assume we are working with zero-coupon instruments for the sake of simplicity— the principles for coupon-paying instruments are the same). If the U.S. Treasury were trying to create such a forward, it would be easy. The Treasury would value the forward as a reduction in its need for 10-year borrowing and an increase in its need for 7-year borrowings, both of which can be valued off the standard U.S. Treasury discount curve. However, a market maker has a lower credit rating and hence higher borrowing costs than the U.S. Treasury has. If it tries to create the forward by buying a 10-year instrument, the price it would need to charge for the forward would be burdened by 7 years' worth of the credit spread between the Treasury and the market maker.

To avoid this, the market maker needs to find a way to borrow for 7 years at essentially a U.S. Treasury rate. Since it has the 10-year Treasury purchased to put up as collateral against its 7-year borrowing, this should be feasible. However, it is an institutional fact that a liquid market does not exist for borrowing against Treasury collateral at a fixed rate for 7 years. It is certainly possible to borrow against Treasury collateral for short periods with great liquidity and the market maker should feel no fear about the ability to continuously roll over this borrowing. However, this introduces a large variance in the possible funding costs due to uncertainty about the direction short-term repurchase rates will take over a 7-year period.

The way around this impasse is for the market maker to buy a 10-year Treasury, borrow a 7-year Treasury, and sell the 7-year Treasury. The 10-year Treasury is financed for 7 years by a series of overnight RPs. The borrowing of the 7-year Treasury is financed by a series of overnight RPs. The market maker has succeeded in achieving the same cost of creating the forward that the Treasury would have, except for any net cost between the overnight RP rates at which the longer Treasury is financed and the overnight RP rate at which the borrowing of the shorter Treasury is financed.

In general, these two RP rates should not differ —on any given day, each represents a borrowing rate for the same tenor (overnight) and with the same quality collateral (a U.S. government obligation). However, the RP market is influenced by supply-and-demand factors involving the collateral preferences of the investors. Some of these investors are just looking for an overnight investment without credit risk so they don't care which U.S. Treasury security they purchase as part of the RP. Other investors, however, are looking to receive a particular U.S. Treasury that they will then sell short—either as part of a strategy to create a particular forward Treasury, or because they think this particular Treasury issue is overpriced and they want to take advantage of an anticipated downward price correction. The higher the demand by cash investors to borrow a particular security, the lower the interest rate they will be forced to accept on their cash. When RP rates on a particular Treasury issue decline due to the demand to borrow the issue, the RP for the issue is said to have *gone on special*.

So the market maker in our example will not know in advance what the relative RP rates will be on the shorter security on which it is receiving the RP rate and the longer security on which it is paying the RP rate. To properly value the Treasury forward created by a market maker, it is necessary to make a projection based on past experience with RP rates for similar securities. This source of uncertainty calls for risk controls, which could be a combination of limits to the amount of exposure to the spread between the RP rates and reserves on forward Treasuries, with reserve levels tied to the uncertainty of RP spreads.

Constant maturity Treasury (CMT) swaps (see Hull [2002, Section 25.4]) are popular products with rate resets based on U.S. Treasury yields. They are therefore valued in the same way as U.S. Treasury forwards. Control of the risk for this product focuses on creating long and short cash Treasury positions and managing the risk of the resulting RP spreads.

8.2.4 Indexed Flows

We will now examine how to extend our methods for handling fixed flows to handling nonfixed flows tied to certain types of indices. Let's start with a simple example. To keep this clear, let's label all the times in our example with specific dates.

Let's say the current date is July 1, 2003. Bank XYZ is due to pay a single flow on July 1, 2005 with the amount of the flow to be determined on July 1, 2004 by the following formula: $100 million multiplied by the interest rate that Bank XYZ is offering on July 1, 2004 for $100 million deposits maturing on July 1, 2005. Since this interest rate will not be known for 1 year, we do not currently know the size of this flow. However, we can determine a completely equivalent set of fixed flows by the following argument and then value the fixed flows by the methodology already discussed.

We write our single flow as the sum of two sets of flows as follows:

	July 1, 2004	July 1, 2005
Set 1	−$100 million	+$100 million × (1 + index rate)
Set 2	+$100 million	−$100 million
Contracted flow	0	+$100 million × index rate

We will argue that the flows in set 1 should be valued at zero. If this is true, then the present value of our contracted flow must be equal to the present value of the second set of flows, which is a set of completely fixed flows.

It can be argued that the present value of the flows in set 1 should be zero because the very meaning of the interest rate that bank XYZ will be offering on July 1, 2004 for $100 million deposits maturing on July 1, 2005 is the rate at which customers of XYZ are willing on July 1, 2004 to pay XYZ $100 million in order to receive a cash flow of $100 million × (1 + rate) on July 1, 2005. So why would we currently value the right to enter into a transaction that will, by definition, be available on that date at anything other than zero?

A second argument can be given for why the present value of the flows in set 1 should be zero. Mathematically, it is equivalent to the argument already given, but it differs in institutional detail and can deepen intuition, so I will provide it.

Let's say we are considering offering a FRA with the following flows:

July 1, 2005

Set 3	+\$100 million × index rate −\$100 million × fixed rate

At what fixed rate would you be willing to enter into this FRA at an up-front cost of zero (which is equivalent to saying it has a discounted present value of zero)? You should only be willing to do this if the fixed rate is one that you can lock into today at zero cost. The only such rate is the one that makes the following set of flows have a discounted present value of zero (see Hull [2002, Section 5.6] for a detailed example).

	July 1, 2004	July 1, 2005
Set 4	−\$100 million	+\$100 million × (1 + fixed rate)

Since both sets 3 and 4 have discounted present values of zero, their sum must also have a discounted present value of zero. The fixed rate is the same in sets 3 and 4 by construction, so the sum is just:

July 1, 2004	July 1, 2005
−\$100 million	+\$100 million × (1 + index rate)

This is the set of flows we wanted to prove has a discounted present value of zero.

One major caveat exists for this approach—it only works when the timing of the index payment corresponds exactly to the index tenor. If, in our example, the payment based on the 1-year index, set on July 1, 2004, had taken place on July 1, 2004 rather than July 1, 2005, the argument would not have worked in eliminating the index rate from the cash flows and we would have ended up with an additional term consisting of the receipt of \$100 million × the index rate on July 1, 2004 and the payment of \$100 million × the index rate on July 1, 2005. The value of this early receipt of payment depends on what the level of the 1-year interest rate will be on July 1, 2004, and the size of the early receipt also depends on what the level of the 1-year interest rate will be on July 1, 2004. This nonlinearity gives rise to convexity, which is very similar to an options position in that no static hedge is possible (a dynamic hedge is required), and the value of the position rises with higher rate volatility.

Other situations also lead to convexity:

- **Positions that have up-front cash settlement without discounting, such as futures.** The value of receiving gains up front is dependent on future rate levels. If changes in the value of the future correlate with changes in rate levels, as they certainly will for an interest rate future, the value will be a nonlinear function of rate levels.
- **Positions where a payment is linearly based on the future rate, rather than the future price, of a bond or swap.** The value of payments based on the future price can be determined by discounted cash flows. However, the future rate is a nonlinear function of the future price.

Hull (2002, Sections 22.6 to 22.8 and 23.16) discusses the issue of convexity adjustments in the valuation of forward risk. Although complete models of convexity adjustments require term structure interest rate options models, Hull offers some reasonable approximation formulas for convexity adjustment in these sections. We will examine a more precise technique for convexity adjustments in Section 10.1.3.

Now that we have found the set of fixed cash flows that are equivalent to an indexed flow, it is important to remember that these fixed flows need to be identified with the same obligor as the indexed flows. Indexed flows are almost exclusively determined for a panel of highly creditworthy banks. For example, LIBOR is determined by a set formula from offering rates of a panel of banks determined by the British Bankers Association. Panels of firms are used because they minimize the fear of firms manipulating the index. If many contractual rates were tied to the rate at which a certain individual bank were offering to pay for deposits, the bank could set its rate a bit higher if it knew this would impact the amount it owes on a large number of contracts. By using a panel of banks and having rules that throw out high and low offers and average those in between, the impact of any one bank on the index rate is lessened.

So the index flows need to be translated into fixed flows representing the average credit discount of a panel of banks. This can lead to risk in three different directions, all of which need to be properly accounted for:

- Different panels are used for different currencies within the same location. There are more Japanese banks in the panel that determines yen LIBOR than in the panel that determines dollar LIBOR; therefore, if Japanese banks are perceived to decline in creditworthiness, it will lead to a higher credit spread applied to the fixed flows that yen LIBOR is equivalent to than for the fixed flows that dollar LIBOR is equivalent to.

- Different panels are used for the same currency within different locations. There are more Japanese banks in the panel that determines the yen Tokyo Interbank Offering Rate (TIBOR) than in the panel that determines the yen LIBOR. Fluctuations in the perceived creditworthiness of Japanese banks lead to fluctuations in yen LIBOR-TIBOR spreads. Firms that have taken the shortcut of valuing all yen index flows the same have suffered significant losses from overlooking this exposure.
- The panel of banks determining an index have a different credit rating than that of an individual obligor. It is important to discount indexed flows at a different set of discount factors than fixed flows of a specific obligor and make sure that exposure to changes in the relationship between these discount factors is kept under control.

8.3   FACTORS IMPACTING BORROWING COSTS

When designing stress tests and setting limits for forward risk for a given product, risk managers must understand the economics of the borrowing costs for that product in order to gauge the severity of stresses the borrowing cost can be subject to. Four key characteristics, which differ from product to product, should be distinguished:

- Section 8.3.1.   How large and diversified is the borrowing demand for the product?
- Section 8.3.2.   To what extent does *cash-and-carry* arbitrage place a lower limit on borrowing costs?
- Section 8.3.3.   How variable are the storage costs that impact the cash-and-carry arbitrage?
- Section 8.3.4.   To what extent are borrowing costs seasonal?

We also discuss the relationship between borrowing costs and forward prices in Section 8.3.5.

8.3.1   The Nature of Borrowing Demand

A source of borrowing demand that exists for all products comes from traders wanting to borrow in conjunction with short selling. For some products—such as stocks, bonds, and gold—this is the only significant source of borrowing demand. At the other extreme are currencies, where there is strong credit demand by businesses and households to finance purchases and investments. Intermediate cases include most physical commodities, such as oil or wheat, where borrowing demand exists to meet immediate consumption needs.

Products for which borrowing demand comes almost exclusively from short sellers tend to have very low borrowing rates most of the time, since there is little competition for the borrowing. This may not be immediately obvious in market quotes if the quotes are made as forward prices rather than borrowing rates. For example, a 1-year gold forward might be quoted at 314.85, a 4.85 percent premium to a \$300 spot price. However, when this is broken apart into a borrowing cost for cash and a borrowing cost for gold, it almost always consists of a relatively high borrowing cost for cash, say, 6 percent, and a relatively low borrowing cost for gold, say, 1 percent. As a result, \$300 today is worth \$300 $\times$ 1.06 = \$318 received in 1 year and 1 ounce of gold received today is worth 1 $\times$ 1.01 = 1.01 ounces of gold received in 1 year, giving a forward price of gold of \$318/1.01 ounces = \$314.85/ounce. Borrowing rates rise as short-selling activity increases. The major risk for short sellers in these products is the *short squeeze* in which borrowing costs are driven sharply upward by a deliberate policy of a government or of holders of the assets seeking to support prices by restricting the supply of available borrowing. The resulting increase in borrowing rates pressures short sellers to abandon their strategy and close out their positions.

Short squeezes are possible for any asset class, but are more difficult to achieve for assets where borrowing demand has a broader base. A government wanting to support the price of its currency may be tempted to tighten the money supply in order to place borrowing cost pressures on the short sellers of the currency, but it will be limited by the fact that these increased borrowing costs will also hurt business firms and consumers who borrow. Even so, a government faced with a run on its currency will still decide on occasion that the desire to pressure short sellers outweighs other considerations, and will either take steps to sharply raise rates or put in place legal measures that discriminate against certain classes of borrowers who are believed to be selling the currency short. An example of the former is the Irish central bank driving short-term rates to 4,000 percent in 1992 in an attempt to teach speculators a lesson (Taleb [1997], p. 212). An example of the latter is Malaysia in 1997 closing its currency borrowing markets to foreign investors.

The possibility of a short squeeze on borrowing rates acts as a brake on those who want to take a position on an asset declining in values, since they are faced with a risk to which those taking a position on the asset price increasing are not subject. Those wanting to position for price increases in a particular asset have the freedom to borrow any other asset (most probably, but not necessarily, a currency) relative to which they believe it will increase in price and exchange one for the other in the spot market. However, those wanting to position for a price decrease in a particular asset must borrow that particular asset. The consequence of this asymmetry for rate scenarios is that the possible short squeeze means the risk of very high borrowing rates needs to be guarded against.

8.3.2   The Possibility of Cash-and-Carry Arbitrage

When available, the possibility of a *cash-and-carry* arbitrage position acts as a lower limit on borrowing costs. A cash-and-carry arbitrage is one in which an asset is either purchased or borrowed at one date and repaid or sold at a later date, being held or stored in between the two dates. The example most often cited is a limit on currency-borrowing rates not to go below zero, since if they did, a trader could borrow the currency at a negative interest rate, hold the currency, and then use the currency held to pay back the borrowing, collecting the negative interest payment as guaranteed profit. A more general result says that a lower limit on negative borrowing costs is the storage cost of the asset. This generalization makes it clear that the specific result for a currency rests on the assumption that currency storage costs are zero (by contrast, a physical commodity such as gold has handling and insurance costs of storage that can lead to negative borrowing costs). Although currency storage costs are almost always zero for large amounts (retail depositors may be charged transactions fees), there have been a few historical exceptions. For example, governments wanting to slow the pace at which foreign deposits are driving up the value of their currency have imposed transaction fees or taxes on large deposits permitting negative borrowing costs.

Cash-and-carry arbitrage is not feasible for all asset classes. Perishable physical commodities, such as live steers or electricity, cannot be stored, so cash-and-carry arbitrage does not place a lower limit on borrowing costs in such markets. Although arbitrage is not available as a limit, some pressure on borrowing costs getting too low will still result from economic incentives for consumers to change the patterns of demand. So if current prices get too high relative to those 6 months forward, beef consumption will be postponed to the point that the spot price will start to decline relative to the forward price, thereby raising the borrowing rate.

8.3.3   The Variability of Storage Costs

Storage costs on physical commodities tend to be reasonably stable, since they are the cost of physical processes such as handling and transportation. Coupon payments on bonds, a storage benefit, are also stable. However, the storage benefit on stocks, the receipt of dividends, can be quite unstable. A financial setback could lead to a sudden drop in dividends. A merger could lead to a sudden increase in dividends, as in the example at the beginning of this chapter. Changes in tax laws applied to dividends have also resulted in substantial sudden changes in stock-borrowing costs. Note that it does not matter whether the contractual borrowing terms call for the stock borrower to receive the dividends or pass them through to the stock lender. If the borrower receives the dividend, then an increase in dividend will cause the lender to demand a higher borrowing rate. When the borrower must pass the dividend through to the lender, then a borrower who has sold the stock short (which is the only economic rationale for borrowing stock) must pay the increased dividend out of her own pocket.

8.3.4 The Seasonality of Borrowing Costs

Interpolation methodology for discount factors and the evaluation of the risk of incorrect interpolation must take into account the seasonality of borrowing costs, which can lead to patterns that would be missed by simple interpolation from adjoining prices. To illustrate this with an extreme example, suppose a stock pays a dividend on exactly every July 15. The value of the dividend to be received on July 15, 2004 will be reflected in the borrowing cost to July 15, 2004, but not in the borrowing cost to July 14, 2004. Without knowing this, no conventional methodology for interpolating between borrowing costs to January 1, 2004 and January 1, 2005 will pick up the sharp difference between the borrowing costs to these two dates.

Most borrowing markets do not hinge on such specific scheduling. However, markets for physical commodities such as oil, and other energy products and agricultural products often reflect seasonal supply and demand factors such as a stronger demand for heating oil as winter approaches and stronger supply of wheat immediately following harvesting months. The seasonality of borrowing costs for physical commodities is closely tied to the possibility of cash-and-carry arbitrage. Commodities capable of storage that permit cash-and-carry arbitrage will have a smaller seasonal component since the storage of supply can be used as a response to seasonal demand. Perishable commodities that do not permit cash-and-carry arbitrage show a stronger seasonal component, since pricing differentials need to become large enough to start shifting demand. In the extreme case of electricity, which cannot be stored for even very short periods of time, seasonality effects can be seen within a single day, with different forward prices for different times of the day based on differing demand by the time of day.

Borrowing rates for gold, stocks, bonds, and currencies generally show far less of a seasonal effect than borrowing rates for physical commodities, both because of the possibility of storage and because the seasonality of supply and demand is weaker than that for physical commodities. However, some seasonal effects can be observed—most prominently turn-of-the-quarter effects in currency borrowing. This effect is a sharp spike in demand for borrowing currency on the last business day of each quarter and particularly the last business day of each year. A more detailed discussion can be found in Burghart and Kirshner (1994).

A particularly pronounced seasonal borrowing effect for currencies was experienced throughout 1999 as fears of computer operational problems starting on January 1, 2000—the Y2K problem—caused a large demand for liquidity over the first few weeks of January 2000. Since firms wanted to lock in the currency availability for this period, they were willing to pay much higher borrowing rates for this period than for any period preceding it or succeeding it.

8.3.5 Borrowing Costs and Forward Prices

As emphasized in Section 8.2, every statement made about borrowing costs can be translated into an equivalent statement about forward prices, and vice versa. In market convention, statements about currencies are usually made in terms of borrowing costs, and statements about physical commodities are usually made in terms of forward prices. Since currencies generally have more widespread borrowing demands than physical commodities, as discussed in Section 8.3.1, physical-commodity-borrowing costs will usually be lower than the borrowing costs for a currency. This is usually expressed in forward price terms by saying that the forward price of a physical commodity is generally higher than its spot price—a condition known as *contango*. However, when a strong demand exists for the availability of a particular physical commodity, its borrowing cost may be driven above the borrowing cost of a currency, resulting in forward prices being lower than spot prices—a condition known as *backwardation*. An example of this relationship is shown in Table 8.4. (This terminology has considerable history behind it. In the 1893 Gilbert & Sullivan operetta *Utopia, Limited*, a character is introduced as a financial wizard with the phrase "A Company Promoter this, with special education, Which teaches what Contango means and also Backwardation.")

A similar situation arises when the borrowing costs are quoted on a net basis in a situation where collateral is being loaned to reduce the credit risk of the borrowing. For example, if a security is being borrowed and cash is being loaned as collateral, there may be no explicit quote on the borrowing cost of the security. Instead, a net rate is quoted as an interest rate on the cash. If a short squeeze develops on the security, making it expensive to borrow, this will manifest itself as a low (possibly negative) interest rate to be paid for the loan of the cash. An identical trade, from an economic viewpoint, is a repurchase agreement. An expensive-to-borrow security will manifest itself through a low to negative rate being paid on the cash side of the transaction.

TABLE 8.4 Examples of Contango and Backwardation

Contango Example	Currency	Commodity	Price
Spot	$100.00	1 unit	$100.00/unit
1 month	$100.50	1 unit	$100.50/unit
2 month	$101.00	1 unit	$101.00/unit
3 month	$101.50	1 unit	$101.50/unit
Backwardation Example	Currency	Commodity	Price
Spot	$100.00	1 unit	$100.00/unit
1 month	$100.50	1.05 units	$95.71/unit
2 month	$101.00	1.10 units	$91.82/unit
3 month	$101.50	1.15 units	$88.26/unit

8.4 RISK-MANAGEMENT REPORTING AND LIMITS FOR FORWARD RISK

Risk-management reports for forward risk must be more detailed than those for spot risk. Not only do the reports involve an extra dimension of time, but they also involve a dimension of credit quality, since the same flow owed to you on the same day has different risks depending on who owes it to you. We'll examine the time dimension first and then the credit quality dimension.

The basic principle of breaking all forward instrument exposures apart into individual flows has already done a lot of the necessary work for risk-management reporting. A complete risk report would just show the amount of net flow exposure for each forward date. The remaining question is what types of date groupings make sense in giving a trading desk and then senior managers a more concise picture of this exposure.

One issue that can lead to some confusion when designing and using risk-management reports for forward risk is that the usage of many close-to-equivalent measures overlaps. This starts with disagreement over the simple convention of what is meant by a long position and a short position. In spot markets, *long* clearly means to own an asset, benefit by a rise in the asset price, and lose from a decline in the asset price, while *short* means exactly the opposite in each respect. In forward markets, some practitioners who think about owning a bond use long in the same way—the long position benefits from bond prices rising and therefore from interest rates falling, and the short position benefits from bond prices falling and therefore from interest rates rising.

Other practitioners with backgrounds in instruments such as swaps and FRAs, where no natural concept of an asset being owned is available, use *long* to mean a position benefiting by interest rates rising and *short* to mean a position benefiting by interest rates falling. Often, all you can do is remind yourself which trading desk you're talking to in order to know which way the term is being used, but insist that everyone must agree to use a firm-wide convention, no matter how much they hate it, when talking to the chairman of the board.

A similar set of differences in convention is at work when describing the size of a position. Some traders have grown up using the term *value of a basis point* (or equivalently *value of an 01*), whereas others refer to a *5-year equivalent, 10-year equivalent,* or *duration.* Tuckman (2002, Chapters 5 and 6) is highly recommended for a detailed and intuitive explanation of these concepts. Table 8.5 illustrates this with a numerical example in which we'll consider a position with just two components—a 5-year flow and a 10-year flow.

As shown in Table 8.5, the different position size measures only differ by a constant factor. The 5-year equivalent of a position is just the value of a basis point of that position divided by the value of a basis point of a 5-year instrument. Any other instrument could be used as a similar common denominator (also known as a *numeraire*). Table 8.5 also shows that the weighted duration is essentially just the value of a basis point divided by minus one basis point ($-.01$ percent). However, note that duration needs to be weighted by the price value of the position, whereas all the other measures are weighted by the par value of the position, reflecting the definition of duration as the price change per dollar of portfolio value. (See Tuckman [2002, p. 98]; see also Tuckman [2002, pp. 120–122] or Hull [2002, Section 5.13] for a proof that the duration of a cash flow is simply equal to its tenor.)

You can check that if the position held was $+100$ of the 5-year flow and -74.536562 of the 10-year flow, using the ratio between values of a basis point, the 5-year equivalent, 10-year equivalent, and duration measures for the portfolio would all come out equal to 0. However, the impact of a 100-basis-point increase would not be 0; it would be $-3.613013 + .74536562 \times 4.725634 = -.090688$. So a position that is completely hedged for a 1-basis-point rate move is not completely hedged for a 100-basis-point move. This nonlinearity stems from the fact that the formula for converting interest rates to prices is not a linear formula. Risk exposure to the size of a move in input variables is known as *convexity risk.* This is a risk that does not exist for spot exposures, which are linear, and is a major issue for options exposures—it will be a principal topic of the next chapter.

The convexity of forwards is much less severe than for options, and it is rare for risk managers to focus much attention on it. In addition to not being a very large effect, it is directly tied to hedging longer positions with shorter positions (since the nonlinear effects grow with time to maturity) and risk reporting will already be directed at the degree of maturity mismatch.

TABLE 8.5 Sample Computation of Forward Risk Positions

	5-Year Flow	10-Year Flow	Portfolio
Amount	+100	−100	
Current zero-coupon rate	6.00%	7.00%	
Current discount factor	1/exp(.06 × 5) = .74081822	1/exp(.07 × 10) = .49658530	
Current value of positions	74.081822	−49.658530	24.423292
Discount factor given 1 basis point increase in zero-coupon rates	1/exp(.0601 × 5) = .74044790	1/exp(.0701 × 10) = .49608897	
Value of portfolio given 1 basis point increase in zero-coupon rates	74.044790	−49.608897	24.435943
Impact of 1 basis point increase in zero-coupon rates	74.044790 − 74.081822 = −.037032	−49.608897− (−49.658530) = .049633	.012601
5-year equivalents	+100	−100 × (.049633/ .037032) = 134.0305	−34.0305
10-year equivalents	+100 × (.037032/ .049633) = 74.536562	−100	−25.390117
Duration	5 years	10 years	
Weighted duration	+74.081822 × 5 = 370.40911	−49.658530 × 10 = −496.58530	−126.17619
Discount factor given 100 basis point increase in zero-coupon rates	1/exp(.07 × 5) = .70468809	1/exp(.08 × 10) = .44932896	
Value of portfolio given 100 basis point increase in zero-coupon rates	70.468809	−44.932896	25.535913
Impact of 100 basis point increase in zero-coupon rates	70.468809 − 74.081822 = −3.613013	−44.932846− (−49.658530) = 4.725634	1.112621

Convexity *is* an important issue for one type of forward risk—credit exposure. Because a credit event, such as the downgrade of a credit rating or, at the extreme, a default event, can cause credit spreads to jump by hundreds or even thousands of basis points, the degree of hedge exposure can be enormous. Reconsider our previous example with the hedge ratio of 100:74.536562, making the position neutral to a 1-basis-point change in the credit spread. In the event of default, there will no longer be any difference between a 5- and 10-year flow—both will just represent claims in a bankruptcy proceeding. If a 30% recovery occurs on these claims, the hedged position will show a loss of $70\% \times (-100 + 74.536562) = -17.8244066$.

This is a risk that investors need to be aware of. This explains why investors in bonds issued by firms with high default risk (known as *high-yield debt*, or, less politely, as *junk bonds*) tend to deal directly with prices and avoid reference to interest rates. For a further discussion of the impact of convexity on credit exposure, see Section 12.1.

Firm-level risk management for forward risk requires decisions about the degree of detail with which exposure to changes in yield curve shape will be represented. Senior management almost certainly only needs to be informed of a few parameters that represent the rate exposure. Many studies have been performed on the historical changes in the shape of many different rate curves and almost all have shown that about 80 to 90 percent of all changes can be explained by just two parameters, and close to 95 percent of all changes can be explained by just three parameters. Although statistical methods can be employed to determine the best two or three principal components, it makes for better intuitive understanding if parameters can be chosen that convey a concrete meaning. Fortunately, almost all studies of yield curve movement show that intuitively meaningful parameters perform almost as well as parameters selected by statistical means (see, for example, Litterman and Scheinkman [1988]). The three parameters that explain most of the change, in order of importance, are:

- A parallel shift parameter
- A parameter to measure the degree of linear tilt of the yield curve
- A parameter to measure yield curve twist, the degree to which the middle of the curve changes relative to the two ends of the curve

The **Rates** spreadsheet illustrates the calculation of the impact of parameter shifts on a portfolio.

Nonstatistical limits on yield curve shape exposure also often start with such overall parameters, but it is usually found to be necessary to have more refined limit measures as well. The debate is often between bucket measures based on groupings of forward risks (for example, 0- to 1-year forwards, 1- to 2-year forwards, 2- to 3-year forwards, and so on) versus bucket measures that break the yield curve exposure down to exposure to yield changes in the most liquid hedging instruments (such as futures contracts out to 5 years and then 7-, 10-, and 30-year swaps). The primary argument in favor of the latter approach is that these are the actual hedging instruments most likely to be used; therefore, limits expressed in these terms are immediately operational (a trader knows what action needs to be taken to close a position) and can more easily be judged as to the viability of limit size relative to customer order flow and market liquidity for that instrument. The primary argument against this approach is that the translation of cash flow exposures into liquid hedging instrument equivalents is not completely determined, and very small changes in the choice of algorithm can lead to large changes in how a position is distributed between different instruments. For further discussion of this choice, see Tuckman (2002, p. 141).

The decision of which currencies, commodities, and equities should be grouped together rests on very similar considerations for yield curves as it does for spot risk (refer to the discussion in Chapter 7). Within a grouping, limits are needed by obligor. You would, at a minimum, want to have limits on the government's curve and the interbank rate curve (also known as the swap curve or LIBOR curve), but would probably want to group together rate curves for other obligors, probably by credit rating and possibly by industry and country.

EXERCISES

8.1 Interpolation

For this exercise, make use of the **DataMetricsRateData** spreadsheet. Suppose you are making a market in 16-, 17-, 18-, and 19-year swaps. Liquid swaps are available at 15 and 20 years. Try out some different interpolation methods and test their effectiveness when using them to derive unwind values.

Here are some suggestions:

■ There isn't enough data on the spreadsheet to see what the impact of initiating a hedge at one point and unwinding in 10 years late would be, so let's make the reasonable assumption that the long-term distribution of rate curve shapes is reasonably stable. So, for example, we'll judge the effectiveness of interpolating the 18-year rate from 40% × the 15-year rate + 60% × the 20-year rate by looking at the long-term distribution of unwind costs of an 8-year rate relative to 40% × the 5-year rate + 60% × the 10-year rate.

- Standard deviation can be used as a reasonable summary statistic for the uncertainty of unwind cost, although you should feel free to explore other possible measures such as the 99th percentile.
- To keep the math easier, ignore any compounding effects—that is, treat the par swap rates as if they were zero-coupon rates. So the gain from buying an 8-year swap at 6% and selling a 5-year swap at 5.70% + 60% of a 10-year swap at 6.10% is just the following: (40% × 5.70% + 60% × 6.10%) − 6% = −.06%.
- You can look at the impact of interpolating with different percentages than those suggested by maturity—for example, consider a 50 percent 5-year, 50 percent 10-year interpolation for an 8-year swap as well as the standard 40 percent 5-year, 60 percent 10-year interpolation.
- You can consider the impact of factoring the 30-year rate into the interpolation—this will lead to the use of a 20-year rate in the unwind.
- Explore how much improvement in reducing hedge uncertainty comes about by interpolation rather than just assuming a flat curve by looking at the degree to which uncertainty is reduced by using both the 5- and 10-year rates in the unwind rather than just the 5-year rate (or just the 10-year rate).

8.2   Stack and Roll

Use the sample stack-and-roll computation in Section 8.2.2 and the rate data history from the **DataMetricsRateData** spreadsheet to calculate two standard deviation reserves for the following products:

- 40-year swap
- 35-year swap
- 33-year swap
- 50-year swap

As in Exercise 8.1, assume that the par swap rates are actually zero-coupon rates to keep the math simpler.

8.3   Rates

Use the **Rates** spreadsheet to calculate risk exposure for a portfolio of forward instruments:

1. Begin by creating a discount curve that can be used in subsequent calculations. Enter a set of benchmark instruments and market prices

into the **Instruments** worksheet and solve for a discount curve that fits these prices, following the spreadsheet instructions. You might, for example, select a set of U.S. Treasury bonds with 1-, 2-, 3-, 4-, 5-, 7-, and 10-year maturities. A reasonable set of parameters is to put an equal weighting of 1 on each of your benchmark instruments and to place a weight of 90 percent on fitting prices and 10 percent on the smoothness of the resulting forward curve, but you are encouraged to try different parameters and see their impact on the resulting discount curve.

2. After creating the discount curve, select a portfolio of instruments for which to calculate risk exposure by placing weights on each instrument (you can also add other instruments beyond the benchmark instruments). Look at the resulting risk exposure by forward bucket and summary exposure to forward shifts, tilt shifts, and butterfly shifts, and try to make intuitive sense of them.

3. By trial and error (or by creating an optimization routine with the Solver), find modifications to your portfolio weights that make parallel shift exposure close to zero, but retain roughly the same tilt exposure and butterfly shift exposure as your original portfolio.

4. Follow the same instructions as for Part 3, but make tilt exposure close to zero and leave parallel shift exposure and butterfly shift exposure roughly the same as in your original portfolio.

CHAPTER **9**

Managing Vanilla Options Risk

Every book should have a hero. The hero of this book is not a person but an equation—the Black-Scholes formula for pricing European-style options. Like every hero, it has its flaws and no shortage of detractors ready to point them out. But with help from some friends, it can recover to play a vital role in integrating all options risk into a unified, manageable framework. This is the theme of this chapter and the next.

Options risk may be subdivided into two categories—the risk of relatively liquid options, termed *plain vanilla* or *vanilla options*, and the risk of less liquid options, termed *exotic options*. Managing options risk for vanilla and exotic options is quite different so we will discuss them in two separate chapters.

Almost without exception, the only relatively liquid options are European-style calls or puts, involving a single exercise date and a simple payoff function equal to the difference between the final price level of an asset and the strike. As such, vanilla options can be priced using either the Black-Scholes formula or one of its simple variants (see Hull [2002, Sections 13.2, 13.4, 13.8, and 22.1 through 22.4]). The only notable exception to the rule that all vanilla options are European style is that some American-style options on futures are exchange traded and liquid. However, the early exercise value of such options—the difference between their value and that of the corresponding European option—is quite small (as discussed in Section 10.5.1). So treating all vanilla options as European-style calls and puts is a reasonable first approximation.

To simplify our discussion of European options, we will utilize the following three conventions:

■ All options are treated as options to exchange one asset for another, which enables us to only consider call options. So, for example, we treat an option to put a share of stock at a fixed price of $50 as being a call option to exchange $50 for one share of stock. This is a more natural way of treating foreign exchange (FX) options than the usual

167

approach, since whether an FX option is a call or a put depends on which currency you use as your base.

- Options prices and strikes will often be expressed as percentages of the current forward price, so a forward price of 100 (meaning 100 percent) will be assumed.
- All interest rates and costs of carry are set equal to zero. This means that the volatilities quoted are volatilities of the forward, not the spot, the hedges calculated are for the forward, not the spot, and option payments calculated are for delivery at the option expiry date. Although almost all options traded are paid for at contract date rather than expiry, discount curves derived from market prices, as shown in Section 8.2, can always be used to find the current spot price equivalent to a given forward payment.

With these three conventions, we can use the following formula for Black-Scholes values:

$$BS(K, T, \sigma) = N(d_1) - KN(d_2) \tag{9.1}$$

Where:

K = Strike as percentage of current forward to time T
T = Time to option expiry in years
N = Cumulative normal distribution
σ = Annualized volatility of the forward
$d_1 = (\ln(1/K) + 1/2\ \sigma^2 T)/\sigma\sqrt{T}$
$d_2 = d_1 - \sigma\sqrt{T}$

This is similar to Equation 13.17 in Hull (2002, Section 13.8). Technically, we are using a model in which the zero-coupon bond price is the *numeraire* (see Hull [2002, Section 21.4]).

Stating the equation in terms of the forward price rather than the spot price is important for reasons other than formula simplification. First, it follows the principle stated and justified in Section 5.2 that all forward risk should be disaggregated from options risk. Second, this has the advantage of not assuming constant interest rates—the volatility of interest rates and their correlation with spot price are all imbedded in the volatility of the forward. The historical volatilities of forwards can often be measured directly. If they cannot be measured directly, they can easily be calculated from the spot volatility, interest rate volatilities, and correlations. Hedges with forwards are often the most liquid hedges available. If a spot hedge is used, then the appropriate interest rate hedges should be used as well, since interest rates and carry costs cannot be assumed to be constant. This combined hedge will be synthetically equivalent to a hedge with a forward.

9.1 OVERVIEW OF OPTIONS RISK MANAGEMENT

Even when we limit our discussion to vanilla options, the vast variety of instruments available makes it unlikely that liquidity of any single instrument will be large. For the options on just a single asset, not only do we face the multiplicity of dates we encountered for forward risk products, but each date also has a multiplicity of possible strikes. Once we take into account that options involve an exchange between pairs of assets, the number of possible contracts expands even more rapidly. For example, if a desk trades 10 different currencies, the number of currency pairs of FX options is 10 × 9 = 90. In fact, the degree of liquidity available for option products is significantly smaller than that for spot or forward products.

When options market trading first began and, to a more limited extent, as options markets continue to develop for new assets, initial market-maker hedging strategies were often a choice between acting as a broker (attempting to find a structure for which a simultaneous buyer and seller could be found) or relying on an initial static hedge with the underlying instrument until a roughly matching option position could be found. The broker strategy is very limiting for business growth. The static hedge strategy can only convert call positions into put positions, or vice versa; it cannot reduce the nonlinear nature of the option position. As such, it can only be used by trading desks that are willing to severely limit the size of positions (thereby limiting business growth) or take very large risks on being right about the maximum or minimum levels to which asset prices will move. Static hedging with limited position size remains a viable strategy for a proprietary desk, but not for a market-making desk.

The development of dynamic hedging strategies was therefore a major breakthrough for the management of options market making. Consider Table 9.1, which extends an example that Hull (2002, Tables 14.1 and 14.4) presents, using Monte Carlo simulation to evaluate the performance of dynamic hedging strategies.

Table 9.1 shows that even a very naïve dynamic hedging strategy, the stop-loss strategy, which calls for a 100 percent hedge of a call whenever the forward price is above the strike and a 0 percent hedge whenever the forward price is below the strike, results in a large reduction in the standard deviation of results—76 percent of option cost relative to 130 percent of option cost for a static hedge. However, an increased frequency of rehedging can only improve stop-loss results up to this point. By contrast, the dynamic hedging strategy corresponding to the Black-Scholes analysis enables standard deviation to get as close to zero as one wants by a suitable

TABLE 9.1 The Performance of Dynamic Hedging Strategies

Price = $49, interest rate = 5 percent, dividend rate = 0, forward price ≈ $50
Strike = $50
Volatility = 20 percent
Time to maturity = 20 weeks (.3846 years)
Drift rate = 13 percent
Option price = $240,000 for 100,000 shares

		Performance Measure (Ratio of Standard Deviation to Cost of Option)		
	Stop Loss	Delta Hedge		
Frequency of rehedging		No. Vol. of Vol.	10% Vol. of Vol.	33% Vol. of Vol.
5 weeks	102%	43%	44%	57%
4 weeks	93%	39%	41%	52%
2 weeks	82%	26%	29%	45%
1 week	77%	19%	22%	47%
1/2 week	76%	14%	18%	43%
1/4 week	76%	9%	14%	38%
Limit as frequency goes to 0	76%	0%	11%	40%

With no hedging, the performance measure is 130 percent.

increase in the frequency of rehedging. You can see why the Black-Scholes approach had such an impact on options risk management.

But almost immediately, this was followed by a backlash, focusing on the unrealistic nature of the Black-Scholes assumptions. Principally, these are:

- Trading in the underlying asset can take place continuously. In fact, a practical limit exists on how frequently trading can occur, which places a lower limit on the standard deviation that can be achieved.
- No transaction costs are involved when trading in the underlying asset. In practice, transaction costs place an even tighter limit on the frequency of rehedging.
- The volatility of the underlying asset is a known constant. If we make the more realistic assumption that volatility is uncertain, with a standard deviation around a mean, we get results like those in the last two columns of Table 9.1, placing a lower limit on the standard deviation that can be achieved.

- The underlying asset follows a Brownian motion with no jumps. In practice, discontinuous jumps in asset prices can occur, even further limiting the degree to which standard deviation can be lowered.

Trading desks that have tried pure Black-Scholes hedging strategies for large positions have generally found that unacceptably large risks are incurred. A related example is the *portfolio insurance* strategy. Many equity portfolio managers were using this strategy in the mid-1980s to create desired options positions through dynamic hedging. In October 1987, the global stock market crash caused liquidity to dry up in the underlying stocks, leading to trading discontinuities that resulted in large deviations from planned option payoff profiles.

As a result, vanilla options market makers have generally moved in the direction of a paradigm in which they attempt to match the options positions bought and sold reasonably closely, enabling basis risk to be taken both over time, while waiting for offsetting trades to be available, and with regard to strike and tenor mismatches. The Black-Scholes model is relied on as an interpolation tool to relate observed market prices to prices needed for the residual risk positions left after offsetting closely related buys and sells. Black-Scholes dynamic hedging is used to hedge these residual risk positions.

Three key tools are needed for managing a vanilla options book using this paradigm:

- A reporting mechanism must be available to measure the amount of basis risk exposure resulting from mismatches in the strike and tenor of options bought and sold. Although summary measures such as *vega* (exposure to a move in implied volatility levels) and *gamma* (the sensitivity of delta to a change in underlying price level) can be useful, the two-dimensional (strike and tenor) nature of the exposure requires a two-dimensional risk measure to be really effective. This measure is the *price-vol matrix* that depicts portfolio valuation sensitivity to the joint distribution of two variables: underlying asset price and implied volatility. It therefore measures exposure to both jumps in underlying asset price and changes in implied volatility. It also measures simultaneous changes in both. We will examine illustrative examples and discuss the use of price-vol matrices in Section 9.4.
- Dynamic delta hedging of the portfolio of bought and sold options needs to be performed. Guidance for this process comes from the Black-Scholes formula. The targeted hedge for the portfolio is a simple summation of the targeted hedges of each individual option position, as determined by Black-Scholes. However, given the reality of transaction costs for executing the delta hedges in the underlying, a

set of guidelines about how often to hedge is necessary. It has been shown, both by theory and trader experience, that hedging guidelines based on the distance between the current delta hedge and the target delta hedge are more effective than guidelines tied to the frequency of hedging. The degree of tolerance for deviation from the target delta determines a trade-off between higher transaction costs (for lower tolerances) and higher uncertainty of results (for higher tolerances). Section 9.5 discusses these delta-hedging guidelines in more detail along with related issues such as what implied volatility to use to determine the target hedge.

■ Options for which liquid market prices are not available are valued based on interpolation from options that do have liquid market prices available. The interpolation methodology translates prices of liquid options into implied volatilities using the Black-Scholes formula, interpolates these implied volatilities to implied volatilities for less liquid options (interpolation is based on both strike and tenor), and then translates implied volatilities to prices of the less liquid options, again using the Black-Scholes formula. Limits and reserves are needed to control uncertainty in the interpolation process. Section 9.6 gives a detailed account of this interpolation method.

Note how closely bound together the three operative legs of this paradigm are. The Black-Scholes formula serves as the glue that binds them together:

■ The price-vol matrix shows how the portfolio valuation will change based on a joint distribution of changes in underlying asset price and implied volatility. However, many (probably most) of the options in the portfolio lack liquid market prices, so their valuation depends on the interpolation step. Furthermore, the calculation of the change in option value for a change of asset price and implied volatility is calculated using the Black-Scholes formula.

■ As will be seen in the detailed discussion of the price-vol matrix, all calculations are done under the assumption that exposure to small changes in underlying asset price have been delta hedged with a position in the underlying asset, so the validity of the price-vol matrix depends on the execution of this dynamic delta hedging.

■ The need for this approach to options risk management is based on the flat rejection of the key assumptions of the Black-Scholes model: continuous rehedging, no transaction costs, no price jumps, and known and constant volatility. How then can we continue to rely on the Black-Scholes model to calculate the impact of changes in underlying asset price, calculate the target delta hedges, and play a critical role in value interpolation? The answer is that position limits based on the price-vol matrix are being counted on to keep risk exposures low enough that deviations from the Black-Scholes assumptions will not have that large an effect. Small risk exposures mean that the size of required delta hedges will be small enough that transaction costs will not be that significant. Small risk exposures mean that the differences between the Black-Scholes model and the presumably much more complex true model (whatever that may be) are small enough to hold down the errors due to valuing and hedging based on a model that is only an approximation to reality.

It is important to be aware of the degree to which this paradigm depends on the availability of market liquidity for hedging instruments. The paradigm works best when reasonable liquidity in vanilla options is available for at least some combinations of strike and tenor. This enables risks to be hedged by actively pursuing the purchase and sale of options to lower exposures as measured by the price-vol matrix. As we will see in Exercise 9.1, price-vol matrix exposures can be held reasonably flat even if only a small number of strike-tenor combinations provide significant liquidity. The valuation of options with other strike-tenor combinations can be interpolated from the liquid set.

If a particular options market does not have liquidity, the paradigm can still work reasonably well as long as the underlying asset has liquidity. The price-vol matrix now serves primarily as a measure of position imbalance. It can serve as a signal to marketers to encourage customer business at some strike-tenor combinations and discourage it at others. It can be used to place limits on new customer business when this would cause risk to exceed management guidelines. It can be used as input to setting limits and determination of reserves against illiquid concentrations of risk. It can also be used as input to calculations of portfolio risks such as value at risk (VaR) and stress tests. Price interpolation, in the absence of liquid market quotations, becomes primarily a mechanism to enforce the consistency of valuations. Delta hedge calculations continue to serve the function of directing dynamic hedging and ensuring the proper representation of options positions in firm-wide reports of spot and forward risk.

It is far more questionable to employ this paradigm in the absence of liquidity in the underlying asset. In this case, it is doubtful that dynamic delta hedging can be carried out in any systematic way, and it probably becomes preferable to analyze positions based primarily on how they will behave under longer-term scenarios, with limits and reserves calculated from this scenario analysis. An example where this may apply is for options written on hedge fund results where there are restrictions on the ability to buy and sell the underlying, which is an investment in the hedge fund. A specific case to illustrate this point is the option Union Bank of Switzerland (UBS) wrote on Long Term Capital Management (LTCM) performance (see Section 4.1.5).

How well does this paradigm work? Trading desks that have years of experience using it have generally been satisfied with the results. But this is insider knowledge and may be specific to conditions in particular markets. How can outsiders get comfortable with these assumptions and how can these assumptions be tested in new options markets to which they might be applied? The best tool available is Monte Carlo simulation, in which all of the Black-Scholes assumptions can be replaced with more realistic assumptions, including limits on hedge frequency, transaction costs, uncertain volatility, non-lognormal changes in the underlying price, and price jumps. In Section 9.3, we examine the results of a typical Monte Carlo simulation to see what it indicates about the feasibility of this risk-management paradigm.

9.2 THE PATH DEPENDENCE OF DYNAMIC HEDGING

To understand options pricing, an important distinction must be made between path-independent and path-dependent options. A path-independent option's payout depends only on what the price of some underlying asset will be at one particular point in time and does not depend on the actual path of price evolution between the current date and that future date. All European-style options are path independent. Exotic options are divided between path-independent and path-dependent options. In Chapter 10 on managing exotic options risk, we will see that path-independent options are generally much easier to risk mange than path-dependent options.

Although, when considered in isolation, European-style options are path independent, once we start to evaluate the impact of dynamic hedging, we find that dynamic hedging makes "every option become path dependent." (This is quoted from Taleb [1997, Chapter 16]. I strongly recommend reading Taleb's Chapter 16 along with this chapter.) This is a direct consequence of the limitations of the Black-Scholes assumptions, since continuous hedging at a known constant volatility would result in a definite value with no variation (hence, you would achieve not just path independence, but independence of the final underlying asset value as well). Sporadic dynamic hedging and stochastic volatility make the realized value of a dynamic hedging strategy dependent on the full price history of the underlying asset. Let's illustrate this with a few examples.

I'll base my first example on one presented in Taleb (1997, p. 270). It is an out-of-the-money call on $100 million par value of a stock with 30 days to expiration that is purchased for $19,000. If no dynamic hedging is attempted, then the option will expire either out of the money for a total loss of the $19,000 premium or in the money with upside potential. The amount of return will be completely dependent on where the underlying asset price finishes in 30 days. Suppose a trader wanting to reduce the uncertainty of this payoff attempts to dynamically hedge her position. Taleb demonstrates a plausible price path for the underlying asset that results in a loss of $439,000, not even counting any transaction costs. The **NastyPath** spreadsheet provided on the accompanying CD-ROM enables you to see the details of this path and experiment with the impact of other possible paths. What is it about the path that leads to a loss that is so large relative to the option's cost? Try to reach your own conclusion. I will provide my answer at the end of Section 9.5.

My second example is drawn from my own experience. In early 1987, I was part of a team at Chase Manhattan that introduced a new product—a term deposit for consumers that would guarantee a return of principal plus a small interest payment, but could make higher interest payments based on a formula tied to the closing price of the Standards and Poor's (S&P) stock index on the maturity date of the deposit. Although the stock market had been showing very good returns in the mid-1980s, stock market participation among smaller investors was still not well developed. Therefore, a product that would be FDIC insured, guarantee against loss, and provide some upside stock participation quickly attracted a sizable amount of investment.

Our hedging strategy for this product was to invest part of the proceeds in standard deposit products, ensuring the ability to return principal plus guaranteed minimum interest, and use the remainder to fund an S&P index call position. As might be anticipated by those who remember the financial events of 1987, this product suffered an untimely demise in the autumn of that year. After the stock market crash of October 19, consumer interest in possible stock market participation sharply diminished so new funds stopped coming in. We also experienced severe losses on our hedging of the existing product, and the postmortem we conducted to determine the reason for these losses produced some interesting results.

Since the equities options markets were at a very early stage of development in 1987, there was virtually no liquidity for options with tenors beyond a few months. Since our market research had determined that there would be little interest in a deposit product with tenors shorter than a year or two, we had decided to initially rely entirely on a dynamic hedging strategy, using a Black-Scholes-determined delta hedge. We were certainly aware of the vulnerability of this approach to high volatility, but we had done extensive research on the historical patterns of stock market volatility and concluded that we could price the product at an implied volatility that allowed a margin for error that would result in hedging losses only in extremely rare cases.

Not surprisingly, our postmortem showed significant losses due to our inability to carry out the delta-hedging strategy during the period of October 19 and the following few days. The cash and futures equities markets during that period were highly illiquid in the face of panicky selling, and there were even some short periods in which the markets were closed in an attempt to restore stability to chaotic trading. Illiquid markets in the underlying during large price moves result in gapping losses to options sellers employing dynamic hedging strategies. We were not alone in this vulnerability. In October 1987, a substantial number of asset managers following portfolio insurance strategies in which they attempted to achieve the payoff profiles of an option through delta hedging experienced heavy losses as a result of this gapping.

What was less expected, though, was our finding that a considerable part of our loss would have been experienced even if the markets had not gapped. Our loss was due to higher than anticipated volatility. This was despite the fact that when we looked over the tenor of our deposit product the average realized volatility was well within the range we had anticipated in pricing the product. Here's where path dependence comes in. The average realized volatility consisted of very high volatility during a short period when the market was plunging sharply, which was preceded and followed by periods of much lower volatility. However, exposure to volatility depends on the relationship between the price level and strike. The higher than average volatility during the period when prices were falling sharply cost us much more than we saved from the lower than average volatility during the other periods.

This phenomenon can be easily illustrated with some simple Black-Scholes calculations. Suppose you have written a 1-year call option with a strike equal to the current forward price. You intend to delta hedge and expect volatility to average 20% over the year. If you are wrong and volatility averages 30%, your expected losses will be $BS(100\%, 1, 30\%) - BS(100\%, 1, 20\%) = 11.923\% - 7.966\% = 3.957\%$. Suppose one-tenth of a year goes by and the forward price is at the same level as when you wrote the option. Your remaining exposure to volatility averaging 30% is $BS(100\%, .9, 30\%) - BS(100\%, .9, 20\%) = 11.315\% - 7.558\% = 3.757\%$. So $3.757\%/3.957\% = 94.9\%$ of your volatility exposure comes in the last 90% of the option's life and only 5.1% comes in the first 10% of the option's life (a consequence of the fact that $\sqrt{.9} / \sqrt{1} = .949$). However, if the price at the end of one-tenth of a year has fallen by 30%, the remaining exposure to volatility averaging 30% is $BS(70\%, .9, 30\%) - BS(70\%, .9, 20\%) = 1.188 - .184 = 1.004$. So $(1.004\%/3.957\%) = 25.4\%$ of your volatility exposure comes in the last 90% of the option's life and 74.6% comes in the first 10% of the option's life. A very similar effect will be seen for a large rise in underlying price.

With the benefit of experience, we concluded that we had badly underestimated the risk of the product. First, we had not taken into account the potential losses from pricing gaps. Second, the chances of volatility being very high during a short time period are much larger than the chances of it being very high during a long time period, so we had not properly calculated our vulnerability to a short period of high volatility combined with a large price move. Third, we had not looked at the impact of other market participants pursuing strategies similar to ours, thereby decreasing liquidity by competing with us for hedges in the underlying when we most needed them.

What would have been a more prudent way of managing this risk? We had been considering, but had not implemented, a proposal from a broker in exchange-traded, shorter-term S&P options for a hedge of our longer-term options with these shorter-term options. See Section 9.6.3 for a discussion of the risk characteristics of this hedge.

9.3 A SIMULATION OF DYNAMIC HEDGING

In the immediately preceding section, we established that, under realistic economic assumptions, dynamically hedged options are path dependent. In the section before that, we observed the need for testing how well the paradigm of managing options risk using Black-Scholes theory works. Both sections point toward using Monte Carlo simulation to see what the probability distribution of results can be for dynamically hedging an options portfolio.

Using Monte Carlo simulation for dynamic hedging options is an invaluable tool for understanding how the management of an options trading book works in practice. When new options products or hedging strategies are proposed, traders and risk managers alike will want to look at simulation results to assess potential pitfalls. Simulation gives the flexibility to take into account the impact on hedging results of real-life constraints such as liquidity constraints on the size of changes in hedges that can be performed in a given time period (or the impact of larger changes on the price at which the hedge can be executed).

Simulation also provides a vital learning tool for people who are unfamiliar with the workings of options markets. Theoretical demonstrations of the power of dynamic hedging rarely carry the conviction that can be provided by observing hundreds of simulation paths that, despite wild gyrations in underlying prices, produce almost identical hedging results. Nothing short of actually suffering through a losing options strategy can convey the pain of an unsuccessful hedge as will observing the losses pile up on a simulation path.

In the course I teach, on which this book is based, I have always insisted that each student personally program and run simulations of a dynamic hedge. I lack a comparable power of persuasion over readers of this book, but I urge each of you to do as much of Exercise 9.2 as you can. Even if you lack the time to program your own simulation, you should at least do Parts 4 and 5 of this exercise using the provided spreadsheets.

What features do we want at a Monte Carlo simulation of dynamic hedging to contain?

- The simulation must be over a sufficiently large number of possible price paths to produce stable statistics. Prices for the underlying variable must be sampled at enough points on each path to allow for rehedging.
- Since volatility of the underlying price is not constant, but is a stochastic variable, a random process should drive it. Data to determine reasonable values of volatility of volatility can be obtained by looking at historical distributions of realized volatility for separate time periods. A separate volatility should be chosen for each path generated.
- The distribution of the underlying price does not necessarily need to be lognormal. Different mixtures of normal and lognormal processes should be tried.
- Rehedges should only be allowed at periodic intervals, and transaction costs of the hedge should be calculated explicitly. Different rules for determining hedge amounts, as discussed in Section 9.5, should be considered.
- When calculating Black-Scholes deltas for rehedging, you generally do not want to take advantage of knowing what volatility is being used for the path, since this would not be available in making actual hedging decisions. Either you want to use the same implied volatility to calculate rehedges on all paths, or you want to use some adaptive rule tying volatility used to the history of price moves on the path up to the time of the rehedge.
- A random process of significant price jumps, where no rehedging is permitted until after the jump is completed, can be used as a simulation of periods of illiquidity.
- When simulating a portfolio of options for one particular expiry date, it is usually convenient to assume that all hedges are performed with a forward with the same expiry to avoid needing to keep track of discounting rates. When simulating options with different expiry dates, some assumptions about discounting rates must be used to arrive at relative prices between forwards.

In effect, we are testing the performance of the Black-Scholes model as a hedging tool by running a Monte Carlo simulation based on a more complex, and presumably more accurate, model of underlying price behavior than Black-Scholes utilizes. Why not just value and hedge options by directly using this more complex and complete model? For two reasons:

- **Computational complexity.** The speed of the computation of the Black-Scholes model for valuation and the fast and direct computation of the target underlying hedge are enormous advantages in providing timely risk information on portfolios of options that may have many thousands of deals outstanding at any given time. By contrast, more complex models can be orders of magnitude slower when computing valuations and often lack a direct computation of target hedges, requiring multiple runs of the valuation algorithm to determine the appropriate hedge. This advantage can particularly be seen in Monte Carlo testing of hedge effectiveness. At each potential rehedge point, the Black-Scholes target hedge is a simple equation; a more complex model may require full recalibration to compute each hedge (see Section 10.3 for a discussion of this point in conjunction with hedging barrier options).
- **Validity.** We don't necessarily know what the correct model is. For testing hedge performance with Monte Carlo, we can make different runs with alternative candidates for the correct model.

As a first example of a simulation, let's look at a comparison between hedging an option using a pure Black-Scholes hedge and hedging using a combination of Black-Scholes delta hedging and hedging with other options. We may suppose that an option has been sold at a strike for which no liquidity is readily available. We can either utilize a dynamic hedging strategy or buy some options at strikes for which liquidity is available and then utilize a dynamic hedging strategy for the residual risk.

For this example, we will assume that a 1-year option has been sold at a strike 5 percent in the money and that 1-year options are available for purchase at strikes at the money and 10 percent in the money. For the second case, we will consider purchasing the same notional amount of options as has been sold, but split 50–50 between the at-the-money option and 10 percent in-the-money option. The reason for thinking that this might be a good hedge is shown in Table 9.4. The price-vol matrix for this portfolio shows very little sensitivity to changes in either the price level or implied volatility. This does not, by itself, prove that the hedge will work well over the life of the option, since it only shows a snapshot at one point in time. In fact, you can see from Tables 9.5 and 9.6 that although this portfolio does continue to show low sensitivity to price on volatility shifts for a substantial time period, this sensitivity increases at some point in its evolution. So we need the Monte Carlo simulation to get a statistical measure of the sensitivity. Table 9.2 shows the results of the simulation.

TABLE 9.2   Monte Carlo Simulation Comparing Pure Dynamic Delta Hedging with Combined Static Option and Dynamic Delta Hedging

	Standard Deviation of P&L		Standard Deviation of P&L			
	Given 0% Standard Deviation of Volatility		Given 33% Standard Deviation of Volatility		Transaction Costs	
Number of rebalancings	Unhedged	Two-sided hedge	Unhedged	Two-sided hedge	Unhedged	Two-sided hedge
10	25.7%	6.4%	50.6%	6.3%	1.5%	0.1%
20	19.8%	5.6%	41.5%	6.7%	2.2%	0.2%
50	12.4%	4.6%	40.9%	5.5%	3.5%	0.4%
100	8.5%	3.6%	42.6%	4.9%	5.0%	0.6%
200	6.3%	2.5%	41.6%	4.8%	7.1%	0.9%
300	5.1%	1.9%	39.9%	3.8%	8.5%	1.1%
400	4.3%	1.8%	40.1%	4.1%	9.9%	1.2%
500	3.9%	1.6%	38.4%	3.9%	11.2%	1.4%
600	3.5%	1.4%	35.9%	3.4%	12.0%	1.5%
700	3.3%	1.3%	41.0%	3.5%	13.3%	1.6%
800	3.2%	1.3%	39.2%	3.7%	14.4%	1.7%
900	2.9%	1.5%	40.0%	3.8%	15.0%	1.9%

All results are shown as a percentage of the cost of the option to be hedged.

The option is a 1-year call struck at the money.

The expected volatility is 20 percent, and all hedges are calculated based on a 20 percent implied volatility.

The two-sided hedge has half a call struck 5 percent above and half a call struck 5 percent below at the money.

Transaction costs are based on a bid-ask spread of one-fourth point per $100.

What conclusions can we reach?

- If the standard deviation of volatility is zero, then both the pure dynamic hedging and the mixed-option/dynamic hedging strategies can achieve as low a standard deviation of results as you like by increasing the frequency of rebalancing the dynamic hedge, although the mixed strategy achieves a given level of standard deviation with far fewer rebalancings than the pure strategy. For either strategy, there is a trade-off between higher expected transaction costs with more frequent rebalancing and lower standard deviations of results. (Standard deviations of total results, including transaction costs, don't differ significantly from the standard deviations without transaction costs, which are shown in Table 9.2.) However, the mixed strategy can achieve a desired level of standard deviation at a far lower transaction cost level than the pure strategy. For example, achieving a 3 percent standard deviation with the pure strategy requires about 900 rebalancings with an associated transaction cost of 15.0 percent. Achieving a 3 percent standard deviation with the mixed strategy requires about 150 rebalancings with an associated transaction cost of about 0.8 percent.

- If the standard deviation of volatility is 33 percent, then there is a lower bound on how much the standard deviation of results can be decreased. For both the pure and mixed strategies, this lower bound is reached at about 250 rebalancings. The lowest level of standard deviation of results that can be achieved by the mixed strategy is about one-tenth of what can be achieved by the pure strategy, roughly 4 percent compared to roughly 40 percent.

- The inability to reduce the standard deviation of results below a lower bound is due to both the uncertainty of volatility and the use of incorrect volatility inputs in forming hedge ratios. However, the first effect is many times larger than the second. A Monte Carlo run with 33 percent standard deviation of volatility, but with hedge ratios on each Monte Carlo path based on the actual volatility of that path results in a lower bound on the standard deviation of results that is only reduced from 40 to 36 percent.

Please note that although we are using standard deviation as a convenient summary statistic to give a rough feel for relative levels of uncertainty, both in this example and others in this book, more detailed analysis would be needed before arriving at any precise conclusions. For example, if a measure was being developed for a risk versus return trade-off as input to a decision on a trading strategy, a more complete set of measures of the probability distribution of returns should be used. The discussion of measures of portfolio risk in Section 11.1.2 gives more of a flavor for these considerations.

These results should not be surprising, given the price-vol matrix in Table 9.4. From the relative insensitivity of portfolio value to a shift in implied volatility, you would expect low sensitivity to the standard deviation of volatility. The small size of the portfolio's convexity translates into small changes in the delta when prices move, so transaction costs should be low. A reasonable inference, which is supported by experience with Monte Carlo simulations, is that a trading desk can estimate its vulnerability to uncertain volatility and transaction costs by forecasting how large its price-vol matrix positions are likely to be given the anticipated flows of customer business and the availability of hedges with liquid options. Management can keep these vulnerabilities under control by placing limits on the size of price-vol matrix positions.

It is important to recognize the distinction between the two aspects of dynamic hedging costs—transaction costs that arise from bid-ask spreads and gamma hedging costs from buying high and selling low that would be present even if all trades were at midmarket. Transaction costs are a direct function of the frequency of rehedging, and a trade-off occurs between higher transaction costs and lower variability of P&L with less frequent rehedging. By contrast, there is no a priori reason to believe that the level of gamma hedging costs will vary in any systematic way with the frequency of rehedging.

A good way to see this latter point is to look at how P&L is related to the gap between actual hedges held and the theoretical hedge called for by the Black-Scholes formula. The expected value of this P&L under the standard Black-Scholes assumption is given by the formula:

$$\sum_{\substack{\text{small time periods}}} (\Delta_{\text{actually held}} - \Delta_{\text{theoretical}}) \times \text{expected price change of underlying forward} \quad (9.2)$$

A full mathematical derivation of this formula can be found in Gupta (1997). I will give an alternative derivation using a simple financial argument. In the presence of the Black-Scholes assumptions, use of the theoretical delta will lead to an expected return of zero, so any holdings above or below the theoretical delta can be regarded as proprietary positions that will lead to the same expected return as an outright position in the underlying forward.

The consequence of this formula for the relation between gamma hedging costs and the frequency of rehedging is that as rehedging becomes less frequent, it widens the gap between $\Delta_{\text{actually held}}$ and $\Delta_{\text{theoretical}}$. However, unless a correlation between the sign of this gap and the sign of the expected price change in the underlying forward is expected for some reason, the expected value of the incremental P&L should be zero. (Although this formula is only strictly correct in the case the Black-Scholes assumptions hold, Monte Carlo simulation with stochastic volatility shows similar results.)

Are there cases where we might expect a relationship between the sign of the delta gap and the sign of expected price changes in the underlying forward? Let's consider a case that will cast an interesting light on a long-standing debate among practitioners. The debate is over what options pricing is appropriate for a market in which the underlying process shows *mean reversion*, resulting in a narrower dispersion of future price levels than would be implied by a pure random walk with the short-term volatility of the underlying process. One group argues that delta-hedging costs are completely a function of short-term volatility, so mean reversion is irrelevant to pricing. The opposing group argues that risk-neutral valuation principles should result in the same pricing of options as would be implied by the probability distribution of final prices (compare the discussion here to Rebonato [1999, Section 2.4]).

Some of this dispute reflects a failure to distinguish between the short-term volatility of spot prices and forward prices. If the market is pricing the mean reversion process into the forward price, we should expect to see a lower historical short-term volatility of forward prices than a historical short-term volatility of spot prices. Equivalently, this can be viewed as a correlation between changes in spot prices and changes in the discount rate of the forwards, a pattern that can be seen in the market for seasonal commodities. When seasonal demand is high or seasonal supply is low, spot prices rise, but so does the discount rate, dampening the rise in forward prices. When seasonal demand is low or seasonal supply is high, spot prices fall, but so does the discount rate, dampening the fall in forward prices. Since the option can be delta hedged with the forward, replication costs will be tied to the volatility of the forward, so we should expect implied option volatilities to reflect the impact of mean reversion relative to the volatility of the spot price.

Suppose that a trader believes that the market has not adequately priced in mean reversion, so he expects that forward prices will show mean reversion. In this case, we cannot resolve the controversy between the two differing views on options pricing by an appeal to the difference between short-term volatility of spot and forward prices. Let us look at the results of a Monte Carlo simulation in which we ignore transaction costs and study the impact of rehedging at a fixed number of evenly spaced intervals. We will calculate statistics for the whole sample of paths, but also for three subsamples:

- The third of paths having the highest finishing forward prices, which we can take as representing upward drift of the forward
- The third of paths having the lowest finishing forward prices, which we can take as representing downward drift
- The remaining third of the cases, which we can take as representing mean reversion

Table 9.3 shows the resulting expected values of a delta-hedging strategy for a written option (for a purchased option, the signs would be reversed).

What conclusions can we draw?

- As you increase the frequency of rehedging, you get the same expected results regardless of drift or mean reversion. This is consistent with the theoretical result that, under the Black-Scholes assumptions,

TABLE 9.3   Impact of Drift and Mean Reversion on Dynamic Hedging Results

	All Paths	Upward Drift	Downward Drift	Mean Reversion
20 rehedges	−.07%	−.33%	−.45%	+.57%
100 rehedges	+.01%	−.06%	−.10%	+.20%
1,000 rehedges	−.01%	0%	0%	−.02%

standard deviation of results goes to zero as the frequency of rehedging increases so the P&L will be the same on every path. It is also consistent with Equation 9.2, since frequent rehedging drives the difference between the $\Delta_{actually\ held}$ and $\Delta_{theoretical}$ terms to zero.

■ As you decrease the frequency of rehedging, you increase the losses from a sold option with drift or a purchased option with mean reversion, and you increase the gains from a sold option with mean reversion on a purchased option with drift. All of these results are consistent with Equation 9.2. For example, here's the reasoning for mean reversion on a sold option: It is likely that one period's up move will be followed by the next period's down move, and vice versa. After an up move, the $\Delta_{theoretical}$ on the sold option will increase, but if no rehedge is performed, due to the infrequency of rehedging, this will make the $\Delta_{actually\ held} - \Delta_{theoretical}$ for the next period be negative. Since the expected price change in the next period is negative, the expected P&L is the product of two negatives, and hence positive.

■ The consequence of the last point for hedging strategies is that if you anticipate mean reversion, you should try to decrease hedging frequency for a sold option (which also saves transaction costs, but increases the uncertainty of return) and to increase hedging frequency for a bought option (but this needs to be balanced against the increase in hedging costs and uncertainty of return). This is intuitively correct. As the option seller, you want to hold off on rehedging since you expect the market to rebound; as the option buyer, you want to take advantage of the market move with a rehedge prior to the expected rebound. Conversely, if you anticipate a drifting market, whether up or down, you should try to decrease hedging frequency for a bought option and increase hedging frequency for a sold option.

■ If you cannot anticipate either drift or mean reversion, there is no difference in gamma hedging costs based on the frequency of rehedging, so the decision rests purely on the trade-off between transaction costs and the uncertainty of return.

9.4   RISK REPORTING AND LIMITS

The best tool for managing residual options risk on a trading desk is the *price-vol matrix*, which depicts valuation sensitivity to joint distributions of two variables, the asset price, and implied volatility. The **PriceVolMatrix** spreadsheet on the accompanying CD-ROM calculates a price-vol matrix for a small portfolio of options. See the accompanying documentation for details. We will note just three important points about the computation:

- All boxes in the matrix represent full valuations using the Black-Scholes model utilizing the shifted volatility level and underlying price level. No approximations are being used in the computation.
- Each box assumes that an underlying position has been put on to neutralize the initial delta position of the options.
- Only the initial delta position is neutralized; no delta rehedging is allowed during a price shift. Therefore, the price-vol matrix represents the potential impact of price jumps that cannot be delta hedged.

For those who respond better to visual presentations than to numerical information, the spreadsheet produces two graphical representations of the price-vol matrix:

- A three-dimensional surface of the P&L consequences of changes in the underlying price and implied volatility
- A chart showing changes in valuation, delta, vega, and gamma as price levels change

The price-vol matrix enables a trading desk manager to see at a glance the *convexity* (the nonlinear impact of large price changes), *vega* (sensitivity to a small change in implied volatility), nonlinearities in vega, and interactions between convexity and vega. The price-vol matrix can pick up discontinuities caused by strikes in a portfolio clustering around certain levels. In order for the price-vol matrix to highlight nonlinear effects, it is best to assume that any linear delta position has already been hedged. To the extent that the trading book chooses not to hedge delta risk, the resulting underlying position should be reported separately and be subject to limits separate from those on options positioning for the reasons given in Section 5.2, concerning the need for clear separation of linear and nonlinear risks.

Traders have recently shown greater focus on the sensitivity of vega to changes in implied volatility and the sensitivity of vega to changes in spot. A sign of this increased focus is that these sensitivities have acquired their own mock Greek names, *vomma*, also known as *wisoo*, and *vanna*, also known as *DdelV*, respectively. Note that the price-vol matrix measures changes in P&L impact due to both vomma and vanna. Also note that the convexity measure goes well beyond a simple P&L impact of *gamma*, which is just the second derivative of price changes, and hence determines the second-order term in the Taylor expansion of option price in terms of underlying price. Since the matrix is filled in by a full revaluation of the Black-Scholes model for each box, the impact of as many terms in the Taylor series as desired can be picked up by a sufficient refinement of the underlying price grid.

We will now use the price-vol matrix to examine some representative option positions as a way to learn both about risk characteristics of the positions and the analytic power of the price-vol matrix:

- ■ **Short a call option.** This is the simplest possible options portfolio. We are short one unit of a 1-year call struck at the money. Figure 9.1 shows the price-vol matrix. Naturally, vega and gamma are both negative, and vega remains negative at all price levels. Negative vega is largest at the money and declines as prices rise and fall, reflecting the decline in the time value of an option as it goes into or out of the money. The negative gamma is reflected in large losses from either up or down price jumps at the current volatility.
- ■ **Call spread.** We are short one unit of a 1-year call option struck at the money and long 1.06 units of a 1-year call option struck at 110 percent of the forward price. Figure 9.2 shows the price-vol matrix. The 1.06 units have been deliberately selected to create a portfolio with zero vega, gamma, and theta. However, as the price-vol matrix shows, this is not the same as saying there is no options risk in the portfolio.

  Focus on the center five boxes in the price-vol matrix of Figure 9.2, representing the current price and implied vol, as well as one shift up and down in price and implied vol, as shown in Table 9.4.

  You can see that this is consistent with vega and gamma being zero, since vega and gamma measure the sensitivity to small changes in volatility and price. However, as you widen your view to the whole matrix, you see both convexity and volatility exposure.

TABLE 9.4   Center Boxes of Price-Vol Matrix

Price	Implied Vol	−2%	0%	2%
−5			−0.01%	
0		0.01%	0.00%	0.00%
5			0.01%	

Discount	5.00%		
Spacing		Volume	-1
Price	5	call/put	call
		Price	100
Volatility		Strike	100
2%		Time	1
Portfolio		Implied vol	20.0%
-7.58%		BS price	-7.58%
-54.0%		Delta	-54.0%
-0.38%		Vega	-0.38%
-2.0%		Gamma	-2.0%
0.015%		Theta	0.015%

Spot-vol matrix

Price	Implied volatilities									Vega	Vega convexity
	-8%	-6%	-4%	-2%	0%	2%	4%	6%	8%		
-25	-5.33%	-5.40%	-5.51%	-5.64%	-5.81%	-6.01%	-6.24%	-6.50%	-6.77%	-0.09%	0.00%
-20	-2.94%	-3.10%	-3.30%	-3.55%	-3.82%	-4.12%	-4.45%	-4.80%	-5.17%	-0.14%	0.00%
-15	-0.80%	-1.10%	-1.43%	-1.79%	-2.18%	-2.59%	-3.02%	-3.46%	-3.91%	-0.20%	0.01%
-10	0.90%	0.46%	0.00%	-0.48%	-0.97%	-1.48%	-1.99%	-2.51%	-3.03%	-0.25%	0.00%
-5	2.01%	1.45%	0.89%	0.33%	-0.24%	-0.81%	-1.38%	-1.96%	-2.53%	-0.28%	0.00%
0	2.42%	1.81%	1.21%	0.60%	0.00%	-0.60%	-1.21%	-1.81%	-2.41%	-0.30%	0.00%
5	2.14%	1.56%	0.97%	0.37%	-0.23%	-0.83%	-1.43%	-2.04%	-2.65%	-0.30%	0.00%
10	1.27%	0.76%	0.23%	-0.32%	-0.88%	-1.45%	-2.03%	-2.62%	-3.20%	-0.28%	0.00%
15	-0.08%	-0.49%	-0.93%	-1.40%	-1.90%	-2.42%	-2.95%	-3.50%	-4.05%	-0.25%	0.01%
20	-1.77%	-2.07%	-2.41%	-2.80%	-3.22%	-3.67%	-4.14%	-4.64%	-5.15%	-0.22%	0.01%
25	-3.67%	-3.87%	-4.13%	-4.43%	-4.78%	-5.16%	-5.57%	-6.00%	-6.46%	-0.18%	0.01%

FIGURE 9.1 Price-vol matrix for being short a call option.

			-1	1.06
Discount	5.00%			
Spacing		call/put	call	call
Price	5	Price	100	100
		Strike	100	110
Volatility	2%	Time	1	1
Portfolio		Implied vol	20.0%	20.0%
	-3.25%	BS price	-7.58%	4.33%
	-16.5%	Delta	-54.0%	37.4%
	0.00%	Vega	-0.38%	0.38%
	0.0%	Gamma	-2.0%	2.0%
	0.000%	Theta	0.015%	-0.014%

Spot-vol matrix

Price	Implied volatilities									Vega	Vega convexity
	-8%	-6%	-4%	-2%	0%	2%	4%	6%	8%		
-25	-0.74%	-0.80%	-0.87%	-0.95%	-1.04%	-1.14%	-1.23%	-1.32%	-1.41%	-0.05%	0.00%
-20	-0.10%	-0.21%	-0.33%	-0.46%	-0.58%	-0.70%	-0.81%	-0.91%	-1.00%	-0.06%	0.00%
-15	0.36%	0.19%	0.03%	-0.12%	-0.26%	-0.38%	-0.49%	-0.59%	-0.67%	-0.07%	0.00%
-10	0.56%	0.36%	0.19%	0.04%	-0.08%	-0.19%	-0.27%	-0.34%	-0.40%	-0.06%	0.00%
-5	0.46%	0.30%	0.17%	0.07%	-0.01%	-0.07%	-0.12%	-0.15%	-0.17%	-0.03%	0.00%
0	0.14%	0.08%	0.03%	0.01%	0.00%	0.00%	0.01%	0.03%	0.05%	0.00%	0.00%
5	-0.27%	-0.20%	-0.13%	-0.06%	0.06%	0.08%	0.15%	0.21%	0.28%	0.03%	0.00%
10	-0.61%	-0.41%	-0.24%	-0.08%	0.21%	0.20%	0.32%	0.44%	0.55%	0.07%	0.00%
15	-0.76%	-0.48%	-0.22%	0.00%	0.46%	0.39%	0.57%	0.73%	0.88%	0.10%	0.00%
20	-0.65%	-0.33%	-0.04%	0.22%	0.85%	0.69%	0.89%	1.09%	1.27%	0.12%	0.00%
25	-0.28%	0.02%	0.31%	0.59%		1.09%	1.31%	1.53%	1.73%	0.12%	0.00%

FIGURE 9.2 Price-vol matrix for a call spread.

The convexity exposure is to a loss on downward price jumps for which the impact of the sold at-the-money option will outweigh the impact of the purchased option at a higher strike. The convexity impact of upward price jumps is a gain, since the effect of the purchased higher strike option will outweigh the effect of the sold at-the-money option.

As prices rise, vega will be positive, reflecting the greater impact of the purchased higher strike option. As prices fall, vega will be negative, reflecting the greater impact of the sold lower strike options.

Option positions that display these characteristics—acting like a bought option to some price levels, with positive vega and gains from convexity, and acting like a sold option at other price levels, with negative vega and losses from convexity—are known as *risk reversals*, since the direction of risk exposure reverses itself with changes in price level (for further discussion of risk reversals, see Taleb [1997, pp. 135, 275–276]).

Here are two stories that illustrate some of the characteristics of risk reversals. The first comes from the Japanese equity derivatives market in the mid-1990s. Many Japanese banks were selling warrants on their stock that had the price-vol profile of a risk reversal. The warrant buyer would have a positive vega and convexity at the stock price levels then prevailing, but would switch to a negative vega and convexity if stock prices were to fall significantly. Rumors in the market indicate that some trading desks purchased these warrants to provide a hedge against the negative vega and convexity exposure they had from other positions in Japanese equity derivatives, but did not adequately plan for what would happen if stock prices plummeted, causing the now negative vega and convexity on the warrant to exacerbate the overall negative vega and convexity of the desk. When Japanese stock prices did experience a sharp decline in 1996, it was accompanied by a rise in implied volatility and a decline in the liquidity of underlying stock positions, so negative vega and convexity positions resulted in large trading losses. Some reports indicate that this was one of the events that contributed to the large losses at UBS (refer to the discussion in Section 4.1.5).

The second story goes back further in time to the early days of options trading. The business executive of a newly formed options business, for which I was in charge of analytics, came to me with a situation that was disturbing him. A recent series of large moves had occurred in this particular market, with large decreases in underlying prices and increases in implied volatility followed by large increases in underlying prices and decreases in implied volatility. The net effect was that prices and implied volatilities had pretty much finished up where they had started. Although the market had retained good trading liquidity throughout, the implied volatility moves were substantial enough to trigger material P&L swings. What was disturbing to the business head was that the trading book had been a loser in both the increase and decrease in implied volatility. The time period that was involved had been short enough that no significant change in the options position had taken place. So how could this pattern be explained?

This trading desk did not yet have a regular price-vol matrix, but my team was able to put one together, which quickly revealed a risk reversal pattern for the portfolio. At the price level that prevailed at the beginning of the period, the portfolio's vega was negative, leading to losses from rising implied volatilities. At the level to which prices then fell, the portfolio's vega was positive, leading to losses from falling implied volatilities. So far, so good. But underlying prices and implied volatilities ended where they began. In an unchanged portfolio, wouldn't the Black-Scholes valuation yield the same option prices at the end of the period as at the beginning of the period given that not enough time had elapsed to make a significant difference? It would be a good exercise to think this through yourself before seeing my answer.

The key to understanding what happened is that the portfolio was not really unchanged since delta hedging had gone on throughout the period. Since the markets had retained liquidity throughout, this delta hedging had been smooth and no gains or losses due to price jumps had occurred. If price jumps had occurred rather than smooth delta hedging, then the portfolio would have come back to its original value.

If this is not clear, follow the example in Table 9.5, which corresponds to short one unit of a 1-year at-the-money call and long one unit of a 1-year call at 80 percent of the current price. Assume that the following four moves take place in sequence: volatilities up 8 percent, prices down 25 percent, volatilities down 8 percent, and prices back up to the original level. Table 9.5 shows the P&L consequences, contrasting a case with price jumps and a case with smooth delta hedging. The computations for Table 9.5 can be found in the **PriceVolMatrixCycle** spreadsheet.

This is the most extreme case in which implied volatility moves completely precede price moves. When implied volatility and price moves are mixed together, the effect is attenuated but not lost. All together, this constitutes another example of the maxim that delta hedging makes all options path dependent.

■ **Calendar spread.** We are short one unit of a 1-year call option struck at the money and long one unit of a 6-month call option struck at the

TABLE 9.5 P&L Consequences of a Cycle in Prices and Volatilities

Moves	With Price Jumps	With Smooth Delta Hedging
Volatilities up 8% (0,0%)→ (0,8%)	−1.06%	−1.06%
Prices down 25% (0,8%)→ (−25,8%)	+0.84% (−.22% − (−1.06%))	0
Volatilities down 8% (−25,8%)→ (−25,0%)	−0.83% (−1.05% − (−.22%))	−0.83%
Prices back up to original level (−25,0%)→ (0,0%)	+1.05%	0
Total	0	−1.89%

money. The price-vol matrix in Figure 9.3 shows positive P&L from price jumps but negative P&L from an increase in implied volatility. This is also reflected in the positive gamma and negative vega measures for the portfolio. Shorter-term options generally have a greater impact on sensitivity to price jumps than longer-term options of the same size, but longer-term options generally have greater exposure to implied volatility than shorter-term options of the same size.

■ **Reduced risk portfolio.** We are short one unit of a 1-year call option struck at 105 percent of the forward price and long .525 units of a 1-year call option struck at the money and .5 units of a 1-year call option struck at 110 percent of the forward price. The price-vol matrix is shown in Figure 9.4. These weights have been deliberately selected to make gamma and vega zero. However, unlike the call spread case, the zero gamma and vega is reflected throughout the price-vol matrix by low exposures at all combinations of price jump and volatility shift. This demonstrates the ability to achieve greater risk reduction by using positions that are symmetric in strike price.

Figures 9.5 and 9.6 show how this position evolves through time. We can see that at the end of .5 years (Figure 9.5), there is still not much risk exposure, but at the end of .9 years, with only .1 year left until option expiration (Figure 9.6), there is some convexity, with gains if prices jump upward and losses if prices jump downward. This shows that even a hedge of options against options that works very well at first cannot be maintained as a purely static hedge. We have already explored the implications of this for options risk management using Monte Carlo simulation in Section 9.3.

		call	call
Discount	5.00%		
Spacing	Volume	-1	1
Price	5 call/put		
Volatility	Price 100	100	
2% Time	Strike 100	100	
	Time 1	1	0.5

	Portfolio		
Implied vol		20.0%	20.0%
BS price	-2.08%	-7.58%	5.50%
Delta	-1.2%	-54.0%	52.8%
Vega	-0.10%	-0.38%	0.27%
Gamma	0.8%	-2.0%	2.8%
Theta	-0.007%	0.015%	-0.021%

Spot-vol matrix

	Implied volatilities										
Price	-8%	-6%	-4%	-2%	0%	2%	4%	6%	8%	Vega	Vega convexity
-25	2.05%	1.99%	1.90%	1.79%	1.66%	1.51%	1.36%	1.19%	1.03%	-0.07%	0.00%
-20	1.90%	1.77%	1.62%	1.46%	1.29%	1.11%	0.92%	0.74%	0.55%	-0.09%	0.00%
-15	1.59%	1.41%	1.22%	1.03%	0.84%	0.65%	0.46%	0.27%	0.09%	-0.10%	0.00%
-10	1.17%	0.98%	0.78%	0.60%	0.41%	0.23%	0.05%	-0.13%	-0.30%	-0.09%	0.00%
-5	0.80%	0.62%	0.45%	0.28%	0.11%	-0.06%	-0.23%	-0.39%	-0.56%	-0.08%	0.00%
0	0.66%	0.50%	0.33%	0.17%	0.00%	-0.16%	-0.33%	-0.49%	-0.66%	-0.08%	0.00%
5	0.83%	0.64%	0.46%	0.28%	0.10%	-0.07%	-0.25%	-0.42%	-0.60%	-0.09%	0.00%
10	1.20%	0.99%	0.78%	0.58%	0.38%	0.18%	-0.01%	-0.21%	-0.39%	-0.10%	0.00%
15	1.65%	1.43%	1.20%	0.98%	0.76%	0.54%	0.33%	0.12%	-0.09%	-0.11%	0.00%
20	2.05%	1.85%	1.64%	1.41%	1.19%	0.96%	0.73%	0.51%	0.29%	-0.11%	0.00%
25	2.37%	2.21%	2.03%	1.82%	1.61%	1.38%	1.15%	0.92%	0.69%	-0.11%	0.01%

FIGURE 9.3 Price-vol matrix for a calendar spread.

Discount

Spacing 5.00%

Price

	Volume	5	-1	0.525	0.5
	call/put	call	call	call	call
Price		100	100	100	100
Volatility	Strike	105	105	100	110
2%	Time	1	1	1	1
Portfolio	Implied vol	20.0%	20.0%	20.0%	20.0%
0.40%	BS price	-5.62%	3.98%	2.04%	
1.7%	Delta	-44.3%	28.3%	17.7%	
0.00%	Vega	-0.38%	0.20%	0.18%	
0.0%	Gamma	-2.0%	1.0%	0.9%	
0.000%	Theta	0.014%	-0.008%	-0.007%	

Spot-vol matrix

Price	Implied volatilities									Vega	Vega convexity
	-8%	-6%	-4%	-2%	0%	2%	4%	6%	8%		
-25	0.02%	0.04%	0.05%	0.06%	0.07%	0.08%	0.09%	0.10%	0.11%	0.01%	0.00%
-20	-0.03%	-0.01%	0.01%	0.02%	0.03%	0.05%	0.06%	0.07%	0.08%	0.01%	0.00%
-15	-0.05%	-0.03%	-0.01%	0.00%	0.01%	0.02%	0.03%	0.04%	0.05%	0.01%	0.00%
-10	-0.04%	-0.02%	-0.01%	0.00%	0.00%	0.01%	0.02%	0.02%	0.02%	0.00%	0.00%
-5	0.00%	0.00%	0.00%	0.00%	0.00%	0.00%	0.01%	0.01%	0.01%	0.00%	0.00%
0	0.03%	0.02%	0.01%	0.00%	0.00%	0.00%	0.00%	0.00%	0.01%	0.00%	0.00%
5	0.04%	0.02%	0.01%	0.00%	0.00%	0.00%	0.00%	0.00%	0.00%	0.00%	0.00%
10	0.04%	0.02%	0.01%	0.00%	0.00%	0.00%	0.00%	0.00%	0.00%	0.00%	0.00%
15	0.01%	0.00%	0.00%	-0.01%	-0.01%	-0.01%	-0.01%	0.00%	0.00%	0.00%	0.00%
20	-0.02%	-0.02%	-0.02%	-0.01%	-0.01%	-0.01%	-0.01%	0.00%	0.00%	0.00%	0.00%
25	-0.05%	-0.04%	-0.03%	-0.02%	-0.02%	-0.01%	0.00%	0.00%	0.01%	0.00%	0.00%

FIGURE 9.4 Price-vol matrix for a reduced risk portfolio.

	Spacing			
Price	5			
Volatility	2%			

	Portfolio	call	call	call
Volume		-1	0.525	0.5
call/put		call	call	call
Price		100	100	100
Strike		105	100	110
Time		0.5	0.5	0.5
Implied vol		20.0%	20.0%	20.0%
BS price	0.44%	-3.53%	2.89%	1.08%
Delta	2.2%	-39.2%	27.7%	13.7%
Vega	-0.01%	-2.7%	0.14%	0.12%
Gamma	-0.1%	1.5%	1.2%	
Theta	0.000%	0.020%	-0.011%	-0.009%

Spot-vol matrix

	Implied volatilities									Vega	Vega convexity
Price	-8%	-6%	-4%	-2%	0%	2%	4%	6%	8%		
-25	0.10%	0.10%	0.11%	0.11%	0.12%	0.13%	0.13%	0.14%	0.15%	0.00%	0.00%
-20	0.00%	0.01%	0.02%	0.03%	0.05%	0.06%	0.07%	0.08%	0.09%	0.01%	0.00%
-15	-0.07%	-0.05%	-0.03%	-0.01%	0.00%	0.02%	0.03%	0.04%	0.05%	0.00%	0.00%
-10	-0.08%	-0.05%	-0.04%	-0.02%	-0.01%	0.00%	0.01%	0.01%	0.02%	0.00%	0.00%
-5	-0.02%	-0.01%	-0.01%	-0.01%	0.00%	-0.01%	-0.01%	0.00%	0.00%	-0.01%	0.00%
0	0.07%	0.04%	0.03%	0.01%	-0.01%	-0.01%	-0.02%	-0.02%	-0.02%	-0.01%	0.00%
5	0.10%	0.06%	0.03%	0.01%	-0.01%	-0.02%	-0.03%	-0.04%	-0.04%	-0.01%	0.00%
10	0.04%	0.02%	-0.01%	-0.02%	-0.04%	-0.05%	-0.06%	-0.07%	-0.07%	-0.01%	0.00%
15	-0.06%	-0.07%	-0.07%	-0.08%	-0.08%	-0.09%	-0.09%	-0.10%	-0.10%	-0.01%	0.00%
20	-0.18%	-0.16%	-0.15%	-0.14%	-0.14%	-0.13%	-0.13%	-0.13%	-0.13%	0.00%	0.00%
25	-0.26%	-0.23%	-0.21%	-0.20%	-0.19%	-0.18%	-0.17%	-0.16%	-0.16%	0.01%	0.00%

FIGURE 9.5 Price-vol matrix for the reduced risk portfolio of Figure 9.4 after .5 years have elapsed.

Discount 5.00%

Spacing	Volume	5		
Price	call/put	call	call	call
		(-1)	(0.525)	(0.5)
Volatility	Price	100	100	100
2%	Strike	105	100	110
	Time	0.1	0.1	0.1
	Implied vol	20.0%	20.0%	20.0%

Portfolio				
0.60%	BS price	-0.81%	1.32%	0.10%
7.4%	Delta	-23.0%	26.9%	3.5%
-0.01%	Vega	-0.10%	0.07%	0.02%
-0.4%	Gamma	-4.8%	3.3%	1.1%
0.003%	Theta	0.037%	-0.026%	-0.008%

Spot-vol matrix

	Implied volatilities										Vega
Price	-8%	-6%	-4%	-2%	0%	2%	4%	6%	8%	Vega	convexity
-25	1.25%	1.25%	1.25%	1.25%	1.25%	1.25%	1.25%	1.25%	1.25%	0.00%	0.00%
-20	0.88%	0.88%	0.88%	0.88%	0.88%	0.88%	0.88%	0.89%	0.89%	0.00%	0.00%
-15	0.51%	0.51%	0.51%	0.51%	0.52%	0.52%	0.53%	0.53%	0.54%	0.00%	0.00%
-10	0.15%	0.15%	0.16%	0.18%	0.19%	0.21%	0.22%	0.24%	0.26%	0.01%	0.00%
-5	-0.12%	-0.08%	-0.05%	-0.02%	0.01%	0.03%	0.05%	0.06%	0.07%	0.01%	0.00%
0	0.03%	0.03%	0.02%	0.01%	0.00%	-0.01%	-0.03%	-0.04%	-0.06%	-0.01%	0.00%
5	0.16%	0.08%	0.00%	-0.06%	-0.11%	-0.15%	-0.19%	-0.23%	-0.26%	-0.02%	0.00%
10	-0.47%	-0.47%	-0.48%	-0.50%	-0.52%	-0.54%	-0.56%	-0.57%	-0.59%	-0.01%	0.00%
15	-1.18%	-1.14%	-1.10%	-1.07%	-1.05%	-1.03%	-1.02%	-1.01%	-1.01%	0.01%	0.00%
20	-1.56%	-1.55%	-1.53%	-1.51%	-1.48%	-1.46%	-1.44%	-1.42%	-1.41%	0.01%	0.00%
25	-1.83%	-1.82%	-1.82%	-1.81%	-1.80%	-1.79%	-1.78%	-1.77%	-1.75%	0.01%	0.00%

FIGURE 9.6 Price-vol matrix for the reduced risk portfolio of Figure 9.4 after .9 years have elapsed.

The price-vol matrix has the great advantage of looking at precise sensitivity to many different values of two variables, but this carries the disadvantage of only being able to consider two variables. This has two consequences: The choice of which two variables to look at is an important one, and the price-vol matrix needs to be supplemented with risk measures that go beyond these two variables.

The selection of the best variables to use in the price-vol matrix can be based on economic insight or on statistical techniques, such as principal component analysis. On the side of asset prices, one question is whether to assume a parallel shift in forward prices. This is equivalent to assuming zero correlation between changes in the underlying asset price and changes in discount curves. Another question is whether to assume constant spreads between different variants of the asset—such as different grades for a physical commodity and different individual stocks relative to a stock market index. For volatilities, the question is whether to assume parallel changes in the volatility surface or whether to assume a statistical relationship based on historical experience.

Looking more closely at the issue of whether to assume a parallel shift in the volatility surface, let's break this down into a time-to-expiry component and a strike component. With regard to time to expiry, the first principal component of changes in volatility surfaces has less tendency to be flat than the first principal component of changes in interest rate curves. Longer-term volatilities often tend to move substantially less than shorter-term ones. Although a time-differentiated shift conveys less immediate intuitive meaning in discussions with senior management than a flat 1 percent shift, the increase in likelihood may outweigh the communications disadvantage. A possible compromise that is reasonably easy to express and often reasonably close to historical experience is a proportional rather than an absolute shift. So if 1-year volatilities are currently 20 percent and 5-year volatilities are 15 percent, a 5 percent proportional shift would move the 1-year volatility up 1 to 21 percent and the 5-year volatility up .75 to 15.75 percent. The **PriceVolMatrix** spreadsheet allows the user specification of either flat or proportional shifts.

With respect to the strike component, a frequently used alternative to a flat shift by instrument is a flat shift by delta. For example, assume that an at-the-money option currently has a 20 percent implied volatility and an in-the-money option with a delta of 75 percent currently has a 19 percent implied volatility, and assume that we are dealing with a currently at-the-money option. Then a volatility shift of down 2 percent combined with a price jump in the underlying asset that makes this option in the money with a 75 percent delta results in an implied volatility of 20% − 2% = 18% if we are assuming a flat shift by instrument. It results in a 19% − 2% = 17% implied volatility if we are assuming a flat shift by delta. The **PriceVolMatrix** spreadsheet allows the user specification of either flat shift by instrument or flat shift by delta.

The driving force behind the use of a flat delta shift is that the factors that generate the shape of the volatility surface by the strike, such as stochastic volatility and the structure of jumps, tend to remain static across changes in the underlying price level. We discuss these factors in Section 9.6.2. Taleb (1997, pp. 138–142) provides a detailed exposition of a flat delta shift methodology and its consequences for hedging. Derman (1999) contrasts flat instrument shifts with flat delta shifts ("sticky-strike" versus "sticky-delta" in Derman's terminology) along with a third possibility, "sticky-implied-tree." Derman presents empirical evidence that differing market environments over time can result in a change in which shift patterns provide the greatest explanatory power.

No matter what selections are made for the price-vol matrix variables, there is clearly enough residual risk to require traders to also look at more detailed risk reports as supplements to price-vol matrices. Certainly, this will include exposure to changes in the shape of the volatility surface, with respect to both time and strikes. The **PriceVolMatrix** spreadsheet includes a calculation of exposure to changes in the volatility surface. These more detailed reports usually only focus on the impact of small one-at-a-time changes, although a particularly significant residual risk might justify a price-vol matrix of its own. For example, an equity options trading desk might want to look at an overall price-vol matrix that considers parallel shifts in all stock market indices as well as price-vol matrices for each individual country's stock index, but would probably only want a simple delta and vega measure to reflect the exposure to each individual stock traded.

Senior management will want to see much less detail than the trading desk regarding options. The primary concern of senior management is making sure that they are comfortable with large macro positions that may be an accumulation of the holdings of many trading desks. As such, the most important measure for senior management is outright exposure to spot positions (for example, JPY/USD FX, S&P index, and gold) or to forward positions (for example, exposure to a parallel shift in the USD interest rate curve). Since options desks hold delta-equivalent positions in these spot and forward markets, including these positions in reports of the total spot, exposure of the firm is necessary in order to ensure an accurate summary. So senior management will generally just be interested in a single out-right position number for each product, along with some measure of vega. For many options positions, the delta will fit the need for an outright position measure. Control of convexity risk around this delta is then left to the trading desk level, probably prescribed by limits on convexity. However, the positions of some complex trading books may not be at all accurately represented by the delta. If a book will gain $100 million for the next 1 point rise in the S&P, but lose $2 million for each point rise after that, representing the position by a +$100 million per point delta will be totally misleading. For senior management purposes, the delta needs to be defined not mathematically, as the instantaneous derivative, but economically, as a finite difference over a selected economically meaningful price movement (a one standard deviation daily price move might be a reasonable choice).

Limit-setting detail for options books lies somewhere between the level needed for trading desk control and that needed for senior management. Some form of limits on price-vol matrix positions is desirable, but separate limits for each matrix box would be overdetailed, whereas a single limit that no matrix box could exceed would be too broad. A limit set high enough to accommodate really unlikely combinations would be too liberal a limit for combinations close to the matrix center. A reasonable compromise is differentiated limits by groups of matrix boxes, where a similar likelihood of outcomes determines grouping. Limits on exposure to changes in the shape of the volatility surface can often be best expressed in terms of a few parameters that determine the shape. For details on possible parameters, see the discussion in Section 9.6.2.

The management of options risk is an inherently dynamic process. Unlike spot or forward risk, you can rarely just put on a hedge once and for all; you must constantly make adjustments. So options traders need measures to show them how their P&L and positions should change as a result of the passage of time or changes in prices. This enables them to prepare for the trading actions they will need to take and serves as a check against actual changes in P&L and positions to highlight anything that is happening that they don't understand. The best-known measures of this type are *theta* (the change in option values with time) and *gamma* (the change in delta with a change in price). However, many other examples are available: for instance, *bleed* (see Taleb [1997, pp. 191–199]) and *Ddeltadvol* (Taleb [1997, pp. 200–201]).

By contrast, corporate risk managers are rarely interested in such measures. Theta cannot be a direct measure of risk since clearly you are not uncertain as to whether time will pass or not. It does measure the possibility of gain or loss if implied volatility fails to be realized over a given time period, but the same risk can be captured in a more comprehensive way by a time-bucketed vega measure. Gamma is only of interest to the extent that it can be used to compute convexity, which is a genuine P&L exposure, but gamma is a reliable indicator of convexity only for very simple portfolios. In general, corporate risk managers expect that trading desk heads will be able to deal with the operational issues of evolving positions. The only exceptions might be changes so large as to make liquidity questionable, which might require limits to be set.

9.5   DELTA HEDGING

In the presence of transaction costs, it is necessary to use optimization to determine a delta hedging strategy. A trade-off exists between achieving a lower standard deviation of results, utilizing more frequent hedging, and achieving a higher expected return, utilizing less frequent hedging, leading to lower transaction costs. Whaley and Wilmott (1994) have shown that the efficient frontier for this problem consists of hedging policies with the following characteristics:

- Hedges will be triggered not by time intervals, but by the distance that the current delta hedge ratio differs from the theoretical delta hedge ratio required by the Black-Scholes formula.
- If transaction costs are only a function of the number of hedge transactions and not the size of the hedge transactions, then whenever a hedge transaction is triggered, the amount will be exactly enough to bring the hedge ratio in line with the desired theoretical ratio. Since the transaction cost is the same no matter how large the amount, you should go to the hedge ratio you would use in the absence of transaction costs.
- If transaction costs are only a function of the size of the hedge transaction, then whenever a hedge transaction is triggered, the amount of the transaction is only large enough to bring the difference between the actual and theoretical hedge ratios down to the trigger point. Since you don't care how many transactions you need to use, only the size of transactions, it makes sense that you will stay as close as possible to the point at which hedge inaccuracy exactly balances between the desire for low standard deviation of results and low transaction costs.
- If transaction costs are a function of both the number and size of hedge transactions, then the optimal rule will be a combination of these two cases, with an outer trigger distance between current and

theoretical delta that institutes a trade to bring the difference down to an inner trigger distance.

Target delta hedges are determined by the Black-Scholes formula as $N(d_1)$, where $d_1 = (\ln(1/k) + \sigma^2 T/2)/\sigma \sqrt{T}$. What value of σ, the volatility of the underlying asset, should be used to determine this target hedge? Options should be valued at the implied volatility that corresponds to the market price at which the position could be exited, but this does not provide any reason for using this implied volatility to determine delta hedges of positions that are not exited. Given that any misestimation of true volatility while determining the hedge will result in unintended proprietary positions in the underlying asset, as per our discussion in Section 9.3, it is best to give traders reasonable latitude to make their best estimate of future volatility as input to the target hedge.

This brings us to the suggested solution we promised to the question in Section 9.2. What causes the large losses from the nasty path? It is caused by the dramatic difference between actual realized volatility and implied volatility. You will see in the **NastyPath** spreadsheet that the option was priced at a 7 percent implied volatility, which was also used in creating the delta hedge. However, the actual price moves of .13 a day correspond to a realized volatility of 2 percent. Had the trader been able to foresee this and form the delta hedges based on a 2 percent volatility, P&L on the trade would have been close to 0 (try this out in the spreadsheet).

Continuing the theme from Section 9.3, concerning what actions to take if a trader believes the underlying price is mean reverting, simulations similar to those reported in Table 9.3 indicate that gains will result from delta hedges based on overestimates of actual realized volatility. If underlying prices are trending (either up or down) rather than mean reverting, then gains will result from delta hedges based on an underestimate of the actual realized volatility. So traders should consider biasing their volatility estimates if they have a view on mean reversion. To get an intuitive understanding of this result, consider what happens if you overestimate volatility. The higher volatility in the denominator of the formula for d_1 will cause the target delta to move less as price movements result in the option moving in or out of the money. If price moves tend to be followed by moves in the opposite direction, as they will be if the price process is mean reverting, then the difference between actual delta and theoretical delta will be in the right direction to create positive P&L.

9.6　BUILDING A VOLATILITY SURFACE

Building a volatility surface for pricing European options is similar to building a discount curve, but it operates in two dimensions rather than one, since volatilities will vary by strike as well as by time. However, the general principle is the same: Build a surface that balances the fitting of known options prices with a smoothness criterion. The smoothness criterion is designed to minimize the risk of loss from hedging options for which market prices are not known with options for which prices are known.

To build the surface in both dimensions simultaneously requires a stochastic volatility model to which you can fit parameters (for example, the Heston model—see Heston [1993]). The more common approach is to build a volatility curve for at-the-money strikes by time period and separately build a volatility curve for a few selected time periods by strike. Arbitrary combinations of time and strike can then be interpolated from already determined points. We will look in turn at the issues of interpolating between time periods, interpolating between strikes, and extrapolating beyond the longest liquid time period.

9.6.1 Interpolating between Time Periods

We have a problem that's extremely similar to the one we faced for discount curves. We have a set of fitting conditions, wanting to choose underlying discount prices (implied volatilities), so that when they're plugged into pricing formulas, they come out with bond prices (option prices) that closely match those observed in the market, and a set of smoothness conditions, wanting to choose discount prices (implied volatilities) that lead to maximum smoothness of forward interest rates (forward volatilities) across periods.

The forward volatility, the amount of volatility expected to take place in some reasonably small time period in the future, is a natural analogy to the forward rate. With forward rates, we discussed whether to have an additional set of constraints stating that all forward rates must be non-negative and examined economic arguments for and against this (refer to Section 8.3.2). With forward volatilities, there isn't any doubt—a negative standard deviation is not a mathematical possibility so the constraints are necessary.

We can set up an optimization to solve for forward volatilities in a completely analogous manner to the optimization we set up to solve for forward rates, with different solutions corresponding to different trade-offs between the tightness of the fitting constraints and tightness of the smoothness constraints and different weights on different fitting constraints based on the liquidity of the price quotes. (Note that it is a more viable possibility with options than with interest rates to just find forwards that exactly fit all available market prices and then interpolate between the forwards. Unlike bonds and swaps, options have no intermediate payments to require a bootstrap. However, optimization still might be desirable as a way of trading off between fitting and smoothness objectives.)

When fitting forward interest rates, we had to preprocess to adjust for the lack of smoothness that we were anticipating based on our economic theories, such as turn-of-the-year effects (see Section 8.3.4). In the same way, forward volatilities need preprocessing. Generally, the opinions of options traders regarding the patterns of forward volatility tend to be much more strongly held than the opinions of interest rate traders regarding forward rates. Opinions on forward volatility center on issues of the flow of information into the markets that will cause price fluctuations. If we look at daily forward volatilities (and traders of shorter-term options often do work at this level of detail), you might find a trader anticipating nearly zero volatility on weekends and holidays (markets are closed, so no new prices can be observed), higher volatility on Mondays and days after holidays than on other weekdays (governments sometimes like to make surprise announcements when markets are closed), lower than normal volatility on days when most traders can be expected to be on vacation or leaving work early (such as the day before a 3-day weekend), and higher than normal volatility on a day when a key economic statistic is scheduled to be announced. For more examples, see Taleb (1997, p. 98), and Burghardt and Hanweck (1993).

The accompanying CD-ROM has two spreadsheets to illustrate fitting a forward volatility curve to observed options prices. The first, **VolCurve**, can be used for all European options other than interest rate caps and floors, and emphasizes the adjustment for anticipated volatility patterns. The second, **CapFit**, is designed for use only for interest rate *caps* and *floors*, which are packages of individual options (known as *caplets* and *floorlets*, respectively). Since liquid prices are generally available only for the options packages and not for the underlying options, an optimization is needed to fit the observed prices of packages with as smooth a forward volatility curve as possible.

9.6.2 Interpolating between Strikes

Now let's turn to building a volatility curve by strike for a given time period. Market prices will be available for certain strikes that we will want to fit. Which variable should play the corresponding role to forward interest rates and forward volatilities as the one for which we try to achieve smoothness? A natural choice is the risk-neutral probability that the underlying variable finishes in a range between two prices. If these ranges are chosen small enough, options at all strikes can be priced to as close a precision as you want based on such probabilities.

If S is the strike and p_i is the risk-neutral probability that the underlying will finish between price P_i and price P_{i+1}, the option price must be bounded by $\sum_i max(P_i - S,0)p_i$ from below and $\sum_i max(P_{i+1} - S,0)p_i$ from above.

Like forward volatilities, probabilities must be constrained to be non-negative. Using this formula allows translation among cumulative probability, probability frequency, and implied volatility by strike as alternative, mutually translatable ways of describing a probability distribution, in much the same way that par rate, zero-coupon rate, forward rate, and discount price are alternatives for describing the discount curve. See the **VolSurfaceStrike** spreadsheet for an illustration of this principle.

Jackwerth and Rubinstein (1996) illustrate an optimization setup to derive probability distributions based on a trade-off between the tightness of fitting constraints and smoothness constraints. When choosing a smoothness criteria, an alternative to just looking at how smooth the changes in probability levels are is to look at how closely the probabilities fit a distribution selected on theoretical grounds (for example, normal or lognormal) as the most likely prior distribution (prior, that is, to any knowledge of the actual options prices). This use of prior distribution ties closely to Baysian statistical methods. In Section III.A of their paper, Jackworth and Rubinstein explore several such smoothness criteria.

A fundamental problem often encountered when trying to derive volatility curves by strike is the relative paucity of market observations available by strike. It is not at all uncommon to find markets in which options prices are available for only three or four different strike levels at a given time period. In such circumstances, a smoothness criteria that does not utilize a prior distribution is of little use—you at least need to restrict your choice to some family of possible candidate distributions on theoretical grounds. Of course, any such choice is a model and should be analyzed for the degree of mispricing possible if the model is wrong by considering how different the volatility curve would be if another plausible model was chosen. Reserves and limits against model error should be considered.

A good discussion of candidate distributions and the theoretical basis for selecting between them can be found in Hull (2002, Sections 20.1–20.3). Let us first state some general facts about the shape of volatility surfaces observed in the markets (these comments can be compared with those in Hull [2002, Sections 15.2–15.3] and Rebonato [1999, Section 4.5]). In this discussion, we will use the term *smile* to refer to a pattern of volatility by strike where volatility rises as strikes move away from at the money in the direction of either in or out of the money. We will use *skew* to refer to a pattern of volatility by strike in which volatility either decreases or increases with increasing strike levels. So skew is primarily a linear relationship and smile is primarily a quadratic relationship. (Market practice from firm to firm, and even desk to desk within a firm may differ in nomenclature. Sometimes *skew* is used to cover all aspects of volatility surface shape, and sometimes *smile* is used to cover all aspects of volatility shape.)

Using these definitions, the observed patterns are:

- Smiles tend to appear in all options markets.
- Equity options markets almost always show a pronounced skew, with volatility decreasing with increasing strikes. The combination of this skew with the smile produces a pattern that can be described as a sharp skew at strikes below at the money and relatively flat volatilities at strikes above at the money.
- No general skew pattern exists in markets for FX options between strong currencies (for example, between the dollar, euro, yen, sterling, and Swiss franc). However, there does tend to be a strong skew pattern (volatility decreases with increased strikes) for FX options between a strong currency and a weaker currency, such as an emerging market currency.
- Skew patterns in interest rate options markets tend to vary by currency, with the strongest patterns of volatilities decreasing with increasing strikes appearing for currencies with low interest rate levels, particularly in yen.

What explanations have been offered for these observed patterns?

- The prevalence of volatility smiles can be explained in two different ways: stochastic volatility and jump diffusion. Stochastic volatility utilizes a probability distribution for the volatility that determines the probability distribution of underlying prices, whereas jump diffusion assumes that some price uncertainty is expressed through price jumps as opposed to a smooth random walk. Both assumptions result in a distribution of final prices with fatter tails than the lognormal distribution used by Black-Scholes. Fatter-tail distributions have little effect on options at close to at-the-money strikes, which are primarily affected by the center of the distribution; however, they have greater effects the more an option is in the money or out of the money, since these options are primarily affected by the size of the tail. The pricing formula for options using either stochastic volatility or jump diffusion (see the equations in Hull [2002, Sections 20.2–20.3]) consists of averages of option prices using the Black-Scholes formula across a range of volatilities. The difference between the two models is the probability weight used in averaging across these volatilities. Stochastic volatility results in a more pronounced smile as the time to option expiry increases, whereas jump diffusion results in a more pronounced smile as the time to option expiry decreases. It may be necessary to combine the two to obtain actual smile patterns observed in market options prices. See Matytsin (1999).

■ The Black-Scholes model assumes a lognormal distribution of the underlying asset price. If the market is assuming a normal, rather than lognormal, price distribution, this will evidence itself as higher implied volatilities for lower strike options and lower implied volatilities for higher strike options when implied volatilities are computed using the Black-Scholes formula. So if the market is assuming that price changes are independent of market level rather than proportional to market level, implying normal rather than lognormal price distributions, this will lead to a skew with volatilities decreasing with increasing strikes. If the market is assuming a distribution intermediate between normal and lognormal, this skew pattern will still exist, but it will be less pronounced. Historical evidence shows support for interest rate movements that are sometimes closer to being independent of the rate level and other times closer to being proportional to the rate level. The skew for implied volatilities of interest rate options is generally believed to be driven primarily by the expectation that rate movements are not completely proportional to the rate level, with the expectation in low-rate environments that rate movements are close to independent of the rate level.

■ The skew pattern in equity markets has sometimes been explained as the outcome of asymmetry of the value of investment in a corporation, which can suddenly collapse as a company approaches the bankruptcy point. Hull (2000, Section 17.7) discusses three alternative models based on this explanation—the compound option model, the displaced diffusion model, and the constant elasticity of variance model.

A more general explanation of skew patterns can be found in analyzing the degree of asymmetry in the structure of a particular market. For a thorough exposition of this viewpoint, see Taleb (1997, pp. 245–252) on which much of my discussion here is based. This asymmetry can be described in two complementary ways: one that focuses on investor behavior and the other that focuses on price behavior.

From an investor behavior viewpoint, in some markets, investment has a structural bias toward one side of the market. Equity markets are a good example. There are far more investors long equity investments than there are investors who have shorted the market; hence, more investors are seeking protection from stock prices falling than are seeking protection from stock prices rising. The reason is that corporate issuance of stock is a major source of supply and corporations are not seeking protection against their stock rising—in fact, they welcome it. So you expect to see greater demand to buy puts on stock at strikes below the current market level, sought by investors protecting their long equity positions, than the demand for calls on stock at strikes above the current market level sought by short sellers to protect their short equity positions. This imbalance in demand drives up implied volatilities on low-strike options relative to high-strike options.

The complementary view from a price behavior viewpoint is that stock market crashes, in which large downward jumps occur in stock prices, are far more common than large upward jumps in stock prices. This can be seen as a consequence of the imbalance in investors who are long stocks relative to those who are short stocks. Falling prices can trigger a selling panic by investors faced with large losses forced to exit leveraged long positions supported by borrowings. There are fewer short sellers and leveraged short positions to cause a panic reaction when prices are rising. A bias toward downward jumps over upward jumps leads to a skew in the distribution of probabilities of price movements that will translate into higher implied volatilities at lower strikes. In addition, the anticipation of possible stock market crashes will exacerbate the demand for crash protection through puts at lower strikes.

A similar structural analysis can be constructed for FX markets for an emerging market currency versus a strong currency. These exchange rates are often maintained at artificially high levels by governments defending the value of the emerging market currency through purchases of the currency, high interest rates, or currency controls. When breaks in the FX rate come, they tend to be large downward jumps in the value of the emerging market currency. There is no similar possibility of upward jumps. This price behavior directly leads to a probability distribution that translates to higher implied volatilities at lower strikes (lower in terms of the value of the emerging market currency). Indirectly, this price behavior encourages holders of the emerging market currency to buy puts at lower strikes, bidding up the implied volatility at these strikes.

Other markets generally tend toward a more symmetric structure. Exchange rates between two strong currencies are usually freer floating with less bottled-up pressures. Thus, no bias exists toward large upward jumps or large downward jumps. Most interest rate markets and commodity markets tend to be roughly evenly divided between longs and shorts—investors who would benefit from upward movement and those who would benefit from downward movement. However, some particular asymmetries can be observed—for example, the large demand by U.S. mortgage investors for protection against falling interest rates leading to accelerated prepayments or a temporary imbalance of the suppliers of a commodity seeking put protection against falling prices relative to the consumers of the commodity seeking call protection against rising prices.

The **VolSurfaceStrike** spreadsheet illustrates both ways in which a probability distribution can be fit to a set of option prices at different strikes. With input on prices at a number of different strikes, it trades off the smoothness of the probability distribution and closeness of price fit. With input on prices at only a few strikes, it fits two parameters—one representing standard deviation of volatility and one representing the degree of proportional versus absolute price change to assume.

9.6.3 Extrapolating Based on Time Period

When we were looking at forward risk, we saw how to create valuation and reserves for a forward that had a longer tenor than any liquid instrument (see Section 8.2.2). The technique was to assume you were going to hedge the longer-term forward with a liquid shorter-term forward and later roll the shorter-term forward into a longer-term forward. The expected cost of the roll needs to be added into the initial cost of the hedge to obtain a valuation, and a reserve can be based on the historical standard deviation of the roll cost.

A similar approach suggests itself for valuing and reserving for long-term options that have a longer tenor than any liquid option. For example, if you want to create a 10-year option in a market that has liquid quotes only out to 7 years, you could begin by hedging with a 7-year option and, at the end of 5 years, roll out of what will then be a 2-year option into the 5-year option you need to exactly match your actual position. Expected differences in implied volatility between 5- and 2-year options determine expected roll costs. Reserves can be based on the historical standard deviation of differences in 2- and 5-year implied vols.

However, options are more complicated because they depend on strike level as well as the time to expiry. The price-vol matrix in Figure 9.7 shows that a ratio of 7-year options to 10-year options selected so as to minimize roll-cost uncertainty when the prices are at 100 leaves large roll-cost uncertainty when prices are above or below 100.

To minimize roll-cost uncertainty over a wide range of prices, you need to hedge with a package of options that differ by both tenor and strike. The price-vol matrix in Figure 9.8 shows the impact of selecting a hedge from a set of 7- and 6-year options at various strike levels, using the **OptionRoll** spreadsheet to select weightings of these options that will achieve minimal roll-cost uncertainty in 5 years. In this example, I have only accounted for roll-cost uncertainty due to shifts in volatility level; a more complete treatment would include shifts in the shape of the volatility surface. Expected roll

Discount	5.00%			
Spacing	Volume			1.34
Price	5	call	-1	call

		call	-1	call
	5 Price	100		100
Volatility	Strike	100	100	100
2%	Time	5	5	2

Portfolio		Impliedvol	20.0%	20.0%	20.0%
-0.14%	BS price		-13.78%	13.64%	
15.7%	Delta		-58.8%	74.5%	
0.00%	Vega		-0.68%	0.68%	
1.0%	Gamma		-0.9%	1.9%	
-0.008%	Theta		0.005%	-0.013%	

Spot-vol matrix

	Implied volatilities								8% Vega	Vega convexity
Price	-8%	-6%	-4%	-2%	0%	2%	4%	6%		
-25	4.26%	3.97%	3.71%	3.47%	3.25%	3.06%	2.89%	2.74%	2.60%	-0.10%	0.00%
-20	2.89%	2.66%	2.45%	2.27%	2.11%	1.97%	1.86%	1.75%	1.67%	-0.07%	0.00%
-15	1.70%	1.54%	1.40%	1.29%	1.19%	1.11%	1.04%	0.98%	0.94%	-0.04%	0.00%
-10	0.78%	0.70%	0.63%	0.57%	0.53%	0.49%	0.46%	0.44%	0.42%	-0.02%	0.00%
-5	0.21%	0.18%	0.16%	0.14%	0.13%	0.12%	0.12%	0.12%	0.12%	-0.01%	0.00%
0	0.02%	0.01%	0.01%	0.00%	0.00%	0.00%	0.00%	0.01%	0.02%	0.00%	0.00%
5	0.20%	0.17%	0.15%	0.14%	0.12%	0.12%	0.11%	0.11%	0.11%	-0.01%	0.00%
10	0.71%	0.64%	0.57%	0.52%	0.48%	0.44%	0.42%	0.40%	0.39%	-0.02%	0.00%
15	1.50%	1.35%	1.22%	1.12%	1.03%	0.96%	0.90%	0.85%	0.82%	-0.04%	0.00%
20	2.48%	2.26%	2.07%	1.90%	1.76%	1.65%	1.54%	1.46%	1.39%	-0.06%	0.00%
25	3.62%	3.32%	3.06%	2.83%	2.64%	2.47%	2.32%	2.19%	2.08%	-0.09%	0.00%

FIGURE 9.7 Hedge of a 10-year option with a 7-year option after 5 years.

Discount 5.00%
Spacing 5
Volatility 2%

	Portfolio			Years						
Volume		-1	-0.6906	5 / 2.5922	-0.6627	0.6714	0.4465	-0.1811	0.4588	-2.3471
call/put		call	call	call	call	call	call	call	call	call
Price		100	100	100	100	100	100	100	100	100
Strike		100	80	90	100	110	120	80	90	100
Time		5	2	2	2	2	2	1	1	1
Implied vol		20.0%	20.0%	20.0%	20.0%	20.0%	20.0%	20.0%	20.0%	20.0%
BS price	-0.72%	-13.78%	-14.42%	38.49%	-6.74%	4.54%	1.95%	-3.65%	5.93%	-17.78%
Delta	-0.8%	-58.8%	-56.9%	180.5%	-36.9%	28.4%	13.7%	-16.1%	33.7%	-126.7%
Vega	0.01%	-0.68%	-0.23%	1.16%	-0.33%	0.34%	0.20%	-0.03%	0.14%	-0.89%
Gamma	-0.1%	-0.9%	-0.6%	3.2%	-0.9%	0.9%	0.6%	-0.2%	0.8%	-4.7%
Theta	0.001%	0.005%	0.004%	-0.022%	0.006%	-0.006%	-0.004%	0.001%	-0.006%	0.034%
Current	0.031%	-15.05%	-14.78%	46.04%	-9.75%	8.16%	4.49%	-3.91%	8.09%	-33.65%

Spot-vol matrix

Implied volatilities

Price	-8%	-6%	-4%	-2%	0%	2%	4%	6%	8%	Vega
-25	0.24%	0.17%	0.10%	0.05%	0.01%	-0.02%	-0.05%	-0.06%	-0.06%	-0.02%
-20	-0.03%	-0.03%	-0.05%	-0.06%	-0.07%	-0.07%	-0.07%	-0.06%	-0.05%	0.00%
-15	-0.08%	-0.07%	-0.07%	-0.08%	-0.07%	-0.06%	-0.05%	-0.03%	-0.01%	0.00%
-10	0.00%	-0.02%	-0.04%	-0.05%	-0.04%	-0.03%	-0.01%	0.01%	0.04%	0.00%
-5	0.10%	0.03%	0.00%	-0.01%	-0.01%	0.00%	0.02%	0.05%	0.08%	0.01%
0	0.12%	0.04%	0.01%	0.00%	0.00%	0.02%	0.04%	0.07%	0.10%	0.01%
5	0.07%	0.01%	-0.01%	-0.02%	-0.01%	0.01%	0.04%	0.07%	0.10%	0.01%
10	0.00%	-0.03%	-0.04%	-0.04%	-0.03%	-0.01%	0.02%	0.05%	0.08%	0.01%
15	-0.02%	-0.04%	-0.06%	-0.06%	-0.05%	-0.03%	-0.01%	0.02%	0.06%	0.01%
20	0.04%	0.00%	-0.04%	-0.05%	-0.06%	-0.05%	-0.03%	-0.01%	0.02%	0.00%
25	0.19%	0.10%	0.04%	-0.01%	-0.03%	-0.04%	-0.04%	-0.03%	0.00%	-0.01%

FIGURE 9.8 Hedge to rollover into a 10-year option.

costs and standard deviations of roll costs must now be computed relative to the weighted average of implied vols of the hedge package.

9.7 SUMMARY

By way of summary, let us see how the paradigm for managing vanilla options risk deals with the criticisms of the Black-Scholes analysis hat have been offered. (Compare the analysis here to Taleb [1997, pp. 110–113].)

- Black-Scholes unrealistically assumes a constant risk-free interest rate and drift rate of the forward. The way we have set up our Black-Scholes model, directly incorporating rate and drift volatility into the volatility of the forward, shows that this criticism is not a serious one.
- Black-Scholes assumes that asset prices are lognormally distributed. This has long ceased to be true in trading practice. With traders valuing positions at each strike at different market-observed volatilities, any probability distribution believed by the marketplace can be accommodated. In Part 2 of Exercise 9.2 you are asked to examine the success of hedging options at one strike with those at another strike, using a Monte Carlo simulation that does not assume asset prices to be lognormally distributed. You will find relatively small uncertainty of hedging results.
- Black-Scholes assumes that hedging in the underlying asset can take place continuously and without transaction costs. These assumptions are closely linked since the presence of transaction costs will certainly force hedging to be less frequent, even if more frequent hedging is theoretically possible. Our Monte Carlo simulations have shown that, with the use of options to hedge other options, the resulting positions can be delta hedged at discrete times, resulting in relatively small uncertainty of hedging results and relatively low transaction costs. Any uncertainty and transaction costs that remain will contribute to wider bid-ask spreads for options.
- Black-Scholes assumes that underlying asset prices will follow a Brownian motion with no sudden jumps. In practice, sudden jumps do occur and these are unhedgeable other than by offsetting options positions. The price-vol matrix reports exposure to price jumps. In Part 1 of Exercise 9.2, you are asked to examine the success of hedging options at one strike with those at another strike, using a Monte Carlo simulation that assumes price jumps will take place. You will find relatively small uncertainty of hedging results.
- Black-Scholes assumes that volatility is constant. This is obviously false. The implications of stochastic volatility for the standard deviation of hedging results have been noted. The price-vol matrix reports exposure to changes in volatility and positions that have small expo-

sure as measured by the price-vol matrix have been shown, using Monte Carlo simulation, to have a relatively small uncertainty of hedging results.

■ Black-Scholes assumes that volatility is known. This is also obviously false. Our Monte Carlo simulations were carried out under the assumption that actual volatility was not known when setting hedge ratios and the resulting uncertainty of hedging results is small.

EXERCISES

9.1

Start with a portfolio consisting of less liquid options as follows:

Volume	1	−1	−1
Call/put	Call	Call	Call
Price	100	100	100
Strike	84	107	114
Time to expiry	1.3	0.7	1.7
Implied volatility	25.9%	24.4%	23.0%

1. Calculate the risk exposure of this portfolio.
2. Use the Solver to minimize risk using more liquid options. The liquid options available are as follows:

Call/put	Call	Call	Call	Call	Call	Call
Price	100	100	100	100	100	100
Strike	100	90	110	100	90	110
Time to expiry	1	1	1	2	2	2
Implied volatility	25.5%	26.0%	24.0%	24.5%	25.5%	23.5%

3. Compare the risk exposure of the risk-minimized portfolio to that of the original portfolio. How much has the risk been reduced? How would you characterize the exposures that remain?
4. Is this a static hedge or will it need to be rehedged through time?
5. Create your own portfolio of less liquid options and go through the same exercise.

9.2

Program a Monte Carlo simulation to compare the results of dynamic hedging on a single option position and on an option hedged by other options. To begin, try to match the results in Table 9.2. Start with eight simulations

($2 \times 2 \times 2$), corresponding to a pure dynamic hedge/two-sided options hedge, 0 percent standard deviation of volatility/33 percent standard deviation of volatility, and 100 rebalancings/500 rebalancings. Use 1,000 paths for each simulation. When using a standard deviation for volatility, apply it at the point that a volatility is assigned to a path (if you let the volatility vary at each rebalancing along the path, the volatilities will average out along the path and little difference will exist between the results of your 0 percent standard deviation and 33 percent standard deviation cases).

For all eight cases, initial price = strike = 100, time = 1 year, average volatility = 20 percent, rate = dividend = 0 percent, and transaction costs are based on one-fourth point per $100 bid-asked spread, so any transaction, either buy or sell, incurs a cost of $.125 per $100 bought or sold (but don't charge any transaction cost for establishing the initial delta hedge).

Use the **OptionMC** and **OptionMCHedged** spreadsheets to check your simulation programs. To do this, run your simulation for just 20 time steps. You can then check a particular path by taking the random numbers drawn for that path and substituting them for the random numbers selected in the spreadsheets. You can then compare results.

Once you match the results from Table 9.2, you should try to expand the runs in the following ways:

1. Four runs with 100 rebalancings/500 rebalancings for the pure dynamic hedge/two-sided options hedge, a 33 percent standard deviation of volatility, and a jump process. Jumps should occur on average once on each path, there should be a 50–50 chance that a jump is up or down, and the average absolute jump size should be 10 percent of the current price with a 33 percent standard deviation around this 10 percent. So a one standard deviation range would be from ($10\% \times \exp[-.33]$) = 7.2%) to ($10\% \times \exp[.33]$) = 13.9%). The volatility of the underlying should be adjusted down from 20 percent to whatever level will leave the average pure dynamic hedging cost equal to what it had been without the jump (you will need to try out a few different volatility levels to determine this).
2. A similar set of runs to test the impact of a volatility skew with a standard deviation of 20 percent.
3. For the case of a pure dynamic hedge, 500 rebalancings, and 33 percent standard deviation of volatility, check the impact of imposing different threshold levels for rehedging on the trade-off between the expected transaction cost and standard deviation of P&L.
4. Examine a sample of 50 individual paths and observe the relationship between the final price of the underlying and the total hedge P&L. Does the observed relationship support the claim in Section 9.3 that "despite wild gyrations in underlying prices, each [simulation

path] produces almost identical hedging results"?

5. What pattern do you observe of hedge ratios along the individual paths? For example, how quickly does the hedge ratio go to 100 percent for paths whose final price is above the strike and to 0 percent for paths whose final price is below the strike?

For Parts 4 and 5 of this exercise, you need to examine individual paths of the Monte Carlo simulation. Use paths taken from the simulation with 0 percent standard deviation of volatility and 500 rebalancings. If you do not have the time or programming background to create your own Monte Carlo simulation, then carry out these parts of the exercise using the **OptionMC1000** and **OptionMCHedged1000** spreadsheets. Use the following input settings: price = $100, strike = 100, time to expiry = 1, implied volatility = 20 percent, volatility = 20 percent, skew = 0 percent, and jump probability = 0 percent.

CHAPTER 10

Managing Exotic Options Risk

We need to first determine what we mean by an *exotic option*. Some articles on options emphasize complex formulas and difficult mathematical derivations as the hallmarks that distinguish exotics from vanillas. The criterion I am using in this book emphasizes market liquidity. If you can readily obtain prices at which the option can be bought and sold, then it counts as a vanilla option; if not, then it is an exotic option.

To understand why I favor this definition, consider a forward starting option as an illustrative example. This is an option priced now, but its strike is not set until some future date. Generally, it is set to be at the money on that future date. There is certainly no complexity about the formula or mathematical derivation of the formula for this product. It is the standard Black-Scholes formula with the strike and underlying price set equal. However, this product has no liquid market, and relating its valuation and hedging to that of ordinary European options is not straightforward. Equivalently, we can say that no clear relationship exists between the volatility that is needed as input to the Black-Scholes formula for the forward-start option and the volatilities implied by the prices of standard European options.

In the two last chapters, on managing forward risk and vanilla options risk, I emphasized the use of methods that maximize the degree to which all transactions can be viewed as being managed within a common risk-measurement framework—a single discount curve for forwards and the price-vol matrix for vanilla options. This common framework increases the chance that exposures on different transactions can be netted against one another and offset by transactions involving the forwards and vanilla options with the greatest liquidity. This paradigm does not work for exotic options since none of them have enough liquidity to provide confidence that risks can be offset at publicly available prices.

Therefore, the emphasis throughout this chapter is on methodology that enables, as much as possible, the risks in an exotic option to be represented as equivalent vanilla option positions. The reasons for this emphasis were discussed in the arguments favoring a more detailed limit approach in Section

5.2, in the broader setting of general risk decomposition. As applied specifically to exotic options, these reasons are:

- It permits the separation of exotic options risk into a part that can be managed with vanilla options and a residual that cannot. It is important to identify and quantify this residual risk so that adequate reserves can be held against it, and to facilitate the management recognition of pricing that is inadequate to support actual hedging costs. Without separating out the part of the risk that can be hedged with liquid vanilla options, it is quite possible that gains from ordinary vanilla risk positions will obscure losses from the truly illiquid residual.
- It encourages as much of the risk as possible to be managed as part of the far more liquid vanilla options position.
- It reduces the risk of having exotic options positions valued with methodology that is inconsistent with that used for valuing the vanilla options positions.
- It consolidates exotic options positions into already well-developed reporting mechanisms for vanilla options—price-vol matrices, volatility surface exposures, deltas, and other Greeks. This has the advantage of building on well-understood reports, thus clarifying the explanation to senior managers. It also guards against large positions accumulating without being recognized by a common reporting mechanism, since all exotics for a given underlying will be consolidated into the same set of vanilla options risk reports.

One approach to accomplishing this objective that we will use repeatedly is the *control variate technique*. The control variate technique uses the best available model to value a particular exotic option, but it also uses the same model to value a related vanilla option (or basket of vanilla options). Since the vanilla options are liquid, they can then be valued directly from the market (or interpolated from direct market prices). The model is only used to value the difference between the exotic and related vanilla. Risk reporting and risk management are similarly divided between reporting and managing the risk of the related vanilla option as we would any other vanilla and creating separate risk reporting and management for the difference between the exotic and related vanilla, thereby reducing the model dependence of valuation. See Hull (2002, Section 18.4) for a discussion that emphasizes the computational efficiency of this technique, which is strongly analogous to the risk-management advantages stressed here.

If the underlying assumptions of the Black-Scholes framework were true, in particular, if volatility was known and constant, the choice of models for exotics would generally be easy. Most exotics can be valued using formulas derived from market assumptions similar to those used in the Black-Scholes analysis of European options. However, when volatility is unknown and variable, there is seldom a direct way of translating a volatility surface used for valuing European options into a single volatility to be used in valuing an exotic. Usually, we will need to rely on more complex formulations tailored to a particular exotic to establish this relationship. Much of this chapter is devoted to developing these formulations for specific exotics.

A distinction that will prove very important when analyzing these models can be made between those where the relationship between the exotic and vanilla is *static* and those where the relationship between the exotic and vanilla is *dynamic*. Static relationships mean that the same vanilla (or package of vanillas) can be used to represent the exotic in vanilla option risk reports throughout the life of the exotic. Dynamic relationships mean that the package of vanillas used may need to change in composition over the life of the exotic.

Static representations have obvious operational advantages. Once it is booked at the inception of a trade, the representation does not need to be updated. Even more important is the simplicity introduced when the potential cost of differences between the actual exotic and its vanilla option representation over the life of the transaction is estimated. As emphasized in Section 9.3, dynamic representation requires simulation to evaluate potential costs. However, the simulation of dynamic changes in vanilla option hedges can be far more computationally difficult than the simulation of dynamic changes in underlying forwards hedges studied in Section 9.3. The reasons for this are discussed in Section 10.3.2.

The ideal of a static representation cannot always be achieved. It will be possible in Sections 10.1 and 10.4 when we are discussing options whose payout depends on prices at a single future time. However, when discussing options whose payout is a function of prices at different times, as is true in Sections 10.2, 10.3, and 10.5, static representation will not be possible. Our alternatives will be either dynamic representation or *quasistatic* representation, in which changes in the representation are minimized, often to only a single change, to simplify calculations of potential cost. We will use the simpler term *static* for the remainder of this chapter, but this is shorthand for *quasistatic representation*, and will pay due attention to the estimation of the cost of the hedge changes.

Table 10.1, which was taken from Smithson (2000), shows the principal forms of exotic products and how widely they are used in different markets.

The study of exotic options in this chapter is divided into five sections, following the categories used in Table 10.1.

- ■ **Section 10.1—single-payout options.** Options whose payoffs are the function solely of the price of an underlying asset at a single future time. We will show how to replicate these options exactly using a basket of forwards and vanilla options. The resulting replication can be

TABLE 10.1 Intensity of Use of Option Structures in Various Markets

	Interest Rate Options		FX Options		Equity Options		Commodity Options	
	OTC	Exchanges	OTC	Exchanges	OTC	Exchanges	OTC	Exchanges
First-generation options								
European style	A	A	A	A	A	O	A	A
American style	A		A		R	A	A	A
Bermuda style	A		A		R		O	
Second-generation options								
Path-dependent options								
Average price (rate)	A		A		A		A	A
Barrier options	A		A		A		A	
Capped	O		O		A		O	
Lookback	R		R		O		R	
Ladder	O		O		A		O	
Ratchet	O		O		A		O	
Shout	R		R		R		O	
Correlation-dependent options								
Rainbow options	R		O		O		O	
Quanto options	A		A		A		A	
Basket options	R		A		A		A	R
Time-dependent options								
Chooser options	R		R		R		O	
Forward start options	R		R		A		A	
Cliquet options	R		R		A		O	
Single-payout options								
Binary options	A		A		A		A	
Contingent premium options	A		A		R		A	

A = actively used; O = occasionally used; R = rarely used; blank = not used

used both to value the exotic and represent it in risk reports. The only residual risk will be the liquidity of the resulting basket, particularly in the replication of binary options. A particular example of an important single payout exotic is a log contract, which makes payments based on the logarithm of the underlying price. Its importance is mostly due to its close linkage to a variance swap, an exotic product not in the Table 10.1 but that shows increasing use. We will also discuss the volatility swap in this section, a close cousin of the variance swap.

■ **Section 10.2—time-dependent options.** Options whose payoffs are the function of the price of a vanilla option at a single future time. As in Section 10.1, we will show how to eliminate all risk of underlying price movement for these exotics by replication using forwards and vanilla options. The residual risk exposure to implied volatility at a future time can be quasistatically hedged with vanilla options. These exotics include forward start options, cliquet options, chooser options, and compound options.

■ **Section 10.3—path-dependent options.** Options whose payoff depends on the price of a single underlying asset at several future times. We will focus on barrier options, but also use the lessons learned to apply to ladder, lookback, double barrier, and partial-time barrier options. We will examine and contrast replication approaches that utilize dynamical hedging with vanilla options and approaches that permit quasistatic hedging with vanilla options.

■ **Section 10.4—correlation-dependent options.** Options whose payoff depends on the prices of several underlying assets securities and that therefore must be priced based on assumptions about correlations. We will examine several important cases: basket forwards and options, quanto forwards and options, diff swaps, mortgage-backed securities, collateralized debt obligations (CDOs), and convertible bonds.

■ **Section 10.5—correlation-dependent interest rate options.** A particular subset of correlation-dependent options are options whose payoffs depend on multiple future interest rates. This includes the important special case of American and Bermudan swaptions.

10.1 SINGLE-PAYOUT OPTIONS

In continuous time finance, the Breeden-Litzenberger theorem states that any option whose payout is a smooth function of a terminal forward price can be perfectly replicated by an (infinite) package of forwards and plain vanilla calls and puts (see Carr and Madan [2002, Section II.A]). The discrete time version states that any option whose payout is a smooth function of a terminal forward price can be replicated as closely as desired by a (finite) package of forwards and plain vanilla calls and puts, with the tightness of fit of the replication dependent on the number of vanilla calls and puts in the package. In both cases, replication is static, meaning the forwards and vanilla calls and puts are purchased at the deal inception and then no further hedging is needed. The terminal payout on the replicating package will match the terminal payout of the exotic option.

The discrete time result can be established in two stages:

- Any smooth function can be approximated as closely as desired by a piecewise-linear function. The tightness of fit depends on the number of pieces of the replication.
- Each piece of a piecewise-linear function can be replicated by adding another vanilla option to a package of options that replicates all of the pieces up to that point. This can be easily seen from an example.

  Consider a function that pays out nothing at prices 100 or below, pays out $2 for every $1 gain in price up to $102, pays out $3.5 for every $1 gain in price from $102 to $105, and pays out $2.3 for every $1 gain in price above $105. This payout can be replicated by buying 2 calls at $100 and 1.5 calls at $102, and selling 1.2 calls at $105, as shown in Table 10.2.

The **BasketHedge** spreadsheet on the accompanying CD-ROM enables you to calculate the vanilla option hedges and the associated valuations based on this discrete time approach. The impact of smiles and skews in the volatility surface of the vanilla options on the valuation of the exotic options can be readily calculated using this spreadsheet.

Even if this is not selected as a desirable hedge from a trading viewpoint, it still makes sense as a way to represent the trade from a risk-management viewpoint for the following reasons:

- It permits realistic valuation based on liquid, public prices. Alternative valuation procedures would utilize an analytic pricing model, which is usually easily derivable, but a level of volatility needs to be assumed

TABLE 10.2 Vanilla Options Replication of a Piecewise-Linear Payout

Price	Payout	+2 Calls at 100	+1.5 Calls at 102	−1.2 Calls at 105
100	0.0	0.0	0.0	0
102	4.0	4.0	0.0	0
105	14.5	10.0	4.5	0
110	26.0	20.0	12.0	−6.0

and no straightforward procedure is available for deriving this volatility from observed market volatilities of vanilla options at different strikes. The hedge package method will converge to this analytic solution as you increase the number of vanilla option hedges used, provided all vanilla options are priced at a flat volatility (it is recommended that this comparison always be made as a check on the accuracy of the implementation of the hedging package method). However, the hedging package method has the flexibility to price the exotic option based on any observed volatility surface (in fact, instead of using the volatility surface, the directly observed vanilla option prices are used, so the pricing is not dependent on any option model).

- The hedge package method gives an easy means of integrating exotic options into standard risk reports, such as price-vol matrices and vega exposure by strike and maturity. Placing as much risk as possible within a single context also increases the chances that risks from one position may offset risks in another position. Only the net risks need to be managed. (See the arguments for requiring internal hedging in Section 5.2.)

- Although the representation will be incomplete due to the use of a finite package of vanilla options, the residual risk can be easily calculated based on an assumed probability distribution of final forward prices multiplied by the amount of mishedge. This is an easier calculation of remaining risk than the analytic method, which requires a Monte Carlo simulation of dynamic hedging.

One objection that is sometimes raised to the static hedging strategy for exotic options is that the required basket of vanilla options is unrealistic, in terms of using options at strikes that have little market liquidity, in terms of the number of different options in the basket, or in terms of the required odd lots of individual options.

Although this objection may have validity in the context of a proposed actual hedge to be placed against a particular deal, it does not carry much force in the context of risk management, in which hedging strategies are utilized as devices for representing risk in standard reports. The tools for managing vanilla European options within a portfolio framework are well established. As was pointed out when discussing dynamic hedging in Section 9.3, good empirical evidence exists that vanilla options at less liquid strikes when statically hedged with vanilla options at more liquid strikes result in dynamic hedging strategies that achieve far greater stability than pure dynamic hedging strategies. As a result, we would argue that risk managers should not hesitate to represent exotic option trades as baskets of vanilla options in a vanilla options portfolio risk report. The advantages are parallel to those cited at the beginning of Section 8.2 for representing an illiquid forward as a static combination of liquid swaps—unified risk reporting increases risk transparency, maximizing liquidity and minimizing transaction costs.

The one point of legitimate concern would be if the resulting representation would be a position too large to be managed with the existing market liquidity. This would be an argument against representing a binary option as a very large position in a very narrow call spread. Instead, liquidity considerations should limit the size of the call spread position that is used as a representation, which in turn limits the narrowness of the call spread used. The resulting residual risks must be managed by the exotics desk through a combination of limits and reserves. We discuss this approach in more detail in Section 10.1.4. Another example would be if the representation revealed heavy reliance on very high- or low-strike vanilla options outside the range at which the firm's vanilla option traders would be comfortable managing the residual risk against more liquid strikes. Note that in both cases, the method of representing exotics exposure as a basket of vanilla options has the advantage of highlighting the regions of illiquidity impacting the exotic, a focus that many analytic pricing methods lack.

These points hold generally for the replication of exotic derivatives with vanilla options. By representing the exotic derivative as closely as possible with a hedge package of vanilla options, you can minimize the remaining basis risk that needs to be managed using techniques specific to the exotic derivative and maximize the amount of risk that can be combined with and managed as part of the vanilla options book, utilizing established risk-management tools such as the price-vol matrix.

Examples of options that can be risk managed in this way are calls on the square, cube, square root, or other power of the excess above a strike, or the corresponding puts. Other mathematical functions, such as the logarithm of the excess above or below a strike are also possible. This style of option, sometimes collectively known as *power options*, has largely fallen out of favor following the Banker's Trust (BT)/Proctor & Gamble (P&G)/ Gibson Greetings blowup of 1994, which is discussed in Section 4.3.1. The lawsuits and allegations prompted by large losses on contracts with complex payoff formulas with no discernible tie to any of the end user's economic motives led to a distrust of such derivatives. Currently, most market makers' client appropriateness rules only permit such contracts in very limited circumstances.

Nonetheless, some power options remain in active use. The most prominent are *log contracts*, which are of particular interest because of their link to valuing and hedging variance swaps, and a type of quanto option that is utilized in the FX and bullion markets. In addition, the convexity adjustments needed for valuing and hedging certain types of forward risk, which we discuss in Section 8.2.4, can usefully be viewed as a type of power option and managed by this technique. We will examine each of these three cases. We will follow this with an examination of the important case of binary options, which illustrate the issue of how to handle liquidity risk arising from static replication. Finally, we will show how binary options can be combined with vanilla options to create other exotics—a contingent premium option and an accrual swap.

10.1.1   Log Contracts and Variance Swaps

A *variance swap* is a forward contract on annualized variance whose payout at expiry is:

$$(\sigma_\rho^2 - K_{VAR}) \times N \qquad (10.1)$$

where σ_ρ^2 is the realized stock variance (quoted in annualized terms) over the life of the contract, K_{VAR} is the delivery price for variance, and N is the notional amount of the swap in dollars per annualized volatility point squared. The holder of a variance swap at expiry receives N dollars for every point by which the stock's realized variance, σ_ρ^2, has exceeded the variance delivery price, K_{VAR}, and pays N dollars for every point by which the stock's realized variance, σ_ρ^2, falls short of the variance delivery price, K_{VAR}. This contract can be generalized to assets other than stocks and amounts other than dollars.

Variance swaps give the holder a vega exposure similar to what she would have by purchasing a vanilla option. However, variance swaps differ from vanilla options in that their vega exposure remains constant over time, whereas vanilla options may go into or out of the money, reducing their vega exposure. This can be a significant advantage to a position taker whose main concern is to find an investment that expresses her economic view of future volatility. It also has the advantage of enabling her to avoid maintaining delta and gamma hedges, which will be seen as a distraction to the real intention, which is just to express a volatility view. The downside is the relative illiquidity of variance swaps versus vanilla options, leading to their being priced with wider bid-ask spreads. The log contract offers a means to link the hedging and valuation of the illiquid variance swap to that of liquid vanilla options, using the basket hedge methodology.

The link between the variance swap and the log contract comes from the following analytic formula for the value of a log contract:

$$ln\ F - 1/2 \int_0^T \sigma^2 dT \qquad (10.2)$$

where ln is the natural logarithm function, F is the current price of the underlying forward to contract expiry T and σ^2 is actual realized variance over that time period. This formula is a direct consequence of Equations 10 and

11 in Demeterfli et al. (1999). A derivation can also be found in Neuberger (1996). Under the Black-Scholes assumptions of known constant volatility, this implies that the log contract should be valued at $\ln F - 1/2\,\sigma^2 T$, an analytic formula used in the **BasketHedge** spreadsheet to check the value derived for the log contract when the volatility surface is flat.

Since we can use the spreadsheet to find a set of vanilla options to replicate the log contract, we now have a hedging strategy for a variance swap. Buy a replicating set of vanilla options for twice the volume of log contracts as the volume of variance swaps sold (twice the volume in order to counteract the $1/2$ in front of the integral in the formula). Delta hedge these vanilla options. Since the log contract is losing value at exactly the rate of $1/2 \int_0^T \sigma^2 dT$, the delta hedging should be producing profits at exactly the rate needed to cover payments on the variance swap.

In practice, this will not work exactly, due to jumps in underlying prices, as explained in Demeterfli et al. (1999, "Hedging Risks"). Monte Carlo simulation would be necessary to quantify the risk of this tracking error. However, the replication of the log contract still offers a good first-order hedge and valuation for the variance swap.

The section "The Difficulty with Volatility Contracts" in the same article discusses why this approach will not work for *volatility swaps*, which differ from variance swaps by having a payout of $(\sigma_p - K_{\mathrm{VOL}}) \times N$ rather than $(\sigma_p^2 - K_{\mathrm{VAR}}) \times N$. No static hedge for the volatility contract exists. In the categorization we are using in this chapter, it is path dependent and needs to be risk managed using the techniques of Section 10.3, utilizing local volatility or stochastic volatility models to determine dynamic hedges. However, its close relation to the variance swap, and thus to the log contract, suggests the use of a control variate approach: Use dynamic hedging just for the difference between the volatility swap and log contract while static hedging the log contract.

Exercise 10.1 asks you to utilize the **BasketHedge** spreadsheet to look at the impact of changes in the volatility surface on the valuation of log contracts and hence on variance swaps. Demeterfli et al. (1999) also has an instructive section on the "Effects of the Volatility Skew" on variance swaps. Log contracts and variance swaps require hedges over a very wide range of strikes and should therefore show valuation sensitivity across the whole volatility surface. This seems reasonable from an intuitive standpoint since changes in volatility impact variance swaps even when the underlying forward price has moved very far away from the current price, leaving a currently at-the-money option very insensitive to vega. So high- and low-strike vanilla options are needed to retain the vega sensitivity of the package.

10.1.2 Single-Asset Quanto Options

In Section 10.4.5, we discuss dual-currency quanto derivatives in which the percentage change of an asset denominated in one currency is paid out in another currency. For example, a 10 percent increase in the yen price of a Japanese stock will be reflected by a 10 percent increase in a dollar payment at a fixed-in-advance dollar/yen exchange rate. We will see that the forward price of a quanto is the standard forward multiplied by $\exp(\rho\sigma_S\sigma_F)$, where exp is the exponential to the base e, σ_S is the standard deviation of the asset price, σ_F is the standard deviation of the FX rate, and ρ is the correlation between them.

A related product is a single-currency quanto derivative in which the asset whose percentage change is to be calculated is also the asset whose exchange rate is fixed. Here are two examples:

- A dollar/yen FX option, which, if the yen rises in value by 10 percent relative to the dollar, will be reflected by a 10 percent payout in yen. Since the yen has gone up in value by 10 percent versus the dollar, the payout in dollar terms is $110\% \times 10\% = 11\%$. In general, for a $p\%$ increase, the payout is $(1 + p\%) \times p\% = p\% + p^2\%$.
- A dollar/gold option struck at $300 per ounce. If gold rises in value by 10 percent to $330 per ounce, the payment is 1 ounce $\times$ 10 percent = .1 ounces of gold. The payout in dollars is therefore .1 $\times$ $330 = $33, which is $300 $\times$ 11%. In general, for a p% increase in gold prices, the payout is $p\% + p^2\%$.

Since just a single asset is involved, the σ_S and σ_F in the quanto formula are the same and ρ is equal to 1, so the standard forward is multiplied by $\exp(\sigma_S^2)$. The **BasketHedge** spreadsheet has a worksheet called **Quanto** that calculates the value of a single-asset quanto using a static hedge basket of vanilla options. As you can see from the spreadsheet, the hedge consists of 101 percent of a standard call at the quanto strike plus calls of 2 percent of the notional at all strike levels above the quanto strike. This gives a payoff, if the asset rises by $p\%$, of $101\% \times p\% + 2\% \times \sum_{i=1}^{p-1} i = 101\% \times p\% + 2\% \times \frac{p^2 - p}{2} = p\% + p^2\%$. When the static hedge cost is computed from a flat volatility surface, the results agree exactly with an analytic formula derived from the forward multiplied by $\exp(\sigma_S^2)$. If higher volatilities are assumed for higher strikes, the cost of the basket hedge will exceed the cost derived from the analytic formula. If lower volatilities are assumed for higher strikes, the cost of the basket hedge will be less than the cost derived from the analytic formula.

10.1.3 Convexity

In Section 8.2.4, on applying mathematical models of forward risk to indexed flows, we raised the issue of convexity or nonlinearity of some index flows and the complications this can entail for valuing and hedging these flows. We pointed out the availability of analytic formulas that approximate the convexity adjustments needed to account for the impact on valuation of the nonlinearity of these flows. These approximation formulas (see formulas 22.15, 22.16, 22.18, 23.32, and 25.3 in Hull [2002]) all require an interest rate volatility as a key input. However, in a world of nonflat volatility surfaces, which implied volatility should be used? Equivalently, what are the strikes of the options contracts that should be used to hedge this exposure?

The basket-hedging methodology we have developed in this section provides a more precise valuation for convexity adjustments, one that is sensitive to the shape of the volatility surface, and also provides details of the required hedge that can be used to represent the exposure in conventional vanilla option position reports, as shown in the **Convexity** worksheet within the **BasketHedge** spreadsheet.

10.1.4 Binary Options

European *binary options* (also known as *digital options* or *bet options*) have highly discontinuous payoffs. The basic form, the *cash-or-nothing option*, which we will focus on in this section, pays either zero if the price finishes below the strike or a set amount if the price finishes above the strike. A variant, the *asset-or-nothing option*, pays zero if the price finishes below the strike or the ending price if the price finishes above the strike. An asset-or-nothing option is simply the sum of a standard vanilla option and a cash-or-nothing option at the same strike that pays the strike price. Table 10.3 illustrates the payouts.

European binary options fulfill the condition of having a payout that is a function of the price of an asset at one definite time. Therefore, it can be treated by the methodology just stated, using a basket of vanilla options to hedge it and using this hedge package to calculate valuation, including skew

TABLE 10.3 Payouts of a Binary Option

Final Price $= S$	Vanilla Call, Strike $= K$	Cash-or-Nothing Call, Strike $= K$, Payout $= K$	Asset-or-Nothing Call, Strike $= K$
$S \leq K$	0	0	0
$S > K$	$S{-}K$	K	S

impact, to calculate remaining risk, and to be incorporated into standard risk reports. However, the discontinuous nature of the payment at the strike leads either to unrealistically large hedge positions in vanilla calls (liquidity risk, since market prices would be impacted by an attempt to transact so many calls) or significant hedge slippage (basis risk) between the binary option and its hedge.

For example, let's say a customer approaches a trading desk wanting to buy a 1-year binary call that will pay $10 million if the Standards and Poor's (S&P) index is above the current 1-year forward level at the end of 1 year and nothing otherwise. The vanilla option decomposition of a barrier option is particularly simple. It can be represented as a call spread between two vanilla options of equal notional size. Assume you buy a vanilla call at a strike just below the current forward level and sell a vanilla option at a strike just above this level with a spread of .01 percent of the price between the two options. You will need to receive $10 million if the index rises by .01 percent above the first strike, since for any index move above the second strike, you are paying as much on the second option as you are receiving on the first. So the notional amount of the call to be bought and sold is $10 million/.01% = $100 billion.

Let us start by assuming that all vanilla calls are priced at a 20 percent flat implied volatility. The straight analytical formula for the value of the binary is the amount to be paid $\times N(d_2)$, the term in the Black-Scholes equation for a vanilla option that gives the risk-neutral probability that the price will finish above the strike. In this case, we have:

$$\$10 \text{ million} \times N(d_2), \text{ where } d_2 = \left(ln(price/strike) - \frac{1}{2}\sigma^2 t \right)/\sigma\sqrt{t}$$

$$= \left(ln(1) - \frac{1}{2}20\%^2 \right)/20\% = 10\% \ N(-.1) = .46017, \text{ giving a price of}$$

the binary of $4,601,700 \hfill (10.3)

Replicating the binary option using a vanilla call spread, the exact choice of vanilla calls to be used makes virtually no difference to the price (as long as we assume a flat implied volatility), but it does make a significant difference to the mix between liquidity risk and basis risk. For example:

- Buy a vanilla call on $100 billion at a strike of 99.995% of the forward level at a price of $BS(99.995\%, 1, 20\%) = 7.9678802\%$ for $100 billion $\times 7.9678802\% = \$7,967,880,200$ and sell a vanilla call on $100 billion at a strike of 100.005% of the forward level at a price of $BS(100.005\%, 1, 20\%) = 7.9632785\%$ for $7,963,278,500, for a net cost of $7,967,880,200 − $7,963,278,500 = $4,601,700.

- Buy a vanilla call on $2 billion at a strike of 99.75% of the forward level at a price of $BS(99.75\%, 1, 20\%) = 8.0812430\%$ for $161,624,900 and sell a vanilla call on $2 billion at a strike of 100.25% of the forward level at a price of $BS(100.25\%, 1, 20\%) = 7.8511554\%$ for $157,023,100, for a net cost of $4,601,800.
- Buy a vanilla call on $500 million at a strike of 99% of the forward level at a price of $BS(99\%, 1, 20\%) = 8.4357198\%$ for $42,178,600 and sell a vanilla call on $500 million at a strike of 101% of the forward level at a price of $BS(101\%, 1, 20\%) = 7.5152765\%$ for $37,576,400, for a net cost of $4,602,200.

Note the inverse relationship between the width of the call spread (.01 percent, .50 percent, and 2 percent, respectively) and the size of the legs of the call spread ($100 billion, $2 billion, and $500 million, respectively).

The first combination offers the smallest basis risk. It will replicate the binary option exactly as long as the S&P index at the end of 1 year is outside the range 99.995% − 100.005%—that is, as long as the S&P index does not finish within about one-half basis point of its current forward level. However, liquidity risk is heavy—purchases and sales in the size of $100 billion would be certain to move market prices if they could be accomplished at all. (Even if the trading desk does not expect to actually buy this call spread, its use in representing the risk profile of the trade will lead to illiquid dynamic hedging requirements.) At the other end of the spectrum, the third combination is of a size that could possibly be transacted without major market movement, but basis risk is now much larger. Exact replication of the binary option only takes place in a range outside 99% − 101% of the current forward, so there are about 100 basis points of market movement on either side of the current forward level in which replication would be inexact. And replication could be *very* inexact. If the index ended at 100.1% of the forward, for example, the customer would be owed $10 million, but the vanilla call at 99% would only pay $500 million × 1.1% = $5.5 million, a net loss of $4.5 million.

Of course, the basis risk can be dynamically hedged with purchases and sales of S&P futures. However, the large payment discontinuity of the binary can lead to unmanageable hedging situations. For example, suppose you are close to expiration and the S&P is 1 basis point below the forward level. If no further movement occurs, you will make about $4.95 million ([99.99% − 99%] × $500 million) on the vanilla call and owe nothing on the binary, but an uptick of just 2 basis points will lead to a loss of about $5 million. Should you put on a delta hedge of a size that will make $5 million for a 2-basis-point uptick? The problem is that a position of this size will cost you $10 million for a 4-basis-point downtick, and you do not gain anything from option payouts to offset this loss. Although in theory, in a world of complete liquidity and no transaction costs, you could put on this hedge only at the exact moment you approach the binary strike and take it off as soon as you move away from that strike; in practice, such strategies are wholly implausible. The actual experience of trading desks caught needing to delta hedge a sizable binary position that happens to be near the strike as expiration approaches is excruciatingly painful. Traders have their choice of gambles, but they must decide on a large bet in one direction or another.

In light of this, risk managers will always seek to place some sort of controls on binary positions. These controls, which may be complementary, come in the form of both limits and reserves. Limits are placed on the size of the loss that can occur for a certain size price move, the maximum delta position that can be required for a hedge, or the maximum gamma (the change in delta) that can be required for a given price move. Delta and gamma limits are based on the anticipated liquidity and transaction costs of the underlying market in which hedging is being done. Limits on loss size are designed to enable traders to take a purely insurance approach to binaries, hoping to come out ahead in the long run. This requires that no one binary be too large. Such an approach needs to be combined with eliminating binaries close to a strike and expiration from delta and gamma reports, so that delta hedging is not attempted. It also requires decisions about how binaries should be combined for limit purposes.

To operate like insurance, binaries need to be widely scattered as to maturity date and strike level, and limits need to bucket strikes and maturities in a manner that forces this scattering. However, bucketing should only combine binaries in one direction (bought or sold)—it is dangerous to permit the netting of one binary with another except when date and strike (and any other contract terms, such as a precise definition of the index) exactly match.

A valuation and reserve policy should also be consistent with the insurance approach to binaries—profit and loss (P&L) should be recognized only to the extent it can come close to being locked in. Gains that have great uncertainty attached to them should only be recognized when realized. This can be accomplished with several methods. I will provide a detailed example of a method that I consider particularly elegant in its capability to balance liquidity and basis risks, its maximal use of static hedge information, and its good fit with dynamic hedging risk reporting. In this approach, every binary has an internal representation assigned to it that is designed to be as close as possible to the binary in its payouts while still being capable of liquid hedging and conservative relative to the binary in that the internal representation will always produce a lower P&L for the firm than the binary. All risk reports for the firm are based on the internal representation, not the true representation of the binary. The valuation difference between the true and internal representation, which by design must always be a positive value to the firm, is booked to a reserve account. Since the reserve is always positive, this policy sometimes results in the firm recognizing windfall profits, but never windfall losses.

Let's see how this policy would work in the case we have been considering. A call spread is selected as the internal representation of the binary by choosing the smallest spread that results in a position size that is considered to be small enough to be liquid, either by representing a real possibility for purchase in the market or by being representable in the firm's risk reports by delta positions that can be achieved with reasonable liquidity. However, rather than choosing a call spread that straddles the binary, and therefore has payouts greater than the binary in some scenarios, we choose a call spread that is on one side of the binary and therefore always has payouts greater than the binary. If 2 percent is the width of the call spread we select as the smallest consistent with a liquid position, then we use as an internal representation a call spread consisting of a sale of $500 million at a strike of 98 percent and a purchase of $500 million at a strike of 100 percent (notice that the internal representation has the opposite sign from the hedge that would extinguish it). The resulting valuation would be $500 million $\times BS(98\%, 1, 20\%) - \$500$ million $\times BS(100\%, 1, 20\%) = \$500$ million $\times 8.9259724\% - \$500$ million $\times 7.9655791\% = \$44,629,900 - \$39,827,900 = \$4,802,000$. This is the valuation of the internal representation. The actual binary continues to be valued at $4,601,700—the difference of $200,300 is placed into a reserve. If the actual sale price of the binary to a customer is $5 million, then only $200,000 of the profit from the difference between the price and valuation goes into immediate P&L recognition; the other $200,000 goes into a reserve against anticipated liquidity costs of managing the binary risk.

What happens to this reserve? There are several possibilities:

- The firm might decide to actually buy the static overhedge, which costs $4,802,000. The internal hedge reports of the firm will not show the net position between the internal representation of the binary and the actual call spread hedge. If the S&P index ends up below 98 percent or above 100 percent, no difference will appear between the eventual payout under the binary and the payin due to the call spread, and the reserve will end up at zero. If the S&P index ends up between 98 and 100 percent, the call spread will have a payin while the binary has no payout. For example, if the S&P index ends at 99 percent, the call spread will pay $5 million, which will be the final value of the reserve. At expiry of the options, this $5 million will be recognized in P&L as a windfall gain.
- The firm might not do any static hedging and just delta hedge based on the internal representation of the static overhedge. Since the static

overhedge was selected to be of a size that enables liquid delta hedging, the results in this case should be close to the results in the case that the static overhedge is actually purchased, but with some relatively small variance. As an example, suppose that we are very close to expiry and the S&P index forward is at 99 percent. Based on the internal representation of the call spread overhedge, the appropriate delta will be a full $500 million long in the S&P index forward and roughly $5 million in dynamic hedging profits should already have been realized but held in reserve. If the index ends at 99 percent, the $5 million in dynamic hedging profits will be taken from the reserve and recognized in P&L as a windfall gain. If the index ends just above 100 percent, the $5 million in dynamic hedging profits realized to date plus the $5 million gain from the 1 percent increase on the $500 million long in the S&P index will be exactly enough to pay the $10 million owed on the binary. Note that keeping the $5 million in dynamic hedging profits realized to date in reserve is necessary to avoid having to reverse a previously recognized gain in order to pay off on the binary.

- Other combinations are possible, such as static hedges that are not overhedges, but all produce similar results.

This technique of representing a binary internally as a static overhedge is sometimes objected to by front-office personnel as trading off a very probable gain in order to achieve security. In this view, the $400,000 that was originally realized on the transaction was real P&L and $200,000 was sacrificed in order to achieve security in the very small minority of cases in which the index finishes very close to the strike. The idea that $200,000 has been thrown away is, in fact, an optical illusion caused by focusing only on those cases in which the index finishes outside the 99 to 101 percent range. The trade still has a $400,000 expected value—it just consists of a sure $200,000 in the vast majority of cases in which the index finishes outside 99% − 101% and a set of windfall profits up to $10 million when the index finishes within this range. The front-office view would be correct if some means were available, such as dynamic hedging, of being almost sure of achieving this $400,000 result in all cases. But it was exactly the lack of such means—the fact that the use of dynamic hedging to try coming close to achieving $400,000 in all cases results in some cases with disastrous losses, which caused us to seek an alternative approach. This reserve methodology can be seen as being consistent with moving the front office away from viewing these trades as normal derivatives trades that can be approached in an isolated manner and toward viewing them as necessarily being part of a widely diversified portfolio of binaries. In this context, over a long enough time period, the sum of occasional windfall gains can become a steady source of income. If limits can ensure a wide enough diversification, then reserves may not be necessary.

So far in the example we have assumed a lack of volatility skew. In the presence of skew, the binary will price quite differently. Let's see the impact of using a 20.25 percent implied volatility for a strike of 99 percent and a 20 percent volatility for a strike of 101 percent. The cost of the 99% vanilla call is now $BS(99\%, 1, 20.25\%) = 8.534331\%$, resulting in a net cost of $5,095,274. Just as with the cases previously discussed, the reduction to a package of vanilla options lets us pick up the impact of volatility skew. We can see that binary options are highly sensitive to skew.

Taleb (1997, Chapter 17) gives a lucid discussion of the practical aspects of hedging binary options. On page 286, Taleb says "the best replication for a binary is a wide risk reversal (that would include any protection against skew). There will be a trade-off between transaction costs and optimal hedges. The trader needs to shrink the difference between the strikes as time progresses until expiration, at a gradual pace. As such an optimal approach consumes transaction costs, there is a need for infrequent hedging." Using a call spread (also known as a *risk reversal*) that is wide reduces the size of the vanilla options that are needed, reducing transaction costs and liquidity concerns, and also capturing the volatility skew more accurately, since a wide spread could utilize more liquid strikes. As we have seen, the width of the spread should not materially impact the total hedge cost.

In many cases, the underlying price will finish nowhere near the strike and no further transactions are needed. However, in those cases where the underlying is threatening to finish close to the strike, the basis risk will get too large and the trader will need to roll from the original call spread into a tighter call spread, incurring transaction costs due to the need to purchase and sell options and because the size of the options transactions is growing as the spread narrows. Factoring this potential transaction cost into the valuation of binary options is an alternative method for establishing a valuation reserve on a binary. As Taleb (1997, p. 286) states, "when the bet option is away from expiration, the real risks are the skew. As it nears expiration, the risks transfer to the pin. In practice, the skew is hedgable, the pin is not." (We have been using *basis risk* for what Taleb terms the *pin risk*.)

10.1.5 Contingent Premium Options

A contingent premium option entails no initial payment by the option buyer, who only pays at option termination under the circumstances that the option finishes in the money. This type of option is popular with some clients because of the deferral of cash payment and because the client will not need to pay for an option that turns out to be "useless," although it should be noted that an option that finishes just slightly in the money will still require a net payment by the option buyer, since the payment due from the option seller will be less than the option's cost. It is easy to see that a contingent premium option is just a standard vanilla option plus a forward to defer payment of the option premium plus a binary option to offset the option premium due in the event the price finishes below the strike of the vanilla option.

10.1.6 Accrual Swaps

Accrual swaps are swaps where interest on one side accrues only when the reference rate is within a given range (see Hull [2002, Section 25.6]). An accrual swap can be represented as a package of binary caps and floors since interest accruing is an all-or-nothing event. Being above the floor rate requires the payment and being above the cap rate cancels the payment, which can be represented by a payment with the opposite sign.

10.2 TIME-DEPENDENT OPTIONS

Now that we have provided a methodology for hedging and valuing the price of a linear underlying instrument at a single future point, we will extend that approach to exotic options whose payoff depends on the price of a vanilla option at a single future point. This dependence on a vanilla option's future price can be decomposed into dependence on the price of the underlying of the vanilla option and dependence on its implied volatility. We can hedge the first element of this decomposition by a direct application of the methodology of the last section, leaving only dependence on implied volatility. To see how to hedge this piece, let us first look at an exotic that is only dependent on implied volatility and has no dependence on the underlying price.

10.2.1 Forward Starting and Cliquet Options

A *forward start option* is specifically constructed to have its price depend entirely on the at-the-money implied volatility of a vanilla option at a specified time. For example, a forward start option could be sold on April 1, 2003 for a 1-year at-the-money option to buy 1,000 shares of IBM that starts on November 1, 2003. The strike of the option will be set on November 1, 2003 at the then underlying price. Hence, no underlying price exposure exists prior to November 1, 2003, and the only exposure prior to that time is to what implied volatility the at-the-money option will sell at on November 1, 2003.

A *cliquet option* is a package of forward start options, usually with one starting just as the previous one expires. For example, a cliquet might consist of 3-month forward start options beginning March 10, June 10, September 10, and December 10, 2003. Since the payoff on each option in the package is determined independently of any other option in the package, a cliquet can be valued by valuing each forward start option separately and then summing.

A natural approach would be to consider valuing a forward start option with an extension of the method we used to roll into a longer-term option (see Section 9.6.3). The only difference is that we need to set up the target price-vol profile that we want to achieve as that of an at-the-money option, regardless of the underlying price level. The accompanying **ForwardStart** spreadsheet shows the details. The essential point is that the difference in the price of the at-the-money option at two different implied volatility levels, σ_1 and σ_2, can just be represented as $BS(100\%, T, \sigma_1) - BS(100\%, T, \sigma_2)$, where T is the tenor of the at-the-money option to be created. Optimal fitting can then find the combination of current options that has close to the desired profile of volatility exposure at the time the forward start expires and the at-the-money option begins.

If you look at the example given in Figure 10.1, you will find that the package of current options that creates the desired profile has a significant weighting at many different strike levels, so it will vary in valuation based on both the current smile and current skew. This is not surprising, given that we are creating an option that has flat exposure to future implied volatility levels at all strikes. The situation parallels that of the log contract, which has flat exposure to variance.

10.2.2 Compound Options

It is now quite straightforward to extend this approach to exotics that depend on both underlying and implied volatility. A call-on-a-call option is one example of a *compound option*, which gives the purchaser of the compound option the right to buy (or sell) a particular vanilla option at a given strike price. It is also known as a *split-fee option* because a major selling point is that a customer who may want an option but is not willing to invest that much in one can put up a smaller down payment to defer his decision. Analytical formulas for compound options, assuming flat volatility surfaces and constant volatility, are well known (see Hull [2002, Section 19.4]). I will make use of these formulas to work through an illustrative example.

Let's say that a customer wants to buy a 1-year at-the-money call on 100 million euro on April 1, 2003 expiring on April 1, 2004. Assuming 20 percent implied volatility, the cost would be 7.97 percent of the principal amount. We'll assume the at-the-money euro exchange rate is $.90. The customer might prefer to pay 4.45 percent to get an option that can be exercised on November 1, 2003. On that date, the customer can either pay 5 percent to get a call on 100 million euro at a strike of $.90 expiring on April 1, 2004, or can choose to let the option expire. The attraction to the customer is that if the euro declines in value by November 1, 2003, the option

FIGURE 10.1 Hedge at rollover of a 1-year option with a forward start in 2 years.

Parameters:

Discount	5.00%
Spacing	5
Volatility	2%

Portfolio and option details (Time in Years):

	Portfolio											
Volume		-1	-1.8054	6.9829	-5.9652	2.7291	0.3272	-0.9075	2.2714	-5.8165	4.9924	-2.3706
call/put		call	call	call	call	call	call	call	call	call	call	call
Price		100	100	100	100	100	100	100	100	100	100	100
Strike		100	80	90	100	110	120	80	90	100	110	120
Time		1	2	2	2	2	2	1	1	1	1	1
Implied vol		20.0%	20.0%	20.0%	20.0%	20.0%	20.0%	20.0%	20.0%	20.0%	20.0%	20.0%
BS price	0.12%	-7.58%	-37.71%	103.69%	-60.70%	18.44%	1.43%	-18.29%	29.36%	-44.07%	20.38%	-4.84%
Delta	30.3%	0.0%	-148.7%	486.3%	-331.8%	115.3%	10.1%	-80.6%	166.9%	-314.0%	176.4%	-49.4%
Vega	0.12%	-0.38%	-0.61%	3.13%	-3.01%	1.37%	0.15%	-0.17%	0.71%	-2.20%	1.77%	-0.66%
Gamma	0.0%	0.0%	-1.7%	8.6%	-8.3%	3.8%	0.4%	-0.9%	3.7%	-11.5%	9.3%	-3.4%
Theta	0.001%	0.000%	0.011%	-0.060%	0.058%	-0.026%	-0.003%	0.006%	-0.027%	0.085%	-0.068%	0.025%
Current	0.105%	-6.86%	-34.12%	93.82%	-54.93%	16.69%	1.29%	-16.55%	26.57%	-39.88%	18.44%	-4.38%

Spot-vol matrix

Price	Implied volatilities									Vega	Vega convexity
	-8%	-6%	-4%	-2%	0%	2%	4%	6%	8%		
-25	0.52%	0.39%	0.28%	0.18%	0.07%	-0.03%	-0.12%	-0.22%	-0.31%	-0.05%	0.00%
-20	-0.14%	-0.06%	-0.04%	-0.04%	-0.07%	-0.10%	-0.14%	-0.17%	-0.22%	-0.01%	0.01%
-15	-0.30%	-0.18%	-0.13%	-0.10%	-0.09%	-0.08%	-0.08%	-0.09%	-0.10%	0.00%	0.01%
-10	-0.12%	-0.10%	-0.09%	-0.07%	-0.05%	-0.03%	-0.01%	0.01%	0.02%	0.01%	0.00%
-5	0.13%	0.02%	-0.03%	-0.03%	-0.01%	0.01%	0.05%	0.08%	0.11%	0.01%	-0.01%
0	0.23%	0.06%	-0.01%	-0.02%	0.00%	0.04%	0.08%	0.12%	0.16%	0.02%	-0.02%
5	0.16%	0.02%	-0.03%	-0.04%	-0.01%	0.03%	0.08%	0.13%	0.18%	0.02%	-0.01%
10	0.02%	-0.04%	-0.07%	-0.07%	-0.04%	0.00%	0.05%	0.11%	0.16%	0.02%	-0.01%
15	-0.03%	-0.06%	-0.09%	-0.09%	-0.07%	-0.03%	0.01%	0.06%	0.12%	0.01%	0.00%
20	0.07%	0.00%	-0.05%	-0.08%	-0.08%	-0.07%	-0.04%	0.01%	0.06%	0.00%	0.00%
25	0.32%	0.17%	0.05%	-0.02%	-0.07%	-0.08%	-0.08%	-0.05%	-0.01%	-0.01%	-0.01%

will seem unattractive and he will have saved money by having paid only 4.45 percent rather than 7.97 percent for the original option. He will only pay more than 4.45 percent if the option really turns out to be valuable. Of course, the downside is that if he does want the option, he will have paid a total of 4.45% + 5.00% = 9.45% for it rather than 7.97%.

When the call-on-a-call option expires on November 1, 2003, the value of the call option that the customer must now decide to purchase or let expire is determined by both the price of the underlying euro exchange rate (forward to April 4, 2004) and the implied volatility for a 6-month option on the euro struck at $.90. The basket hedging procedure used in Section 10.1 can find a set of vanilla option hedges that eliminate the risk of the uncertainty of the underlying euro exchange rate. However, exposure to the uncertainty of the 6-month implied volatility on November 1, 2003 will remain. This implied volatility exposure can be hedged by the same option roll approach used in Section 10.2.1. The **Compound** worksheet of the **BasketHedge** spreadsheet calculates the vanilla option hedge against the underlying price and also calculates the price-vol matrix exposure of the resulting hedged position. This price-vol matrix can then be used as input to the **ForwardStartOption** spreadsheet to compute a hedge on the residual forward starting volatility risk.

Exercise 10.1 takes you through pricing this call-on-a-call option in the **BasketHedge** spreadsheet. For a flat volatility surface, the basket hedge reproduces the analytical value, but different valuations are produced in the presence of smile and/or skew. Further steps in the exercise have you utilize the spreadsheet to calculate hedges and valuations for other compound options and chooser options in which the decision on whether an option should be a call or a put can be deferred.

10.3 PATH-DEPENDENT OPTIONS

So far we've dealt strictly with exotic options whose payment is based on the price of an asset at a single time period, that is, European-style options. Now we want to look at how an option that is based on the prices of a single asset at many time periods can be handled. Barrier options are a good example to focus on for the following reasons:

- They illustrate dependence on the entire volatility surface, both in terms of time and strike level.
- They have a large range of variants.
- They are overwhelmingly the most traded exotic options among FX options and are also used with equities, commodities, and interest rates.

■ They can be used as building blocks to form static hedges for other exotic options, such as lookback and ladder options.

A *barrier option* is one whose payoff is equal to that of a standard call or put, but that only pays off under the condition that some price level (called the *barrier*) has been breached (or not) at some time period prior to the time the call or put payoff is determined. Options that only pay if a barrier has been breached are called *knock-in* (*down and in* if the barrier is below the asset's price at the time the option in written—*up and in* otherwise). For example, a 1-year down-and-out call on the S&P index with a barrier of 1,050 will have no payout if the S&P index goes below 1,050 at any time during the year. Options that only pay if a barrier has not been breached are called *knock-out* (either *down and out* or *up and out*). Variations include *double barrier options* that either knock out if either a down-and-out or an up-and-out condition has been reached or knock in if either a down-and-in or up-and-in condition has been reached. Another variation is a *partial-time barrier*, where the barrier condition can be activated only during a specified time period that begins after the option start date and/or ends before the option termination date. A variation that can be combined with all of these options is a fixed rebate to be paid if an option is knocked out.

We will first show that standard analytic models for barrier options are inadequate, both for valuation and risk representation, in the presence of nonflat volatility surfaces for vanilla options. We will therefore need to turn our attention to two alternative approaches to valuing and hedging barriers: dynamic hedging utilizing both vanilla options and the underlying and quasistatic hedging with vanilla options. One particular quasistatic hedging approach, developed by Peter Carr, is particularly useful for developing an intuitive understanding of the risk profile of barrier options. We will then demonstrate how to statically hedge lookback and ladder options with barrier options and how to handle rebates. Finally, we will briefly discuss how the methods developed for standard barrier options can be applied to the broader class of single-asset exotic options, including double barriers and partial-time barriers.

One noticeable difference between this section and all of our previous discussions of options is that we are concerned with the *drift*, which can be thought of either as the difference between the risk-free rate and the dividend rate, or more generally as the discount rate between forward prices at different expiries. Up until now, we didn't need to worry about drift because we were only considering options whose value would be determined by the asset price at a single point in time; hence, all hedges could be based on a forward with a single expiry date. Since we are now considering options that depend on price behavior at several points in time, hedges may need to involve forwards for different expiry dates and the relation between forward prices can no longer be ignored.

10.3.1 Standard Analytic Models for Barriers

Good analytic models based on partial differential equations (PDEs) have been developed for barrier options (see Hull [2002, Section 19.6] for the equations). Analytic models have great advantages in terms of computational speed relative to Monte Carlo and tree-based models. The ease of calculating a valuation by just plugging input variables into a formula explains much of the success of the Black-Scholes equation. The formulas for barrier options require a bit more computation than Black-Scholes, but they are still quite manageable. However, the analytic models for barriers have the drawback that they need to assume a single level of volatility, and there are no good rules for translating a volatility surface observed for European options into a single volatility to be used for a particular barrier option. In fact, cases can be shown where no single volatility assumption can be utilized with the standard analytic approach to give a reasonable price for the barrier option. We will illustrate this point with the following example. Consider an at-the-money 3-month up-and-out call that knocks out at a barrier 20 percent above the strike. Its valuation at different volatility levels, using the standard analytic formula shown in Hull (2002), is shown in Table 10.4.

Note that the analytic result has option values that first increase as the volatility level rises, since rising volatility causes the call value to increase. At higher volatility levels, the option values decrease as the volatility level rises, since rising volatility increases the probability of a knock-out. Since the barrier level starts far away from the current price, it is only at high volatilities that the impact of rising volatility on the probability of a knock-out dominates the impact of rising volatility on the value of the call.

The methods for utilizing the full volatility surface, which we will discuss shortly, would agree with these analytical results for flat volatility surfaces. However, if we assume a nonflat volatility surface, with an implied volatility of 20 percent for a European call struck at 100 and 18 percent for a European call struck at 120, approaches that utilize the full volatility surface (either the Derman-Kani dynamic hedging approach or the Carr static hedging approach) would price the barrier option at 3.10, which is 10 percent higher than the 2.81 maximum value the barrier option reaches at any volatility level using the analytic approach. The reason for this is that the lower volatility as you approach the barrier decreases the chance of penetrating the barrier without simultaneously lowering the value of the call.

This example also shows why the analytic method is inadequate for representing the risk in standard option reports. The analytic method does not give any breakdown of how much of the risk should be represented as sen-

TABLE 10.4 Value of a Barrier Based on Analytic Formula

Volatility	Value of Up-and-Out Call
1.00%	0.1995
2.00%	0.3989
3.00%	0.5984
4.00%	0.7979
5.00%	0.9973
6.00%	1.1968
7.00%	1.3962
8.00%	1.5956
9.00%	1.7942
10.00%	1.9897
11.00%	2.1772
12.00%	2.3499
13.00%	2.5008
14.00%	2.6242
15.00%	2.7166
16.00%	2.7771
17.00%	2.8070
18.00%	2.8087
19.00%	2.7858
20.00%	2.7421
21.00%	2.6816
22.00%	2.6080
23.00%	2.5245
24.00%	2.4340
25.00%	2.3390
26.00%	2.2415
27.00%	2.1432
28.00%	2.0455
29.00%	1.9492
30.00%	1.8552

sitive to changes in the at-the-money vanilla options versus how much should be represented as sensitive to changes in the out-of-the-money vanilla options.

10.3.2 Dynamic Hedging Models for Barriers

Dynamic hedging models price barrier options (or any other exotic option whose payoff is a function of a single underlying asset) based on the cost of dynamically hedging the exotic with a portfolio of the underlying asset and vanilla European options. This is analogous to the Black-Scholes model pricing of vanilla European options based on the cost of dynamically hedging with the underlying asset. These models utilize the full set of the current prices of vanilla European options, so they make use of the full volatility surface along with a theory of how these vanilla option prices can evolve with time. If you utilize an actual dynamic hedging strategy consistent with the model, you will be successful in replicating the model's price for the exotic to the extent that the model's theory about the evolution of the vanilla options prices is correct and that transaction costs are manageable.

Two principal types of dynamic hedging models are used for exotics:

- **Local volatility models that assume that volatility is a known and unvarying function of time and the underlying price level.** These models are natural extensions of the Black-Scholes model, which assumes that volatility is known and unvarying, but which also assumes it is the same at all times and underlying price levels. Based on the assumption of the local volatility model, you can derive a definite price at any future time and the underlying price level of any vanilla or exotic option. The cost of the dynamic hedge therefore differs from the originally derived price only to the extent that future volatilities prove to follow a varying function of time and underlying price level (or that transaction costs are significant).
- **Stochastic volatility models that assume that volatilities will vary over time and that might include price jumps, based on some assumed model.** The cost of the dynamic hedge differs from the derived price to the extent that the process of actual volatility variation differs from that assumed by the model (or that transaction costs are significant).

A relatively straightforward implementation for a local volatility model is the trinomial tree approach of Derman and Kani (1994), which builds the unique trinomial tree for modeling the price diffusion of the underlying asset that meets the following two criteria:

- Volatility is a known and unvarying function of time and the underlying price level.
- The tree correctly prices *all* European calls and puts on the underlying asset at different strike levels and times to expiry.

A thorough discussion of the Derman-Kani approach and its application to barrier pricing can be found in Chriss (1997, Chapters 9 and 11). If any reader wants to implement this model, I would strongly recommend reading Chapter 5 of Clewlow and Strickland (1998), which provides wonderfully detailed instructions and examples.

A general introduction to stochastic models can be found in Derman and Kani (1998). A frequently used computationally tractable stochastic volatility model is that found in Heston (1993). A model that is attracting current interest is the *variance gamma model*, which is explained in Madan, Carr, and Chang (1998). The course notes for Jim Gatherall's Case Studies and Financial Modeling course at the Courant Institute, which can be found on his Web page, and Lee (2001) contain insightful analysis on the differences between local volatility and stochastic volatility models in the pricing of exotic options. Matytsin (1999) suggests that a combination of stochastic volatility and jump processes are needed to explain observed volatility surfaces implied by the vanilla option prices. The jump processes are needed to explain the steepness of smile and skew observed at shorter-term maturities, whereas stochastic volatility is needed to explain the steepness of smile and skew at longer-term maturities.

Dynamic hedging utilizes the full volatility surface in pricing barrier options. It can be readily employed for representing the barrier option in risk reports through its vanilla option hedges. Dynamic hedging can also be applied to any derivative based on a single underlying. Its drawback is its vulnerability to incorrect assumptions about volatility evolution and possible instability of the hedge representation.

Once an exotic has been priced by a given model, the exotic can be hedged by a set of vanilla options that have the same sensitivity to the model's input parameters as the exotic. So long as the model's input parameter remain unchanged, the hedge does not require changing. However, changes in observed vanilla option prices may require changes to input parameters to fit current prices, and once parameters change, the hedge may need adjustment.

How stable is the resulting representation? To what degree does it require frequent and sizeable adjustments in the options hedges that can result in hedge slippage as a result of both transaction costs (generally considerably higher for options than for the underlying) and the instability of the hedge against parameter changes? Although trading desks may gain experience with the stability of particular models in particular markets through time, it is difficult to obtain a risk measure in advance. The projection of hedge changes through Monte Carlo simulation, which has proved very useful in establishing results for the hedging of vanilla options with other vanilla options, is orders of magnitude more difficult to achieve for exotics. This is because each step on each path of the Monte Carlo simulation requires recomputation of the hedge. When the only hedge change is in the underlying, this is a very simple calculation of the $N(d_1)$ in the Black-Scholes formula. When the hedge change is in an option, a complete recalculation of the model being used to link the vanilla options and the exotic option together is required.

10.3.3 Static Hedging Models for Barriers

The uncertainty surrounding the hedging costs of using dynamic hedging for barriers provides the motivation to search for static or near-static hedging alternatives. Static hedging models price barrier options based on the cost of a replication strategy that calls for an almost unvarying hedge portfolio (at least of the vanilla options; it would be possible to use a dynamic hedge of the underlying, although the particular static hedging models we discuss only utilize vanilla options in the hedge portfolio). These models utilize nearly static hedge portfolios both as a way to reduce transaction costs and as a way to reduce dependence on assumptions about the evolution of volatility. Three approaches to the static hedging of barriers can be distinguished:

- The approach of Derman, Ergener, and Kani, which is broadly applicable to all exotic options whose payoff is a function of a single underlying asset, but has considerable exposure to being wrong about future volatility levels.
- The approach of Carr, which is more specifically tailored to barrier options, utilizing an analysis of the Black-Scholes formula to form a hedge portfolio that is immune to changes in overall volatility level and volatility smile. However, the Carr approach is still vulnerable to changes in the volatility skew. It is easier to implement than the Derman-Ergener-Kani approach for barriers in the absence of drift (that is, forward equal to spot) and produces a very simple hedging portfolio that helps develop intuitive understanding of the risk profile of the barrier.
- Approaches that utilize optimal fitting give solutions close to those provided by the Carr approach for single barriers in the absence of drift, but are more flexible in handling drift and are less vulnerable to changes in volatility skew. Optimal fitting can be generalized to broader classes of exotics, but with less ease than the Derman-Ergener-Kani approach.

All three approaches are based on the idea of finding a basket of vanilla options that statically replicate the differences between the barrier option and a closely related vanilla option. To facilitate the discussion, we will confine ourselves to the case of a knock-out call, since a knock-in call can be handled as a vanilla call less a knock-out call, and all options can be treated as call options to exchange one asset for another (refer back to the introductory section of Chapter 9). The idea is to purchase a vanilla call with the same strike and expiration date as the knock-out being sold and then reduce the cost of creating the knock-out by selling a basket of vanilla options (this basket may have purchases as well as sales, but the net initial cash flow on the basket is positive to the barrier option seller). The basket of vanilla options must be constructed so that:

- It has no payoff if the barrier is never hit. In this case, the payout on the barrier option, which has not been knocked out, is exactly offset by the payin from the vanilla call that was purchased, so nothing is left over to make payments on the basket.
- Its value when the barrier is hit is an exact offset to the value of the vanilla call. When the barrier is hit, you know you will not need to make any payments on the barrier option so you can afford now to sell the vanilla call you purchased. You do not want to later be vulnerable to payouts on the basket of vanilla options you sold so you must purchase this basket. In order for cash flows to be zero, the basket purchase price must equal the vanilla call sale price.

You can guarantee the first condition by only using calls struck at or above the barrier in the case of a barrier higher than the current price and by only using puts struck at or below the barrier in the case of a barrier lower than the current price. If the barrier is never hit, then you certainly won't be above the up barrier at expiration, so you won't owe anything on a call, and you certainly won't be below the down barrier at expiration, so you won't owe anything on a put.

All three static hedging techniques take advantage of knowing that at the time you are reversing your position in these vanilla options, the underlying must be at the barrier. A useful analogy can be made between these approaches to static hedging and the one we examined for forward start options in Section 10.2. For forward start options, we purchased an initial set of vanilla options and then had a fixed date on which we would make a single switch of selling our initial package of vanilla options and buying a new vanilla option. For barrier options, we cannot know in advance what the time of the switch will be, but we can know what the forward price of the underlying will be at the time of the switch. As with forward starts, we confine ourselves to one single switch out of the initial vanilla option hedge package. All of these approaches therefore share many of the advantages we saw for the static hedge technique for forward starts:

- A clear distinction between the portion of expected cost that can be locked in at current market prices of vanilla options (including current volatility surface shape) versus the portion that requires projections of what the volatility surface shape will be at the time of the switch.
- An estimate of uncertainty for establishing limits and reserves can be based on readily observable historical market data for possible

volatility surface shapes. The impact of uncertainty is easy to calculate since it only needs to be computed at one particular point.

- Future liquidity costs, such as the potential payment of bid-ask spread, are confined to a single switch.
- Although it is to be expected that trading desks will, in practice, adjust the static hedge as market circumstances evolve, it remains useful as a risk-management technique to evaluate the consequences of an unadjusted hedge.

The three approaches differ in how they attempt to ensure that the option package will be equal in value to the vanilla call at the time the barrier is hit. The Derman-Ergener-Kani approach (see Derman, Ergener, and Kani [1995]) uses a package of vanilla options that expire at different times. The algorithm works backwards, starting at a time close to the expiration of the barrier option. If the barrier is hit at this time, the only vanilla options still outstanding will be the vanilla call and the very last option to expire in the package. Since both the underlying price is known (namely, the barrier) and the time to expiry is known, the only remaining factor in determining the values of the vanilla options is the implied volatility, which can be derived from a local or stochastic volatility model (if it is derived from a stochastic volatility model, it will be based on expected values over the probability distribution). Thus, the Derman-Ergener-Kani approach can be viewed as the static hedging analog of the dynamic hedging approaches we have been considering.

Once the prices of the vanilla options at the time the barrier is hit are calculated, you can easily determine the amount of the option that is part of the basket that needs to be sold in order to exactly offset the sale of the vanilla call with the purchase of the option in the basket. You then work backwards time period by time period, calculating the values of all vanilla options if the barrier is hit at this time period and calculating what volume of the new option in the basket is needed to set the price of the entire basket equal to the price of the vanilla call. At each stage, you only need to consider unexpired options, so you only need to consider options for which you have already computed the volumes held.

The following points about the Derman-Ergener-Kani approach should be noted:

- If the barrier is hit in between two time periods for which vanilla options have been included in the package, the results are approximated by the nearest prior time period. The inaccuracy of this approximation can be reduced as much as you want by increasing the number of time periods used.

- The approach can easily accommodate the existence of drift (dividend rate unequal to risk-free rate), since a separate computation is made for each time the barrier could potentially be hit.
- Since the approach relies on the results of a local or stochastic volatility model to forecast future volatility surface levels and shapes, it is vulnerable to the same issue as when these models are used for dynamic hedging—the hedge only works to the extent that the assumptions underlying the model prove to be true. As Derman, Ergener, and Kani state, "The hedge is only truly static if the yield curve, the dividend, and the volatility structures remain unchanged over time. Otherwise, the hedge must be readjusted." This is illustrated in Table 10.5, which shows the potential mismatch in unwind cost at a period close to expiry based on differences between model-assumed volatilities and actual volatilities at the time the barrier is hit.

Note that the Derman-Ergener-Kani approach is vulnerable to model errors relating to both the level of volatility surface and shape of volatility surface.

The Carr approach (see Carr, Ellis, and Gupta [1998]) avoids this dependence on projecting future volatility surfaces and is much simpler to implement, but at a price—it cannot handle volatility skews (though it can handle volatility smiles) and its simplicity depends on the absence of drift (dividend rate equals risk-free rate).

The Carr approach achieves a degree of model independence by using a framework that corresponds directly with the Black-Scholes equation and determining a hedge package that will work, providing no drift or volatility skew is present. In these circumstances, one can calculate exactly a single vanilla put that will be selling at the same price as the vanilla call in the

TABLE 10.5 Unwind Costs of Derman-Ergener-Kani Hedge of Barrier Option

Strike at the money, barrier at 95% of forward, and 3 months to expiry
Down-and-out call value at initial 20% volatility is 3.1955
Unwind with 1 month to expiry

Volatility at Unwind	Unwind Gain or Loss
10.00%	.4479
15.00%	.2928
20.00%	.0000
25.00%	−.3595
30.00%	−.7549

case that a down barrier is hit. It is based on the principle of put-call symmetry. In the following boxes, we first explain how the principle of put-call symmetry can be derived from the Black-Scholes equations and then show how the exact Carr hedges can be derived from put-call symmetry.

PUT-CALL SYMMETRY

The principle of put-call symmetry says that if you have two strikes, K_1 and K_2, whose geometric average is the forward price, that is, $\sqrt{K_1 K_2} = F$, then the current price of a call strike at K_1 for expiry T, $C(K_1,T)$ and the current price of a put struck at K_2 for the same expiry T, $P(K_2,T)$ are related by the equation:

$$C(K_1,T)/\sqrt{K_1} = P(K_2,T)/\sqrt{K_2}$$

This formula is a direct and easy consequence of the Black-Scholes formula. From Hull (2002, Section 13.8), the Black Scholes formula for the price of a call and put based on the forward price is:

$$C(K_1,T) = e^{-rt}(FN((ln(F/K_1) + \sigma^2 T/2) / \sigma\sqrt{T}$$
$$- K_1 N((ln(F/K_1) - \sigma^2 T/2 / \sigma \sqrt{T}))$$

$$P(K_2,T) = e^{-rt}(K_2 N((ln(K_2/F) + \sigma^2 T/2) / \sigma\sqrt{T}$$
$$- FN((ln(K_2/F) - \sigma^2 T/2) / \sigma \sqrt{T}))$$

But since $F = \sqrt{K_1 K_2}$,

$$K_2/F = K_2/\sqrt{K_1 K_2} = \sqrt{K_2}/\sqrt{K_1} = \sqrt{K_1 K_2}/K_1 = F/K_1$$

So,

$$C(K_1,T)/\sqrt{K_1} = e^{-rt}(\sqrt{K_2} N((ln(F/K_1) + \sigma^2 T/2) / \sigma\sqrt{T})$$
$$- \sqrt{K_1} N((ln(F/K_1) - \sigma^2 T/2 / \sigma \sqrt{T}))$$

And substituting F/K_1 for K_2/F,

$$P(K_2,T) / \sqrt{K_2} = e^{-rt} (\sqrt{K_2} N((ln(F/K_1) + \sigma^2 T/2) / \sigma \sqrt{T})$$

$$- \sqrt{K_1} N((ln(F/K_1) - \sigma^2 T/2) / \sigma \sqrt{T}))$$

$$= C(K_1,T) / \sqrt{K_1}$$

Since we have utilized the Black-Scholes formula in our derivation, this result only holds under the Black-Scholes assumption of a flat volatility surface for the expiry time T or if the deviation from flat volatility surface is exactly the same at strike K_1 and K_2. However, since the forward is the geometric average of these two strikes, this is equivalent to saying that one strike is the same percentage above the forward as the percentage the other strike is below the forward. For their volatilities to be equal, the volatility surface must have a smile shape, not a skew shape, using the terminology of Section 9.6.2.

DERIVING THE CARR HEDGE

Since no drift is present, the forward price is equal to the spot price, which is the barrier level, H. Since the call is struck at K, we can find a reflection strike, R, such that $\sqrt{KR} = H$ and, by put-call symmetry,

$$\sqrt{R}Call(K) = \sqrt{K}Put(R) \quad \text{Since} \quad \sqrt{KR} = H, R = H^2/K, \sqrt{R}$$

$= H/ \sqrt{K}$, you need to purchase $\dfrac{\sqrt{K}}{\sqrt{R}} = \dfrac{K}{H}$ puts struck at H^2/K.

For an up barrier, one must separately hedge the intrinsic value and the time value of the vanilla call at the time the barrier is hit. The intrinsic value can almost be perfectly offset by selling binary options that pay $2 \times I$, the intrinsic value. Any time the barrier is hit, there will be nearly a 50–50 chance that the binary will finish in the money, so its value is close to $50\% \times 2 \times I = I$. In fact, the standard lognormal pricing of a

(continued)

DERIVING THE CARR HEDGE (continued)

---

binary results in assuming slightly less than a 50 percent chance of finishing above the barrier so we need to supplement the binary with I/H of a plain vanilla call struck at the barrier. The exact value of the binary

is $2 \times I \times N\left(-\dfrac{\sigma\sqrt{T}}{2}\right)$ and the value of the vanilla call struck at

the barrier, and hence exactly at the money when the barrier is hit, is

$$(I/H) \times H \times \left(N\left(\frac{\sigma\sqrt{T}}{2}\right) - N\left(-\frac{\sigma\sqrt{T}}{2}\right)\right)$$

$$= I \times \left(1 - 2 \times N\left(-\frac{\sigma\sqrt{T}}{2}\right)\right)$$

The sum of these two terms is then I.

The Carr approach has several advantages:

- It shows that it is at least plausible to price the barrier based on options with tenor equal to the final tenor of the barrier, indicating that this is probably where most of the barrier's risk exposure is coming from.
- Having a large binary component of the hedge is an excellent means of highlighting and isolating the pin risk contained in this barrier that dies in the money. Techniques we have already developed for managing pin risk on binaries can now easily be brought into play. For example, we could establish a reserve against the pin risk of the binary (see Section 10.1.4). This approach is quite independent of whether the trading desk actually sells a binary as a part of the hedge—the risk of the binary is present in any case.
- Because the Carr approach uses a small number of options in the hedge package, it is very well suited for developing intuition about how changes in the shape of the volatility surface impact barrier prices.
- Even if you choose to hedge and price using a dynamic hedging approach, the Carr methodology can still be useful as a control variate. Dynamic hedging can be employed for the difference between the barrier and the static hedge determined by the Carr approach. By choosing an initial hedge that, on theoretical grounds, we expect to be close to a good static hedge, we expect to minimize the degree to

which changes in option hedges are required. However, by using dynamic hedging, we allow for as much protection as the accuracy of the model provides against uncertainty in skew and drift.

- Neither the presence of volatility smiles nor the uncertainty of future volatility smiles impacts the Carr approach. Since it deals with options that are symmetrically placed relative to the at-the-money strike, all smile effects cancel out.

The simplicity of the Carr approach is lost in the presence of drift or volatility skew. (See the appendix to Carr and Chou [1996] for a method of using a large number of vanilla options to create a volatility-independent static hedge of barrier options in the presence of drift. See Carr [2001] for a method of handling volatility skew.)

To appreciate how the Carr model performs and gain the benefit of its insight into the risk structure of barriers, you should study the **CarrBarrier** spreadsheet provided on the accompanying CD-ROM. The spreadsheet shows the hedge structure for all eight possible simple barrier structures and the result of the barrier unwind for a specified scenario. Exercise 10.2 guides you through some sample runs. Here are some of the points you should be looking for:

- The one common element in all eight variants is the use of the reflection option—the one that utilizes the principle of put-call symmetry. It captures the time value of the barrier option at the point the barrier is hit.
- The sample run displayed in Figure 10.2 shows that on unwind, for the down call and up put cases, the reflection option exactly offsets the value of the option that needs to be purchased for the in cases and needs to be sold for the out cases. For the up call and down put cases, a binary piece also needs to be offset, but the reflection option offsets the entire time value. In Figure 10.3, in which the only change from Figure 10.2 is that the volatility at unwind has been raised, the binary piece (the sum of the binary and binary correction) is unchanged from Figure 10.2, but the time value has increased exactly equally for the vanilla option and the reflection option.
- The time value when the barrier is hit depends on how far the barrier is from the strike. In the Figure 10.2 example, the up barrier of 110 is further from the 100 strike than the 95 down barrier is, so the up reflection options have far less value than the down reflection options. You can think of the reflection option as taking value away from the out option and transferring it to the in option.
- The up call and down put cases are ones with binary components, since these in options will begin life already in the money and these

out options cause an in-the-money component to be extinguished. The size of the binary component at the time the barrier is hit is the exact difference between the strike and barrier. It is divided into two pieces —the principal piece is the binary option and the secondary piece is the vanilla option used to supplement the binary. The total value of these two components at initiation will be less than the potential value on hitting the barrier, precisely reflecting the (risk-neutral) probability that the barrier will be hit.

■ By trying different values for barrier-hitting scenarios, you will see that as long as volatility skew and drift are both equal to zero, the total impact of buys and sells in all eight cases is always zero. That is, the hedge works perfectly regardless of the assumptions made as to the time remaining when the barrier is hit, the at-the-money volatility, the volatility smile, or the risk-free rate. However, if either drift or volatility skew differs from zero, gains and losses will occur when the barrier is hit, varying by case. Examples are shown in Figures 10.4 and 10.5. It would clearly be a relatively easy task to calculate the size of potential losses based on assumptions about how adverse drift and skew could be at different possible times the barrier is hit. This could serve as input for the determination of reserves and limits.

■ When the initial volatility skew, volatility smile, and drift are set equal to zero, pricing given by the standard analytic formula for barriers (shown on the top line in each column) exactly equals the total creation cost of the Carr hedges, as can be seen from the zero on the line labeled "difference." When any of these values is different from zero, the Carr hedge gives a different value than the analytic formula. For example, Figure 10.6 shows a case that corresponds to the one analyzed in Table 10.4, showing a 3.104 value for the up-and-out call in the presence of a volatility skew compared with a 2.7421 value using the analytic formula. Note that the presence of volatility skew (or drift) in the initial conditions does not imply that the Carr hedge will not work. Only conditions at the time the barrier is hit determine the efficiency of the hedge.

A more general approach to static hedging that can handle all drift and volatility shape conditions is optimization, in which a set of vanilla options is chosen that fits as closely as possible the unwind of the barrier option at different possible times, drifts, volatility levels, and volatility surface shapes that may prevail when the barrier is hit. The optimization approach is discussed in Dembo (1994). Often no perfect static hedge can be found, but in these cases the optimization produces information on the distribution of possible hedge errors that can be useful input for determining a reasonable reserve. A similar approach can be taken to many different types of exotic structures.

	100.00
Price	100.00
Strike	100.00
Up Barrier	110.00	vanilla
Down Barrier	95.00	digital
Time to Expiry	0.25	correct dig
Rate	0.00%	reflect
Drift	0.00%	total
ATM Volatility	20.00%	difference
Vol Smile	0.00%	reflect point
Vol Skew	0.00%	

		cdo	cdi	cuo	cui	pdo	pdi	puo	pui
vanilla		3.1955	0.7923	0.6343	3.3535	0.0778	3.9100	3.8791	0.1087
digital		-3.9878	0	-3.9878	0	-3.9878	0	-3.9878	0
correct dig		0	0	3.1581	-3.1581	3.2171	-3.2171	0	0
reflect		0	0	0.0867	-0.0867	-0.0994	0.0994	0	0
		0.7923	-0.7923	0.1087	-0.1087	0.7923	-0.7923	0.1087	-0.1087
total		-3.1955	-0.7923	-0.6343	-3.3535	-0.0778	-3.9100	-3.8791	-0.1087
difference		0.0000	0.0000	0.0000	0.0000	0.0000	0.0000	0.0000	0.0000
reflect point		90.25	90.25	121	121	90.25	90.25	121	121

at barrier

		cdo	cdi	cuo	cui	pdo	pdi	puo	pui
Time to Expiry	0.25	vanilla	-1.8881	1.8881	-10.9539	10.9539	-6.8881	6.8881	-0.9539	0.9539

		cdo	cdi	cuo	cui	pdo	pdi	puo	pui
Time to Expiry	0.25	vanilla	-1.8881	1.8881	-10.9539	10.9539	-6.8881	6.8881	-0.9539	0.9539
Rate	0.00%	digital	0	0	9.6012	-9.6012	5.1994	-5.1994	0	0
Drift	0.00%	correct dig	0	0	0.3988	-0.3988	-0.1994	0.1994	0	0
ATM Volatility	20.00%	reflect	1.8881	-1.8881	0.9539	-0.9539	1.8881	-1.8881	0.9539	-0.9539
Vol Smile	0.00%	total	0.0000	0.0000	0.0000	0.0000	0.0000	0.0000	0.0000	0.0000
Vol Skew	0.00%									

forward	100
up forward	110
down forward	95

FIGURE 10.2 Carr static hedge.

Parameter	Value	
Price	100.00	
Strike	100.00	
Up Barrier	110.00	vanilla
Down Barrier	95.00	digital
Time to Expiry	0.25	correct dig
Rate	0.00%	reflect
Drift	0.00%	total
ATM Volatility	20.00%	difference
Vol Smile	0.00%	reflect point
Vol Skew	0.00%	

at barrier

Parameter	Value	
Time to Expiry	0.25	vanilla
Rate	0.00%	digital
Drift	0.00%	correct dig
ATM Volatility	40.00%	reflect
Vol Smile	0.00%	total
Vol Skew	0.00%	

forward	100
up forward	110
down forward	95

Data table (first):

	cdo	cdi	cuo	cui	pdo	pdi	puo	pui
vanilla	3.1955	0.7923	0.6343	3.3535	0.0778	3.9100	3.8791	0.1087
digital	-3.9878	0	-3.9878	0	-3.9878	0	-3.9878	0
correct dig	0	0	3.1581	-3.1581	3.2171	-3.2171	0	0
reflect	0.7923	-0.7923	0.0867	-0.0867	-0.0994	0.0994	0.1087	-0.1087
total	0.0000	0.0000	-0.1087	0.1087	-0.7923	0.7923	0.0000	0.0000
difference	-3.1955	-0.7923	-0.6343	-3.3535	-0.0778	-3.9100	-3.8791	-0.1087
reflect point	90.25	90.25	121	121	90.25	90.25	121	121

Data table (at barrier):

	cdo	cdi	cuo	cui	pdo	pdi	puo	pui
vanilla	-5.5195	5.5195	-14.2920	14.2920	-10.5195	10.5195	-4.2920	4.2920
digital	0	0	9.2034	-9.2034	5.3983	-5.3983	0	0
correct dig	0	0	0.7966	-0.7966	-0.3983	0.3983	0	0
reflect	5.5195	-5.5195	4.2920	-4.2920	5.5195	-5.5195	4.2920	-4.2920
total	0.0000	0.0000	0.0000	0.0000	0.0000	0.0000	0.0000	0.0000

FIGURE 10.3 Carr static hedge with higher volatility at unwind.

Parameters

Price	100.00	
Strike	100.00	
Up Barrier	110.00	vanilla
Down Barrier	95.00	digital
Time to Expiry	0.25	correct dig
Rate	0.00%	reflect
Drift	0.00%	total
ATM Volatility	20.00%	difference
Vol Smile	0.00%	reflect point
Vol Skew	0.00%	

	cdo	cdi	cuo	cui	pdo	pdi	puo	pui
vanilla	3.1955	0.7923	0.6343	3.3535	0.0778	3.9100	3.8791	0.1087
digital	-3.9878	0	-3.9878	0	-3.9878	0	-3.9878	0
correct dig	0	0	3.1581	-3.1581	3.2171	-3.2171	0	0
reflect	0.7923	-0.7923	0.0867	-0.0867	-0.0994	0.0994	0.1087	-0.1087
total	-3.1955	-0.7923	-0.6343	-3.3535	-0.0778	-3.9100	-3.8791	-0.1087
difference	0.0000	0.0000	0.0000	0.0000	0.0000	0.0000	0.0000	0.0000
reflect point	90.25	90.25	121	121	90.25	90.25	121	121

at barrier

Time to Expiry	0.25	vanilla
Rate	0.00%	digital
Drift	0.00%	correct dig
ATM Volatility	20.00%	reflect
Vol Smile	0.00%	total
Vol Skew	10.00%	

	cdo	cdi	cuo	cui	pdo	pdi	puo	pui
vanilla	-1.9757	1.9757	-10.8303	10.8303	-6.9757	6.9757	-0.8303	0.8303
digital	0	0	9.2028	-9.2028	5.0002	-5.0002	0	0
correct dig	0	0	0.3988	-0.3988	-0.1994	0.1994	0	0
reflect	1.8010	-1.8010	1.0830	-1.0830	1.8010	-1.8010	1.0830	-1.0830
total	-0.1746	0.1746	-0.1457	0.1457	-0.3739	0.3739	0.2527	-0.2527

forward	100
up forward	110
down forward	95

FIGURE 10.4 Carr static hedge with nonzero skew at unwind.

253

Block 1 — parameters

Price	100.00	
Strike	100.00	
Up Barrier	110.00	vanilla
Down Barrier	95.00	digital
Time to Expiry	0.25	correct dig
Rate	0.00%	reflect
Drift	0.00%	total
ATM Volatility	20.00%	difference
Vol Smile	0.00%	reflect point
Vol Skew	0.00%	

	cdo	cdi	cuo	cui	pdo	pdi	puo	pui
vanilla	3.1955	0.7923	0.6343	3.3535	0.0778	3.9100	3.8791	0.1087
digital	-3.9878	0	-3.9878	0	-3.9878	0	-3.9878	0
correct dig	0	0	3.1581	-3.1581	3.2171	-3.2171	0	0
reflect	0.7923	-0.7923	0.1087	-0.1087	0.7923	-0.7923	0.1087	-0.1087
total	-3.1955	-0.7923	-0.7210	-3.2668	0.0216	-4.0094	-3.8791	-0.1087
difference	0.0000	0.0000	-0.0867	0.0867	0.0994	-0.0994	0.0000	0.0000
reflect point	90.25	90.25	121	121	90.25	90.25	121	121

Block 2 — at barrier

Time to Expiry	0.25	vanilla
Rate	0.00%	digital
Drift	-3.00%	correct dig
ATM Volatility	20.00%	reflect
Vol Smile	0.00%	total
Vol Skew	0.00%	

	cdo	cdi	cuo	cui	pdo	pdi	puo	pui
vanilla	-1.6691	1.6691	-10.2694	10.2694	-7.3790	7.3790	-1.0913	1.0913
digital	0	0	9.0057	-9.0057	5.4972	-5.4972	0	0
correct dig	0	0	0.3610	-0.3610	-0.2179	0.2179	0	0
reflect	2.1120	-2.1120	0.8243	-0.8243	2.1120	-2.1120	0.8243	-0.8243
total	0.4429	-0.4429	-0.0784	0.0784	0.0123	-0.0123	-0.2671	0.2671

forward	100
up forward	109.17809
down forward	94.290165

FIGURE 10.5 Carr static hedge with nonzero drift at unwind.

254

Parameters (at initiation)

Price	100.00	
Strike	100.00	
Up Barrier	120.00	vanilla
Down Barrier	90.00	digital
Time to Expiry	0.25	correct dig
Rate	0.00%	reflect
Drift	0.00%	total
ATM Volatility	20.00%	difference
Vol Smile	0.00%	reflect point
Vol Skew	-10.95%	

	cdo	cdi	cuo	cui	pdo	pdi	puo	pui
vanilla	3.9244	0.0633	2.7421	1.2456	0.8479	3.1399	3.9875	0.0003
digital	-3.9878	0	-3.9878	0	-3.9878	0	-3.9878	0
correct dig	0	0	0.8708	-0.8708	3.7355	-3.7355	0	0
reflect	0	0	0.0130	-0.0130	-0.0935	0.0935	0	0
total	0.1266	-0.1266	0.0000	0.0000	0.1266	-0.1266	0.0000	0.0000
difference	-3.8611	-0.0633	-3.1040	-0.8838	-0.2192	-3.7686	-3.9878	0.0000
reflect point	0.0633	-0.0633	-0.3618	0.3618	0.6287	-0.6287	-0.0003	0.0003
	81	81	144	144	81	81	144	144

at barrier

Time to Expiry	0.25	vanilla
Rate	0.00%	digital
Drift	0.00%	correct dig
ATM Volatility	20.00%	reflect
Vol Smile	0.00%	total
Vol Skew	0.00%	

	cdo	cdi	cuo	cui	pdo	pdi	puo	pui
vanilla	-0.7124	0.7124	-20.1473	20.1473	-10.7124	10.7124	-0.1473	0.1473
digital	0	0	19.2024	-19.2024	10.3988	-10.3988	0	0
correct dig	0	0	0.7976	-0.7976	-0.3988	0.3988	0	0
reflect	0.7124	-0.7124	0.1473	-0.1473	0.7124	-0.7124	0.1473	-0.1473
total	0.0000	0.0000	0.0000	0.0000	0.0000	0.0000	0.0000	0.0000

FIGURE 10.6 Carr static hedge with nonzero skew at initiation.

The **OptBarrier** spreadsheet illustrates how optimization can be used to find a static hedge for a barrier option. If the possible conditions when the barrier is hit are restricted to zero drift and volatility smile but no skew, then the Excel Solver will find a set of vanilla options that almost exactly matches the barrier unwind for all volatility levels and times to expiry (although the particular set of hedges chosen may lack the clarity of insight that the Carr hedges offer). Of course, this is not a surprise since we know from the Carr approach that a perfect static hedge is possible under these circumstances. When different nonzero drift and volatility skew conditions are allowed, the match of the barrier unwind is no longer as exact.

The spreadsheet determines how much this slippage can be across all the specified cases of hitting time, skew, and drift. As with the Carr approach, this information can then be used to set reserves and limits. The difference from the Carr approach is the objective to find a hedge that minimizes the amount of this slippage. Exercise 10.3 guides you through some sample runs.

As a concluding note, observe that there is a lower limit on the uncertainty of unwind costs for any static hedging approach. Any dynamic hedging model can be used to compute the unwind cost of a selected static hedging strategy. So any difference in the pricing of barrier options between different dynamic hedging models translates into uncertainty of unwind costs. Practical experience with dynamic hedging models shows that differences in assumptions (for example, stochastic volatility versus local volatility and the frequency of jumps) give rise to substantial differences in barrier options prices utilizing the same input for current vanilla options prices. So you can search for static hedges that minimize the uncertainty of unwind costs, but an irreducible uncertainty will always remain that can only be controlled through limits and reserves. Static hedging greatly simplifies the calculations needed for limits and reserves.

10.3.4 Barrier Options with Rebates, Lookback, and Ladder Options

We will show how to use barrier options to create a static hedge for barrier options with rebates, lookback, and ladder options. Thus, we can transfer the techniques we have studied for using vanilla options to represent and hedge barrier option positions to create vanilla option representations and hedges of barrier options with rebates, lookback, and ladder options.

The use of a rebate feature in a barrier option can be regarded as a binary option triggered by a barrier. For example, suppose you have a down-and-out call that pays a rebate of $2 million if the down barrier is hit and the call is cancelled. This can be viewed as the sum of a down-and-out call with no rebate and a down-and-in binary option that pays $2 million if the barrier is hit. However, since a binary option can be represented by being long one vanilla call and short another vanilla call, as discussed in Section

10.1.4, a down-and-in binary can also be treated as being long one down-and-in call and short another down-and-in call. So the rebate can be hedged and valued through the methodology we have already developed for barriers without rebates.

Lookback options come in two varieties: those that pay the difference between the maximum price that an asset achieves during a selected period and the closing price and those that pay the difference between the maximum price that an asset achieves during a selected period and a fixed strike. Symbolically, the lookback either pays $S_{max} - S_T$ or $\max(0, S_{max} - K)$. We can reproduce the payoffs of a lookback of the first type exactly by buying a lookback of the second type with a strike equal to the current price of the asset (S_0), selling the asset forward to time T and buying a forward delivery of S_0 dollars at time T. Since S_{max} is certainly $\geq S_0$, $\max(0, S_{max} - S_0) = S_{max} - S_0$, the total payoff of this combination at time T is:

$$\max(0, S_{max} - S_0) - S_T + S_0 = (S_{max} - S_0) - S_T + S_0 = S_{max} - S_T \qquad (10.4)$$

So if we can hedge the second type of lookback option by static hedging with barriers, we can create the first type of lookback option by static hedging with barriers as well.

Lookback options have a closely related product called *ladder options* that pay $\max(0, S_{max} - K)$ rounded down by a specified increment. For example, if $K = 100$ and $S_{max} = 117.3$, the lookback call of the second type would pay 17.3, a ladder with increments of 1 would pay 17, a ladder with increments of 5 would pay 15, and a ladder with increments of 10 would pay 10. Since a lookback call can be approximated as closely as we want by a ladder with a small enough increment, it is sufficient to show how to statically hedge a ladder with barriers.

It is easy to create a static hedge for a ladder option using up-and-in binary options. For each ladder rung, you buy an up-and-in binary option of the same tenor that pays the increment conditional on the rung being breached at some point during the life of the option. For example, if $K = 100$ and we have a ladder with increments of 5, we buy an up-and-in binary option having a payoff of 5 and a barrier of 105, another with a payoff of 5 and a barrier of 110, and so on. If the highest level the underlying reaches during the life of the ladder option is 12, then 10 will be owed on the ladder option, but the binary up-and-ins with barriers of 105 and 110 will both have been triggered for a payment of $5 + 5 = 10$.

10.3.5 Broader Classes of Path-Dependent Exotics

Now that we have looked at several dynamic hedging and static hedging alternatives for managing risk on standard barrier options, we want to examine how these approaches can be generalized to the full universe of single-asset exotics. We will focus most of our attention on double barriers and partial-time barriers, since these are reasonably popular products and since any techniques that are flexible enough to handle these variants would be flexible enough to handle any product.

Double barriers knock out (or knock in) if either a higher or lower barrier is crossed. An example would be a 1-year call option struck at 100 that knocks out if the price during the year is ever either above 120 or below 80. Partial-time barriers have a restricted time period during which the barrier provision applies. An example would be a 1-year call option struck at 100 that knocks out if the price is below 90 any time between the end of month 3 and the end of month 9. If the price goes below 90 prior to month 3 but then goes back above 90 by the end of month 3, no knock-out occurs. Similarly, if the first time the price goes below 90 is after month 9, no knock-out occurs.

The greatest flexibility is offered by dynamic hedging, using either local volatility or stochastic volatility models, and by the Derman-Ergener-Kani approach to static hedging. Both can be easily generalized to double barriers and partial-time barriers. Local volatility models that solve for the exotic option values on a tree constructed to fit vanilla option prices can be easily adapted to solve for virtually any set of payoffs. Stochastic volatility models, which may require Monte Carlo simulation solutions, can easily handle any deterministic payout. The Derman-Ergener-Kani static hedging algorithm can solve for hedge packages that give zero unwind costs for double barriers and partial-time barriers just as easily as for standard barriers. The **DermanErgenerKaniDoubleBarrier** and **DermanErgenerKaniPartialBarrier** spreadsheets illustrate this computation. An interested reader could use these spreadsheets as a guide to program a general calculator for applying the Derman-Ergener-Kani method to more complex barriers.

The drawbacks of dynamic hedging and Derman-Ergener-Kani static hedging that we analyzed for standard barriers apply in a more general setting as well. It will still be difficult to project the potential effects of hedge slippage for dynamic hedging. This is a heightened concern for double barriers since they have a reputation among exotics traders as particularly treacherous to dynamically hedge since they are almost always threatening to cross one barrier or the other. The dependence of Derman-Ergener-Kani on the model used to calculate the hedge ratios, and hence its vulnerability to being wrong about future volatility levels, remains true for the expanded product set.

Peter Carr and his collaborators have done a lot to expand the applicability of his static hedging approach beyond standard barriers. In particular, Carr, Ellis, and Gupta (1998, Section 3.1) have developed a static hedge for double barriers and Carr and Chou (1997) have developed a static hedge for partial-time barriers. Similar results are presented in Andersen and

Andreasen (2000). These hedges offer one of the major advantages of the Carr hedge for standard barriers—protection against shifts in volatility levels. However, they do not offer another major advantage of the Carr hedge for standard barriers—they are not simple to compute and do not provide much intuitive insight into the risk structure of the exotic being hedged. The specialized nature of each construction does not offer significant guidance as to how to build hedges for other exotics.

Optimal fitting would seem to offer the best hope for an easy-to-generalize static hedge that will minimize sensitivity to model assumptions. However, unlike the Derman-Ergener-Kani method, which automates the selection of the vanilla options to be used in hedging a particular exotic, the optimal fitting approach relies on practitioner insight to generate a good set of hedge candidates. A poor choice of possible hedges results in a poorly performing static hedge. A possible solution is to try to generalize the Derman-Ergener-Kani approach to fit to a range of volatility surfaces rather than to a single one. Some promising results along these lines have been obtained by Allen and Padovani (2002, Section 6). A copy of this paper is on the accompanying CD-ROM.

10.4   CORRELATION-DEPENDENT OPTIONS

Valuation and hedging strategies for derivatives whose payoff is a function of more than one underlying asset are critically dependent on assumptions about correlation between the underlying assets. With only a few exceptions (which are discussed in Section 10.4.3), there is an absence of sufficiently liquid market prices to enable implied correlations to be inferred in the way implied volatilities can be derived from reasonably liquid prices of vanilla options. So much of the focus of risk management for these derivatives revolves around controlling the degree of exposure to correlation assumptions and building reserves and limits against the differences between actual realized and estimated correlations.

An important distinction within derivatives with multiasset payoffs should be made between those whose payoff is based on a linear combination of asset prices (for example, the average of a set of prices or the difference between two prices) and those whose payoff is based on a nonlinear combination of asset prices (for example, the maximum of a set of prices or the product of two prices). When the payoff is based on a linear combination of asset prices, risk management is considerably simpler, even if the payoff itself is a nonlinear function of the linear combination of asset prices, such as an option on the average of a set of prices. We therefore discuss these two types of derivatives in separate sections. A final section discusses options that depend on a different type of correlation—the correlation between underlying asset value and the probability of option exercise.

10.4.1   Linear Combinations of Asset Prices

Derivatives whose payoff depends on a linear combination of asset prices share several important characteristics that simplify their risk management:

- If the payoff function is a linear function of the linear combination of asset prices, then the derivative does not have any option characteristics and can be perfectly hedged with a static portfolio of the underlying assets. In such cases, the valuation of the derivative is independent of correlation assumptions. This is not true of derivatives whose payoff function is a linear function of a nonlinear combination of asset prices, such as a forward based on the product of an asset price and an FX rate (a so-called quanto) that requires dynamic hedging.
- Even when the payoff function is a nonlinear function of the linear combination of asset prices, such as an option on the average of a set of prices, and therefore requires dynamic hedging, the rules for dynamic hedging are particularly simple to calculate.
- Even when dynamic hedging is required, it is often possible to make very good approximations of valuation and the risk of incorrect correlation assumptions using a standard Black-Scholes model.

We will examine each of these characteristics more closely. We will then make use of the approximation technique discussed previously to answer questions about how the risk of these derivatives should be managed.

Derivatives Whose Payoffs Are Linear Functions of Linear Combinations of Asset Prices
In principle, any derivative whose payoff is a linear function of a linear combination of asset prices, such as a forward on the average price of a basket of assets, can be statically hedged by buying the properly weighted basket of forwards. In practice, this could be operationally difficult for a basket composed of a very large number of assets, and a market maker may choose to hedge with a differently weighted basket selected to statistically track the derivative payoff closely, with a resulting possibility of tracking error. However, in either case, the performance of this hedging strategy will not be influenced by the level of correlations of assets within the basket. In particular, the valuation of a basket should not be influenced by whether the assets in the basket are well diversified or highly concentrated. Both well-diversified and highly concentrated baskets should be valued as the weighted average of the valuations of the individual components.

At first, this may seem to violate intuition, since firms devote considerable resources to calculations such as value at risk (VaR) that rate highly concentrated baskets as riskier than well-diversified baskets. Shouldn't some penalty in valuation be applied for an asset basket that carries more risk?

The answer from capital market theory is that only systemic risk, which is not capable of being diversified away, should be penalized and that the role of tools such as VaR is to make certain that a firm has considered the proper hedges against risk that can be diversified away. So a trader entering into a forward on the average price of a basket will be charged a higher risk premium by his firm's risk systems for running an open position (that is, not putting in place the basket hedge) in a highly concentrated basket than in a well-diversified basket. But in either case, he has the ability to put on the hedge closing out the position, so concentration should only play a role in the evaluation of the risk of running an open position, not in the valuation of the derivative. A particularly clear discussion of this point can be found in Varian (1987, "Value Additivity Theorem").

As Varian emphasizes, this principle only applies as long as payoffs are linear and ceases to apply when payoffs are nonlinear. This is true both for nonlinearity of the payoff function, such as an option on the average price of a basket of stocks, and the nonlinearity of a combination of asset prices, such as a forward on the maximum price of a set of stocks. As soon as nonlinearity is introduced, considerations that only play a role in the risk assessment of linear products begin to play a role in valuation. For example, the probability of extreme tail events based on the correlation of default probabilities plays no role in the valuation of a CDO based on a basket of loans and/or bonds so long as the CDO divides ownership of the basket proportionally. (A CDO is an example of an asset-backed security; see Section 8.1.9.) However, CDOs often divide the ownership of the basket into tranches, with some tranches paying all credit losses up to a certain level and other tranches paying only losses above that level. This enables the investor market to be segregated more efficiently by creating some bonds that are tailored to investors seeking lower credit risk and other bonds that are tailored to investors willing to take on more credit risk in return for adequate compensation. Tranching CDOs introduces nonlinearity of payoffs. As a result, valuation is dependent on the probability of extreme tail events based on the correlation of default probabilities. For further discussion of this point, see Section 12.1.

A second point to note is that the arbitrage principle only applies if the assets comprising the basket are sufficiently liquid. If not, investors who would have a hard time acquiring a diversified basket of assets may be willing to pay a premium to receive a payment on an index based on the average price of such a basket. This offers a profit opportunity to market makers who can efficiently acquire diverse baskets that other market participants would find difficult to replicate. The market maker can then offer to pay an index based on its earnings on the basket and build a premium into the index. This diversification premium has definitely been observed in the default swaps market.

Rules for Dynamic Hedging

The required dynamic hedges for an option on a linear combination of asset prices are very easy to determine. Standard deltas can be derived from option pricing models, and the delta hedge can then be formed by multiplying this delta times the linear weights of each asset in the basket. This simplifies ongoing hedging calculations and the calculation of required hedges in Monte Carlo simulations of hedging strategies.

Consider an at-the-money 1-year option on a 5,000-share stock basket consisting of 20 percent IBM, 45 percent GE, and 35 percent Merck. If the volatility of the basket is assumed to be 25 percent, the delta, using the Black-Scholes formula, is 55 percent. The hedge should be:

$$5,000 \times 55\% \times 20\% = 550 \text{ shares of IBM}$$
$$5,000 \times 55\% \times 45\% = 1,237.5 \text{ shares of GE}$$
$$5,000 \times 55\% \times 35\% = 962.5 \text{ shares of Merck} \qquad (10.5)$$

Approximation of Option Values

The calculation of the value of an option on a linear combination of asset prices can be reasonably approximated by calculating the volatility of the underlying basket based on the weights of each asset in the basket, the implied volatilities of each asset, and the assumed correlations between assets. This calculated volatility can then be used as input to the Black-Scholes formula for the basket option.

Continuing the previous example, assume that the volatility of IBM stock is 30 percent, the volatility of GE stock is 33 percent, and the volatility of Merck stock is 28 percent, with correlations between IBM and GE of 60 percent, between IBM and Merck of 50 percent, and between GE and Merck of 40 percent. Then the volatility of the basket can be estimated as:

$$
\begin{aligned}
&\text{SquareRoot } [(20\% \times 30\%)^2 + (45\% \times 33\%)^2 + (35\% \times 28\%)^2 \\
&+ 2 \times (20\% \times 30\% \times 45\% \times 33\% \times 60\% + 20\% \times 30\% \\
&\times 35\% \times 28\% \times 50\% + 45\% \times 33\% \times 35\% \times 28\% \times 40\%)] \\
&= 25.2\%
\end{aligned}
\qquad (10.6)
$$

This is only an approximation for two reasons. The first reason is that the representation of an asset's distribution by a single implied volatility is only accurate if the implied volatility surface for that option is flat, that is, the same at all strike prices. However, as discussed in Section 9.6.2, this is rarely the case. The second reason is that even if we had an example in which the implied volatility surfaces of the options on all the individual assets were flat, meaning that the market was pricing them all as if they were lognormally distributed, a linear combination of lognormal distributions is not lognormal, so the implied volatility surface for the basket option would not be flat and thus could not be represented by a single volatility.

For assets with reasonably flat implied volatility surfaces, this approximation technique will give accurate enough results to be useful as a way of building intuition about the degree to which basket option prices depend on the implied volatilities of the individual assets and on the assumed correlations between them. This is how we will make use of this approximation in the remainder of this section.

Actual valuations require more accurate numerical techniques. In practice, two are generally used. One technique is a Monte Carlo simulation in which each asset process is specified by a full distribution that corresponds to the implied volatility surface for that asset, following the approach discussed in Section 10.3.2. Assumed correlations between assets can be enforced by the technique discussed in Hull (2002, pp. 412–413). This technique is flexible enough to support more complex assumptions, such as correlations that vary based on the price level or price movement of the component assets. Finally, the value of the basket can be computed along each sample path and the resulting value of the option can be calculated.

The flexibility to have correlation vary with price level or price movement can be important since large downward price moves tend to be accompanied by higher correlation than ordinary price moves. This can result in baskets being priced at higher volatility skews than individual components of the basket since it increases correlation and hence increases volatility at lower price levels. For further discussion of this point, see Derman and Zou (2001).

The Monte Carlo approach affords great flexibility, including the incorporation of stochastic volatility and price jump assumptions. Its drawback is difficulty in valuing American-style options that require the determination of optimal early exercise strategies. Recent developments in Monte Carlo modeling do allow approximations of American option valuation—see, for example, Broadie, Glasserman, and Jain (1997).

The alternative approach for American-style options on baskets is the three-dimensional tree approach described in Hull and White (1994). This approach enables the combination of two trinomial trees that have been fitted to the full implied volatility surface, using the techniques discussed in Section 10.3.2, to be combined into a single tree based on assumed correlations, which can vary by node. Basket values can then be computed on the combined tree and option values determined by working backwards on the tree. This approach has the advantage of greater precision in determining early exercise strategies. The disadvantages are that it is only computationally feasible for baskets involving two assets and it is restricted to using local volatility models to replicate the implied volatility surface, which lacks the flexibility to incorporate stochastic volatility or price jumps. A possible combination of the two methods for more than two assets would be to determine the option price for the final exercise using the more precise Monte Carlo method and estimating the extra value due to possible early exercise using the three-dimensional tree technique using the first two principal components of the assets as the two variables to be modeled on the tree.

10.4.2   Risk Management of Options on Linear Combinations

We will now take advantage of the simple formula available to approximate the value of an option on a linear combination of assets to examine how risks arising from positions in these options should be managed.

One possible risk-management technique is pure dynamic hedging of options positions in a particular linear combination. This is operationally straightforward, as discussed in Section 10.4.1. However, it encounters the same deficiencies of reliance on the delta-hedging strategy that we discussed in Section 9.1. The same arguments favoring the use of other options in hedging that were given in Section 9.1 apply, but it is unusual to find any liquidity in options on asset combinations. This suggests the use of options on individual assets comprising the basket as part of the hedge.

Consider the following simple example. An option has been written on the average of two assets, A and B. Compare the simulation results of a pure dynamic hedge with the underlying stocks with the simulation results of a hedge that involves first purchasing options on assets A and B and then dynamically hedging the resulting position with the underlying stocks.

Suppose a 1-year at-the-money option has been written on the average of the prices of two stocks, A and B. Assume that both A and B have 20 percent volatility on average with a 33 percent standard deviation of volatility and that correlation between the two assets averages 0 percent with a 33 percent standard deviation. We will simulate two hedging strategies: Use a pure dynamic hedge with the underlying stocks, or first purchase an at-the-money option on A and an at-the-money option on B and then dynamically hedge the resulting position with the underlying stocks. The ratio of the notional of purchased options on individual stocks to the notional of the sold basket option we will use is 70 percent, split equally between the option on A and the option on B. This 70 percent ratio is suggested by the average volatility of the basket option being $\sqrt{(50\% \times 20\%)^2 + (50\% \times 20\%)^2}$ = 14.14%, which is just a little bit more than 70 percent of the 20 percent average volatility of the individual stocks. Simulation starting with different ratios of individual stock options to the basket options confirms that 70 percent is the ratio that results in the lowest standard deviation of the

TABLE 10.5 The Impact of Hedging Basket Options with Single Stock Options

	Standard Deviation	Transaction Costs
Dynamically hedge with underlying stocks only	28.7%	2.3%
Purchase at-the-money options on stocks A and B and then dynamically hedge	14.0%	1.9%

dynamic hedging results. Table 10.5 compares the results between the two hedging strategies.

Although a substantial reduction in uncertainty and transaction costs results from utilizing an option in the constituent stocks as a hedge, it is not as large a reduction as was shown for hedging vanilla options with vanilla options at other strikes in Table 9.2. Even if we were certain of the correlation, the static hedge utilizing the purchase of at-the-money options on stocks A and B can only reduce the standard deviation to 12.2 percent. The intuitive reason for this is that the relationship of one strike being located midway between two other strikes is obviously stable, whereas the underlying stock options can move into or out of the money without a similar move on the part of the basket option. For example, if stock A's price rises by 20 percent and stock B's price falls by 20 percent, the previously at-the-money call options on stock A and B will now be substantially in and out of the money, respectively. In both cases, their sensitivity to volatility will be considerably reduced from the time of initiation. This is not true for the basket option, which will still have its same initial sensitivity to volatility since it is still at the money relative to the average price of A and B.

A possible remedy would be to dynamically change the amount of single stock options being used to hedge in response to changes in relative volatility sensitivity of the basket option and single stock options. This has many similar virtues and drawbacks with the proposal to dynamically hedge barrier options with vanilla options that was considered in Section 10.3.2. One advantage in this case is that it is considerably easier to calculate the required option hedges in the Monte Carlo simulation, provided you are willing to accept the degree of approximation of the simple formula.

Whether employing static hedging or dynamic hedging with single-asset options, the following rules should apply:

- Any residual exposure to the uncertainty of correlation should be reflected in reserve policies and limits, since this is an exposure that cannot be hedged with liquid instruments.

- Residual unhedgeable exposure to the uncertainty of single-asset volatility should be quantified, as shown in the Monte Carlo example in Table 10.5, and reflected in reserve policies and limits.
- Valuation procedures and risk measurement should be in agreement. If implied volatilities of individual assets are used as an input to the valuation of a basket option, then the exposure to changes in each constituent asset's implied volatility should be reflected, either statically or dynamically, in price-vol matrix reports and other volatility exposure measures computed for the individual asset. Similarly, delta exposure should be reflected in individual underlying asset position reports. If this principle is not followed, valuation exposure to changes in the price or volatility of an asset can grow without control by being included in more and more basket products.
- In some cases, individual asset volatility may be so slight a contribution to the risk of a basket option that it is not worth the effort of utilizing the implied volatility as an input to valuation or reflecting exposure to volatility changes in individual asset risk reports. The basket option will then effectively be managed as if it was an option on a separate underlying unrelated to the single-asset options. Note that this does not change the use of the individual underlying to perform delta hedging.

The **BasketOption** spreadsheet on the accompanying CD-ROM shows the calculation of basket option exposures to changes in correlation and individual asset volatility under the approximation of the simple formula. Table 10.6 shows some sample results for an equally weighted two-asset basket

TABLE 10.6   Sensitivities of Option on Basket

Correlation Level	1% Shift in Volatilities	10% Shift in Correlation
90%	0.97%	0.51%
75%	0.94%	0.53%
50%	0.87%	0.57%
25%	0.79%	0.62%
0%	0.71%	0.69%
−25%	0.61%	0.79%
−50%	0.50%	0.95%
−75%	0.35%	1.30%
−90%	0.22%	1.85%
−95%	0.16%	2.31%
−98%	0.10%	2.90%

with both assets having a 20 percent volatility. The impacts shown are for a 1% shift in the volatilities of both assets (for example, 20% + 1% = 21%) and a 10% shift in correlation (for example, 75% + 10% = 85%).

Note how the relative contribution of individual stock volatility relative to correlation declines sharply as correlation levels become negative. This is very relevant for options on the spread between two asset prices, since the hedge basket then consists of a positive position in one asset and a negative position in the other. If the assets are strongly correlated, their positions in the basket will show high negative correlation. In these cases, hedging the individual option volatilities is questionable.

One reporting issue for all multiasset derivatives is whether to take correlation into account when reporting delta and vega exposure of the derivative. As a concrete example, consider a forward on the average of two stocks, A and B, whose prices are 90 percent correlated. If the overall basket position has an exposure of $1 million for a 10 percent rise in the average price, should you show the exposure to A as $500,000 or as something closer to $1 million to reflect the probability that a rise in the price of A will be accompanied by a rise in the price of B? Clearly, for purposes of the firm's consolidated risk-management reports, $500,000 is the right figure since the consolidated reports will also be showing a $500,000 exposure to B and these two positions will contribute to the consolidated reporting of total exposure to a 10 percent increase in stock prices. If you used a position closer to $1 million for the A exposure, it would have the absurd result, when combined with exposure to B, of showing an exposure greater than $1 million to a 10 percent increase in stock prices. However, including a correlation may be appropriate for specially tailored reports for traders who want a quick rule of thumb about how much the basket price will move when stock A's price moves (perhaps because A's price is more liquid than B's). A particular example that has attracted industry attention is the sensitivity of convertible bond prices to changes in the underlying stock price, which we discuss further in Section 10.4.4.

A particular example of a basket option is an Asian option on a single asset. An Asian option is an option on the average price of the asset over a specified set of observations. This is equivalent to an option on a basket of forwards where all the forwards are for the same underlying asset. Obviously, one would expect correlations on such forwards to be quite high. In fact, the conventional Asian option pricing formula assumes a correlation of 100 percent (see Hull [2002, Section 19.10]), which is equivalent to assuming constant interest rates, which is slightly inaccurate. Note that the time period over which each forward will contribute volatility to the basket is different, which is a key element to be taken into account in the pricing of the option.

10.4.3   Index Options

As a generalization, we have stated that most multiasset derivatives are illiquid. But this rule has clear exceptions—most prominently, options on interest rate swaps and options on equity indices. Options on interest rate swaps, also known as *swaptions*, are mathematically and financially equivalent to options on a basket of forwards so they reflect an implied correlation. This special case is treated at length in Section 10.5. Options on stock indices, such as the S&P 500, Nasdaq, FTSE, and NIKKEI, are among the most widely traded of all options. Comparing implied volatilities of stock index options with implied volatilities of options on single stocks that are constituents of the index will therefore yield implied correlation levels. We look at the risk-management consequences, which can also be applied to other liquid index options such as options on commodity baskets and FX baskets.

The first principle is that the valuation of a reasonably liquid index option should always be directly based on market prices for the index option and not derived from prices for options on individual stocks in the index and a correlation assumption. Correlation assumptions, no matter how well based in historical analysis and economic reasoning, should never be allowed to replace a market-derived implied correlation to assess the price at which risk can be exited. This is just an application of the same reasoning that says that reasonably liquid options need to be valued using implied volatilities, not volatility assumptions based on history.

This does not mean that room is not available for models that analyze the index option price in terms of its constituent parts. Traders frequently employ trading strategies based on how rich or cheap the implied correlation is relative to correlations based on historical and economic analysis. When they conclude that implied correlations are too low, they buy the index option and sell options on individual stocks in the index, hoping to gain if realized correlation is higher than implied. This is called a *convergence position*. When they conclude that implied correlations are too high, they buy options on individual stocks and sell the index option. This is called a *divergence position*. Corporate risk managers need to make a judgment about how high or low realized correlation can go in measuring the riskiness of these positions.

Index options are also potentially useful in hedging illiquid basket options. For example, if a market maker has written an option on an average of 50 stocks, all of which are components of the S&P index, hedging the volatility risk of the basket option by buying an option on the S&P 500 index is likely to leave less residual risk than buying options on the 50 individual stocks and it will certainly be far more efficient from an operational risk viewpoint (an error is more likely tracking 50 options positions in single stocks than 1 options position in the index). Also in favor of the index option hedge is that index options are almost always more liquid than single stock options.

However, if the option written was on the average of two stocks that are components of the S&P 500 index, hedging the volatility risk of the basket option by buying options on the two single stocks is likely to leave less residual risk than buying an option on the S&P 500 index. At some point between 2 and 50 stocks, the index hedge is less uncertain than the individual stock hedge, but it needs to be found empirically through simulation. Simulation is also necessary to measure the residual uncertainty of the index stock hedge for purposes of calculating reserves and limits. The most accurate means of simulation is a Monte Carlo with dynamic hedging in an underlying asset package for which the deltas on individual stocks are computed as the net of the delta on the basket option and the delta on the index option. An approximation that is much easier to compute and reasonably accurate for large baskets is to assume no delta hedging and just compute the tracking error between the two options that occurs at the final payoff.

10.4.4 Options to Exchange One Asset for Another

At the beginning of Chapter 9, we stated that all vanilla options could be viewed as the option to exchange one asset for another. It is equally true, following a result of Margrabe, that every option to exchange one asset for another can be evaluated by the Black-Scholes option formula used for vanilla options (see Hull [2002, Section 19.11]). So why should we try to view these as multiasset options? Because by bringing in a third asset that plays no role in the original contract, we can in some cases increase the liquidity of the option's valuation. This can most easily be seen by a concrete example.

Consider an option to exchange 10,000 ounces of gold for £4.5 million. Clearly, this option will be exercised if and only if an ounce of gold at the expiration of the option is worth more than £450. Equally clearly, this contrast has absolutely no reference or relationship to dollars. However, it can be viewed, as a mathematical equivalence, as a spread option on the difference between the dollar price of 10,000 ounces of gold and the dollar price of £4.5 million. To see this equivalence, consider the following:

- The option will be exercised if and only if an ounce of gold is worth more than £450. This is equivalent to saying it will be exercised if and only if the dollar price of an ounce of gold is worth more than the dollar price of £450, which is equivalent to saying it will be exercised if and only if the dollar price of an ounce of gold minus the dollar

price of £450 is greater than 0. Multiplying by 10,000, this is equivalent to saying it will be exercised if and only if the dollar price of
10,000 ounces of gold minus the dollar price of £4.5 million is greater
than 0.

- If the option is exercised, it can be exercised by buying 10,000 ounces
of gold for its then current market price in dollars, exchanging the
gold under the options contract for £4.5 million, and selling the £4.5
million for its then current market price in dollars. The (necessarily
positive) difference between the dollar sale price and the dollar purchase price represents the payoff of the option.

What has been gained by introducing dollars into the picture? If sterling
options on gold have no liquid market, but dollar options on gold and dollar-
sterling options have a liquid market, then the gold-sterling spread option
can be valued and risk managed based on the implied volatilities of dollar-
gold and dollar-sterling vanilla option hedges. Some residual uncertainty will
still exist due to the assumed correlation level, but this residual uncertainty
may be less than the uncertainty of an illiquid gold-sterling exchange option.
As we saw in Table 10.6, this will depend on the gold and sterling-dollar
prices not being too highly correlated with one another. If they are highly
correlated, implying a very negative correlation for the long and short positions in the spread basket, then little can be gained from being able to hedge
the sensitivity to implied volatilities of dollar-gold and dollar-sterling.

A particular case of an option to exchange one asset for another that
draws considerable attention is the large market in convertible bonds.
Convertible bonds offer the bondholder an option to exchange the bond for
a fixed number of shares of the firm issuing the convertible bond. Convertible bonds generally have reasonably liquid markets, so there is rarely a
valuation advantage to viewing them as spread options. However, when
determining trading strategies and evaluating risk exposures, it is often convenient to assess the dependence of convertible bond valuations on the
implied volatility of the equity option (more precisely, the equity-cash
option), the assumed volatility of the option on a straight (nonconvertible)
bond issued by the firm, and the assumed correlation between the bond and
the stock.

As discussed in Section 6.3, one trading strategy often pursued is to try
to take advantage of the implied volatility for an equity option on the stock
of a particular firm being higher than the equity volatility implied by the price
of a convertible bond issued by that firm. A trader may decide that buying
a convertible is an inexpensive way of buying volatility on the firm's equity
price. Or a trader might choose to run a basis position long the convertible
bond and short the equity option. Risk analysis of such positions should be

sensitive to the reasonableness of assumptions about the volatility of the bond option and the correlation between the bond and stock that have been used to conclude that the convertible bond's equity volatility is cheap. The valuation of a convertible should always be based on observed market prices, not on assumptions about correlation.

Another issue that frequently arises in the management of convertible positions is determining the correct delta to use in hedging a convertible position with stock. It has often been observed that when stock prices are so low that the convertible is far from its exercise price, the actual response of the convertible price to changes in the stock price is far larger than would be expected from a delta derived from a model that only accounts for volatility of the stock price. The explanation of this observation can be found in the correlation between the bond and stock. When stock prices are far below its exercise prices, a convertible bond ought to behave very much like a straight bond, but both the bond and stock price will be impacted in similar ways by changes in the outlook for the firm's earnings (this is discussed in more detail in Section 12.2.3).

If a convertible bond behaves more like a straight bond than a stock, then a straight bond would seem like a better hedge. However, there might be reasons for using the stock as a hedge, such as greater liquidity or ease in borrowing the stock relative to the straight bond. In such instances, hedging ratios should certainly reflect the assumed correlation between stock and bond prices. But you must be careful to remember that the correlation assumption drives this delta. For example, if the firm's risk reports show a sensitivity to credit spread for the convertible, also showing a high sensitivity to stock price for the convertible in the firm's risk reports would involve a double count of the sensitivity to the bond price—once directly and once though the bond-stock correlation.

10.4.5 Nonlinear Combinations of Asset Prices

When a derivative's payoff is the function of a nonlinear combination of a set of asset prices, none of the three simplifying characteristics that hold for a linear combination can be assumed to be in force. This can be illustrated by a single concrete example—a *quanto* forward whose payoff is calculated by the product of an asset price and FX rate.

On January 25, 2002, stock in the Sony Corporation was trading at 6,080 yen per share and the yen was trading at 134.79 yen per dollar. So the then current dollar price of a share of Sony stock was 6,080/134.79 = $45.11. The 6-month forward price for Sony stock on that date was also roughly 6,080 yen per share and the 6-month forward exchange rate was 133.51 yen per dollar. Suppose a customer comes to a market maker looking to purchase 1,000,000 shares of Sony stock for 6-month forward delivery at a dollar price. Possible contracts (see Reiner [1992] for a full discussion) could be:

- Make the purchases at a dollar price fixed in advance. The market maker has a static hedge available (it is an exchange of assets, as discussed in Section 10.4.4). She can purchase 1,000,000 shares for 6-month forward delivery at 1,000,000 × 6,080 = 6,080,000 yen and purchase 6,080,000 yen for 6-month forward delivery at 6,080,000/ 133.51 = $45,539,660, which is the price, without profit margin, she should charge the customer.
- Make the purchase at a dollar price based on the exchange rate, which will be in effect in 6 months. The market maker has a static hedge available. She can purchase 1,000,000 shares for 6-month forward delivery at 1,000,000 × 6,080 = 6,080,000 yen. The dollar price will be determined in 6 months based on the then prevailing exchange.
- Agree that the dollar price per share will differ from the current 6-month forward price of 6,080/133.51 = $45.54 per share by the percentage change in the yen price per share. So if the yen price in 6 months is 6,080 × 110% = 6,688, the price per share to be paid will be $45.54 × 110% = $50.094. This is a quanto.

No static hedge is available for a quanto. The market maker can begin with a purchase of 1,000,000 shares for 6-month forward delivery for 6,080,000 yen and a 6-month forward exchange of 6,080,000 yen for $45,539,660. However, if the forward share price rises by 10 percent, she now has FX risk on an additional 1,000,000 × 6,080 × 10% = 608,000 yen and must enter into a forward exchange of these yen for dollars. If the forward FX rate rises by 10% to 133.51 × 110% = 146.86 yen per dollar, she now has stock price risk of an additional 10%, since her stock price hedge is for a fixed amount of yen and what she needs is a hedge for a fixed amount of dollars. As the yen weakens against the dollar, she needs to increase the amount of hedge denominated in yen to maintain the dollar amount of the hedge. This pattern, a change in one asset price requiring a dynamic change of the hedge amount of the other asset, is typical of derivatives with payoffs based on the product of two asset prices.

The formula for valuation of a quantoed forward, under the assumption of a bivariate lognormal distribution, is the price of a standard forward multiplied by $\exp(\rho\sigma_S\sigma_F)$, where σ_S is the volatility of the stock price denominated in yen, σ_F is the volatility of the FX rate (that is, the yen price denominated in dollars), and ρ is the correlation between the stock price denominated in yen and the FX rate. (A brief explanation of this formula can be found in Hull [2002, Sections 21.7–21.8]. A more detailed derivation can be found in Baxter and Rennie [1996, Section 4.5].) Two important consequences follow from this formula. First, the value of the derivative, even though it is not an option, is dependent on the volatilities of the assets and the correlation. Second, if the correlation is zero, then the valuation formula for a quanto is the same as the valuation formula for a standard forward, so the total impact of the dynamic hedging required must balance out to zero (however, this dynamic hedging could still result in transaction costs).

A derivative with very similar characteristics to a quanto is a difference swap, in which the payoff is based on the future difference between interest rates in different currencies multiplied by a notional principal denominated in one of the currencies. For example, the difference between a dollar interest rate and a yen interest rate may be multiplied by a dollar notional amount. The future dollar interest rate multiplied by the dollar notional amount represents a quantity that can be statically hedged, but a yen interest rate multiplied by a dollar notional amount is a quantoed combination that requires dynamic hedging of both the yen interest rate and the dollar/yen FX rate. For more details, see Hull (2002, Section 21.8) and Baxter and Rennie (1996, Section 6.5).

Once the bivariate lognormal assumption is dropped, more complex valuation algorithms are required. Both the Monte Carlo and trinomial tree approaches discussed in Section 10.4.1 have the flexibility to be directly applied to quantos or any other derivative based on a nonlinear combination of asset prices. Both approaches build probability distributions for each asset separately and can incorporate a full volatility surface (and, in the case of Monte Carlo, can incorporate stochastic volatility and price jumps). Both approaches can factor in any desired correlation assumptions between assets. Both approaches can then compute any desired function of the asset prices, no matter how complex, based on the individual asset prices at each node (and Monte Carlo can incorporate full price histories of the assets if they play a role in the function).

Nonlinear functions of multiple asset prices can range from the simplicity of the maximum or minimum price of a basket of assets to the complexity of an involved set of rules for successively dropping high and low prices out of a basket on which an average is being calculated. Some assets in the basket may represent quantoed translations from other currencies. As a further step, options can be written on any of these nonlinear functions, and exotic features such as barriers can be introduced. So long as the Monte Carlo or tree is valuing the nonlinear function correctly, it should also value the option correctly. A general designation for derivatives based on nonlinear functions of multiple asset prices and their derived options is a *rainbow contract*.

Hedging considerations for derivatives on nonlinear combinations are exactly parallel to those for derivatives on linear combinations, so the approach in Section 10.4.2 can be applied. The only difference is that the simple approximation formulas used in that section do not apply. Computations of sensitivities to shifts in asset prices, implied volatilities, and assumed correlations generally need to be evaluated by rerunning the Monte Carlo or trinomial tree valuation model with shifted inputs.

Another interesting example that is similar in structure to the quanto is counterparty credit exposure on a derivative such as an interest rate swap of a FX forward. As discussed in Section 12.4, counterparty credit exposure can grow or diminish through time as a function of the interest rate or FX rate driving the value of the derivative. This credit exposure can be hedged by the purchase of credit derivatives or the short sale of bonds issued by the counterparty. The total value of the credit exposure is then the product of the value of the derivative and the credit spread on the counterparty. Similar to a quanto, a dynamic hedge is required. A change in the value of the derivative requires a change in the size of the credit hedge and a change in the size of the credit spread requires a change in the size of the derivative hedge.

In Section 9.3, we examined a case of mean reversion in which there is a narrower dispersion of final underlying price levels than would be implied by a pure random walk and we questioned whether dynamic hedging costs would be a function of the higher short-term volatility or the lower long-term dispersion. Our answer, based on both Monte Carlo simulation and theory, was that sufficiently frequent rehedging makes dynamic hedging costs depend entirely on short-term volatility, but a trader who wanted to take advantage of anticipated lower long-term dispersion could do so by rehedging less frequently (but with an attendant trade-off of a higher uncertainty of hedging costs).

Let's ask a parallel question for correlation. Suppose you anticipate that two assets will have a strong correlation in terms of long-term trend, but very little correlation in terms of short-term moves. If you are dynamically hedging a position whose valuation depends on correlation, will your dynamic hedging costs be a function of the low short-term correlation or the high long-term correlation?

You shouldn't be surprised to find that the answer is the same for correlation as it is for single-asset volatility. If you rehedge often enough, only the short-term correlation impacts hedging costs. If you want to take advantage of the anticipated long-term trend, you must hedge less frequently and accept a higher uncertainty of hedging costs in exchange for expected hedging costs being influenced by the longer-term correlation.

Many people find this conclusion highly nonintuitive. Consider an example. Suppose you are hedging the counterparty credit risk on an FX forward and that over the life of the forward the exposure continues to grow while the credit rating of the counterparty continuously deteriorates, but the individual moves are uncorrelated. As the exposure grows, you are going to have to buy more credit protection, and it may be hard to believe that you will not have to pay for this increased credit protection at the higher price levels brought on by the deteriorating credit rating.

To help see how this works mechanically, I have provided the **CrossHedge** spreadsheet, which enables you to enter a price history of six prices for each asset and which looks at the hedging of an exotic paying the product of the two asset prices. The spreadsheet shows the hedging and its costs under two assumptions: if the price moves between the two assets are completely uncorrelated and if the price moves between the two assets are perfectly correlated. The complete lack of correlation is implemented by having each price move on the first asset precede in time each price move on the second asset, so there is time to change the hedge quantity before the second asset's price changes. (Remember that for a payoff tied to the product of two asset prices, a change in the price of one asset requires a change in the hedge quantity of the other asset.) Perfect correlation is implemented by simultaneous changes in prices.

Figure 10.7 shows the case of deteriorating credit on counterparty credit risk. The first asset is the exposure amount and the second asset is the discount on the counterparty's bonds. As credit deteriorates, the discount goes all the way to 100 percent, corresponding to the worst possible case of default with no recovery. Despite the fact that the exposure is steadily growing while the discount is steadily increasing, the change in the value of the product is completely hedged in the uncorrelated case. Examining the impact of the individual hedges should impart a better sense of how the hedge works —each change in credit quality and exposure has been hedged by having the right size hedge in place at the time of the change.

10.4.6 Correlation between Price and Exercise

Standard option pricing assumes a correlation of 100 percent between price and exercise—that is, option buyers will exercise their options when, and only when, the price of the underlying asset makes it profitable to exercise. However, in some instances, it can be argued that a correlation of less than 100 percent should be assumed. These arguments rely on a combination of historical experience, showing that a previous correlation has been less than perfect, and on a behavioral analysis of the option buyers, demonstrating that they have motivations that conflict with optimal option exercise. In terms of game theory, standard option analysis, which assumes a correlation of 100 percent, is equivalent to a zero-sum game in which a loss by the option seller is exactly offset by a gain for the option buyer. A correlation of less than 100 percent corresponds to a non-zero-sum game.

Start / End price path

	Asset1	Asset2
Start	10	5
1	20	10
2	30	30
3	40	50
4	50	80
End	60	100

		P&L
Quanto		-5,950
Hedges	Asset1	1,750
	Asset2	4,200
	Total	0

Uncorrelated

	Prices Asset1	Prices Asset2	Asset1 Buy/Sell	Asset1 Price	Asset1 Proceeds	Asset2 Buy/Sell	Asset2 Price	Asset2 Proceeds
Start	10	5	5	10	-50	10	5	-50
	20	5	0	20	0	10	5	-50
1	20	10	5	20	-100	0	10	0
	30	10	0	30	0	10	10	-100
2	30	30	20	30	-600	0	30	0
	40	30	0	40	0	10	30	-300
3	40	50	20	40	-800	0	50	0
	50	50	0	50	0	10	50	-500
4	50	80	30	50	-1,500	0	80	0
	60	80	0	60	0	10	80	-800
End	60	100	20	60	-1,200	0	100	0
	60	100	-100	60	6,000	-60	100	6,000
Total					1,750			4,200

Correlated

	Asset1 Buy/Sell	Asset1 Price	Asset1 Proceeds	Asset2 Buy/Sell	Asset2 Price	Asset2 Proceeds
Start	5	10	-50	10	5	-50
1	5	20	-100	10	10	-100
2	20	30	-600	10	30	-300
3	20	40	-800	10	50	-500
4	30	50	-1,500	10	80	-800
End	20	60	-1,200	10	100	-1,000
	-100	60	6,000	-60	100	6,000
Total			1,750			3,250

		P&L
Quanto		-5,950
Hedges	Asset1	1,750
	Asset2	3,250
	Total	-950

FIGURE 10.7 Cross-hedge of deteriorating credit on a growing counterparty exposure.

276

Table 10.7 shows the impact of different correlation assumptions, multiplying the payoff based on price and exercise by the probability and summing to get an expected return.

For example, it may be argued that a municipality that has the option to require early repayment of a fixed-rate term deposit without paying any penalty, which is equivalent to a swaption, will only exercise this option in response to a change in its cash needs, which are uncorrelated with interest rate levels. Support for this analysis should certainly include historical studies of how similar municipalities have exercised these options. However, even reasonable explanations of behavior and historical precedent may be questionable evidence. In the absence of any actual legal constraint or internal costs that exercise would entail, it is possible that institutions will become more efficient exercisers of options over time, as they gain financial sophistication or as large economic movements (for example, unusually high interest rates on new deposits) create increased incentives to focus attention.

Such arguments may become more plausible when the option must be exercised by a large group of individuals. Correlation now becomes a

TABLE 10.7   Correlation between Price and Exercise

Standard Option

Price	Exercise	No Exercise		Probability			
110	−10	0	×	50%	0	=	−5
90	+10	0		0	50%		

No Correlation

Price	Exercise	No Exercise		Probability			
110	−10	0	×	25%	25%	=	0
90	+10	0		25%	25%		

Some Correlation

Price	Exercise	No Exercise		Probability			
110	−10	0	×	35%	15%	=	−2
90	+10	0		15%	35%		

Negative Correlation

Price	Exercise	No Exercise		Probability			
110	−10	0	×	15%	35%	=	+2
90	+10	0		35%	15%		

question of what proportion of a population will exercise options in a timely fashion, and their diversity of circumstances will argue for less than perfect correlation. An example would be a pension plan that guarantees some minimum return on a particular investment strategy. If option exercise were a zero-sum game, the individual investors would withdraw from the plan whenever the investment was below the minimum return in order to collect the guarantee. However, financial institutions that provide these guarantees value them based on behavioral assumptions about the individual participants, whose varied circumstances with regard to age, career, and tax status make the cost of exercising the option different for each subgroup.

An important example of an option exercised by a large group of individuals is the very sizable market in asset-backed bonds, where each bond is backed by a pool of mortgages, automobile loans, or other consumer loans. Although these assets often provide consumers the legal right to prepay the loan without penalty, individual circumstances often get in the way of an economically efficient exercise of this right. First, refinancing a loan often involves substantial personal costs (for example, legal fees, title searches, and the time devoted to the transaction). For an institution on a large loan, these would probably be insignificant relative to gains from exercise, but this may not be true for an individual. Second, some consumers may not be able to refinance due to a deteriorating credit rating or decrease in asset value. Others may have strong personal motives that outweigh the costs of financing, such as a required move or a divorce forcing a home sale that causes a desirable rate mortgage to be prepaid or the desire to trade a car for a newer model.

Given the enormous size of this asset class and the plausibility of less than perfect correlations, financial firms have invested and continue to invest large amounts of money in research to develop accurate models of this correlation. For some assets, such as automobile loans, the general conclusion is that correlation tends to be close to zero. For mortgages, correlation is definitely strongly positive—falling mortgage rates trigger massive refinancings and rising mortgage rates trigger considerably slow refinancings. However, correlation is certainly far from perfect and the stakes in properly identifying which mortgage bonds represent good investments are sufficiently high to support detailed research trying to predict the relationship between refinancing behavior and prevailing mortgage rates by population subcomponent, such as the geographic region or size of mortgage. The relationships developed are often quite complex. The behavior depends not just on current mortgage rates, but also past mortgage rates and yield curve shape. Consumers are found to be sensitive not only to the current refinancing advantage, but also to beliefs as to whether that advantage will be growing, since the costs of refinancing are high enough to cause consumers to attempt to minimize the number of times they refinance. Another factor, known as *burnout*, indicates that a consumer population that has already experienced a period of low rates will show lower refinancing response (as a proportion of mortgages still outstanding) in a subsequent low rate period. This is presumably due to the proportion of those who did not refinance the first time who cannot afford to refinance. Monte Carlo models of the correlation are used to project consumer behavior under a variety of possible future interest rate movements, and bonds are ranked on the basis of *option-adjusted spread* (OAS)—the spread the bond is earning over a comparable maturity Treasury after taking into account the cost of the refinancing option based on the assumed correlation.

Why does this spread remain? One reason is certainly that these correlation relationships are only estimates based on past data that could prove to be wrong. When unanticipated shifts in consumer behavior on refinancings are observed, such as a prolonged period of very low rates resulting in greater consumer education about refinancings, leading to refinancing levels that substantially exceed those predicted by models based on past data, OAS can show large rapid increases. To some extent, this will later reduce as Monte Carlo models are updated to accommodate the new experience, but some OAS increase may persist, reflecting an increase in uncertainty over the accuracy of such models.

10.5 CORRELATION-DEPENDENT INTEREST RATE OPTIONS

Throughout Chapter 9 on vanilla options and in Sections 10.1 and 10.2, we have dealt with options whose underlying can be regarded as a forward to a set future date. As we discussed at the beginning of Chapter 9, all uncertainty about discounting rates for these models can be collapsed into the volatility of the forward. However, some options have payoffs that depend on forwards for several different future dates (but with all forwards on the same spot underlying). The primary example would be an American option that gives the option holder freedom to determine the timing of payoff. More complex dependence on different forwards can be seen in the products we examined in Section 10.3, such as barrier options.

Options that depend on forwards for several different future dates can usefully be viewed as options on multiple underlyings with all relationships between these forwards built into the correlation structure assumed between the forwards. Indeed, this is the approach to multifactor interest rate models that has predominated over the past decade in the form of the Heath-Jarrow-Morton (HJM) models (see Hull [2002, Section 24.2]) and the LIBOR market models, also known as Brace-Gatarek-Musiela (BGM) models (see Hull [2002, Section 24.3]).

Should we then just view these products as a particular class of options with multiple underlyings and consider their risk-management issues as already having been dealt with in Section 10.4? One reason for not availing ourselves of this convenient shortcut is that the large volume of these options that actively trade encourages extra effort to try to find a simpler structure and faster computation time for subsets of this product. Another reason is that this represents the only class of multiasset options where some reasonable liquidity exists in products that require correlation inputs to value, so it is worth studying how much information on correlation can be extracted from observed market prices.

Three levels of models are essentially available, of increasing mathematical and computational complexity. The simplest level includes the binomial and trinomial tree models in which the relationship between different forwards is treated as constant. In Section 10.5.1, we examine risk management using these models and the conditions under which more complex models are required. The second level includes the single-factor interest rate models in which the relationship between different forwards is treated as stochastic. In Section 10.5.2, we examine risk management using these models and the conditions under which the third level of full-blown multifactor HJM or BGM models are required. Finally, in Section 10.5.3, we look at how much correlation information can be extracted from observed market prices.

10.5.1 Models in Which the Relationship between Forwards Is Treated as Constant

We have already encountered binomial and trinomial tree models in which the relationship between forwards is treated as constant—the local volatility models discussed in Section 10.3.2. Recall that this section was devoted to options whose payoff depends on the underlying price of a single asset at several different times. Because values of the asset at several different times are involved, we needed to be concerned with hedging and valuation depending on several different forwards. However, the only way to avoid treating these different forwards as multiple assets is to assume that a constant relation exists between them. This is in effect what is done in the local volatility models of Section 10.3.2, since the only variable changing on the tree is the spot price of the asset and all forward prices are derived based on fixed interest rate relationships between forward and spot prices.

In this section, we study the simplest, most widely traded, and best known version of a product that depends on the underlying price of a single asset at several times—the *American option*. American options differ from European options by a single added feature: the right of the option buyer to exercise the option at any time. A simple variant restricts the right to exercise to several specified times and is variously known as a *semi-European, semi-American,* or (as a geographic middleground between European and American) *Bermudan option.*

American and Bermudan options have long been valued using binomial trees (the Cox-Ross-Rubinstein model) and more recently using trinomial trees to allow for nonflat volatility surfaces. (See Hull [2002, Sections 18.1– 18.5] for the mathematics of the binomial tree. See Clewlow and Strickland [1998, Chapter 5] for the use of trinomial trees to incorporate the volatility surface.) The key assumption is that the relationship between the forwards remains fixed. Most typically, this is represented by a constant interest rate and forward drift (or constant dividend rate, with *drift* defined as the interest rate less the dividend rate). However, any constant set of relationships between forwards can be accommodated with no increase in complexity or cost of computation, as discussed in Hull (2002, Section 18.4).

Four factors drive the value of early exercise (all of this discussion is for calls—we are continuing our convention from Chapter 9 of treating all options as calls):

- **Price.** When prices rise, it increases the probability of price levels high enough to warrant early exercise, so early exercise value increases.
- **Volatility.** The more volatile the price, the greater the incentive not to exercise early in order to take advantage of the time value of the option. However, high volatility means a greater percentage of price moves will be large enough to warrant early exercise. So the two impacts of higher volatility run in opposite directions. In practice, the second effect is usually larger, and higher volatility increases early exercise value.
- **Financing cost.** The higher the net cost of funding the delta hedge of the option, the greater the incentive to exercise early. However, if net financing cost is earning the option buyer money on his delta hedge, it discourages early exercise. An equivalent way of viewing this is through the drift of the forward. If drift is positive, this decreases the incentive to exercise the call early since it is likely the call will be worth more after the upward drift. If drift is negative, this increases the incentive to exercise the call early since it is likely the call will be worth less after the downward drift.
- **Discount rate.** Early exercise allows earlier receipt of option payoffs. This is more valuable the higher the discount rate, so high discount rates encourage early exercise.

The **AmericanOption** spreadsheet illustrates the computation of American option values using a Cox-Ross-Rubinstein binomial tree. It focuses on the computation of the early exercise value, defined as the excess value the American option possesses over the corresponding European option. Figure 10.8 shows some sample results.

strike	100	100	100	100	100	100	100
time	1	1	1	1	1	1	1
volatility	20%	20%	20%	20%	20%	20%	30%
rate	0%	1%	0%	0%	5%	10%	0%
drift	0%	0%	-1%	-5%	0%	0%	-1%
European price	7.97%	7.89%	7.44%	5.57%	7.58%	7.21%	11.37%
American price	7.97%	7.90%	7.52%	6.09%	7.66%	7.40%	11.45%
Early exercise	0.00%	0.01%	0.08%	0.51%	0.09%	0.19%	0.08%
vega	0.40%	0.39%	0.39%	0.38%	0.38%	0.36%	0.39%
Early exercise as % of:							
European price	0.00%	0.17%	1.05%	9.23%	1.13%	2.65%	0.70%
Vega	0.00%	3.46%	19.72%	136.95%	22.74%	53.11%	20.16%
American / European Delta	100.02%	100.24%	100.96%	110.39%	101.63%	103.96%	100.58%
American / European Vega	100.00%	100.18%	99.99%	99.84%	101.15%	102.68%	100.08%
Rate sensitivity per $1mm	$136	$163	$202	$214	$201	$219	$291
Drift sensitivity per $1mm	$778	$844	$1,044	$1,267	$971	$1,037	$956

FIGURE 10.8 Early exercise values and hedges for American option.

Note from Figure 10.8 the relatively small impact of discount rates on early exercise relative to drift. Since exchange-traded American options are all options on a fixed forward, they all have zero drift, so early exercise value is quite small. This explains the claim made at the start of Chapter 9 that exchange-traded American options have little valuation difference from European options.

Hedges can be established for the impact on the early exercise value of all four of these factors, as illustrated in Figure 10.8. For delta and vega, we calculate the ratio of American option delta and vega to the corresponding European option delta and vega, enabling the American to be represented in delta reports and price-vol matrices for the corresponding European option. For discount and drift, the sensitivity of the early exercise value to a 100 basis point shift is calculated and can be used to establish a hedge. This is a comparable situation to vega hedging an option you are valuing using the Black-Scholes model—the theory behind the model says volatility is constant, but you are going "outside the model" to hedge against volatility uncertainty. Here we are determining the early exercise value using a model that says that discount rate and drift are constant, but we are establishing a hedge against an uncertain discount rate and drift.

The critical assumption when calculating these hedges is that discount rate and drift risk can be valued and hedged as variables independent of the spot price risk. Equivalently, the assumption is that the level of forward rates is uncorrelated with the shape of the forward rate curve. This assumption is reasonable for most equities, questionable for FX and commodities (refer back to our discussion of mean reversion in Section 9.3), and certainly false for interest rate options, since high correlation will exist between the rate determining the payoff and the rates determining the discount and drift.

Is it possible that the impact of this correlation is small enough to ignore for practical purposes? As shown in Figure 10.8, when drift is positive or zero or when it is not too negative, the total size of the early exercise value is not too large so any impact of correlation can probably be ignored. When drift is quite negative, early exercise value becomes significant and it is likely that the impact of correlation between interest rates needs to be taken into account. To do so requires some type of term structure model—the factors influencing choices between these models is discussed in the next section.

This is particularly true for options on bonds or on swaps, where the *pull to par* causes drift to be very negative. Because the duration of a bond or swap gets shorter as time passes, the impact of interest rates on prices is continuously declining. So an option holder faced with an early exercise decision knows that the current price premium is likely to diminish through time —if interest rates don't move further in her favor, current rate levels will translate into a smaller price advantage in the future. This is true both for options that pay on rising interest rates and those that pay on falling interest rates, since both high bond prices based on low interest rates and low bond prices based on high interest rates move in the direction of par if rates stay the same as time to maturity diminishes.

If any substantial reduction in the duration of an underlying bond or swap occurs during the tenor of an option, this negative drift will require a term structure model. If no substantial reduction in duration occurs over the option tenor, then a Cox-Ross-Rubinstein model with the duration held constant can be used as a reasonable approximation. A rule of thumb that is often used is that this approximation is suitable as long as the duration of the underlying at the start of the option life is at least 10 times as great as the option tenor. So this rule of thumb would allow the use of a Cox-Ross-Rubinstein model for a 6-month option on a 10-year bond, but would insist on a term structure model for a 1-year option on a 5-year bond.

10.5.2 Term Structure Models

Broadly speaking, term structure models come in two varieties: single-factor models that assume that the correlation between all forwards is 100 percent and multifactor models that can accommodate less than perfect correlation structures. Both types of model can handle a correlation between the underlying of the option and drift. Multifactor models are obviously more accurate, but add a considerable cost in computation time and complexity. Since American and Bermudan options on swaps and bonds are by far the most utilized exotic in the interest rate options market, there is a strong incentive to try to use single-factor models for this product as long as accuracy is reasonable.

A critical fact about interest rate options, which any term structure model needs to deal with, is that options of the same tenor for bonds (or swaps) of different maturities tend to have lower interest rate volatilities for the long maturity. This can be confirmed both by observations of implied volatilities from market quotes and from historical volatility observations of par bond or swap yields. (For example, Table 10.8 shows annualized volatilities by tenor based on 6 years of dollar par swap yields between 1996 and 2001—see the **DataMetricsRatesData** spreadsheet for the underlying data.)

Broadly speaking, this fact can be explained by some combination of the following two theses:

- Forward rates are less than perfectly correlated with one another and the longer the bond maturity, the more its volatility is dependent on the correlation between forwards.
- Longer-term forwards have lower volatility than shorter-term forwards.

The latter theory implies that interest rates are mean reverting, since it requires the standard deviation of longer-term forwards to be lower than that

TABLE 10.8 Annualized Volatility of Dollar Par Swap Yields

Tenor	2 Years	3 Years	4 Years	5 Years	6 Years	7 Years	8 Years
Annualized Volatility	16.95	16.24	15.95	15.81	15.26	15.18	14.88

Tenor	9 Years	10 Years	12 Years	15 Years	20 Years	30 Years
Annualized Volatility	14.72	14.65	14.25	13.50	12.87	11.99

produced by a pure random walk driven by the volatility of shorter-term forwards. To see the interaction between the correlation and volatility of longer-term forwards when explaining swaption volatility, see Section 10.5.3.

Because it assumes that all correlation between forwards is 100 percent, a single-factor model must utilize the lower volatility of long-term forwards to drive the observed volatility structure of swaptions. To what extent does forcing one of these two levers to bear all of the explanatory weight distort valuation and hedging? In principle, to answer this question, build the best multifactor term structure model you can; calibrate both this multifactor model and the single-factor model that is proposed for production use to the current set of vanilla cap, floor, and European swaption prices; and then compare their output in valuing exotic products.

Although this is too daunting a computational task to attempt here, I will give a flavor of what this analysis is like for one very simple case: a 3-year time horizon; three liquid vanilla products—a 1-year caplet on a 1-year LIBOR, a 2-year caplet on a 1-year LIBOR, and a 1-year swaption on a 2-year swap; and a flat implied volatility surface with respect to strike. We will assume the 2-year swap is on a 1-year LIBOR. We will take advantage of the equivalence between swaps and packages of forward rate agreements (FRAs), as noted in Section 8.1.6. The notation we will employ is to label a FRA by the time at which its rate is determined and the time at which it settles. So a 2–3 FRA has a rate determined at the end of 2 years based on what would then be the 1-year rate.

The model will be calibrated to the current 1-year LIBOR, 1–2 FRA and 2–3 FRA, the 1-year volatility of the 1–2 FRA, the first-year volatility of the 2–3 FRA, the second-year volatility of the 2–3 FRA, and the 1-year correlation between the 1–2 FRA and the 2–3 FRA. In addition to valuing the liquid vanilla products, we will value four exotics:

- A 2-year Bermudan swaption that can either be exercised at the end of year 1 based on the then prevailing 2-year LIBOR or at the end of year 2 based on the then prevailing 1-year LIBOR

- A 2-year caplet on a 1-year LIBOR that can knock out depending on the level of a 1-year LIBOR in 1 year
- A forward start caplet on a 1-year LIBOR that has a 1-year tenor and begins in 1 year with a strike set to the then 1-year LIBOR
- A 1-year tenor option on the spread between a 2-year LIBOR and a 1-year LIBOR

Our full term structure model is in the **TermStructure** spreadsheet. It is a simple Monte Carlo implementation. It takes advantage of the fact that only two exercise points are available for the Bermudan to value it by the following trick. At the end of 2 years, exercise is a simple decision. If you are in the money at the end of 1 year, you have a choice between early exercise, which gives you a 2-year par swap, or waiting a year, which is equivalent to a 1-year caplet on a 1-year LIBOR. So you just choose the maximum value between the 2-year swap and the 1-year caplet on the 1-year LIBOR.

Using a flat initial rate curve of 1-year LIBOR = 1–2 FRA = 2–3 FRA = 7 percent, two scenarios can be computed as shown in Table 10.9, which can be verified with the spreadsheet.

Notice the following:

- The inputs have been deliberately chosen to calibrate to the same vanilla option prices in both scenarios.

TABLE 10.9   The Valuation of Interest Rate Volatility Products under Two Scenarios

	Scenario 1	Scenario 2
Inputs		
First-year volatility of 1–2 FRA	20.00%	20.00%
First-year volatility of 2–3 FRA	19.50%	14.00%
Second-year volatility of 2–3 FRA	14.83%	20.00%
First-year correlation of 1–2 FRA and 2–3 FRA	50.00%	100.00%
Valuations		
1-year caplet on 1-year LIBOR	.519	.519
1-year swaption on 2-year swap	.810	.810
2-year caplet on 1-year LIBOR	.559	.559
Bermudan swaption	.936	.949
Knock-out caplet	.400	.447
Forward start option	.645	.541
Spread option	.518	.153

- The higher correlation in scenario 2 must be balanced by lower volatility of the longer-term 2–3 FRA in the first year in order to match the 1-year swaption price. This must be followed by higher volatility in the second year when its time to maturity is shorter so that the combined first- and second-year volatilities fit the price of the 2-year caplet.
- Despite a very large difference in correlations between the two scenarios, the Bermudan swaption values close to equal in both scenarios. This reflects a trade-off between lower volatility of the 2–3 FRA in the first year, which decreases the value of early exercise, and higher volatility of the 2–3 FRA in the second year, which increases the value of the option in those cases in which early exercise does not occur.
- The knock-out caplet also shows values close to equal in both scenarios. Lower correlation increases the chances that a high 2-3 FRA, which leads to a higher caplet value, will be accompanied by a 1-2 FRA that is low enough that the caplet will not knock out. This leads to a higher caplet value but is offset by the lower second-year volatility that accompanies the lower correlation.
- Lower correlation causes the forward start option to have a higher value by adding volatility in the relation between the strike and forward to the volatility of the forward.
- The largest difference between the two scenario valuations is for the spread option, which is the product most directly tied to yield curve shape rather than level. It values much higher when lower correlation permits greater variability in shape.

This single case is consistent with the intuition of most practitioners in the interest rate options market. For Bermudan swaptions, a one-factor model can be calibrated to current vanilla prices and give reasonable results, but as you move toward products that are more dependent on the future shape of the yield curve, multifactor models become more of a necessity. Although this demonstration for a two-period case is far from conclusive for longer-term swaptions, see Andersen and Andreasen (2001) for similar conclusions in a more general setting. This spreadsheet can be useful for gaining intuition about the direction and order of magnitude of correlation assumptions on different interest rate exotics.

When multifactor models are utilized, traditionally the primary choice has been between models that assume a normal distribution of the short-term rate, such as Hull-White (see Hull [2002, Sections 23.9–23.12]), and models that assume a lognormal distribution of the short-term rate, such as Black-Derman-Toy or Black-Karasinski (see Tuckman [1996, pp. 102–109] for a succinct and balanced presentation, and references to more detailed papers).

The discussion on which of these approaches to use has often centered on whether one believes that normal or lognormal distributions of rates give closer correspondence to historical experience. This line of argument is getting to seem rather dated in light of the almost universal adoption of full volatility surfaces that accommodate mixtures of normal and lognormal assumptions in equity, FX, and commodity options models (see Section 9.6.2). As we discussed with barrier options in Section 10.3.1, not getting the shape of the implied volatility surface correct can result in major errors in the valuation of exotics. Bermudans share a key characteristic of barriers in that the strike level that determines the termination of the option can be different than the strike level that determines the value of the option, making the correct fitting of the relative volatility between these two strike levels an important determinant of valuation. A more modern approach to utilizing the full implied volatility surface when creating a single-factor interest rate options model can be found in Khuong-Huu (1999).

Other factors that go into the choice and accuracy of a single-factor model include:

- The Hull-White model offers a strong computational advantage in that the forward value of a bond or swap can be computed by analytic formula for any node of the tree (see Hull [2002, Section 23.9]). By contrast, lognormal models of the short rate must extend the tree all the way out to the maturity of the bond or swap and solve backwards on the tree to determine a forward value.

- It is possible for interest rates to become negative in some portion of the tree in normal models of the short rate. If you believe this is economically unrealistic (refer back to the discussion in Section 8.3.2), then you would want to get estimates of the degree of impact this could have on valuations and hedges (see Rebonato [1998, 13.9] for a balanced discussion of this issue and other strong and weak points of the Hull-White model).

- The limitation of having just a single factor to calibrate with leads to conflicts between the desire to correctly fit observed prices of potential hedging instruments and the desire to avoid unrealistic evolutions of the rate curve (see Rebonato [1998, 12.5 and 13.9] for an extended discussion).

- Black-Derman-Toy is a binomial tree model, in contrast to the trinomial tree models of Hull-White and Black-Karasinski, and is far easier to implement and maintain than the trinomial tree models. The price paid for this convenience is that the speed of mean reversion is determined and cannot be set as an input parameter. Overcoming this weakness was the primary motivation for the introduction of Black-Karasinski (see Hull [2002, Section 23.13]). As a result, Black-

Derman-Toy can only calibrate to a limited subset of vanilla options on any given run. For instance, in our two-period example, it could only calibrate to the 1-year swaption on a 2-year swap and the 2-year caplet, but not to the 1-year caplet. This could potentially reduce the number of possible hedging instruments that have been correctly priced by the model (see Rebonato [1998, 12.5] for further discussion).

■ All of the single-factor models share the issue that shifts in rate levels will cause shifts in the package of vanilla options that form a good hedge for an American or Bermudan option. (See Table 10.10 for an illustrative example.) It is almost certainly computationally intractable to run a Monte Carlo simulation to estimate the impact of such shifts in options hedges on future transaction costs and hedge slippage. About the best that can be done is to use a Monte Carlo simulation to estimate the hedge slippage of holding an initial static hedge determined by the initial rate level. To my knowledge, little work has been done to determine optimal static hedges of American or Bermudan options. A promising avenue to pursue would be to apply the Black-Ergener-Kani static hedging technique to one of the single-factor trees.

Table 10.10 is based on a 10-year annually exercisable Bermudan call option on a 10-year swap with a coupon rate of 7 percent and flat volatility surface at 20 percent. As should be expected, falling rates increase the value of the call, making early exercise more likely and thus increasing the impact of early volatility relative to later volatility. Rising rates decrease the value of the call, making early exercise less likely and thus increasing the impact of late volatility relative to earlier volatility. It is then easy to solve for a set of European options with similar exposure to the forward volatility curve.

TABLE 10.10 Impact of Rate Levels on the Forward Volatility Curve Dependence of a Swaption

Years	Flat Rate Level =	5%	7%	9%
1		1%	0%	0%
2		12%	4%	0%
3		13%	8%	3%
4		13%	11%	6%
5		12%	12%	8%
6		11%	13%	13%
7		11%	13%	15%
8		10%	13%	17%
9		9%	13%	19%
10		8%	12%	20%

However, a package of vanilla options that matches the distribution of exposure at one rate level will no longer match the exposure at a different rate level.

10.5.3   Relation between Swaption and Cap Prices

Since a European option on a swap or bond can be a reasonably liquid instrument, and since we can view it as equivalent for valuation purposes to an option on the baskets of FRAs, which the swap is equivalent to, we can try to extract information on market-implied correlations between FRAs from liquid prices. How much correlation information can we extract? Not that much, unless we are willing to make some additional assumptions.

To see why, let's start by considering a simplified market in which only two FRAs trade a 1–2 year and a 2–3 year. The natural options would be a 1-year caplet on the 1–2 year, a 2-year caplet on the 2–3 year, and a 1-year swaption on the combination of 1–2 year and 2–3 year. To price these three options, we need inputs for the following underlying variables: the volatility of the 1–2-year FRA in year 1, the volatility of the 2–3-year FRA in year 1, the correlation between these two FRAs in year 1, and the volatility of the 2–3-year FRA in year 2. Unfortunately, four underlying variables are present and only three options need to be priced. So it will not be possible to extract a correlation from the prices, as we have seen in the example of the previous section, unless we are willing to place some tight restrictions on the possible structure of FRA volatilities.

When we move to more realistic market assumptions, the situation does not improve. The **Swaptions** spreadsheet can take price inputs for 1-year LIBOR caplets from 1 to 10 years and all possible swaption prices involving an integral number of years less than or equal to 10 (for convenience, the prices are quoted as the equivalent Black-Scholes implied volatility). Based on an assumption as to correlation structure, the spreadsheet uses the Excel Solver to find a structure of underlying FRA volatilities that explains the prices. From your experimentation with the spreadsheet (see Exercise 10.8), you can confirm that a wide range of different correlation assumptions is consistent with a single set of prices. We have assumed zero volatility skew and smile throughout this discussion, but changing this assumption will not improve the situation.

It is possible to come to conclusions about the probability of different underlying FRA volatility structures based on historical observation, and this may result in constraints that would at least give a tight range of possible market-implied correlations. For example, one proposal that has both intuitive appeal and some empirical support is to assume that the volatility of FRAs is a function of how far they are from maturity. So the volatility of a 2–3-year FRA in its second year, when it is in the final year of its life, should be the same as the first-year volatility of a 1–2-year FRA and the third-year volatility of a 3–4-year FRA. The intuition behind this assumption is that new information has its greatest impact on nearby borrowing rates, so we should expect to see greater volatility in nearby rates and lower volatility as you go farther out in maturity (this is equivalent to assuming mean reversion of interest rates, as we saw in Section 10.5.2). So if the caplet volatility in the market for a 1–2-year FRA is 23 percent, but is 22 percent for a 2–3-year FRA, it is reasonable to assume that this 22 percent can be decomposed into a 21 percent volatility in the first year, when the FRA still has over a year to go, and a 23 percent volatility in the second and last year.

This assumption is powerful enough to enable all FRA correlations to be derived from swaption prices. To see this, consider that if you have N different FRAs for which you provide volatility assumptions, this can provide pricing for $\frac{N^2 + N}{2}$ different swaptions (N in period 1, $N - 1$ in period 2, and so on— $\sum_{i=1}^{N} i = \frac{N^2 + N}{2}$). The total number of correlations that can be specified between FRAs is $\frac{N^2 - N}{2}$, since the N correlations of a FRA with itself must be 100 percent and a correlation between FRA_i and FRA_j must equal the correlation between FRA_j and FRA_i. If you specify that FRA volatility is completely determined by time to maturity, it reduces the number of volatilities that can be specified to N. The total of specified volatilities plus specified correlations is then $N + \frac{N^2 - N}{2} = \frac{N^2 + N}{2}$. So if all $\frac{N^2 + N}{2}$ swaption prices are specified, a unique set of FRA volatilities and correlations that can explain them must exist.

However, it is possible that placing severe constraints on the relationship between different FRA volatilities will not leave enough freedom to find implied correlations that fit market swaption prices. It can also be the case that caplet volatilities decline too steeply with time to be consistent with the assumption of FRA volatility being a function only of time to maturity (compare this with the discussion in Ricardo Rebonato [1998, Section 4.5]).

EXERCISES

10.1   Using the BasketHedge Spreadsheet

1. For a flat volatility assumption (that is, smile = 0 and skew = 0), check the calculation of the square root option in the **Main** worksheet against another pricing method. The method could be analytic

(that is, based on solving a PDE), use Monte Carlo simulation, or use a binomial or trinomial tree. Whatever method you choose, make sure you check its accuracy by pricing ordinary options and comparing the answers to the Black-Scholes formula.

2. Pick another type of nonlinear payoff. Change Column C in the **Main** worksheet to calculate a hedge and pricing. Check the results for a flat volatility assumption against another pricing method, as in Part 1 of this exercise.

3. Check the impact of smile and skew on the pricing of each of the following:
   a. The square root option
   b. The option you priced in Part 2 of this exercise
   c. The single-asset quanto priced in the **Quanto** worksheet
   d. The log contract priced in the **Log** worksheet
   e. The convexity risk hedge priced in the **Convexity** worksheet
   f. The call-on-a-call option priced in **Compound** worksheet

4. Change Column C in the **Compound** worksheet to price:
   a. A put-on-a-call compound option
   b. A call-on-a-put compound option
   c. A chooser option that as of the first expiry time (B1) turns into whichever is more valuable between a call and a put priced at the same strike (B5) to a second expiry time (B4) (see Hull [2002, Section 19.5]).

5. For a call-on-a-call option and all three of the options in Part 4 of this exercise, use the **Compound** worksheet to determine how much sensitivity remains to future implied volatility after exposure to the price level has been hedged.

10.2 Using the CarrBarrier Spreadsheet

Using the same price strike, up barrier, down barrier, and original time to expiry as the one used in Figure 10.2, perform the following:

1. Test the validity of the claim that unwind P&L is zero whenever drift and skew at unwind are zero. Try different combinations of time to expiry, at-the-money volatility, smile, and rate at the time the barrier is hit. Also try different combinations of drift and skew at the time the option is originated.

2. What conclusions can you draw about the pattern of dependence of unwind P&L on different values of drift?

3. What conclusions can you draw about the pattern of dependence of unwind P&L on different values of skew?

10.3   Using the OptBarrier Spreadsheet

Take a down-and-out call case that you have analyzed using **CarrBarrier** and analyze it using **OptBarrier**. Use the optimization criterion of 100 percent of the maximum absolute error:

1. First use **OptBarrier** with four possible times and four possible at-the-money volatilities, but only one possible smile, skew, and drift—smile, skew, and drift are all set to zero. Confirm that the values you derive for the option price are close to those that **CarrBarrier** derived.
2. Change skew to a single value of 10 percent and see what option values result.
3. Change drift to a single value of −3 percent and see what option values result.
4. Change skew to have two values—one 0 and one 10 percent—and see what option values result and what the resulting degree of uncertainty of closeout cost is. Compare this uncertainty of forward cost to that of the **CarrBarrier** for the same level of skew and drift.
5. Change drift to have two values—one 0 and one −3 percent—see what option values result and what the resulting degree of uncertainty of closeout cost is. Compare this uncertainty of forward cost to that of the **CarrBarrier** for the same level of skew and drift.

10.4   Using the DermanErgenerKani Spreadsheet

1. Use the spreadsheet to check the results given in Table 10.5. Then examine the impact on unwind P&L of deviations between the assumptions about unwind conditions in C8:C12 and the actual unwind conditions in C17:C21. Create a table to show the impact of changes in rate, drift, smile, and skew.
2. Verify that any changes made in initial conditions in B8:B12 will only change the initial price of setting up the hedge and will not have any impact on unwind P&L.

10.5   Using the BasketOption Spreadsheet

1. Check on the sensitivities shown in Table 10.6.
2. Create some examples to check that the General Case and the 3 Asset Case give the same answers for cases with just two or three assets.
3. Using the General Case, tabulate the rate of change in base case volatility and sensitivity to changes in volatility and correlation as the number of assets increases. How does this differ at base correlation rates of 0, 25, and 50 percent?

10.6   Using the CrossHedge Spreadsheet

Try different price paths for the two assets and confirm that they always show zero P&L for the uncorrelated case. What patterns do you observe for the P&L in the correlated case (for example, what distinguishes cases that lead to gains from cases that lead to losses; what influences the size of the gains or losses)?

10.7   Using the TermStructure Spreadsheet

1. Reproduce the results in Table 10.9, which will verify that two different combinations of volatility and correlation input can produce the same valuations for vanilla products but different valuations for exotic products.
2. Find other combinations of volatility and correlation inputs that produce the same valuations for the vanilla products and determine the sensitivity of the exotic products to these inputs.
3. Create your own exotic product by specifying a different payout structure in column J and determine its sensitivity to different combinations of input volatility and correlation that leave vanilla product pricing fixed.

10.8   Using the Swaptions Spreadsheet

Start with input swaption and FRA rates as follows:

- All FRA rates at 7.00 percent.
- Swaption volatilities from Table 10.11.

These swaption volatilities display the usual pattern observed in the market of declining as swap tenor increases:

1. Input correlations of 90 percent for all combinations and use the Solver to find a set of FRA volatilities that correspond to this case.
2. Replace all the 90 percent correlations with 80 percent correlations and use the Solver to find a set of FRA volatilities that correspond.
3. You now have two different sets of FRA volatilities that can explain the same set of swaption volatilities—one based on higher correlation levels than the other. What are the patterns of difference you see between these two sets of volatilities and how would you explain the linkage between these patterns and the difference in correlation levels?

TABLE 10.11 Swaption Volatilities Input for Exercise 10.8

Option Expiry	Swap Tenor									
	1	2	3	4	5	6	7	8	9	10
1	16.000%	14.700%	13.700%	12.800%	12.400%	12.000%	11.700%	11.500%	11.300%	11.100%
2	17.700%	15.100%	13.700%	13.100%	12.600%	12.100%	12.000%	11.800%	11.600%	
3	17.100%	15.100%	14.000%	13.200%	12.600%	12.500%	12.400%	12.200%		
4	17.200%	15.000%	13.800%	12.900%	12.800%	12.700%	12.500%			
5	16.200%	14.200%	13.100%	12.700%	12.800%	12.600%				
6	14.800%	13.300%	12.900%	12.900%	12.700%					
7	14.400%	13.400%	13.200%	12.900%						
8	14.900%	13.700%	13.100%							
9	14.000%	12.900%								
10	13.000%									

CHAPTER 11

VaR and Stress Testing

We now turn to the risk-management techniques that focus on risk aggregation—those that attempt to reduce risk by creating portfolios of less than completely correlated risks and achieve risk reduction through diversification. The key step is to develop measures of the overall risk of a firm's portfolio that fully reflect the impacts of correlation and diversification. These measures can then be factored into limits and incentives that encourage the proper balancing of potential return and contribution to portfolio risk. In this chapter, we investigate portfolio risk measures for market risk; in the following chapter, we consider portfolio risk measures for credit risk.

Measuring the overall risk of a firm's positions can be done in two principle ways: a statistically based approach called *value at risk* (VaR) or an approach based primarily on economic insight rather than statistics called *stress testing* or *scenario analysis*. We will discuss the potential uses of such overall measures of firm risk in some detail, but first we will explore the methodology required to make such measurements. For the time being, we will just point out two major advantages of overall firm risk measures relative to more traditional measures of risk such as the value of a basis point, or delta or vega:

- Traditional measures do not allow senior managers to form conclusions as to which are the largest risks currently facing the firm. For example, it is not possible to meaningfully compare the value of a basis point in two different currencies, because this comparison does not reflect the relative size of potential interest rate moves in the two currencies. Both VaR and stress testing provide a measure that combines the size of the position and the size of the potential market move into a potential impact on firm profit and loss (P&L). Moreover, both produce a measure that can compare risks between disparate businesses, such as interest rates and equities.
- Traditional measures do not interact with one another. Should you add up the risks under different measures into some total risk?

Clearly, this would be wrong because it would ignore the effect of correlation between market factors. Both VaR and stress-testing account directly for correlations between market factors.

We first discuss the methodology of statistical measurement, VaR, and then discuss the methodology for nonstatistical measurement, stress testing.

11.1   VAR METHODOLOGY

Strictly speaking, VaR is a measure of the worst loss that can occur at a given confidence level. However, the statistical methodology used to determine VaR can also be used to calculate broader measures of the distribution of potential losses. In Section 11.1.1, we first look at the methodology for calculating the distribution and in Section 11.1.2 we turn to the question of how best to summarize it.

Since statistical risk measures first began to be calculated by financial firms about 20 years ago, three methods have dominated:

- The direct measurement of P&L distribution
- The calculation of P&L distribution based on historical statistics representing the variance and covariance of market variables and the current size of position exposures to each of these market variables. So if s_i represents the firm's exposure to each market variable, σ_i represents the volatility of each market variable, and $\rho_{i,j}$ represents the correlation coefficient between each pair of market variables. The volatility of overall firm P&L is calculated as:

$$\sqrt{\sum_{i,j} s_i s_j \sigma_i \sigma_j \rho_{i,j}} \qquad (11.1)$$

  The P&L distribution can now be calculated from this volatility.
- The simulation of P&L distributions based on a selected set of possible moves of market variables and the current size of position exposure to each of those market variables. So if s_i represents the firm's exposure to each market variable, $m_{i,j}$ represents the size of the move of each market variable in each considered scenario and p_j represents the probability assigned to each scenario, with:

$$\sum_{j} p_j = 1 \qquad (11.2)$$

Then the P&L movement in each scenario is calculated by:

$$\sum_i s_i m_{i,j} \qquad (11.3)$$

The P&L distribution is calculated by multiplying each of these terms by its respective p_j.

Let us consider the advantages and disadvantages of each of these three methods.

The use of direct measurement of P&L distribution is still widely used, as can be seen from the frequent use of histograms of daily P&L distributions published in annual reports of financial firms, as illustrated in Figure 11.1. It has the advantage of simplicity of calculation, not having to make any use of models or statistical assumptions. It also has the ability to capture effects of the trading culture, which the other methods do not. For example, does management respond to periods of greater market volatility by reducing position size? If they do, this will mitigate some of the earnings volatility resulting from market volatility.

Direct measurement of P&L distribution is also the only method that is available for measuring risk when access to details of trading positions is not available. For example, a hedge fund investor probably does not have any access to details of the investment holdings of the hedge fund. To estimate its risk, her only alternative is to measure historical P&L distribution of the fund.

However, direct measurement of P&L distributions cannot take into account the possibility that current position taking may be radically different than historical position taking. Corporate risk managers and regulators will insist on risk measures that fully reflect the current portfolio composition whenever available. This renders direct measurement of the P&L distribution close to useless as a standalone risk measure, although it is still valuable as a complement to other measures.

The use of the variance-covariance method has now been virtually abandoned by sophisticated financial firms in favor of simulation methods. The primary reason for this is that relative to the simulation method, the variance-covariance method provides very little flexibility in evaluating the contribution of nonlinear positions, notably options positions, to P&L distributions. As we will see, simulation provides the flexibility to tailor the degree of detail used in calculating nonlinear positions to the degree of accuracy required for particular portfolios. Detail can range from simple factor

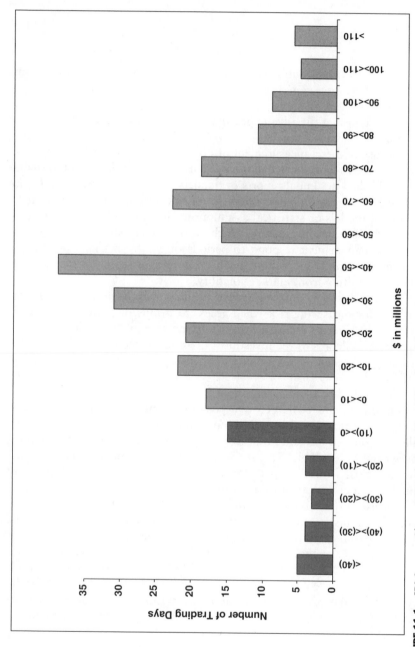

FIGURE 11.1 JPMorgan Chase 2001 daily market risk relegated revenues (from annual report).

approximations (using delta, gamma, vega, and so on) to a full valuation of each individual option, with several gradations available in between. By contrast, variance-covariance cannot go beyond factor approximation. Secondary reasons are:

- The greater difficulty that the variance-covariance method has in dealing with the fat-tailed distributions normally encountered in financial markets.
- The inability of variance-covariance to pick up the phenomenon, often observed in financial markets, that the largest changes in variables often cluster together (such as the high correlation between stock markets in different countries in the 1987 stock crash) to a greater degree than will be indicated by correlation coefficients (that is, the joint distribution is not bivariate normal).
- The realization that almost all the benefits of simplicity and speed of computation claimed for variance-covariance relative to simulation are based on fallacious comparisons. As will be apparent in our discussion of simulation methodology, the degree of simplicity and speed of computation are largely determined by the choice of the user. To achieve the same level of accuracy, simulation is at least as simple and fast to compute as variance-covariance. Unlike variance-covariance, simulation offers the flexibility of increasing accuracy as a trade-off against simplicity and computation time, but having more flexibility can surely not count as a disadvantage.

Currently, the primary users of variance-covariance are smaller firms that do not hold significant options positions and that want to outsource the market data component of their VaR computations. For such firms, variance-covariance offers the distinct advantage that they only need to obtain volatilities and correlations rather than the day-by-day pricing histories required for simulation, a considerable savings in the amount of data to be transferred. One company that provides such an outsourcing service is RiskMetrics, which maintains volatilities and correlations for thousands of instruments and publishes extensive documentation on their methodologies.

In Exercise 11.1, you have a chance to see an example of how variance-covariance computes VaR and why a simulation calculation that is as simple computationally and superior in flexibility is always available. I will therefore not spend any more time on variance-covariance or the various tricks that have been devised to provide the capability to approximate options positions and incorporate fat tails within it. For readers who want to pursue this approach, I recommend reading Dowd (2002, Chapter 5).

11.1.1 Simulation of the P&L Distribution

Remember that the simulation approach consists of determining a number of possible scenarios, to be indexed by j, determining the size of the move of each market variable in each scenario $m_{i,j}$, and then calculating:

$$\sum_i s_i m_{i,j} \qquad\qquad (11.4)$$

as the firm's total P&L movement in each scenario. The steps in a P&L simulation consist of determining a set of scenarios specified by the size of the move in each of a set of key market variables and a probability to be assigned to each set and a translation from the size of the move of key market variables to price changes for all positions. For example, the key market variables for a set of bond positions could be interest rates for 10 key tenors and the full set of market variables could be prices for individual bonds. Two alternative approaches exist for the first step: historical simulation and Monte Carlo simulation. The decisions to be made for the second step do not depend on the choice made for the first step. We will discuss each step in some detail.

Step 1: Determine Key Market Probabilities   The historical simulation approach is quite simple. A group of historical periods is chosen and the observed size of market move in each of these historical periods constitutes the scenarios. So, for example, you could choose 300 scenarios consisting of all the most recent 1 business day changes in market variables. The changes in market variables from June 7, 1999 to June 8, 1999 would be one scenario, the change from June 8, 1999 to June 9, 1999 would be another scenario, and so forth. Or one could choose all the 10 business day changes.

Scenario probabilities can be assigned based on the perceived relevance to the current market situation. For example, greater probability weight could be assigned to more recent historical periods.

Historical simulation offers a large advantage in terms of simplicity—simplicity of implementation, simplicity of assumptions, and simplicity of explanation. The advantage in terms of assumptions is that no modeling assumption needs to be made beyond the assumption that the immediate future will resemble the past. No parameterization of either variance or correlation is needed, and no assumptions are made about the distribution shape (such as normality). If fat tails or the clustering of large moves between variables is present in the historical data, they will be reflected in the simulation.

The advantage in terms of explanation is that any questions raised by traders or managers concerning a VaR that seems too high can be easily traced to a subset of specific historical dates, which would show large losses against the current firm holdings. Disagreement can be quickly focused on the accuracy of data for a few specific dates or on arguments about the probabilities to be assigned to the repetition of particular historical events. By contrast, the variance-covariance approach and the Monte Carlo simulation approach make it far more difficult to resolve such questions.

This advantage of the simplicity of historical simulation also underlies its primary disadvantage: The VaR produced is dominated by market moves on a few specific historical days. If a particular combination of market events did not occur in the historical period being considered, it cannot contribute to VaR. It is difficult to overcome this problem by just expanding the historical period you are considering. Data availability tends to get sparse once you go back more than a few years, because of the failure to retain data, because data becomes more difficult to "clean" the further back you go in time, and because some currently traded instruments may not have histories that go back that far.

This disadvantage of generating scenarios utilizing the historical method is the primary argument in favor of the Monte Carlo method. The Monte Carlo method starts with a specification of the key market variables, which is similar to that of the variance-covariance approach, but it may have a richer specification of each single variable than just a volatility. An example would be a multiparameter specification that allows the generation of distributions that are skewed or fat tailed. A Monte Carlo generation of distributions that fit specified parameters can be achieved though stochastic volatility and jump process specifications, similar to those we have discussed in Section 9.3, or they can utilize processes specially designed to find distributions that match parameters, such as those discussed in Shaw (1997). Monte Carlo techniques are then used to generate a set of scenarios that fits the desired statistical specifications.

Usually, users of Monte Carlo simulation want to take advantage of the flexibility it offers to generate many more scenarios than can be practically generated with historical simulation. This has led to the incorrect assertion that Monte Carlo simulation *requires* more scenarios than historical simulation. Rather, Monte Carlo simulation offers the flexibility of achieving greater accuracy if the greater expense of running more scenarios is justified by the increase in accuracy. Standard computerized techniques for improving the trade-off between accuracy and speed for Monte Carlo can also be employed (such as stratified sampling, low-discrepancy sequences, and importance sampling—see Hull [2002, Section 18.7]).

Advantages that Monte Carlo simulation offers are as follows:

- **The ability to select the most suitable technique to estimate each parameter.** Volatilities and correlations can be forecast using statistical techniques such as generalized autoregressive conditional heteroscedasticity (GARCH) (for a discussion of the most common statistical methods used in forecasting volatilities and correlations, see Hull [2002, Chapter 17] or Jorion [2001, Chapter 8]). If implied volatilities are available, they can be substituted for or blended with statistical measures. (Should implied volatility always be used when available? We'll examine this question at the end of this section). The choice can be separately made for each variable, though you do need to be careful not to generate impossible or implausible combinations of correlation coefficients. (For a discussion of how to avoid creating impossible correlation matrices, see Dowd [1998, Chapter 3, Section 5, and Chapter 5, Section 2.3.2].)

■ **The ability to select the most relevant data set for estimating each parameter.**   You might have 10 years of good historical data for 1 variable and only 2 years for another. Historical simulation would force you to use only 2 years' worth of data for both. Monte Carlo simulation lets you choose the data set individually for each variable and choose the weighting of data individually.

■ **The ability to select the most relevant data set for estimating different aspects of a single variable.**   For example, volatility could be based on recent data or derived from an implied volatility while higher-order parameters of the distribution are estimated from longer data periods. Recent data is often considered a better predictor of near-term future volatility, but shape parameters, such as fatness of tails, are hard to discern from a small data set

■ **Greater flexibility in handling missing data.**   Data for individual dates can be missing because a particular market was closed for a holiday or because of errors in data gathering. In fact, all sources of market data, whether data vendors, brokers, or databases internal to the firm, are notoriously poor in quality and require major data scrubbing efforts. But some data will not have sufficient duplication of sources to scrub successfully and must be regarded as unavailable. If a data series is unavailable for a particular time period, Monte Carlo simulation can exclude this period for the calculation of this data series without excluding this period from the calculation of other variables for which data is available. Historical simulation lacks this flexibility; it must either completely include or completely exclude a particular day's data.

■ **Greater flexibility in handling asynchronous data.**   Correlations observed between variables that are sampled at different times of the day can be highly misleading and lead to significant misstatements of risk. Monte Carlo simulation has the flexibility to measure correlations for each individual pair of variables based on quotations from the best time of day to represent that particular pair, or by basing the correlation on a multiday time interval, which will tend to smooth out asynchronous effects.

- **The ability to combine histories.** Consider corporate bonds held in the firm's portfolio. By historical experience, one knows that some of these bonds may suffer a ratings downgrade and a subsequent large fall in price. But it may be that none of the bonds currently held has previously suffered such a downgrade since the firm avoids holding such bonds. Historical simulation would show no ratings downgrade events for these bonds. But Monte Carlo simulation could be used to combine ratings downgrade possibilities based on the history of a large pool of bonds with the specific pricing history of the actual bonds held. Another example would be a foreign exchange (FX) position held in a currency that has been pegged at a fixed exchange rate to the dollar by government intervention. You may have no historical example of this particular currency devaluing, yet want to include some probability of devaluation. Monte Carlo simulation could incorporate a devaluation event, possibly parameterized by devaluation experience in other currencies, as a jump process superimposed on the specific history of this FX rate.

Reproducing any desired correlation matrix in a Monte Carlo simulation using the Cholesky decomposition method described in Hull (2002, Section 18.6) is a straightforward task. But covariance matrices employ correlations based on multivariate normal distributions and therefore do not capture any relationships that are extremely unlikely under this hypothesis, such as the clustering of large changes in variables. Addressing these concerns requires more refined data analyses. For example, different correlation matrices could be used depending on the size of price moves. Days in which price moves are larger would use a correlation matrix derived from a sample of days with large moves.

Given all these advantages to Monte Carlo simulation in its flexibility to handle data and estimation issues, it is preferable, and sometimes even unavoidable, to still employ some Monte Carlo simulation techniques when you have chosen historical simulation as your primary methodology. Consider these examples:

- A certain stock held in your portfolio has only recently been issued. To develop a past history for the price of this stock for use in historical simulation, you may represent it by some formula based on a selected stock index. But if you are long this stock and short this index, you would measure your position as having no risk during the period when it is represented by the index. To avoid this, you need to introduce a random element into your generation of the stock's price history, basing the size of the random element on observed changes during the period since the stock began trading. But this is precisely the Monte Carlo approach.

■ If two stocks have begun trading in a very tightly related fashion since a merger announcement, you would not want to reflect their previous, more volatile arrangement as part of the history that determines VaR. So you must generate the price of one stock as a function of the other. If you are to avoid treating a merger arbitrage position as having zero risk, you must introduce a random element as in the previous case.

■ The examples of handling a ratings downgrade risk and an FX devaluation risk, discussed in the last bullet point under the advantages of Monte Carlo, are good candidates to receive Monte Carlo treatment in a historical simulation.

Similarly, Monte Carlo simulation techniques can be used to fill in missing data in historical simulations. Also, historical simulations can be modified to choose a volatility for a particular instrument based on any of the techniques mentioned in the first bullet point under the advantages of Monte Carlo. All that is required is to multiply each historical observation for the instrument by the ratio between the desired volatility and the volatility over the historical period. This transformation leaves all shape characteristics of the historical distribution, such as the fatness of tails and the correlation structure, intact. This approach is illustrated in the **VaR** spreadsheet on the accompanying CD-ROM.

Just as we can modify historical simulations to include some of the advantages of Monte Carlo, we might want to modify Monte Carlo to include some of the advantages of historical simulation. Beyond simplicity, the primary advantage of historical simulation is the more refined way in which it handles multivariate correlation. By utilizing actual daily simultaneous price moves across the set of all relevant market variables, nonlinear impacts of arbitrarily great complexity are directly incorporated. This points toward a modification of Monte Carlo in which all individual variables are generated by standard Monte Carlo techniques and all correlations between variables are based on historical simulation. This approach, roughly following Shaw (1997), works as follows.

First, you perform a standard historical simulation, with equal probabilities assigned to each day's history. Then each individual variable is regenerated using a Monte Carlo method based on whatever estimation technique is considered the most appropriate, such as GARCH, implied volatilities, or a multiparameter specification. Different methods can be individually tailored to different variables. The use of the historical simulation values is to determine which values of the variables occur simultaneously based on rank order.

For example, suppose you have a historical simulation with 850 days. Monte Carlo simulation is used to generate 850 values of each variable. If a particular historical date consisted of the 4th highest value of variable 1, the 38th highest value of variable 2, the 625th highest value of variable 3, and so on, then you would create a simulation instance with the 4th highest value of the 850 Monte Carlo simulations of variable 1, the 38th highest value of the 850 Monte Carlo simulations of variable 2, the 625th highest value of the Monte Carlo simulations of variable 3, and so on.

Although this approach retains many of the advantages of Monte Carlo simulation, it cannot incorporate them all. It lacks the flexibility to base some correlations on one data set and other correlations on another data set. It requires complete data for every variable in every day to be included in the dates determining the correlation structure. And it has the same problems as historical simulation with asynchronous data.

Finally, let's examine the question of whether implied volatility should always be preferred to historical volatility when it is available. In Chapters 9 and 10, I argue strongly for always valuing options at volatilities implied from liquid market prices. But this is a pricing argument; we need to determine prices at which a longer-term volatility risk can be exited in order to convert longer-term risks into shorter-term risks (refer to Section 1.3). VaR is already dealing with shorter-term risks, usually overnight, and is not being used to price risk but to measure it. Implied volatilities can be used as an indicator of overnight volatility, and arguments may be made for believing they carry a great deal of information. But arguments also can be made against giving much weight to implied volatilities; they sometimes have more to do with supply and demand factors than forecasts of price variation, as discussed in Section 9.6.2. The decision must be based on belief about their predictive value, as no pricing argument exists for using them.

Step 2: Determine Price Changes for All Positions   When computing VaR for spot positions, the translation from key market variables to the full set of price changes is quite direct. Spot positions such as spot FX or the holding of an individual stock or stock index, or spot gold or spot oil, is just directly multiplied by the generated price change from Step 1.

Computation for forward positions is less straightforward. If you are currently holding a Treasury bill maturing 1 month from now, you don't want to apply to it the price move you observed for that Treasury bill on a date 6 months ago. This is because at that point the Treasury bill had 7 months to maturity, and you expect 7-month instruments to demonstrate much larger price changes than 1-month instruments. You want to utilize yield curve parameters as key market variables and then multiply those yield curve parameters by the appropriate value of a basis point measure of a forward position. This has the important advantage of not having to separately price each interest rate instrument, but instead works with a summary description of the entire position.

Issues are most complex for option positions (in which we include any nonlinear payoff positions). The conceptually simplest and most accurate approach would be to value each individual option separately based on the changes in the key market variables of forward price and implied volatility. Even such a simple approach has complications, since for each scenario it is necessary to choose a volatility at which to evaluate the option. This requires deciding which point on the implied volatility surface is the right one to apply. Suppose you are repricing an option with 1 year to expiry, a strike of 100, and a current underlying price of 80. Which implied volatility shift do you use when sampling from a period 6 months ago when the underlying price was 100? Most practitioners would opt for looking at the shift in options with a 1-year expiry and a strike of 125, since that would give the same *moneyness*, that is, a strike 25 percent above the current spot. But this is clearly open to interpretation and a variety of theories on what drives options pricing (see Derman [1999]). Very similar considerations apply to option-adjusted spreads on mortgage and mortgage-backed securities, which should be related to the security that had a comparable relationship to the prevailing new mortgage rate. The reasoning is similar, since option-adjusted spreads represent the market pricing of uncertainty in option exercises by homeowners.

Although the simplest approach is the most accurate, it is clearly also the most costly, and the heavy expense of doing a full individual revaluation of each option position is what was primarily responsible for incorrect claims that simulation methodology for VaR was inherently expensive to perform. In fact, simulation methodology can achieve better accuracy than variance-covariance at no greater cost by the easy trick of representing option portfolios by summary statistics of deltas, gammas, and vegas and multiplying these by the appropriate price change, half the square of the change in price, and the change in implied volatility, respectively. This simplified representation makes options positions no more computationally difficult for simulation than linear positions, so it is a matter of trade-off in desired accuracy versus the cost to be determined for each options position.

Intermediate approaches can also be used. One that can provide quite accurate approximations is to interpolate results based on a price-vol matrix representation of the options portfolio, as per Section 9.4. If a reasonably detailed price-vol matrix is already being calculated as part of the trading desk's own risk reporting, this is a good way of taking advantage of a large number of full revaluation runs that are already being made (since each bucket of the matrix requires all options in the portfolio to receive a full revaluation) without needless duplication of effort. As we noted in Section 9.4, the price-vol matrix can potentially capture all higher-order terms in the Taylor series of both the underlying price and the volatility, as well as cross-terms between them. It will not capture impacts such as nonparallel shifts in volatility surface, so these sensitivities will need to be separately accounted for.

Whatever approximations are used should be occasionally tested against a full revaluation by individual options to see if a finer degree of detail is needed. The scenarios involving the very largest shifts should probably always be evaluated by full revaluation by individual options. This is a form of importance sampling (see Hull [2002, Section 18.7]). One possible implementation would be to first use a selected approximation technique to simulate all possible shifts. Then focus on the ones that produce the highest P&L changes, which will have the greatest influence on the VaR measure, and recalculate these using the full revaluation of each option.

Choices as to whether to work with a full revaluation of individual option positions, a price-vol matrix, or summary sensitivity statistics should be solely motivated by trade-offs between the computation time and expense versus accuracy. In all cases, the ultimate accuracy of P&L simulations rests on the accuracy of the models the firm uses to value transactions. This is true whether the models are used directly in full revaluation or indirectly in supplying the deltas, gammas, vegas, and price-vol matrices that are multiplied by positions in simulations or in variance-covariance calculations. Reviews of the accuracy of the firm's models should always consider their impact on risk calculations such as VaR and stress tests along with their impact on valuations and limit calculations.

Another important determinant of the cost of calculating simulations and the cost of storing the data needed as input to these simulations is the degree of detail with which positions and market prices are recorded. At one extreme, it would be foolish not to keep separate prices and positions for each different currency for spot FX; there are just not that many different currencies and movements between them that can be significant. At the other extreme, it would be equally foolish to store market data on forward rates for all possible tenors, that is, 365 days × 30 years. Most of these rates are just being produced by interpolation anyway, so you might as well store just the 20 to 50 liquid rates on the curve that all the others are calculated from. In between, trade-off decisions must be made. For example, do you want to track individual histories on every stock you hold, or do you want to keep track of just indices with individual stocks represented through their betas relative to the index? If you choose the latter approach, then a separate estimate needs to be made of the VaR due to idiosyncratic stock risk.

Finally, we note that some of the determinants of exotic derivative prices are not market variables whose price history can be observed and thus are not suitable for inclusion in a VaR analysis. Consider an option on a basket of stocks. The impact of changes in the prices of the stocks and in the implied volatilities of each stock in the basket can be computed and included in the VaR. But there will probably be no liquid market quotations for the implied correlations impacting this option. Analysts are occasionally tempted to substitute changes in historical correlation for unobservable changes in implied correlation. I would argue that this is an error.

If the basket option has 3 years remaining, you should presumably look at the change from 1 business day to the next of a change in the 3-year historical correlation. But since these two 3-year periods will share all but 1 day at the beginning and end in common, the change in correlation that you will measure must be tiny. We know from experience that implied volatility can change far more rapidly than a similarly computed change in historical volatility, and I do not know of any reason why correlations should behave differently. If, on the other hand, you decided to choose a much shorter period for computing the historical correlation in order to increase the potential size of the change from day to day, how would the choice of period be justified? I believe it is better to acknowledge that such nonmarket observables cannot be included in VaR analyses and that their risks should be accounted for separately through reserves and stress tests.

Another factor that some risk managers have been trying to incorporate into VaR is liquidity considerations. Rather than using overnight price moves to represent each instrument, price moves over a longer period will be used to represent less liquid instruments. If this is not handled carefully, it can result in under-representation of illiquid risks. For example, you might have a short position in a very liquid government bond and a smaller long position in a less liquid corporate. If you compute VaR based on a 1-day move for the government bond and a 2-day move for the corporate bond, this could show less risk than a 1-day move for both. This is because the larger moves for the corporate bond have the same effect in the computation as increasing the size of the position. A better approach is to separately calculate a liquidity penalty, as an add-on to VaR, for the cost of exiting less liquid positions, using a formula similar to that proposed for liquidity reserves in Section 5.1.2. For more on liquidity adjustments to VaR, see Dowd (2002, Chapter 9).

11.1.2   Measures of the P&L Distribution

Simulation is ideally suited to producing full P&L distributions, since individual cases are simulated and probabilities are assigned to each case. Although the full distribution can be represented graphically, such as by a histogram like that in Figure 11.1, some type of summary statistics are desirable to convey information succinctly. In practice, the primary focus has been on producing a single summary measure: the percentile loss. For example, the VaR at the 99th percentile would be the amount of loss that will only be equaled or exceeded 1 percent of the time. Although less well known, another summary measure that is very useful is the *shortfall VaR*, which is the average loss conditional on being beyond a given percentile. For example, the shortfall VaR at the 99th percentile is the probability-weighted average of all losses greater than the VaR at the 99th percentile.

Computation of both VaR and shortfall VaR at any selected percentile is very direct from a simulation. If we have simulated 1,000 equally probable P&Ls, we only need to sort them. The 990th P&L in the sort is the 99th percentile VaR. The average of the 991st through the 1,000th P&L in the sort is the 99th percentile VaR shortfall. The **VaR** spreadsheet on the accompanying CD-ROM demonstrates this calculation for both historical and Monte Carlo simulation.

Despite the VaR measure being better known than the shortfall VaR measure, the latter has several advantages that recommend it as a superior summary statistic. They are:

- Shortfall VaR is sensitive to the entire tail of the distribution, whereas VaR does not change even if large increases take place in some of the losses beyond the cutoff percentile at which the VaR is being measured. This can be quite dangerous if it encourages businesses to tailor products to produce risks that escape the VaR measure by being too far out in the tail.
- In practice, shortfall VaR has proved to be a more stable measure than VaR in showing less sensitivity to data errors and less day-to-day movement due to seemingly irrelevant changes in input data. Presumably, this is due to a greater tendency to average out the noise in the data.
- With VaR, apparently negative diversification effects can arise, as shown in Table 11.1, in which the 99th percentile of the combined portfolios, a loss of $42 million, is greater than the sum of the 99th percentile losses in the 2 separate portfolios: $20 million + $20 million = $40 million. Shortfall VaR never displays negative diversification effects.

Negative portfolio effects are undesirable both from the standpoint of clarity of exposition, when explaining risk measures to managers, and from the standpoint of control structure. Even if all units of the firm are within allocated VaR risk limits, the firm itself may be outside its risk limits. Negative portfolio effects are associated with risk measures that have been termed *incoherent* in the terminology of Artzner, Delbaen, Eber, and Heath (1997). By contrast, shortfall VaR and stress scenario measures are coherent and cannot have negative diversification effects. For further discussion of coherent risk measures, see Dowd (2002, section 2.3)—note that Dowd's terminology for *shortfall VaR* is *expected tail loss* (ETL).

TABLE 11.1 Negative Portfolio Effects

	Portfolio A	Portfolio B	Combined Portfolio A and B
Third worst case for A	−20 million	+10 million	−10 million
Second worst case for A	−25 million	−17 million	−42 million
First worst case for A	−30 million	−10 million	−40 million
Third worst case for B	−7 million	−20 million	−27 million
Second worst case for B	−10 million	−40 million	−50 million
First worst case for B	+5 million	−60 million	−55 million
99th percentile (third worst case)	−20 million	−20 million	−42 million

Given these drawbacks of VaR, why has it been so widely adopted as a risk measure? The real question senior managers and regulators would like to ask is "what is the worst loss that can possibly occur?" This is a question that does not admit a concrete answer, so a confidence interval needs to be specified, which presumably leads to questions like "what is the worst loss that will happen no more than 1 percent of the time?" This is the question to which VaR is the answer. But it seems doubtful that management really wants to convey indifference to the size of the losses beyond this threshold.

Based on these considerations, I would recommend shortfall VaR as a more desirable summary statistic. If management or regulators still want to know the VaR, then I would recommend estimating it by a properly selected shortfall VaR. For example, a good estimate of the 99th percentile VaR is the 97.6th percentile shortfall VaR. The two measures are almost exactly equal for normal distributions and using the 97.6th percentile shortfall VaR as an estimator provides greater stability, avoids negative diversification effects, and eliminates incentives to hide risk in the tails.

If you want to use simulation results to project possible extreme results, that is, at very large percentiles, then you need to extrapolate beyond the historical data set. For example, if you want to produce a VaR or shortfall VaR at 99.99 percent, you need to forecast what will happen 1 out of every 10,000 days. But you will almost certainly be working with far less than 10,000 days of historical data. We discuss later, in Section 11.3, the reasonableness of calculating such extreme measures, but for now, let's see how it can be done if needed.

Extrapolation beyond the historical data set requires statistical tools from *Extreme Value Theory* (EVT). A very brief summary of the principal EVT techniques most often used in VaR analysis appears in the following box.

KEY RESULTS FROM EVT

The results from EVT that are most often used in portfolio risk measurement are estimates for VaR and shortfall VaR at percentiles far out on the tail of the distribution. For example, you can find the formulas for these estimates along with derivations as numbers (6) and (10), respectively, in McNeil (2000). I will state them in slightly altered notation, which is designed to make them easier to utilize in a standard VaR framework.

Let VaR_p and ES_p stand for the VaR and shortfall VaR at any given percentile p. Let u be a percentile at which we can directly measure VaR_u by standard simulation. The formulas are:

$$\text{VaR}_p = \text{VaR}_u + (\beta/\xi)(((1-p)/(1-u))^{-\xi} - 1)$$
$$\text{ES}_p = (\text{VaR}_p + \beta - \xi\text{VaR}_u)/(1 - \xi)$$

The estimation procedure requires a choice of a base percentile u as well as a choice of the parameters β and ξ. A good discussion of the most frequently used methods for determining these parameters and how much confidence may be placed in the estimation procedure can be found in Diebold, Schuermann, and Stroughhair (2000). An example using these formulas can be found in the **EVT** spreadsheet.

The use of EVT involves many issues, such as the need to make assumptions that are nearly impossible to test and the difficulty in estimating parameters. But its virtue is that, if such data extrapolations need to be made, it provides a smooth and consistent methodology that is superior to the alternative of extrapolating based on empirical curve fitting. A brief and lively discussion of these issues with plentiful references can be found in Embrechts (2000). As Embrechts indicates, EVT is even more problematic when used with high-dimensional data that combines in a nonlinear fashion. This is a good description of the VaR of a large firm's portfolio, with options valuation providing the nonlinearity. So direct application of EVT to the VaR measure for the portfolio is highly questionable. More reasonable is the application of EVT to each individual input variable in a Monte Carlo simulation, combined with as much structural modeling of correlation as possible.

As with any model, a VaR model needs to have its predictions tested against real results to see if it is sufficiently accurate. This process is sometimes known as *backtesting*, since you are looking back to see how the model would have performed in the recent past. It has been particularly emphasized for VaR models, owing to insistence by regulators that if firms are to be allowed to use internally built models for the calculation of regulatory capital, they must be able to demonstrate that the models fit real results. The suggested regulatory backtest is a straightforward comparison between the 99th percentile produced by a VaR model on each day during a specified period (since it is this percentile that determines regulatory capital) and the actual P&L on each day. The model is considered satisfactory (or at least erring acceptably on the side of too much capital) if the number of days on which the P&L exceeds the predicted 99th percentile is not statistically significantly greater than 1 percent. Although this approach has the virtue of simplicity, it is statistically quite a blunt instrument. Much more information can be extracted by comparing VaR projections to actual results at many different percentiles. More detail on backtesting can be found in Jorion (2001, Chapter 6) and Dowd (2002, Chapter 10).

A methodological question is whether to backtest against actual reported P&L or against P&L that has been adjusted for components that the VaR cannot reasonably be expected to pick up. Such components are revenue from newly booked transactions and revenue from intraday or (when running VaR for periods longer than a day) intraperiod trading. The argument in favor of using unadjusted P&L in the comparison, besides the simplicity of computation, is that these are all real components of P&L that can be quite difficult to identify, so it is better to be aware of the extent to which your model is underpredicting actual reported loss events. An argument for making at least the largest of these adjustments is that without getting the target data to line up with the forecasting process, you are working with a suboptimal diagnostic tool.

11.2 STRESS TESTING

Stress testing involves using economic insight rather than strict reliance on statistics to generate scenarios against which to measure firm risk. From a computational standpoint, it is simply another variant of simulation; it just uses a different method to generate the scenarios of underlying market variables. But after that, the other two steps in simulation analysis, translation to all market variables and the calculation of firm P&L, can be carried out exactly as with simulation VaR; indeed, the exact same system can be used for both.

The advantage of using stress testing as a supplement to VaR is that it can pick up possible extreme events that can cause large losses to the firm's positions that may be missed by a purely statistical approach. The disadvantage is that once we leave the realm of statistics, we must substitute a standard of plausibility for one of probability, and plausibility is a very subjective notion. However subjective, plausibility must still be insisted upon. Without such a standard, stress testing becomes equivalent to the child's (and childish) game, "who can name the largest number?" No one ever wins, because one can always be added to the last number named. And you can always specify a stress test that is one shade more extreme than the last one specified.

Working out plausible combinations of the entire set of key variables that can impact a large firm's trading position is hard work and requires a lot of attention to detail. One aid is to split the work up between a senior group that determines a global scenario for the most important variables and specialist groups that work out the consequences of that global scenario for less important variables. Global scenarios generally reflect major shifts in economic conditions: a stock market crash, an oil embargo, or a series of large credit defaults.

One question to consider is why bother departing from statistics? Couldn't we just rely on Monte Carlo simulation to generate highly unlikely but still plausible scenarios? The answer is clearly no, for several reasons:

- Some scenarios represent such sharp breaks with history that no analysis of past experience can offer a complete story. Economic forecasting based on hard-to-quantify judgment is required. When firms were worried in 1999 about the potential impact on the financial markets of the Y2K systems bug, no purely historical analysis could offer any guidance. When many of the nations of Europe adopted a common currency, a scenario based on the possible collapse of that currency could not be based on any clear historical precedents.

- Some scenarios do not relate to public price observations at all, so they cannot be based on historical records of price changes. If a firm has an inventory of options on stock baskets whose pricing depends on long-term correlations for which no liquid public prices exist, a scenario for a market event that would cause the portfolio to be revalued must be formed based on market knowledge. For example, a wave of mergers might drive up the input level of correlations used in valuations. Both the judgments about how plausible a given level of merger activity might be and how much this might impact the firm's internal valuation policies must be based on the knowledge and experience of individuals.

- Many scenarios require judgment about the impact of large declines in market liquidity that often accompany extreme price moves. Record keeping on price liquidity is extremely sparse relative to record keeping on price levels, so it is doubtful that any such scenario could be constructed based on historical statistics.

- Some scenarios focus on the plausibility of contagion, or chain reactions of changes in one market spilling over into other markets through investor behavior. For example, this may be caused by fear that a stock market crash will spur sales of bonds by firms needing to meet margin calls. Refer back to the discussion in connection with Long Term Capital Management (LTCM) in Section 4.2.1. Such scenarios must be constructed based on knowledge of the current composition of investor portfolios. Historical statistical analysis is likely to be of limited value.

But the need for judgment in forming some stress scenarios does not imply that historical data could not be the sole driver of some scenarios and a contribution to most of the others. We first examine how scenarios principally based on judgment can be designed and then discuss methods that can be used to supplement these with scenarios based primarily on historical data.

Some points that should be considered in scenario generation:

- Given the difficulty of developing hypothetical scenarios, it is unreasonable to think that more than a handful (say, between 10 and 20) can be in use at any one time. Given all the potential combinations of events in markets, it is important to focus on those possibilities that are most significant to the types of positions your firm generally holds.

- Anchoring the assumptions for the move of a particular variable to the largest move previously observed historically is a good preventative against playing the "who can name the highest number?" game and overcoming some of the inherent subjectivity. But care should be taken to consider a broad enough range of evidence. For example, if the largest previous daily decline in one country's broad stock market index has been 10 percent and that of the stock index in another country with a similar level of economic development has been 15 percent, there is a presumption in favor of using 15 percent as a historical worst case for both.

- The most important choices are always about which variables can plausibly move together, not about the size of the moves. History can be some guide, particularly experience in prior large moves; the history of statistical correlations is virtually worthless. It is important to consider linkages that are caused by investors as well as linkages caused by economics.

- Large moves in variables are closely associated with market illiquidity. The size of the variable moves chosen should correspond to moves that occur from the time a liquidity crisis begins to the time it ends; prices recorded in between these times often have little meaning, since you cannot really do any significant size of business at them. Since record keeping relating to market liquidity is usually sparse, the choice of the starting and ending points for a liquidity crisis usually depends on the institutional memory of the people involved in the trading business.

Supplementing hypothetical scenarios with those developed primarily on historical data is desirable for a few reasons. The intensity of effort that goes into developing a hypothetical scenario limits the number that can be used at any given time, which leaves open the possibility that some plausible large risks have been ignored. Also, having a more methodical process in place for searching for plausible extreme events may lessen some of the concern about the subjective nature of scenario generation.

We can distinguish two general approaches to forming hypothetical scenarios based on historical data:

- **A complete replay of a previous stressful event, like the 1987 stock market crash or the 1997 Asian crisis.** The fact that such an event has actually occurred is a strong argument for the plausibility of a similar event occurring in the future. Although some arguments always are made along the lines of circumstances having changed so much since the time of the event to make a similar event unlikely, it should be remembered that the standard is plausibility, not probability. Thus, arguments against reoccurrence should be fairly overwhelming in order to rule it out. The simulation process for a prior event is pretty simple: Select the proper start and end dates based on when market liquidity was restored, make sure you've stored or have researched the historical values of the market variables, and do some artful creation of variables for which you don't have historical values. For example, no significant liquid emerging market debt existed in 1987, so you have to create prices based on how emerging market debt fared in subsequent large stock market downturns.
- **Factor-push methodology.** This involves selecting a number of key factors, determining a plausible up and down move for each factor, and then evaluating all possible combinations of these moves. Those that produce the largest negative P&Ls become plausible stress scenarios. The advantage of this approach is that it investigates a large number of possible scenarios (2^f where f is the number of factors) while requiring decision making or statistical analysis around a small number of inputs: the plausibility ranges for each factor. (See Wilson [1998, Section 3.3.4.iv] and Dowd [2002, Section 11.3.1]).

Two principal criticisms of factor-push methodology have been made. The first is that it does not follow from each individual factor move being plausible that each combination of these factor moves is plausible. This would be particularly true if the factors selected were closely related; it would be totally implausible for the 2-year Treasury rate to make its largest plausible up move while the 3-year Treasury rate is making its largest plausible down move. So factors must be selected to be relatively independent of one another (though complete independence is not necessary since we're dealing with the qualitative notion of plausibility rather than quantitative probabilities). For example, one factor might represent overall rate levels while another represents the slope of the rate curve, while a third represents the spread between dollar and euro rate levels. But even with relatively independent factors, all of them moving to their plausible extremes at the same time may be implausible.

The second criticism of factor-push methodology is that it assumes that the worst-case P&L always occurs at the extremes of the factor range. Although true for linear products, it may not be true once options are involved (for example, there might be a big digital options payment that will not be received at either extreme, but will be received at some points in between). A potential method for dealing with both criticisms is Monte Carlo simulation, which can search for worst-case combinations anywhere within the ranges prescribed by the individual factor plausibility bounds, but can also screen out combinations that fall below some rough measure of combinatorial plausibility. As one example, you might put a limit on the total gross amount of up plus down moves across all factors.

Since factor-push is searching for worst-case combinations rather than trying to compute statistical measures, the desire is to compute all 2^f P&Ls or, in the Monte Carlo approach, to compute a very large number of possible combinations. This can be very resource intensive if a full P&L simulation is needed for each case. One must take advantage of the relative independence of factors to compute P&Ls by segment (such as equities, interest rates, and FX) and compute combinations by summation.

The need to use relatively independent factors means that factor-push-generated scenarios will not pick up many details that are considered important in VaR and in fully specified stress scenarios, such as precise yield curve shape. But factor-push still represents an important tool for identifying the combinations of broad economic factors that are of greatest concern. Once identified, they could be further fleshed out by detailed scenario specification. At the same time, it should be recognized that stress scenarios will never reflect the full amount of detail that a purely statistical method such as VaR can encompass. A large position that is long one stock and short a closely related stock has virtually no chance of having its risk properly measured by a stress scenario. Too many possible positions of this type exist to think that each will be accounted for among a relative handful of scenarios. VaR, by statistically summarizing over a large number of scenarios based on detailed price histories, is capable of reflecting such risks.

One point of contention between traders on one side and risk managers and regulators on the other side is the assumption that no delta rehedging of options positions will take place during the unfolding of a stress scenario (a parallel contention occurs about the same assumption when used for the largest moves seen in VaR simulation). Traders rightly point out that they often have firm rules and limits that would require them to perform a delta rehedge when underlying prices move sufficiently. However, the reason risk managers and regulators often insist on assuming no rehedging is the fear that the lack of market liquidity in a crisis will prevent rehedging from being executed successfully.

11.3   USES OF OVERALL MEASURES OF FIRM POSITION RISK

In an excellent article, Wilson (1998) distinguishes several possible uses of VaR: preventing embarrassing losses, creating operational risk limits, comparing risk, determining capital adequacy, and measuring performance (see Section 3.2 of Wilson's article). I will use Wilson's framework, stating my own opinions on the usefulness of both VaR and stress testing for these purposes, and compare my views to his.

Certainly, a major concern that firms have looked to VaR and stress testing to help mitigate is the risk of embarrassing losses such as those discussed in Chapter 4. I would agree with Wilson that many of those disasters are due to issues of improper controls (for example, Barings or Allied Irish) or improper valuation (for example, Kidder Peabody or Union Bank of Switzerland [UBS]) that cannot be controlled by VaR or stress testing. Improper controls and valuation lead to positions being incorrectly reported, and VaR and stress testing cannot overcome issues of deliberate or inadvertent errors in input. If you look at the disasters covered in Chapter 4, only two resulted from unexpectedly large market moves interacting with correctly reported positions: LTCM and Metallgesellschaft (MG). Even for cases like these, I share Wilson's skepticism about the usefulness of standard VaR as a controlling mechanism since market moves that cause losses of sufficient size to threaten a firm's stability are generally radical departures from recent historical experience.

This still leaves the possibility of using stress testing or an extreme value version of VaR as a good controlling mechanism for those embarrassing losses that are based on large market moves. For the reasons I have given in Section 11.2, I believe stress tests based on economic insight are far more likely than statistical methods to produce useful measures for controlling extreme market moves.

When it comes to risk comparability, both VaR and stress offer the advantages I emphasized at the beginning of this chapter, allowing meaningful comparison and aggregation between different businesses. As Wilson states, traditional risk measures, such as the value of a basis point or vega, "provide little guidance when trying to interpret the relative importance of each individual risk factor to the portfolio's bottom line or for aggregating the different risk categories to a business unit or institution level." The ability that VaR and stress provide to make such comparisons and aggregation

> *correctly allows an institution to gain a deeper understanding of the relative importance of its different risk positions and to gauge better its aggregate risk exposure relative to its aggregate risk appetite. VaR accomplishes these objectives by defining a common metric that can be applied universally across all risk positions or portfolios: the maximum possible loss within a known confidence interval over a given holding period. Besides being able to be applied universally across all risk categories, including market, credit, operational, and insurance risks, this metric is also expressed in units that are (or should be) meaningful at all levels of management: dollars (or pounds, francs, etc.) It therefore serves as a relevant focal point for discussing risks at all levels within the institution, creating a risk dialogue and culture that is otherwise difficult to achieve given the otherwise technical nature of the issues.*

Given this ability to place different risks on a common footing, it is quite natural to want to place limits on businesses based on VaR and stress scenario losses. Stress scenario losses offer the added benefit of controlling against at least some forms of financial disaster. However, this does not provide a complete solution to the control of a trading business, and other non-statistical limits are needed as well. Wilson emphasizes the speed of calculation and the ease of understanding and communication as the reasons for needing other limits besides VaR. I would emphasize, as I did in Section 5.2, the need to match position taking to expertise and to assure adequate diversity of trading styles.

A supplement to the use of limits to control risk is the provision of an adequate capital cushion against potential losses. This cushion is required for both earnings volatility and protection against large market moves. Earnings volatility measurement aligns well with VaR, while the impact of large market moves is a risk better measured by stress scenarios. Although I believe this to be a sound argument for basing internal measures of capital adequacy on both VaR and stress loss, regulators have strongly favored VaR as the measure upon which to base the capital required for regulatory purposes. Since the capital required for regulatory purposes can have a direct impact on the firm's stock price performance, regulators have been wary of any tie to a measure such as stress, which directly relies on human judgment, for fear that management will manipulate it. VaR has been viewed as preferable based on the relative difficulty of manipulating a statistical measure. VaR is viewed as at least capturing relative differences in the level of risk. Translation into a required capital cushion against large, unexpected moves is then approximated through multiplication by an essentially arbitrary constant. For a more detailed discussion of the regulatory capital standards revolving around VaR, see Jorion (2001, Chapter 3).

For performance measurement, the critical objective is to have a means of adjusting the P&L performance of the firm and of business units for the level of risk taken in achieving this performance. As with the capital cushion, the risk taken is both a function of earnings volatility and of vulnerability to unexpectedly large market moves, arguing for using a mix of VaR and stress loss in developing this measure. But the subjectivity of stress scenarios, combined with the sole reliance of regulatory capital on VaR, has led almost all firms to the decision to base this risk measure completely on VaR. The firm at which I have worked for the past several years, Chase Manhattan (now JPMorgan Chase) has been very unusual in utilizing both VaR and stress in this measure. I will relate some of the history that led Chase management to conclude that stress loss was worth utilizing despite the disputes between the central risk-management group and business units, which are inevitable when experience and judgment are a significant determinant of a performance measure.

When the Asian credit crisis in the fall of 1997 started to spread to other emerging market economies, we noticed that the losses being experienced by Chase trading desks very closely matched the projections of the hypothetical flight-to-quality stress scenario we had constructed. The match was not just for the firm as a whole, but for individual business units. This experience persuaded management to experiment with tying the risk adjustment of business units to stress losses as an incentive to reduce vulnerability to large market shocks. As business adjusted to the new performance measure in early 1998, we noticed a significant impact in terms of strategies to continue to meet P&L targets with less reliance on positions that were vulnerable to these shocks. The result was that Chase weathered the fall of 1998 market shock due to Russian default and the unraveling of LTCM with much smaller losses than in the fall of 1997 crisis and with smaller losses than almost all of our largest competitors (see O'Brien [1999]). Continued experience with the impact of this decision since then has continued to confirm its value.

The mechanisms for adjusting P&L return for risk, which include calculating risk-adjusted return on capital (RAROC) and shareholder value added (SVA), are not topics I will address in this book. Interested readers are referred to Jorion (2001, Chapter 17).

In reporting the contribution of product lines, trading desks, and risk components to overall firm risk, varying approaches can be taken:

- Each component can be represented by the scenario risk measure it would have as a standalone portfolio. This is the easiest approach to implement and certainly gives a good indicator of relative risk, but it fails to capture any correlation effects with other risk components that contribute to overall firm risk.

■ Each component can be represented by the impact the full elimination of that risk component would have on total firm risk. This captures correlation effects, but may be unrealistic in that the full elimination of a business line may not be a feasible alternative.

■ Each component can be represented by its marginal impact on total firm risk. This captures correlation effects and gives a good measure of the immediate impact on firm risk of adding to or offsetting some of a component's risk, but it is very dependent on the current mixture of risk components. A very risky business line may get represented as having a small contribution to risk just because it has low correlation with the current mix of risk for the firm. It may be best to use a standalone risk measure in conjunction with a marginal impact measure to make sure that components that can potentially make large contributions to risk receive timely management focus.

The marginal impact measure has a nice side benefit. When you take the weighted sum of marginal impact, weighted by current positions, you get the total risk measure for the firm. This makes the marginal impact a convenient tool for exercises such as allocation to a business line of firm capital where you need the sum of the parts to equal the whole. In order to have this property, a risk measure need only satisfy the condition that it scales directly with position size; that is, a position with the same composition but k times as large has a risk measure k times as large as the original position. This homogeneity condition is clearly met by both VaR and stress-testing measures.

To see that the weighted by position sum of the marginal impacts equals the total risk, first write the risk measure of the portfolio as $R(x_1, x_2, \ldots x_n)$ where x_i is a component of the portfolio. By hypothesis, $R(kx_1, kx_2, \ldots, kx_n) = kR(x_1, x_2, \ldots, x_n)$. Taking the derivative of both sides with respect to k, the left-hand side by the chain rule, we obtain:

$$\sum_i x_i \frac{\partial R(kx_1, kx_2, \ldots, kx_n)}{\partial kx_i} = R(x_1, x_2, \ldots, x_n) \qquad (11.5)$$

Setting $k = 1$,

$$\sum_i x_i \frac{\partial R(x_1, x_2, \ldots, x_n)}{\partial x_i} = R(x_1, x_2, \ldots, x_n) \qquad (11.6)$$

which states that the sum of the marginal impacts weighted by position equals the total risk. Further discussion of marginal VaR analysis can be found in Litterman (1997A). Litterman (1997B) demonstrates how to gain intuitive understanding of the sources of risk by creating a portfolio with a small number of components that replicates a large portion of the total VaR of a firm.

EXERCISES

11.1

Using the data in the **VaR** spreadsheet (with equal weights on all days) and a 10 percent position in each of the 10 variables, calculate the 99th percentile VaR using the following 5 methods:

    a. Variance-covariance.
    b. Historical simulation using a single-point estimate of the 99th percentile.
    c. Historical simulation using 2.33 × the standard deviation of the daily total portfolio valuations as the 99th percentile.
    d. Historical simulation using a single point estimator of the 99th percentile and substituting the historical volatility over the most recent 100 business days for the historical volatility over the full data set, but using the full data set to simulate results.
    e. A Monte Carlo simulation.

    Your answers to a, c, and e should be very close to equal. Why? What does this tell you about the relative ease of implementation of the three methods?

11.2

Try the same exercise as in 11.1 with a combination of investment percentages that you choose yourself. Can you find a combination without any short positions (all investment percentages positive) that gives a high diversification benefit (cell D24 of the **Var-CoVVaR** worksheet in the **VaR** spreadsheet)?

11.3

Look at the **Ratios** worksheet in the **VaR** spreadsheet. What does it tell you about how fat tailed the time series used in these calculations is? At what percentile level do you begin to see a significant impact of the fat tails?

CHAPTER 12

Credit Risk

The field of credit risk management has undergone major transformations over the 1990s. Traditional commercial bank lenders, whose focus used to be almost exclusively on the analysis of individual borrowers with a small dose of limits to avoid excessive concentration in a region or industry, have increasingly viewed overall portfolio management as a major part of their function. This has opened the door to rapid growth in the use of quantitative risk aggregation techniques. At the same time, the introduction of an array of vehicles for transferring credit risk between creditors—the increased use of loan sales, loan syndication, and short sales of bonds, along with the introduction of many varieties of credit derivatives, asset-backed securities, and collateralized debt obligations—has served as a tool for portfolio management. It has also opened the door to risk decomposition techniques.

As with market risk, the use of risk decomposition to price the cost of exiting risk positions holds out the promise of transforming long-term risk into short-term risk. The potential benefits of this transformation mirror those for market risk—the possibility of using abundant data on short-term price movements as opposed to using sparse data on long-term risks over credit cycles, the ability to receive much earlier feedback on investment strategies that are not working, and the ability to use short-term value at risk (VaR) analysis for risk aggregation.

Although widespread agreement seems to exist on the benefits of quantitative risk aggregation when applied to credit risk, the use of risk decomposition to transform long-term risks into short-term risks is far more controversial. Strong proponents tend to come from investment banks. Their approach could be telescoped into the motto "What credit risk? All I see is market risk." In other words, once you obtain liquid daily prices for credit exposure, you can just view this as another asset class, such as foreign exchange (FX), interest rates, equities, and commodities, to be managed using market risk techniques. Those resisting this idea tend to come from commercial banks. Their motto could be expressed as "We only lose money when borrowers default." So any analysis that is not sufficiently long term to get to default experience will be inadequate.

Some of the controversy over the transformation to short-term risk can be attributed to arguments over the degree of liquidity of credit. Even with the new means of transferring credit risks that have been introduced, there is still far less liquidity in the external price quotes that can be obtained for loan prices than for equity prices. Bond prices fall somewhere in between, but even with these prices, quotes tend to be sparse except for the very largest names. Loans are also more flexible instruments than stocks or bonds, since they are subject to continual renegotiation between the borrowers and a small group of lenders who develop a private knowledge of the borrower's business.

Some of this controversy can be traced to a difference in credit culture. Commercial bankers' views are shaped by their greater experience in the less liquid, more private environment of loans, and investment bankers' views are influenced by their greater experience in the more liquid, more public environment of bonds.

Political interests also drive some of this controversy. Commercial bankers seek to hold onto the competitive advantages of not having to publicly recognize profit and loss (P&L) on changes in market value on the bulk of their loan portfolio. Investment banks, which are required to publicly recognize P&L based on changes in market value on all their assets, would prefer that the commercial banks be on a level playing field with regard to accounting.

Finally, some of this controversy is due to the large convexity risk on credit instruments, as discussed in Section 8.4. A market risk approach that is well adopted to exposures to stocks, currencies, commodities, and forwards free of credit risk may leave too much exposure to the large sudden price jumps that result from defaults or credit downgrades.

In this chapter, we outline both risk management approaches to credit risk: one based on short-term exposure to changes in market prices and the other based on the long-term risk of default. However, first we need a fundamental framework within which we can discuss these risks. Ultimately, the cost of credit risk must be based on expectations and uncertainty concerning loss from default. Without the possibility of default, credit instruments would just be priced based on the risk-free discount curve. Default loss can be analyzed into three components as follows:

$$D(I) = P_D(B) \times L_D(I) \times A_D(I) \qquad (12.1)$$

Where

I is a credit instrument.
B is the borrower on the instrument.
$D(I)$ is the default loss on the instrument.

$P_D(B)$ is the probability that the borrower will default.
$L_D(I)$ is the percentage loss on the instrument conditioned on default.
$A_D(I)$ is the amount that will be owed on the instrument conditional on default.

We use $P_D(B)$ instead of $P_D(I)$ because cross-default legal provisions come close to guaranteeing that a borrower will either default on all or none of its debt.

For many instruments, $A_D(I)$ is a fixed amount—the amount of currency borrowed. The two major exceptions are:

- **Lines of credit, which enable a borrower to draw funds as needed up to some maximum amount, subject to various terms and conditions.** From a completely pessimistic view, $A_D(I)$ would be set for a credit line equal to the maximum amount that can be drawn, since just prior to default a borrower will likely try to maximize the use of all available sources of credit. However, this fails to take into account some of the contractual terms that the lender can employ to limit credit line usage when the credit rating of the borrower is declining. It is thus possible that $A_D(I)$ will be less than the maximum amount that can be drawn.
- **Counterparty credit risk on derivatives, for which the amount owed depends on the replacement value of the derivative at the time of default.** For example, consider a forward FX agreement of company XYZ to buy $200 million dollars at 100 yen to the dollar. If XYZ defaults when the forward dollar (to the contracted date) is selling at 90 yen to the dollar, finding another counterparty to take over this contract will cost (100 yen − 90 yen) × $200 million = 2 billion yen, which is the $A_D(I)$ for this case. But if XYZ defaults when the forward dollar is selling at 110 yen to the dollar, you would actually receive 2 billion yen as an inducement to find another counterparty to take over the contract. This is not a windfall gain, since you would need to pay a similar amount to the bankruptcy trustees for XYZ to settle your contract with XYZ. The $A_D(I)$ for this case is zero.

We will focus first on those instruments for which $A_D(I)$ is a fixed amount. At the end of the chapter, we will return to the subject of lines of credit (Section 12.3) and counterparty credit risk (Section 12.4). With $A_D(I)$ fixed, what remains to be determined are $P_D(B)$ and $L_D(I)$, the probability of default and loss conditional on default, respectively.

We will first examine credit risk based on short-term exposure to changes in market prices. Afterwards, we will take up the approach based on the long-term risk of default.

12.1 SHORT-TERM EXPOSURE TO CHANGES IN MARKET PRICES

As noted in the introduction to this chapter, the potential advantage of a market-based approach is to be able to base risk analysis on the more abundant data of short-term price movements and take advantage of the VaR and stress testing mechanisms already developed for managing market risk. The drawbacks are the relative illiquidity of credit instruments and the large convexity risks of credit instruments.

Another potential advantage of a market-based approach is its relative simplicity. We can draw on the mechanics developed for the analysis of forward risk, such as the extraction of discount factors from the most liquid prices, and then use these discount factors to price all other sets of cash flows (see Section 8.2). However, two issues complicate the application of this technique:

- It cannot distinguish the effects of default probability and loss given default—in other words, you can extract information from market prices on $P_D(B) \times L_D(I)$, but cannot distinguish between $P_D(B)$ and $L_D(I)$.
- Not all cash flows received at the same time can be valued using the same discount factor.

Let's examine these two issues. To get a clear view of the entanglement of default probability and loss given default in market prices for credit instruments, let's consider the simplest possible case. Suppose company XYZ has a 2-year zero-coupon bond that is trading at $85.50 per $100.00 par amount, while a 2-year zero-coupon government bond is trading at $90.00 per $100.00 par amount. The $4.50 haircut on the corporate bond implies that the market is pricing the bond as if the expected loss from default over a 2-year period would be 5% ($90 × 95% = $85.50). However, this loss could consist of $P_D(B) = 5\%$, $L_D(I) = 100\%$, or $P_D(B) = 10\%$; $L_D(I) = 50\%$; or any other combination that results in $P_D(B) \times L_D(I) = 5\%$. If we were only concerned with linear credit risk, this wouldn't make a difference—all we really need to know is to price all 2-year cash flows owed by XYZ at a 5% discount from 2-year risk-free cash flows. However, we will need the distinction when we start to account for convexity, as you will see shortly.

The ability to value all cash flows received on the same date using the same discount factor is a vital assumption in the methodology used to maximize liquidity in the forwards markets, as discussed in Section 8.2. The reason this assumption breaks down for credit instruments relates to provisions of bankruptcy law. In almost all jurisdictions, the claim for a 2-year coupon due on a 5-year bond is not the same in bankruptcy as the claim for the same amount of principal on a 2-year bond. The common rule for bankruptcy is that the holder of a bond or loan can make a claim on the principal, but not on any coupon interest. Offsetting this loss of interest that can be claimed is the ability to call for immediate payment of principal, regardless of maturity.

For bonds or loans trading close to par—that is, the coupon on the bond is close to the current par coupon—the advantage and disadvantage almost cancel out. A 5-year bond loses 5 years' worth of coupons, but can accelerate principal due by 5 years, while a 2-year bond loses only 2 years' worth of coupons, but can accelerate principal due by only 2 years. The par coupon can be thought of as the rate of interest that exactly compensates an investor, at current market discount factors, for deferral of receiving principal; therefore, foregoing coupons on the par coupon bond will precisely offset the acceleration of principal. For similar reasons, a floating rate bond or loan, whose coupon resets to current market levels, should have the advantage of principal acceleration closely balance out the loss of coupon payment.

However, for bonds or loans selling at a premium, either because of a fixed coupon higher than the current par coupon or a floating rate at a positive spread to current market levels, the bankruptcy rules will cause more of a loss on default than that felt by a par bond or loan. Conversely, a bond or loan selling at a discount will experience less of a loss on default than that experienced by a par bond or loan. As a result, the rule that all cash flows on the same date are equivalent, regardless of what package they are part of, breaks down. A coupon payment is worth more in default if it is packaged as part of a discount bond than a coupon payment for the same date that is packaged as part of a premium bond.

Exercise 12.1 familiarizes you with the mathematics needed to deal with this situation. The **CreditPricer** spreadsheet used in the exercise takes as input the current risk-free zero-coupon curve, an assumed set of annual default rates, and an assumed loss given default rate, and computes the resulting par curve for a corporate bond and resulting spreads to the risk-free par curve. The calculation looks at the value of payments received if no default occurs plus the accelerated principal payments received if default occurs. The exercise demonstrates that spreads to the risk-free par curve will differ for differing assumptions of loss given default. This shows that it is not just the product $P_D(B) \times L_D(I)$ that matters in this case, but also the individual components, since the value of the principal acceleration depends on the loss given default assumption. The exercise also shows you how to use the same spreadsheet to solve for market-implied default rates based on an observed par curve and an assumed loss given default rate. It further shows that if prices are available for several coupons with the same maturity, then information about the split between $P_D(B)$ and $L_D(I)$ can be extracted.

To illustrate the difficulty that convexity poses for credit risk management based on short-term exposure to market prices, consider the following simple example. Consider two obligations of company XYZ: a 2-year zero-coupon bond and a 10-year zero-coupon bond. Assume that a risk-free 2-year zero is trading at $90 per $100 par value and a risk-free 10-year zero is trading at $60 per $100 par value. If the expected loss from default for XYZ is roughly 1 percent a year, we would expect to see a haircut for the 2-year zero of $90.00 $\times$ 2% = $1.80 and a haircut for the 10-year zero of $60.00 $\times$ 10% = $6.00. If market confidence in XYZ worsened slightly, expected loss from default might rise from about 1 percent a year to about 1.1 percent a year, resulting in a haircut for the 2-year zero of $90.00 $\times$ 2.2% = $1.98 and a haircut for the 10-year zero of $60.00 $\times$ 11% = $6.60. Therefore, the 2-year zero has moved by $1.98 $-$ $1.80 = $0.18 and the 10-year zero has moved by $6.60 $-$ $6.00 = $0.60, a ratio of $0.60/$0.18 = 3.33 (which could also be derived as a ratio of the durations multiplied by the present values, [10 $\times$ $60]/[2 $\times$ $90]).

If you want to hedge against small moves in a credit spread, you would sell short $30 million 10-year bonds against a long position of $100 million 2-year bonds. But what happens if XYZ defaults? You have losses on $100 million balanced by gains on only $30 million. The right ratio for hedging short-term market movements is an extremely poor ratio for hedging default, due to the severe convexity. For large moves that do not go all the way to default, as might be associated with a credit downgrade, a mismatch will still occur, but it will be less severe. The example demonstrates that risk management utilizing short-term exposures to changes in market price is not sufficient by itself; it needs to be supplemented by an analysis of ultimate default risk.

Another shortcoming of basing risk analysis exclusively on short-term exposure to market prices is that it is insufficient to determine the adequacy of capital due to the inability to distinguish between the probability of default and rate of loss given default and the need to take into account the correlation between defaults. Consider a portfolio of loans and bonds for which you are trying to decide whether you have adequate capital protection for the coming year. If market prices are telling you that $P_D(B) \times L_D(I)$ for the next year averages 2 percent for the portfolio, does it matter what the values of $P_D(B)$ and $L_D(I)$ are? Let's take a simple case with only two loans, each for $100 million, and assume that $P_D(B) \times L_D(I) = 2$ percent for each loan and that zero correlation exists between their defaults. Assume you are holding $75 million in capital and want to know the probability that this amount of capital will be adequate. In Table 12.1, we examine two different cases, in which different assumptions about the composition of $P_D(B)$ and $L_D(I)$ lead to different probabilities of capital adequacy. In the interest

TABLE 12.1 Impact on the Probability of Losses Exceeding Capital

	Case 1		Case 2	
$P_D(B) \times L_D(I)$	2%		2%	
$P_D(B)$	2%		4%	
$L_D(I)$	100%		50%	
Probabilities				
2 defaults	2% × 2% =	0.04%	4% × 4% =	0.16%
1 default	2 × 2% × 98% =	3.92%	2 × 4% × 96% =	7.68%
0 defaults	98% × 98% =	96.04%	96% × 96% =	92.16%
		100.00%		100.00%
Expected Loss from Default				
2 defaults	0.04% × $200 mil. =	$0.08 mil.	0.16% × $100 mil. =	$0.16 mil.
1 default	3.92% × $100 mil. =	$3.92 mil.	7.68% × $50 mil. =	$3.84 mil.
		$4.00 mil.		$4.00 mil.
Probability of Losses Exceeding $75 Million Capital				
2 defaults		0.04%	0.16%	
1 default		3.92%		
		3.96%	0.16%	

of simplifying the example, we will ignore the uncertainty around the expected value of $L_D(I)$.

An enormous difference appears in the probability of losses exceeding capital based on a different mix between the probability of default and loss given default. However, market prices for individual loans and bonds are primarily based on the product of the probability of default and loss given default, with only slight sensitivity to the mix between the two, as shown in Exercise 12.1. Increasing the number of loans, introducing nonzero correlations between defaults, and adding the volatility of $L_D(I)$ does not change this conclusion.

Correlation levels between loans will obviously have a major influence on capital. Increasing correlation between defaults from 0 to 100 percent in Case 2 of Table 12.1 would increase the probability of losses exceeding $75 million capital from 0.16 to 4.00 percent, since all of the default cases would now be joint default cases with losses of $100 million. Intermediate positive correlations between 0 and 100 percent would result in intermediate levels of the probability of exceeding the capital level. Increasing the number of loans does not change this conclusion. Note that what is important is the correlation of default, not the correlation of short-term moves in credit spread, again showing that an analysis based on short-term exposure to market prices is insufficient and must be supplemented by an analysis of ultimate default risk.

So far we have argued that we must look beyond a pure market-price-based approach to credit risk and take the ultimate default risk into account in order to deal with the issues of hedging convexity risk and deciding on the adequacy of capital. When dealing with complex credit derivatives, even market valuation requires the consideration of ultimate default risk. To illustrate with a simple example, consider a collateralized loan obligation (CLO) based on the exact same basket of loans we considered in the previous capital adequacy example. If the shares in the CLO are simple proportional shares in the basket, then CLO valuation is exactly equivalent to the sum of the market valuation of the individual loans (refer to Section 10.4.1 for a discussion of this point). However, suppose the CLO is structured in two tranches: one tranche of $75 million that absorbs all losses in the basket until it is exhausted and a second tranche of $125 million that absorbs all remaining losses. Now the valuation of the tranche is a direct analogue to the discussion of the adequacy of $75 million in capital, with expected credit losses by tranche corresponding to the two cases discussed previously, as shown in Table 12.2.

A 100 percent correlation between defaults in Case 2 will raise the expected loss of the $125 million tranche to 4.00% × $25 million = $1 million, since all of the default cases will now be joint default cases with losses of $100 million.

Another example where market valuation requires the consideration of ultimate default risk would be a nonstandard default swap that pays a fixed dollar amount in the event of default. Since standard default swaps tie loss in the event of default to loss in the event of default on loans and bonds, market prices for all standard credit instruments entangle default probabil-

TABLE 12.2 Impact on the Pricing of CLO Tranches

Case 1	Case 2
Expected Loss of $75 Million Tranche	
	0.16% × $75 mil. +
3.96%× $75 mil. = $2.97 mil.	7.68% × $50 mil. = $3.96 mil.
Expected Loss of $125 Million Tranche	
0.04% × $125 mil. +	
3.92% × $25 mil. = $1.03 mil.	0.16% × $25 mil. = $0.04 mil.
$4.00 mil.	$4.00 mil.

ity and loss in the event of default. To value a default swap that pays a fixed amount requires a default probability in isolation, so valuation based on standard market prices is not possible.

12.2   THE LONG-TERM RISK OF DEFAULT

We will now examine the risk management approach to credit risk that is based on the long-term risk of default. As discussed in the preceding section, this approach is at least needed as a supplement to risk management based on short-term exposure to change in market prices. However, it can also be used as a standalone method. Two fundamental variants exist. One is based on the statistical analysis of the historical experience of occurrence of default and loss in the event of default. The second is based on representing a firm's debt holders as having sold a put on the value of the firm and using option theory to analyze the probabilities of default and loss in the event of default. No matter which of these two methods is chosen, statistical analysis is relied upon to estimate correlations between defaults.

Our discussion is divided into five sections:

- **Section 12.2.1.**   The statistical approach to estimating the occurrence of default.
- **Section 12.2.2.**   The statistical approach to estimating loss given default. We also cover issues relating to possible correlation between the occurrence of default and loss given default in this section.
- **Section 12.2.3.**   The options theory approach to estimating the occurrence of default and loss given default.
- **Section 12.2.4.**   The statistical approach to estimating correlations between defaults.
- **Section 12.2.5.**   The computation of portfolio risk based on these estimates.

The amount of literature on these issues is large and growing. I provide references throughout to what I consider the most complete sources of public information on specific topics. For a reader looking for an overview at a greater level of detail than I am providing here, I recommend Saunders and Allen (2002).

12.2.1   The Statistical Approach to Estimating the Occurrence of Default

The statistical study of default probability generally centers on transition matrices published by the credit agencies—Standard and Poor's (S&P) and Moody's. These matrices show the probability over a fixed time period that a credit rated in one category at the beginning of the period will default during the period or will transition to another credit rating category at the end of the period. Tables 12.3 and 12.4 show a sample 1-year transition matrix published by S&P (1996) based on about 20 years' worth of data and a cumulative transition matrix that only looks at default. Both rating agencies also publish matrices covering many different transition periods (for example, 2-year transitions, 3-year transitions, and so on), matrices with finer credit rating graduations, and matrices based on subsets of this historical data.

Any analysis of the default probability of a particular credit facility must involve assigning it a gradation of credit risk and then associating a default

TABLE 12.3 One-Year Transition Matrix

Initial Rating	Rating at Year End							
	AAA	AA	A	BBB	BB	B	CCC	Default
AAA	90.81%	8.33%	0.68%	0.06%	0.12%	0.00%	0.00%	0.00%
AA	0.70%	90.65%	7.79%	0.64%	0.06%	0.14%	0.02%	0.00%
A	0.09%	2.27%	91.05%	5.52%	0.74%	0.26%	0.01%	0.06%
BBB	0.02%	0.33%	5.95%	86.93%	5.30%	1.17%	0.12%	0.18%
BB	0.03%	0.14%	0.67%	7.73%	80.53%	8.84%	1.00%	1.06%
B	0.00%	0.11%	0.24%	0.43%	6.48%	83.46%	4.07%	5.20%
CCC	0.22%	0.00%	0.22%	1.30%	2.38%	11.24%	64.86%	19.79%
Default	0.00%	0.00%	0.00%	0.00%	0.00%	0.00%	0.00%	100.00%

Source: Standard & Poor's, Credit Week, April 15, 1996.

TABLE 12.4 Cumulative Default Rates

Initial Rating	Number of Years							
	1	2	3	4	5	7	10	15
AAA	0.00%	0.00%	0.07%	0.15%	0.24%	0.66%	1.40%	1.40%
AA	0.00%	0.02%	0.12%	0.25%	0.43%	0.89%	1.29%	1.48%
A	0.06%	0.16%	0.27%	0.44%	0.67%	1.12%	2.17%	3.00%
BBB	0.18%	0.44%	0.72%	1.27%	1.78%	2.99%	4.34%	4.70%
BB	1.06%	3.48%	6.12%	8.68%	10.97%	14.46%	17.73%	19.91%
B	5.20%	11.00%	15.95%	19.40%	21.88%	25.14%	29.02%	30.65%
CCC	19.79%	26.92%	31.63%	35.97%	40.15%	42.64%	45.10%	45.10%

Source: Standard & Poor's, Credit Week, April 15, 1996.

probability with that credit risk. The most straightforward approach, and the one often used in practice, is to rely on the credit grade assigned by one of the two rating agencies and then utilize the transition matrix published by that rating agency to determine a default probability associated with the rating and tenor. A large number of variants exist around both of these steps. Here are some of the major differences in approach and the issues surrounding them:

- Large lending firms may have their own internal data on defaults and transitions that they may want to use to supplement the publicly available data that comes from S&P and Moody's. However, even if this data has been well maintained, a trade-off exists between using data that is more relevant to the particular class of borrowers who are customers of a particular firm and the loss of accuracy that comes from the utilization of a smaller sample.

- If default and transition data is available broken out by country and industry, this could be used to refine the data available from S&P and Moody's. One criticism of S&P and Moody's data is that they are largely based on experience with U.S. firms. However, the same points about small data samples raised in the last bullet may be relevant here.

- Default and transition data from different sources can be blended, such as averaging S&P and Moody's data, or rating agency and private data.

- Trade-offs between using multiyear default data based on the direct observation of cumulative default rates versus generating multiyear cumulative default rates by the matrix multiplication of 1-year transition matrices. The direct use of cumulative default rates suffers from a diminishing data pool for longer tenors and greater potential inaccuracy from withdrawn ratings (firms whose ratings are no longer tracked) (see Gupton, Finger, and Bhatia [1997, 6.3.2]). Matrix multiplication assumes a Markovian process, where no serial correlation exists between transitions. Alternatively, it could be desirable to derive 1-year transition matrices that are consistent with observed longer-term cumulative default and transition behavior (see Gupton, Finger, and Bhatia [1997, 6.4]). However, there is data suggesting that serial correlation between transitions does exist (see Bahar and Nagpal [2000]).

- Default rates and transition matrices could be adjusted for the current stage in the economic cycle, based on historical observation of differences during recession and growth periods.

- The classification of credit exposures into rating categories could use blended information from the ratings services or could rely on internal ratings of a firm's credit officers. It could also combine internal and external ratings. The advantage of internal ratings is they have the capability to leverage detailed knowledge built up on the particular names a firm lends to. However, care must be taken to ensure that internal ratings are updated with sufficient frequency. Also, a mismatch may appear between ratings determined by internal processes and default and transition data tied to rating agency categories. To make sense of this, an effort must be made to conform the internal ratings categories used as closely as possible to ratings agency definitions.

A frequently expressed concern is that credit ratings are not updated often enough to fully reflect the probability of default. This applies equally to credit rating agency ratings and internal ratings. It reflects the nature of the rating process, which, because of the serious consequences to a firm's financial health a ratings change can entail, requires that changes be thoroughly deliberated and well documented.

An alternative would be to infer default probabilities from market prices, which are subject to far more rapid change. For a firm with publicly traded debt, implied default probabilities can be backed out of market prices, based on an assumption of loss given default, using the methodology illustrated in Exercise 12.1. Transition probabilities for downgrades can then be determined by looking at historical statistics for debt with a similar default probability. The downside is that changes in debt prices may reflect many factors other than changes in market sentiment about default probability—technical liquidity factors or changes in the willingness to take on risk can dominate. This is not a valuation process where we are trying to determine an exit price, as would be the case if we were focused on managing short-term market risk, so we are faced with a real choice of whether to base a longer-term forecast of default on market prices. It is very analogous to the decision we discussed in Section 11.1, regarding whether to base a VaR calculation on volatilities implied by market prices or those obtained from historical observation.

Even when a firm has publicly traded debt, it may not be very liquid and may not provide an up-to-date assessment of market sentiment on the firm's credit risk. Stock prices are generally far more liquid, leading to attempts to extract credit default information from stock prices, as is discussed further in Section 12.2.3.

12.2.2   The Statistical Approach to Estimating Loss Given Default

Statistical estimates of loss given default have been published by the credit rating agencies. A few other published studies are available as well. Gupton, Finger, and Bhatia (1997, Chapter 7) offers a good discussion of the public

TABLE 12.5 Comparison of Rates of Loss Given Default

Seniority Class	Number of Observations	Average Loss Given Default	Standard Deviation
Senior secured bank loans	119	30.5%	22.5%
Senior unsecured bank loans	33	47.9%	28.6%
Senior secured bonds	115	46.2%	26.9%
Senior unsecured bonds	278	48.9%	25.5%
Senior subordinated bonds	196	61.5%	23.8%
Subordinated bonds	226	67.3%	20.2%
Junior subordinated bonds	9	82.9%	10.9%

Source: Moody's, "Bank Loan Loss Given Default," November 2000, and "Corporate Bond Defaults and Default Rates 1938–1995," January, 1996. Reprinted with permission from Moody's Investors Service.

data available. A recent aggregation of public data can be found in Altman, Resti, and Sironi (2001, Appendix III.1). Table 12.5 provides results from the Moody's study for bond defaults occurring from 1970 to 1995, as reported in Gupton, Finger, and Bhatia (1997). Distinctions are drawn based on the relative seniority of debt, with bank loans regarded as a separate seniority class from bonds. Bank loss data is drawn from the Moody's (2000) study that covers a period from 1989 to 2000. Published studies usually show recovery rates, which are 100 percent minus the loss given default rate, but I have translated into loss given default.

The measurement of historical loss given default can be performed in two different ways. One, which is used in the Moody's study, is to observe the drop in market prices for an instrument about 1 month after the announcement of default. The second is to track all cash eventually received in the settlement of claims and to present value these future receipts back to the date of default, utilizing a discount rate that suitably reflects the uncertainty of recovery. Gupton, Finger, and Bhatia (1997, Section 7.1) cites academic studies that conclude that the "bond market efficiently prices future realized liquidation values," supporting a rough equivalence of these two methods. All losses should be expressed as a percentage of par, given that bankruptcy law uses par amount of the instrument as the basis for a claim (as discussed in Section 12.1).

Parallel to our discussion on the estimation of the risk of default, firms may want to supplement published data on loss given default with their own internal data. This is particularly an issue with non-U.S. debt and bank loans. Published data on loss given default is heavily weighted toward the U.S. market, but bankruptcy laws and procedures differ substantially by country and may thus be expected to impact recovery rates. The lower loss given default rate on bank loans can be presumed to be due to the attention banks pay to the negotiation of security against default. However, this attention may vary between banks and, even within a bank, by loan type.

An issue that has drawn significant recent attention is the correlation between the occurrence of default and rate of loss given default. This is the focus of a report submitted by Altman, Resti, and Sironi (2001) to the International Swaps and Derivatives Association. This study finds significant negative correlation between the occurrence of default and recovery rate, which translates to a strong positive correlation between the occurrence of default and loss given default. This is not surprising on economic grounds, since an economic recession is likely to trigger more defaults while also negatively impacting the ability of a bankrupt firm to realize value on its remaining assets. This correlation has much the same effect as an increase in the level of correlation between defaults, since both result in more clustering of default losses. For example, if we're projecting the possible default losses for the next year, we might experience a good period for the overall economy that leads to few defaults and small losses on the defaults that do occur, or we might experience a recession that leads to many defaults and a high level of losses on these defaults. To the extent default losses cluster, it implies the need for added capital to guard against large losses and a lower valuation of the senior tranches in CDOs, as discussed in Section 12.1.

12.2.3   The Option-Theoretic Approach

In the option-theoretic approach, a firm's equity is viewed as a call option on the value of the firm's assets with a strike price equal to the face value of the firm's debt. This is equivalent to viewing the equity owners of a firm as having a put option to pay off the debt holders with either the face value of the debt or the total value of the firm's assets, whichever is smaller. So the total economic value of the firm's debt to the debt holders must be the face value of the debt less the value of this put option.

The advantage of the option-theoretic approach is that it can derive default probability and recovery rates from variables that can be observed in the market. By utilizing market information, it is hoped to reduce the time lag in recognizing changes in default probabilities. This time lag is inherent in the statistical approach, which requires time for credit analysts to react to new information. In addition, the option-theoretic approach is the only one that can link together credit valuation and equity valuation into a single coherent theory.

Let us first look at a very simple version of the options model, which can be found in Hull (2002, Section 26.5). This model has four key simplifying assumptions:

- The firm has only a single class of debt outstanding, a zero-coupon debt, and the firm will not issue any new debt before this debt matures.
- If the firm defaults, this will only occur at the time of the maturity of this debt.
- The firm's behavior, such as the riskiness of its investments, will not be impacted by how close it is to default.
- No intermediate payments, such as dividends, will be made to equity holders.

At the price of these simplifying assumptions, the model only requires four inputs—the time to maturity of the debt, the market value of the firm's assets, the present value of the firm's debts, and the volatility of the firm's assets. The model can give explicit formulas, in terms of these four inputs, for the probability the firm will default, the loss given default, the required interest rate spread over the risk-free rate for the firm's debt, and the market value of the firm's equity and debt.

Using notation close to that in Hull, we'll denote:

V_0: The current market value of the firm's assets
D_0: The present value of the firm's debt, which matures at time T, discounted at the risk-free interest rate
σ_V: The volatility of the firm's assets
P_D: The probability of default
L_D: The loss in the event of default

Viewing the equity as a call option on the firm's value with a strike price of the face amount of the debt, we can write a formula for the current market value of the firm's equity as:

$$E_0 = V_0 N(d_1) - D_0 N(d_2)$$

Where

$$d_1 = (\ln(V_0/D_0) + \sigma^2{}_V T/2)/\sigma_V \sqrt{T}$$

$$d_2 = d_1 - \sigma_V \sqrt{T} \tag{12.2}$$

The current market value of the firm's debt is just $V_0 - E_0$.

Following the standard Black-Scholes analysis, $N(d_1)$ is the delta, the partial derivative of E_0 with respect to V_0, and $N(d_2)$ is the probability that the strike price will be exceeded at time T. But this is the probability that the firm will not default so:

$$P_D = 1 - N(d_2) \tag{12.3}$$

If no default occurs, the debt holders receive the face value of the debt and, if default does occur, the debt holders receive the recovery rate times the face value of the debt, so we can write the market value of the debt as:

$$V_0 - E_0 = ((1 - P_D) + P_D(1 - L_D))\, D_0 \qquad (12.4)$$

Substituting from Equations 12.2 and 12.3,

$$V_0(1 - N(d_1)) + D_0 N(d_2) = ((1 - P_D) + (1 - N(d_2))\,(1 - L_D))\, D_0 \quad (12.5)$$

Solving this equation for L_D, we get:

$$L_D = 1 - (V_0/D_0)((1 - N(d_1))/(1 - N(d_2)) \qquad (12.6)$$

If the debt were truly risk free, its market value would be D_0. The credit spread on a zero-coupon instrument can be written as s, where the market value (MV) of the instrument is the face amount (F), discounted by $r + s$, where r is the risk-free rate.

Thus,

$$MV = Fe^{-T(r+s)}$$
$$e^{-Ts} = MV/Fe^{-Tr}$$
$$s = -\ln (MV/Fe^{-Tr})/T \qquad (12.7)$$

We know the market value of the debt is $V_0 - E_0$ and the present value of the debt discounted by the risk-free rate, Fe^{-Tr}, is D_0.

Thus,

$$s = -\ln ((V_0 - E_0)/D_0)/T = \ln (D_0/(V_0 - E_0))/T \qquad (12.8)$$

Two of the four required inputs, T and D_0, are easy to determine, provided all the firm's debts are reported in some publicly filed statement. To use the model as an approximation when several maturity dates are available for debt and the debt has scheduled coupon payments, T can be calculated as the weighted average duration of the debt.

In theory, you could obtain V_0 by summing the market prices of all the firm's equity and debt and estimate σ_V by looking at the historical volatility of this sum. In practice, most firms have some amount of debt that is not publicly traded and for which a market price would therefore not be available.

Inputs that can be obtained easily are the market price of equity, E_0, and the volatility of equity price, σ_E, which can be based on both historical observation and implied volatility from equity options. To obtain V_0 and σ_V from E_0 and σ_E, solve the simultaneous equations:

$$E_0 = V_0\, N(d_1) - D_0\, N(d_2) \tag{12.9}$$

and

$$\sigma_E\, E_0 = N(d_1)\, \sigma_V\, V_0 \tag{12.10}$$

The latter equation can be derived from Ito's lemma and the fact that $N(d_1)$ is the partial derivative of E_0 with respect to V_0. The **MertonModel** spreadsheet takes E_0, σ_E, D_0, and T as input and solves for V_0, σ_V P_D, L_D, MV, and s.

To remove the simplified assumptions of the model considered thus far, we could move to a Monte Carlo model that reproduces many possible future paths of the firm's asset value. The growth rate of the asset value assumed would be the risk-free rate by the usual risk-neutral valuation argument. It is easy in the context of a Monte Carlo model to build in payments due to different maturities of debt with coupons, build in rules for when default will occur (such as when the net worth of the firm is below a certain threshold), and build in rules for the distribution of asset value in the event of default to different seniority levels of debt. It is also easy to build in behavioral rules for the firm's response to different levels of net worth (such as increasing asset volatility as the net worth gets close to the default threshold or issuing new debt as it gets further from the default threshold) and build in rules for dividend policy. By summing over all paths in the Monte Carlo model, it is easy to compute the expected default rates by time period, recovery rates in the event of default by time period and seniority level, and the market value of equity and of each combination of maturity and seniority level of debt. Required spreads over the risk-free rate for each combination of maturity and seniority level of debt can be computed from the market value. When the assumptions of the simple options model are input to the Monte Carlo model, the same result is obtained as from the simple model.

When this model is implemented, a problem immediately appears. If the default threshold is set greater than zero and if asset values are assumed to follow paths without jump processes, then the required spread over the risk-free rate can be driven as close to zero as desired by increasing the frequency with which observations of the asset value are taken. Increasing the frequency of observation increases the probability of default, but it also causes the loss in the event of default to approach zero by dividing up the assets of the firm among the creditors while they are still sufficient to pay off the creditors in full. This shows that the key issues in determining default loss are behavioral rather than financial—that is, they depend critically on how transparent the operations of the firm are to creditors and how much control the creditors can exercise in forcing bankruptcy in a timely fashion. This may differ significantly by government jurisdiction. The role governments may play in providing help for firms close to default may also differ. So the usefulness of options models for determining default probabilities and values is questionable.

A recent approach to dealing with this issue is to treat the default threshold as a stochastic variable with statistical properties that result in the probabilities of default and loss given default that match observed values. Since a statistical measurement of past experience is being used in driving the default process, this can be seen as a hybrid between a statistical approach and an option-theoretic approach. For details, see Pan (2001). An implementation of this algorithm, with all input data and computational details fully disclosed, is available on the Web site www.creditgrades.com.

Even simple options models can still play a useful heuristic role in helping to understand the default process. This is the role they play in the models of the KMV Corporation, the leading consulting firm in using options models to study default behavior. Crosbie (1999) summarizes the KMV methodology.

The KMV approach is to utilize a model somewhat like the simple option model we have discussed, but the objective is to use it not to try to directly measure default probability, but rather to produce a measure called *distance to default*, which is then used to project default probabilities based on an empirically fitted statistical model. The insight behind this is that, whereas the behavioral nature of default requires the use of statistical observation of past experience, the options model output can be a valuable input to this process when used comparatively to judge which firms are relatively more likely to default than others. In this approach, statistical models, not option-theoretic ones, are employed in estimating loss in the event of default.

KMV presents the following points in favor of this use of the option model:

- Because the model is based on equity market prices, which are continuously observable, it is more likely to represent the latest available information than the ratings of just a single firm's credit officers or a rating agency or on statistical models based on accounting information that is only available periodically. It can also be applied to any public company, even one that does not have publicly rated debt, since it is based on equity prices.
- The model takes into account both the capital structure of a firm and its business and industry risk. Capital structure is represented by the

leverage, the ratio of total firm value to equity. Business and industry risk is represented by the volatility of asset values. (For example, you can expect much more volatility from a firm in a high-tech industry than a utility, or much more volatility from a firm in an emerging market country than one in an established industrial country.)

The distance to default is measured by the number of standard deviation movements it would take to put a firm at the point where default is a serious possibility. In terms of the simple model we presented, it would be $(V_0 - D_0)/(V_0 \, \sigma_V)$, which is calculated in the **MertonModel** spreadsheet. The actual model used by KMV to calculate the distance to default is more complex than our simple model in several ways. To highlight a few:

- Our simple model assumes that default can only occur when firm asset value is insufficient to make a required payment. The KMV model recognizes that firms can be forced to default when their asset values decline sufficiently below the present value of required future payments. Based on empirical studies, KMV has set the default point, which in our model is D_0, as the sum of short-term debt, representing required current payments, and one-half of long-term debt, representing payments that will be required in the future. In this way, assets can decline below the required future payments by some amount, but not too far, before default is threatened.
- The KMV model can handle more liability classes than just straight debt and equity; it can also accommodate hybrid classes—convertible debt and preferred stock.
- KMV regards equation 12.10 as too simplistic, since it does not take into account the impact of varying leverage levels through time on the relationship between equity volatility and asset volatility. KMV uses a more complex model to reflect this factor. In particular, the concern is that for a firm whose performance is trending downward, the decline in equity value will result in current leverage being higher than its leverage has been in the past. If asset volatility is estimated from its historical equity volatility and its current leverage, this will tend to understate historical asset volatility, resulting in understating the default probability. The converse of this effect will result in overstating the default probability for a firm whose performance is trending upward. As Crosbie (1999) states, this "biases the probabilities in precisely the wrong direction."

KMV's solution is a more granular approach in which a time series of historical daily asset returns is constructed from historical daily equity returns and Equation 12.2, based on an initial guess at σ_V. These daily asset returns can then be used to compute a new guess at σ_V, leading to a new series of daily asset returns. The process is repeated until it converges (see Crosbie [1999, p. 173]).

12.2.4 The Statistical Approach to Estimating Correlations Between Defaults

Let's begin with some points on which almost everyone who has worked on this topic can agree:

- Strong evidence supports a positive correlation between defaults—that is, that defaults tend to occur in clusters. For example, Table 12.6, from Moody's (2002), of default percentages by year for ratings categories Baa, Ba, and B, shows much higher default rates in recession periods, such as 1989 to 1991, and in 2001, than in periods of economic growth, such as 1993 to 1999.

- Estimating this correlation based on the joint default history of firms with the same credit rating is unsatisfactory. Grouping together all firms with the same credit rating ignores factors such as whether firms are in the same industry or whether firms are located in the same geographical region, but these factors are widely believed to influence joint default correlation. See Gupton, Finger, and Bhatia (1997, Section 8.2).

- The direct estimation of joint default correlation by examining historical defaults categorized by rating, country, and industry is not a feasible approach. Default is a relatively rare event and with this fine a segmentation, there would not be enough observation to allow robust statistical inference. A way around this impasse is to estimate correlation for a variable that can be more frequently observed and can then be utilized to produce default correlations.

For KMV, asset returns are a very natural choice for such a variable, since they are directly tied to defaults through the distance-to-default measure and its statistical relationship to default probability. KMV utilizes the methodology we discussed in Section 12.2.3 to de-lever equity returns directly observed in the market and compute asset returns. It is an easy step from creating a time series of asset returns for a large universe of borrowers to compute correlations between asset returns for those borrowers. Monte Carlo simulations of correlated movements in asset returns, which we discuss in the next section, can then be used to calculate the percentage of cases that result in joint default, enabling a default correlation to be computed. The actual methodology employed by KMV does not directly calculate asset return correlations between pairs of borrowers. Instead, a factor

TABLE 12.6 Default Percentages by Year

	Rating		
Year	Baa	Ba	B
1970	0.28%	4.19%	22.78%
1971	0.00%	0.43%	3.85%
1972	0.00%	0.00%	7.14%
1973	0.47%	0.00%	3.77%
1974	0.00%	0.00%	6.90%
1975	0.00%	1.04%	5.97%
1976	0.00%	1.03%	0.00%
1977	0.28%	0.53%	3.28%
1978	0.00%	1.10%	5.41%
1979	0.00%	0.49%	0.00%
1980	0.00%	0.00%	5.06%
1981	0.00%	0.00%	4.49%
1982	0.31%	2.78%	2.41%
1983	0.00%	0.94%	6.31%
1984	0.37%	0.87%	6.72%
1985	0.00%	1.80%	8.22%
1986	1.36%	1.78%	11.80%
1987	0.00%	2.76%	6.27%
1988	0.00%	1.26%	6.10%
1989	0.61%	3.00%	9.29%
1990	0.00%	3.37%	16.18%
1991	0.29%	5.43%	14.56%
1992	0.00%	0.31%	9.05%
1993	0.00%	0.57%	5.86%
1994	0.00%	0.24%	3.96%
1995	0.00%	0.70%	4.99%
1996	0.00%	0.00%	1.49%
1997	0.00%	0.19%	2.16%
1998	0.12%	0.64%	4.15%
1999	0.11%	1.03%	5.88%
2000	0.39%	0.91%	5.42%
2001	0.30%	1.19%	9.35%

Source: Moody's, "Corporate Bond Defaults and Default Rates 1938–1995," and "Default and Recovery Rates of Corporate Bond Issuers: 2000." Reprinted with permission from Moody's Investors Service.

analysis is used in which composite asset returns are calculated for sectors —countries and industries as well as groupings of countries and industries. Historical asset return correlations can then be computed between sectors. Asset return correlations between borrowers can then be easily computed based on the statistical relationship between each borrower's asset return and those of the country and industry sectors. The KMV approach to correlations is described in more detail in Saunders and Allen (2002, pp. 160–165).

The CreditMetrics™ approach to estimating default correlations is very similar to KMV's, except that correlation between equity returns is used as a proxy for correlation between asset returns. Gupton, Finger, and Bhatia (1997, Section 8.5) provides great detail on this process.

The default probability implied by credit spreads is another natural candidate to be used. The drawback is that this involves a much smaller universe of borrowers for whom liquid public debt prices are available relative to the number of borrowers for whom liquid equity prices are available. Strong evidence shows that implied default probabilities from credit spreads significantly overstate realized default rates (see Hull [2002, Sections 26.3–26.4]). As a result, firms may decide to use implied default probabilities as indicators of relative credit quality, but may choose to adjust the overall default probability by a factor that lowers these probabilities to anticipated rates of actual default. Further details and references can be found in Saunders and Allen (2002, Chapter 5).

Whichever variable is used to provide the linkage, the key to transforming shorter-term correlations into longer-term default correlations is a simulation of movements through time. Because of the relative infrequency of default, even high short-term correlations transform into much smaller default correlations (see Saunders and Allen [2002, pp. 160–161]).

12.2.5 The Computation of Portfolio Risk

Where we stand based on the preceding sections is that a variety of methods have been presented for estimating default probability and loss given default for individual borrowers and for estimating the short-term correlation between borrowers for some variable that can be linked to longer-term defaults. We now focus on analyzing methods that can provide this linkage and also produce calculations of portfolio risk very similar to the portfolio risk measures that were provided for market risk in Chapter 11.

Let's begin by assuming that all of this analysis will be provided by Monte Carlo simulation. For many of the same reasons stated in our analysis of VaR in Section 11.1, simulation is the most accurate method of generating portfolio risk measures. It has the flexibility to incorporate almost any assumption about statistical distributions we want to make. Later in this section, we will discuss possible shortcuts to the calculation of portfolio risk under more restrictive distributional assumptions. However, simulation is always the benchmark against which the accuracy of other approximations can be tested. The reason why we only consider Monte Carlo simulation for credit risk, while we considered the alternatives of Monte Carlo simulation and historical simulation for market risk VaR, is that the longer time periods involved in credit risk simulations mean that not enough nonoverlapping historical data points will be available to derive a historical simulation.

A Monte Carlo simulation will follow a key variable, whether it is asset value or default probability, for each borrower to whom credit has been extended. The simulation will be based on assumptions about the volatility of asset returns or transaction matrices for default probabilities and assumptions about short-term correlations between the borrowers. If asset value is being used as the key variable, it must be converted into default probabilities, using a statistical relationship such as the one developed by KMV between an asset's distance to default and probability of default. Defaults can then occur at random, based on the probability of default. In the event of default, a random sample is drawn based on the mean and standard deviation of the loss given default for a given seniority class of instrument (if instruments of different seniority are outstanding to the same borrower, a correlation should be enforced between the degree to which the loss given default on each instrument exceeds or is below the average).

A Monte Carlo model meeting this description has many possible applications. It can be used with just two borrowers to translate a short-term correlation of assets values or credit spreads into long-term default correlations. It can also be used with an entire portfolio of assets to generate statistics on expected credit losses and the full distribution of credit losses, such as losses at the 99th percentile. It can be used for valuing a tranched CDO by tracking losses to each tranche along each of the paths and then calculating the expected losses on each tranche.

A Monte Carlo simulation provides a complete analytic solution to the evaluation of purchased credit protection. Consider, for example, a loan to company ABC for which full credit protection has been purchased from company XYZ, either in the form of a default swap or as a loan guarantee. No loss to the portfolio will occur if ABC defaults as long as XYZ does not default as well, since in this circumstance, XYZ must pay all the costs of the ABC default. The portfolio will not experience a loss if XYZ defaults as long as ABC does not default, since in this circumstance, the guarantee will not need to be invoked. Loss will only occur if both default. The Monte Carlo simulation easily represents this by calculating the probability of joint default, taking the proper correlation between the firms into account, and it can embed this in the overall calculation of the full distribution of credit losses for the portfolio.

Thus far we have been discussing a Monte Carlo simulation that only deals with a single time period in which the relevant outcomes are for each credit to either default or not default. This can be extended in one of two directions. One direction would be the simulation of an end-of-period change in credit grade and credit spread in addition to default. This extension requires a tie between the key variable being simulated and credit grade and credit spread. This relationship is straightforward for implied default probabilities and is provided for asset values by KMV's statistical linkages of the distance to default to credit rating and credit spread. The other direction would be multiperiod simulation. Multiperiod simulation could be achieved by just computing default loss distributions at different points along the simulation path. However, full accuracy requires some simulation of possible changes in the overall economic climate, factoring in features such as the increased probability of an economic downturn following a period of sustained economic growth (see Wilson [1998, pp. 111–112]). Extended models may be needed to value more exotic credit derivative products. An example would be a CDO where the tranche payments are tied to the number of defaults rather than the size of default losses (for example, one tranche pays all losses on the first three defaults to occur, and the other tranche pays all other defaults) or an option on a credit spread.

A Monte Carlo simulation of individual loans becomes computationally infeasible for loan portfolios with very large numbers of very small loans. This is certainly true for retail loans such as home mortgages or credit cards. In such cases, the portfolio needs to be analyzed into segments that can be treated as roughly homogeneous. For example, a portfolio of home mortgages could be divided into segments grouped by geography and home value. Each segment now must be treated as a single loan in the Monte Carlo simulation of the entire firm's loan portfolio. But unlike a true individual loan, which is in either one of two states, default or nondefault, a grouping of small loans must be represented by a percentage of loans that default in a particular time period. An analysis of the history of default patterns can establish statistics to drive the simulation, including correlations with default levels between two segments and between the segment and individual loans being simulated. The best way to derive historical correlations may be through a mutual dependence on macroeconomic factors, such as growth rates in the economy. See Wilson (1998, p. 111). For a general overview of a simulation of defaults on retail credits, see Risk Management Association (2000).

One way in which the use of simulation for credit risk differs from its use for market risk VaR is that the expected value of the distribution plays a significant role. Since market risk VaR is computed over very short time periods, expected value can either be ignored or else has only a minor impact. The far longer time horizon of credit risk simulation requires that expected credit loss be accounted for. Expected credit loss should be taken as a charge against earnings, either in the form of a reduction in valuation for a portfolio that is marked to market or in the form of a loan loss reserve for a portfolio that uses accrual accounting. Capital should be allocated based on the unexpected losses—the distribution of returns around the expected losses. Many firms allocate capital based on an amount needed to cover losses at a particular percentile level, often 99.97 percent, based on the ratings agency standard of a .03 percent probability of default in a year being equivalent to an AA credit rating (see Saunders and Allen [2002, p. 207]).

Estimation techniques that avoid the full cost of Monte Carlo simulation are available if simplifying assumptions are accepted. Usually the simplifying assumption is that the distribution of losses is multivariate normal. With this assumption, the formula for the standard deviation of losses for a single borrower is:

$$\sigma_i = \sqrt{P_D(1 - P_D)\overline{L_D}^2 + P_D\sigma_{L_D}^2} \qquad (12.11)$$

where $\overline{L_D}$ is the expected value of the loss given default.

See Saunders and Allen (2002, Equation 11.4, pp. 158–159) for the derivation of this equation. If we have estimates of default correlations, then the standard deviation of loss on the portfolio can be estimated based on the standard deviation of loss on each borrower and the correlation between defaults. Note that some Monte Carlo simulation must be used to estimate default correlation based on short-term correlation of asset returns or equity returns or implied default probabilities. The formula for portfolio standard deviation is:

$$\sqrt{\sum_{i,j} s_i s_j \sigma_i \sigma_j \rho_{i,j}} \qquad (12.12)$$

This is the same formula used for VaR in the variance-covariance approach. Percentiles of unexpected loss are then calculated from the standard deviation based on the shape of the normal distribution.

The degree of error introduced by such approximations needs to be periodically tested against full Monte Carlo simulations. Simulation can capture the detailed consequences of assumptions about the credit risk process that approximation methods will miss. An example would include the ability to capture correlation between default probability and loss given default (see Section 12.2.2). Another example would be the ability to capture dependence of correlation on the level of default probabilities (which might occur if equity return correlations tend to increase in economic downturns). When capital is computed based on percentiles like 99.97 percent, which are beyond the range of observation, the accuracy of even Monte Carlo simulations must be questioned. Simply increasing the number of paths cannot overcome the limitation of input data that does not include catastrophic events. As with VaR, the possibility of employing extreme value theory is a consideration (see Section 11.1).

Parallel to the discussion in Section 11.2 of stress testing as a complement to VaR for market risk, it is often desirable to complement the statistical analysis of credit risk for a portfolio with a stress test based on economic insight. This is especially true in evaluating the risk of credit concentration to firms doing business within a particular country. Credit concentration within a country leads to the risk of correlated outcomes since all firms may be impacted by how well the country's economy performs. This type of correlation risk is very much the same type of risk as the risk of credit concentration within an industry or within a geographical region of a country. All of these correlation risks can be reasonably measured by statistical means. But country risk has an additional dimension. The possibility exists that all firms, individuals, and government bodies within a given country will be prohibited from meeting their contractual obligations. This can arise from the imposition of exchange controls by the government as a defensive measure against adverse currency flows, or from government renunciation of foreign debts, or from disruption of normal contractual relationships due to war or revolution. This form of risk represents a major political discontinuity that statistical analysis of historical economic data will shed little light on. It can best be quantified by looking at the extent of damage in past incidents of political disruption in other countries combined with subjective assessment of the likelihood of occurrence based on economic and political insights into the current conditions within a particular country. See Calverley (1985).

12.3 LINES OF CREDIT

Two principal forms of credit lines are available—those used for working capital and those used as backstops for commercial paper issuance.

Working capital credit lines give a borrower the flexibility of only paying full interest on the amount of funds it needs at a particular point of time without losing the security of knowing that it can draw down a precommitted amount as needed.

Commercial paper backup lines act as a safety net for commercial paper issuers. Commercial paper issuance typically occurs for very short time periods, often only a few days, to accommodate the liquidity needs of commercial paper investors. The tenor of the commercial paper is usually shorter than the borrowing need of the commercial paper issuer, leaving the issuer vulnerable to an inability to roll the paper over at maturity, but also leaving the investor vulnerable to not being paid back in the event of rollover failure. The backup line gives assurance to both the borrower and investor in the event of a liquidity squeeze. A backup line is consequently insisted on by rating agencies as a prerequisite for an investment-grade credit rating on a firm's commercial paper. Usage on commercial paper backup lines is virtually zero, except in the rare case of rollover difficulty.

In measuring the loss given default of credit lines, average usage is obviously of little value, since it fails to deal with the high correlation between line usage and credit deterioration. The key is how much usage will there be if default occurs. As noted previously, backup line usage averages close to zero, but when the lines are used, it is because credit difficulties make rolling commercial paper problematic. If only 1 percent of all commercial paper issuers default, but all of these have their lines drawn by 100 percent just prior to default, and if 0 percent usage appears on the remaining 99 percent of issuers, then the overall line usage will be only 1 percent, but default losses will be just as great as if overall line usage is 100 percent.

If credit lines are viewed simply as an option to draw funds exercisable by the borrower, then line usage should be assumed to be 100 percent in the event of default. However, this option is not unconstrained, given that covenants that form part of the contract for the line give lenders the opportunity to reduce line availability in the event of credit deterioration. There will, on one hand, be competitive pressures on the bank not to exercise its full rights under these covenants to avoid damaging the particular relationship and to maintain a reputation with customers as being reliable in a crisis. On the other hand, a bank can pressure a customer to renegotiate loan terms. Araten and Jacobs (2001) aptly describe credit line usage in the event of default as "the outcome of the race between the bank and the borrower with regard to the draw-down of unused commitments in adverse circumstances."

When a result is the product of complex behavioral assumptions, it is not surprising to see that the dominant method of analysis is historical statistical study. Araten and Jacobs (2001) published the most complete analysis based on a study of 399 defaulted borrowers at Chase Manhattan Bank over a 5¾-year period, ending in December 2000. Their main results are shown in Table 12.7.

As would be expected, average usage upon default rises with the time elapsed between when a line is committed and when default occurs. This is because the longer the time period elapsed, the more likely that a borrower who started as higher grade and subject to fewer covenants has slipped downward in credit grade. Similar reasoning explains the finding that average usage upon default tends to rise with a higher initial credit rating. Of course, it is less likely that a higher-rated credit will default compared to a lower-rated credit, but for those who do default, the lower level of covenants results in higher usage.

12.4 COUNTERPARTY CREDIT RISK

Counterparty credit risk requires input from both disciplines of market risk and credit risk. Loss will occur only in the event of counterparty default, so a credit risk assessment is required; however, the size of potential loss is not

TABLE 12.7 Average Usage Conditional on Default by Facility Risk Grade and Time to Default for Revolving Credits

(Number of observations in parentheses)

Facility Risk Grade	Time to Default (in Years)					
	1	2	3	4	5–6	Total
AAA/AA		12.1% (1)				12.1% (1)
A	78.7% (3)	75.5% (6)	84.0% (1)			77.2% (10)
BBB+/BBB	93.9% (1)	47.2% (7)	41.7% (5)			55.5% (15)
BBB/BBB−	54.8% (18)	52.1% (20)	41.5% (9)	100% (2)		52.2% (52)
BB	32.0% (81)	44.9% (84)	62.1% (45)	37.5% (3)	100% (2)	46.4% (231)
BB−/B+	39.6% (129)	49.8% (100)	62.1% (37)	76.0% (17)	68.3% (4)	50.1% (295)
B/B−	26.5% (86)	39.7% (22)	37.3% (5)	62.6% (25)	100% (4)	30.7% (115)
CCC	24.5% (100)	26.7% (14)	9.4% (1)	97.8% (2)		24.6% (115)
Total	32.9% (418)	46.6% (254)	62.1% (103)	68.7% (59)	71.8% (59)	43.4% (834)

fixed, as with bonds and loans, but is determined by how much a derivative contract is worth at the time of default. The estimation of potential moves in derivatives contract values is traditionally a concern of market risk.

The standard approach to handling this interaction between market and credit risk is to separate the two contributions into independent factors that can be worked on separately. In this model, the market risk discipline considers market risk factors alone when assessing the size of potential moves in derivatives contract value. Based on a set probability threshold (such as the 99th percentile), the near-maximum amount that can be lost in the event of counterparty default is calculated. This near-maximum amount of loss in the event of default is then treated as the equivalent of the principal of a loan, which is also the maximum amount that can be lost in the event of default (assuming no recovery). Credit risk personnel is expected to evaluate the reasonableness of taking on the risk of this loss just as if they were evaluating making a loan of that size. For decisions that depend more on portfolio considerations, such as measures of the total credit risk of the firm or measures of whether the firm is receiving an adequate return on the credit risk it is taking to a particular counterparty, the expected amount of loss and standard deviation of loss in the event of default must be computed and factored into the calculations we discussed in Section 12.2.5.

This approach depends critically on the following independence assumptions:

- The probability that the counterparty will default cannot depend on the value of the market variables underlying the derivative, so the derivative contract and instruments priced off the same market variables cannot be a significant enough portion of the counterparty's business to induce a correlation between the size of the move and likelihood of loss.
- The timing of default must be independent of the size of market moves.

A primary motivation for managing market exposures through derivatives is to reduce the amount of credit exposure that needs to be taken in order to obtain a desired market position. Given this motivation, an essential component of managing a derivatives business is minimizing the amount of credit exposure, and many tools have been designed to accomplish this objective. The key tools for minimizing exposure are:

- Transacting many derivatives positions with a given counterparty under a single master agreement, and permitting positions on which the counterparty owes money and those on which it is owed money to be netted in the event of default, thereby reducing exposure

- Periodic settlement of outstanding exposures, either through cash payments or the posting of collateral

Standalone derivatives positions can have near-maximum and expected exposures calculated by fairly simple approximation methods, which are covered in Hull (2002, Section 27.5). However, the ability to take into account credit exposure reduction techniques such as netting and collateral posting requires full-scale simulation, using a methodology similar to the simulation that generates VaR. The primary difference is that credit exposure needs to be calculated over much longer time periods than VaR. A firm can exit its market risks, so it only needs to simulate VaR for the period prior to the potential exit, but it has longer contractual commitments to the credit risk on derivatives.

Some of the key points that need to be considered in designing a simulation are:

- Paths on which the firm owes money to the counterparty need to count as zero in calculations of average exposure, since no windfall gain occurs when a counterparty to which you owe money defaults —you still owe the money to the bankruptcy trustees.
- The assumption most often used in these models is that each market variable follows a random walk centered around the current path of market forward prices for that variable. Assumptions regarding price volatilities and correlations are subject to the same set of arguments discussed in Section 11.1.1, but are modified to the longer term of the simulations needed for credit exposure. In particular, if implied volatilities are used, the full maturity structure of the implied volatility surface should be considered when projecting longer-term price behavior. As with VaR, no definitive pricing argument governs the choice between historical or implied volatilities. By similar reasoning, no definitive pricing argument favors centering the simulation on market forward prices and a case can be made for choosing other processes.
- The use of a random walk model implies that the uncertainty about market variables will grow with the square root of elapsed time in the simulation model. If exposure is a fixed function of a market variable, as it is for FX forwards, equity forwards, and commodity forwards, then near-worst-case and expected credit exposures will also grow roughly with the square root of time. But for products where exposure is not a fixed function of a market variable, such as interest rate swaps and bonds, this will not be the case. Interest rate swaps and bonds exposure, relative to rate uncertainty, declines through time

as the duration diminishes. Increasing uncertainty at first dominates these offsetting effect and credit exposure increases, reaches a peak, and then declines through time as the impact of decreasing duration dominates.

■ Potential exposure reflects the cost of replacing a derivative with another counterparty. Liquidity costs for less heavily traded derivatives should be reflected through assumed bid-ask spreads or through lengthening the time over which near-worst-case market moves are measured to reflect not just the time to default, but also the added time until a replacement can be found after default.

■ The use of measures to mitigate counterparty credit risk, such as requiring a cash settlement or the posting of collateral after exposure grows to a certain point, should be reflected by incorporating collateral posting into the simulation. This should include simulating the posting of collateral based on contractual triggers plus a delay to reflect the time period it is estimated it will take to enforce the posting. This delay includes the time it takes to detect the nondelivery of required collateral, communicate with the counterparty, and reach a decision to liquidate the position. Market impacts on the value of collateral should also be incorporated in the simulation, reflecting both the uncertainty of market value and any correlation that may exist between collateral value and derivative exposure.

■ Netting the exposure between different derivatives with the same counterparty should only be permitted in circumstances where netting is legally enforceable (this varies by country, based on differing bankruptcy laws).

A more detailed description of the simulation methodology can be found in Brindle (2000).

In some cases, the required independence assumption breaks down. In some equity derivatives and credit derivatives, close ties exist between the counterparty's credit and the variable determining the valuation of the derivative. The most extreme example is a company writing a put on its own stock—it will owe the most in the circumstances it is most likely to default. A less extreme case would be a Brazilian bank writing a default swap on another Brazilian bank. Their economic conditions are likely to be closely correlated, giving rise to the probability that a large exposure will correlate with a counterparty default.

Sometimes the exposure of a counterparty to a country's economic circumstances is strong enough to call into doubt independence for even interest rate and FX derivatives. An example that caused major losses in 1998 was Russian banks' FX forwards to deliver dollars against rubles. When the ruble collapsed against the dollar, the Russian banks lacked the economic strength to deliver the promised dollars. This has led to concerns about the validity of the independence assumption on *wrong-way* derivatives, where a firm will owe money when its home currency is weak.

When the independence assumption breaks down, market and credit risk considerations need to be combined into a single model. Such a model would be a combination of the Monte Carlo simulation of default loss discussed in Section 12.2.5 and the Monte Carlo simulation of credit exposure caused by market movements that we outlined earlier in this section. In this model, each Monte Carlo path simulates both the movements of interest rates, FX rates, equity and commodity prices that determine the size of exposure to a derivative counterparty, and changes in asset value or credit spread of the counterparty that determine whether and when default will occur. Assumptions can be provided about correlation between the driving variable behind default and the market risk factors. Although a detailed historical analysis of the correlations may not be easy to achieve, it is certainly possible to make reasonable assumptions for the strong correlations that cause concerns about wrong-way exposure.

For example, there will probably be a widespread consensus about a high correlation between declines in the dollar value of the Brazilian currency and increases in the default probability of a Brazilian-based company with substantial dollar borrowings. Even if not enough liquidity exists in the company's debt and equity prices to enable a measurement of historical correlation, there should be agreement on the direction and approximate magnitude of assumed correlation. This will have the desired effect of increasing the average size of exposure on those simulation paths that result in default.

The estimation of correlation will be even more direct for counterparty exposure on credit derivatives, since now correlations are between the credit risk of the counterparty and the credit risk of the firm on which the credit derivative is written. The estimation of these correlations was discussed in Section 12.2.4. This is, in fact, the case we have already covered in Section 12.2.5 when we discussed the estimation of risk on a loan for which credit protection has been purchased. Being able to combine this in a single Monte Carlo analysis with the calculation of exposure on other derivatives with the same counterparty enables the proper calculation of netting effects.

Shortcuts for wrong-way exposure calculations that approximate the impact of full Monte Carlo simulation have been developed. For a discussion with further references, see Winters (1999).

The management of counterparty exposure utilizing the market-based credit spread approach we discussed in Section 12.1 requires the use of dynamic hedging techniques originally developed for multiasset exotic derivatives such as quantos. The size of market exposure at any instant is the product of the credit spread of the counterparty and the size of the credit exposure. As we illustrated in Section 10.4.5, this requires dynamic hedging, with a change in derivative value requiring a change in the size of the credit hedge, and a change in the credit spread requiring a change in the size of the derivative hedge. Essentially, this method amounts to replacing the derivative with another counterparty, not all at once on default, but gradually as the original counterparty's credit worsens. Correlation assumptions, driven by wrong-way exposure concerns, will have the intuitively correct effect of increasing the expected cost of the dynamic hedge.

EXERCISES

12.1

Using the **CreditPricer** spreadsheet, begin with the following input:

	Risk-Free Zero-Coupon Rate	Risky Par Rate
1	7.00%	8.00%
2	7.50%	8.60%
3	7.75%	8.90%
4	8.00%	9.20%
5	8.15%	9.40%
Loss given default 60.0%		

1. Solve for the default rates and spreads to the risk-free par curve that corresponds to this case.
2. Change the loss given default to 30 percent and double the default rates. Solve for the risky par bond rates. How does the spread to the risk-free par curve differ from that in the previous step? This shows that it is not just the product of default rate and loss given default that impacts the valuation of risky cash flows.
3. Assume that the company whose risky par rate curve was shown previously also has a 5-year bond with a 9 percent coupon that is priced in the market at 98.56. Assuming a constant loss given default irrespective of the time at which default occurs, determine a unique loss given default and a set of default rates from this information. What if the 9 percent coupon 5-year bond is selling at 98.46?

Spreadsheet Calculators

This book is accompanied by a CD-ROM containing Microsoft Excel spreadsheets that can be used to experiment with many of the concepts covered in the text. Most of the book's exercises are built around these calculators. Full documentation of the spreadsheets is contained in an accompanying Word document on the CD-ROM. In this appendix, I will give a brief description of the spreadsheets that are available. They are listed in the order you will encounter them in the text.

I have chosen to build all of these calculators in Excel with minimal use of user-defined functions for two reasons:

- By using Excel rather than a programming language, I am hoping to maximize the number of readers who will be able to follow the calculations.
- By minimizing user-defined functions, I am making the machinery of the computations as visible as possible.

These calculators have all been built specifically to illustrate the material of this book (and the course I teach on which the book is based). They are *not* designed to be used to actually manage risk positions. Specifically, they don't include the sort of detail, such as day count conventions, that is important in a trading environment. This sort of detail can be distracting when trying to learn broad concepts. For similar reasons, I have often chosen simple alternatives over more complex ones to illustrate a point. For example, I have chosen to represent volatility smile and skew through a simple formula that favors the ease of seeing the approximate impact of changes in input variables over the accuracy of a more complex representation.

Using such calculators for actual trading would require programs that are easily scalable—that is, can readily accommodate adding a larger number of positions. I have deliberately sacrificed scalability for the ease of handling a small number of positions. Scalability nearly always requires the use of a programming language as opposed to a primarily spreadsheet-based approach. For readers who want to pursue building more robust calculators, these spreadsheets should be able to serve as good sources for parallel tests of computations, particularly since Excel gives an immediate display of all the numerical results of the intermediate stages of the calculations.

The spreadsheets, in the order of the corresponding material in the text, are as follows.

The **WinnersCurse** spreadsheet illustrates the mechanism of the winner's curse in auction situations, as explained in Section 2.4.

The **Rates** spreadsheet can be used to either value and compute risk statistics for a portfolio of linear instruments (such as forwards, swaps, and bonds) based on an input set of forward rates or it can determine a set of forward rates that achieve an optimum fit with a given set of prices for a portfolio of linear instruments while maximizing the smoothness of the forward rates selected. This is discussed in Sections 8.2.1 and 8.4.

The **Bootstrap** spreadsheet produces a comparison between the bootstrap and optimal fitting methodologies for extracting forward rates from an observed set of swap rates. This spreadsheet was used to produce Figure 8.1.

The **DataMetricsRateData** spreadsheet contains a historical time series of U.S. interest rate data from August 26, 1996 to October 30, 2001, which was generously provided by RiskMetrics. It is used in Exercises 8.1 and 8.2.

The **NastyPath** spreadsheet is an illustration of the size of losses that can be incurred when dynamically delta hedging an option. The example follows the dynamic delta hedging of a purchased call option over the 30 days of its life. This is discussed in the example in Section 9.2.

The **PriceVolMatrix** spreadsheet computes the price-volatility matrix and volatility surface exposure for a small portfolio of vanilla European-style options. It illustrates the material discussed in Section 9.4.

The **PriceVolMatrixCycle** spreadsheet is a particular run of the **PriceVolMatrix** spreadsheet that has been used to produce Table 9.5.

The **VolCurve** spreadsheet fits a forward volatility curve to observed options prices. This spreadsheet is designed for European options other than interest rate caps and floors. This is discussed in Section 9.6.1.

The **CapFit** spreadsheet fits a forward volatility curve to observed options prices for interest rate caps. Since caps are baskets of options, with each option within the basket termed a *caplet*, the spreadsheet needs to break each cap apart into its constituent caplets and price each one individually. This is discussed in Section 9.6.1.

The **VolSurfaceStrike** spreadsheet interpolates implied option volatilities by strike for a given tenor, utilizing the methods discussed in Section 9.6.2. The interpolation can be performed in two modes:

- Implied volatilities are input for enough strikes to allow for reasonable interpolation.
- Implied volatilities are input for only three strikes.

The **OptionRoll** spreadsheet is a variant of the **PriceVolMatrix** spreadsheet. It differs in the form of the optimization, which is set up to calculate a hedge that will minimize a future roll cost. It illustrates the material discussed in Section 9.6.3.

The **OptionMC** spreadsheet calculates a single path of a Monte Carlo simulation of the delta hedging of a vanilla European-style call option position. It is designed to help you check your work for the Monte Carlo simulation exercise in Chapter 9.

The **OptionMC1000** spreadsheet is identical to the **OptionMC** spreadsheet except that it is set up for 1,000 time steps instead of 20 time steps.

The **OptionMCHedged** spreadsheet is a variant on the **OptionMC** spreadsheet. It calculates a single path of a Monte Carlo simulation of the delta hedging of the European-style call option hedged by two other call options with the same terms but different strike prices.

The **OptionMCHedged1000** spreadsheet is identical to the **OptionMCHedged** spreadsheet except that it is set up for 1,000 time steps instead of 20 time steps.

The **BasketHedge** spreadsheet calculates and prices a piecewise-linear hedge using forwards and plain vanilla European options for any exotic derivative whose payoffs are nonlinear functions of the price of a single underlying asset at one particular point in time. The spreadsheet consists of a **Main** worksheet that can be used for any payoff function and other worksheets that contain illustrations of how the **Main** worksheet can be used to hedge particular payoff functions. The particular functions illustrated are a single-asset quanto, a log contract, interest rate convexity, and a compound option. This is discussed in Section 10.1.

The **ForwardStartOption** spreadsheet is a slight variant on the **PriceVolMatrix** spreadsheet that can be used for the risk management of forward starting options using the method discussed in Section 10.2.

The **CarrBarrier** spreadsheet compares the pricing of barrier options using Carr's static hedging replication with those computed using standard analytic formulas. The cost of unwinding the static hedge is also calculated. This is discussed in Section 10.3.3.

The **OptBarrier** spreadsheet illustrates the use of optimization to find a hedge for a down-and-out call barrier option, as discussed in Section 10.3.3.

The **DermanErgenerKani** spreadsheet calculates the pricing of knock-out barrier options using the Derman-Ergener-Kani static hedging replication. The cost of unwinding the static hedge is also calculated. It illustrates the material discussed in Section 10.3.3.

The **DermanErgenerKani20** spreadsheet also calculates the pricing of knock-out barrier options using the Derman-Ergener-Kani static hedging replication. It displays intermediate results more explicitly than the **DermanErgenerKani** spreadsheet, but is less flexible for expansion to a larger number of time steps.

The **DermanErgenerKaniDoubleBarrier** spreadsheet calculates the pricing of double barrier knock-out barrier options using the Derman-Ergener-Kani static hedging replication. The cost of unwinding the static hedge is also calculated. This is discussed in Section 10.3.

The **DermanErgenerKaniPartialBarrier** spreadsheet calculates the pricing of partial barrier knock-out barrier options using the Derman-Ergener-Kani static hedging replication. The cost of unwinding the static hedge is also calculated. This is discussed in Section 10.3.

The **BasketOption** spreadsheet computes an approximate value for the volatility to be used to price an option on a basket of assets and also computes the sensitivity of this volatility to changes in the volatility of the underlying asset and in the correlation between assets. This is discussed in Section 10.4.1.

The **CrossHedge** spreadsheet simulates the hedging of a quanto that pays the product of two asset prices. The hedge is simulated using two different assumptions, if the asset price moves are completely uncorrelated and if the asset price moves are completely correlated. This is discussed in Section 10.4.5.

The **AmericanOption** spreadsheet calculates risk statistics for the early exercise value of American call options, as discussed in Section 10.5.1.

The **TermStructure** spreadsheet illustrates the difficulties involved in pricing yield-curve-shape-dependent products. It shows that different combinations of input parameters that result in the identical pricing of European caps/floors and swaptions can lead to very different pricing of yield-curve-shape-dependent products. This is discussed in Section 10.5.2.

The **Swaptions** spreadsheet calculates current swaption volatilities from current forward rate agreement (FRA) levels, forward FRA volatilities, and correlations between FRAs. Using the Solver, it can find forward FRA volatilities that will reproduce observed current swaption volatilities, as discussed in Section 10.5.3.

The **VaR** spreadsheet computes VaR using three different methods—historical simulation, Monte Carlo simulation, and variance covariance. It enables the user to compare results obtained through the three methods and explore possible modifications. This is discussed in Sections 11.1 and 11.3.

The data sample used in these calculations consists of 10 series of daily data from August 22, 1996 to November 30, 2001, which was generously provided by RiskMetrics. The 10 series selected have been chosen to provide a cross-section of data from the equity, rates, currency, and credit markets from the United States, Europe, and Japan.

The **EVT** spreadsheet uses the extreme value theory formulas from the box "Key Results from EVT" in Chapter 11 to calculate VaR and shortfall VaR for selected percentiles.

The **CreditPricer** spreadsheet translates between par yields and default rates for risky bonds and also prices risky bonds based on the derived default rates, as discussed in Section 12.1.

The **MertonModel** spreadsheet calculates default probabilities and the distance to default using the simplified model documented in Section 12.2.3.

Allen, Steven, and Otello Padovani. 2002. Risk management using quasi-static hedging. *Economic Notes* 31, no. 2:277–336.

Almgren, Robert, and Neil Chriss. 2001. Optimal execution of portfolio transactions. *Journal of Risk* 3, no. 2:5–39.

Altman, Edward, Andrea Resti, and Andrea Sironi. 2001. Analyzing and explaining default recovery rates. ww.defaultrisk.com/pp_recov_28.htm.

Andersen, Leif, and Jesper Andreasen. 2001. Factor dependence of Bermudan swaptions: fact or fiction? *Journal of Financial Economics* 62, no. 1:3–37.

———. 2000. Static barriers. *Risk* 9:120–122.

Anson, Mark. 1999. *Credit Derivatives.* New Hope, PA: Frank J. Fabozzi Associates.

Araten, Michel, and Michael Jacobs. 2001. Loan equivalents for revolving credits and advised lines. *The RMA Journal* 5:34–39.

Artzner, Philippe, Freddy Delbaen, Jean-Marc Eber, and David Heath. 1997. Thinking coherently. *Risk* 11:68–71.

Asiaweek. 1996. Perils of Profit. July 5th.

Bahar, Reza, and Krishan Nagpal. 2000. Modeling the dynamics of rating transition. *Credit* 3:57–63.

Baxter, Martin, and Andrew Rennie. 1996. *Financial Calculus.* Cambridge: Cambridge University Press.

Bennett, Oliver. 2001. Splitting headaches. *Risk* 7:36–37.

Brigo, Damiano, and Fabio Mercurio. 2001. *Interest Rate Models: Theory and Practice.* New York: Springer.

Brindle, Andy. 2000. Calculating with counterparties. *Risk* 1:100–103.

Broadie, Mark, Paul Glasserman, and Gautam Jain. 1997. Enhanced Monte Carlo estimates of American option prices. *Journal of Derivatives* 5, no. 1:25–44.

Burghardt, Galen, and Gerald Hanweck. 1993. Calendar-adjusted volatilities. In *Volatility: New Estimation Techniques for Pricing Derivatives*, edited by Robert Jarrow. London: Risk Books.

365

Burghart, Galen, and Susan Kirshner. 1994. One good turn. *Risk* 11:44–54.

Calverley, John. 1985. *Country Risk Analysis*.London: Butterworths.

Carr, Peter. 2001. Closed form barrier option valuation with smiles. www.math.nyu.edu/research/carrp/.

Carr, Peter, and Andrew Chou. 1996. Breaking barriers. www.math.nyu.edu/research/carrp/.

———. 1997. Hedging complex barrier options. www.math.nyu.edu/research/carrp/.

Carr, Peter, and Dilip Madan. 2002. Towards a theory of volatility trading. www.math.nyu.edu/research/carrp/.

Carr, Peter, Katrina Ellis, and Vishal Gupta. 1998. Static hedging of exotic options. *Journal of Finance* LIII, no. 3:1165–1190.

Cass, Dwight. 2000. The devil's in the details. *Risk* 8:26–28.

Chew, Lillian. 1996. *Managing Derivatives Risks*. Hoboken, NJ: Wiley.

Chriss, Neil. 1997. *Black-Scholes and Beyond*. Chicago: Irwin.

Clemen, Robert. 1996. *Making Hard Decisions*. 2nd ed. Belmont, CA: Duxbury Press.

Clewlow, Les, and Chris Strickland. 1998. *Implementing Derivatives Models*. Hoboken, NJ: Wiley.

Counterparty Risk Management Policy Group. 1999. Improving counterparty risk management practices. www.defaultrisk.com/pp_other_08.htm.

Crosbie, Peter. 1999. Using equity price information to measure default risk. In *The Handbook of Credit Derivatives*, edited by Jack Clark Francis, Joyce Frost, and Gregg Whittaker. New York: McGraw-Hill.

Crouhy, Michel, Dan Galai, and Robert Mark. 2001. *Risk Management*. New York: McGraw-Hill.

Cruz, Marcelo. 2002. *Modeling, Measuring, and Hedging Operational Risk*. Hoboken, NJ: Wiley.

Culp, Christopher, and Merton Miller. 1995A. Metallgesellachaft and the economics of synthetic storage. *Journal of Applied Corporate Finance* (winter): 62–75.

———. 1995B. Hedging in the theory of corporate finance: A reply to our critics. *Journal of Applied Corporate Finance* (spring): 121–127.

Dawes, Robyn. 1988. *Rational Choice in an Uncertain World*. San Diego: Harcourt Brace Jovanovich.

Dembo, Ron. 1994. Hedging in markets that gap. In *Handbook of Derivatives and Synthetics*, edited by Robert A. Klein and Jess Lederman. Chicago: Probus.

Demeterfli, Kresimir, Emanuel Derman, Michael Kamal, and Joseph Zou. 1999. Guide to variance swaps. *Risk* 6:54–59.

Derman, Emanuel. 1999. Regimes of volatility. *Risk* 4:55–59.

———. 2001. Markets and models. *Risk* 7:48–50.

Derman, Emanuel, and Joseph Zou. 2001. A fair value for the skew. *Risk* 1:111–114.

Derman, Emanuel, and Iraj Kani. 1994. Riding on a smile. *Risk* 2:32–39.

———. 1998. Stochastic implied trees. *International Journal of Theoretical and Applied Finance* 1, no. 1:61–110.

Derman, Emanuel, Deniz Ergener, and Iraj Kani. 1995. Static options replication. *Journal of Derivatives* 2, no. 4:78–95.

Diebold, Francis, Til Schuermann, and John Stroughair. 2000. Pitfalls and opportunities in the use of extreme value theory in risk management. In *Extremes and Integrated Risk Management*, edited by Paul Embrechts. London: Risk Books.

Dixit, Avinash, and Robert Pindyck. 1994. *Investment Under Uncertainty*. Princeton: Princeton University Press.

Dowd, Kevin. 1998. *Beyond Value at Risk*. Hoboken, NJ: Wiley.

———. 2002. *Measuring Market Risk*. Hoboken, NJ: Wiley.

Dwyer, Paula. 1996. Sumitomo's descent into the abyss. *Business Week* (July 1).

Eichenwald, Kurt. 1995. *Serpent on the Rock*. New York: HarperBusiness.

Elden, Lars, and Linde Wittmeyer-Koch. 1990. *Numerical Analysis*. Boston: Academic Press.

Embrechts, Paul. 2000. Extreme value theory: Potential and limitations as an integrated risk management tool. *Derivatives Use, Trading, and Regulation* 6:449–456.

Falloon, William. 1998. The devil in the documentation. *Risk* 11:32–35.

Fay, Stephen. 1996. *The Collapse of Barings*. London: Richard Cohen Books.

French, Simon. 1986. *Decision Theory*. Chichester: Ellis Horwood.

Gillen, David, Yoolin Lee, and Bill Austin. 1999. J. P. Morgan's Korean debacle. *Bloomberg* 3:24–30.

Group of Thirty. 1993. Global derivatives study group: practices and principles.

Gumerlock, Robert. 1999. The future of risk. *Euromoney* 6:112–114.

Gupta, Ajay. 1997. On neutral ground. *Risk* 7:37–41.

Gupton, Greg, Christopher Finger, and Mickey Bhatia. 1997. Creditmetrics™ —technical document. www.defaultrisk.com/pp_model_20.htm.

Hansell, Saul. 1997. Joseph Jett: A scoundrel or a scapegoat? *New York Times*, 6 April.

Haug, Espen. 1998. *The Complete Guide to Option Pricing Formulas*. New York: McGraw-Hill.

Henderson, Schuyler. 1998. Credit derivatives: Selected documentation issues. *Journal of International Banking and Financial Law* 9.

Heston, Steven. 1993. A closed-form solution for options with stochastic volatility. *Review of Financial Studies* 6, no. 2:327–343.

Hoffman, Douglas. 2002. *Managing Operational Risk*. Hoboken, NJ: Wiley.

Holland, Kelley, and Linda Himelstein. 1995. The Banker's Trust tapes. *Business Week* (October 16).

Hull, John. 2000. *Options, Futures, and Other Derivatives*. 4th ed. Upper Saddle River, NJ: Prentice Hall.

———. 2002. *Options, Futures, and Other Derivatives*. 5th ed. Upper Saddle River, NJ: Prentice Hall.

Hull, John, and Allen White. 1994. Numerical procedures for implementing term structure models II: two-factor models. *Journal of Derivatives* 2, no. 2:37–48.

Hull, John, and Wulin Suo. 2001. A methodology for assessing model risk and its application to the implied volatility function model. www.rotman.utoronto.ca/~hull/DownloadablePublications/.

Jackwerth, Jens, and Mark Rubinstein. 1996. Recovering probability distributions from option prices. *Journal of Finance* 51, no. 5:1611–1631.

Jameson, Rob. 1998A. Operational risk: getting the measure of the beast. *Risk* 11:38–41.

———. 1998B. Operational risk: playing the name game. *Risk* 10:38–42.

Jarrow, Robert, ans Stuart Turnbull. 1999. *Derivative Securities*. Cincinnatti, OH: South-Western College Pub.

Jett, Joseph, with Sabra Chartrand. 1999. *Black and White on Wall Street*. New York: William Morrow.

Jorion, Philippe. 2001. *Value at Risk*. 2nd ed. New York: McGraw-Hill.

Kagel, J. H., and Alvin Roth. 1995. *Handbook of Experimental Economics*. Princeton: Princeton University Press.

Khuong-Huu, Philippe. 1999. Swaptions on a smile. *Risk* 8:107–111.

King, Jack. 2001. *Operational Risk*. Hoboken, NJ: Wiley.

Kooi, Mari. 1996. Analyzing Sumitomo. http://risk.ifci.ch/134800.htm.

Kotowitz, Y. 1989. Moral hazard. In *The New Palgrave: Allocation, Information, and Markets*, edited by John Eatwell, Murray Milgate, and Peter Newman. New York: Norton.

Lee, Roger. 2001. Local volatilities under stochastic volatility. *International Journal of Theoretical and Applied Finance* 4:45–89.

Leeson, Nick, with Edward Whitley. 1996. *Rogue Trader*. Boston: Little, Brown.

Lindley, D. V. 1985. *Making Decisions*. 2nd ed. Hoboken, NJ: Wiley.

Litterman, Robert. 1997A. Hot spots and hedges, part 1. *Risk* 3:42-45.

———. 1997B. Hot spots and hedges, part 2. *Risk* 5:38-42.

Litterman, Robert, and Jose Scheinkman. 1988. Common factors affecting bond returns. *Journal of Fixed Income* 1, no. 1:54–61.

Lowenstein, Roger. 2000. *When Genius Failed*. New York: Random House.

Ludwig, Eugene. 2002. Report on Allied Irish Bank. http://www.sunspot.net/business/bal-allfirst,0,4619625.special?coll=bal-business-indepth.

Madan, Dilip, Peter Carr, and Eric Chang. 1998. The variance gamma process and option pricing. www.math.nyu.edu/research/carrp/.

Malcolm, Fraser, Pawan Sharma, and Joseph Tanega. 1999. _Derivatives: Optimal Risk Control_. London: Prentice Hall.

Matytsin, Andrew. 1999. Modeling volatility and volatility derivatives. www.math.columbia.edu/~smirnov/Matytsin.pdf.

Mayer, Martin. 1995. Joe Jett: Did the computer make him do it? _Institutional Investor_ 3:7–11.

———. 1997. _The Bankers: The Next Generation_. New York: Truman Talley Books.

McKay, Peter. 1999. Merrill Lynch to pay fines of $25 million for scandal. _Dow Jones Newswires_ (July 1).

McNeil, Alexander. 2000. Extreme value theory for risk managers. In _Extremes and Integrated Risk Management_, edited by Paul Embrechts. London: Risk Books.

Mello, Antonio, and John Parsons. 1995. Maturity structure of a hedge matters. _Journal of Applied Corporate Finance_ (spring): 106–120.

Moody's. 2000. Bank loan loss given default. http://www.defaultrisk.com/pp_recov_16.htm.

———. 2002. Default & recovery rates of corporate bond issuers. http://www.defaultrisk.com/pp_other_16.htm.

Neuberger, Anthony. 1996. The log contract and other power options. In _The Handbook of Exotic Options_, edited by Israel Nelken. Chicago: Irwin.

Norris, Floyd, and Kurt Eichenwald. 2002. Fuzzy rules of accounting and Enron. _New York Times_, 30 January.

O'Brien, Timothy L. 1999. Taking the danger out of risk. _New York Times_, 28 January.

O'Kane, Dominic, and Robert McAdie. 2001. Trading the default swap basis. _Risk_ 9, Lehman Brothers-sponsored article.

Pan, George. 2001. Equity to credit pricing. _Risk_ 11:99–102.

Perold, Andre. 1998. Capital allocation in financial firms. Harvard Business School working paper.

———. 1999A. Harvard Business School Case Study (9-200-007) of Long-Term Capital Management (A).

———. 1999B. Harvard Business School Case Study (9-200-009) of Long-Term Capital Management (C).

Raiffa, Howard. 1970. _Decision Analysis_. Reading, MA: Addison-Wesley.

Rawnsley, Judith. 1995. _Total Risk_. New York: HarperCollins.

Rebonato, Riccardo. 1998. _Interest-Rate Options Models_. 2nd ed. Hoboken, NJ: Wiley.

————. 1999. *Volatility and Correlation*. Hoboken, NJ: Wiley.

————. 2001. Model risk. *Risk* 3:87–90.

Reiner, Eric. 1992. Quanto mechanics. *Risk* 3:59–63.

Risk Management Association. 2000. *Credit Risk Capital for Retail Products*.

Rubinstein, Reuven. 1981. *Simulation and the Monte Carlo Method*. Hoboken, NJ: Wiley.

Saunders, Anthony, and Linda Allen. 2002. *Credit Risk Measurement*. Hoboken, NJ: Wiley.

Schutz, Dirk. 2000. *The Fall of UBS*. New York: Pyramid Media Group.

Shaw, Julian. 1997. Beyond VaR and stress testing. In *VaR—Understanding and Applying Value-at-Risk*. London: Risk Publications.

Shirreff, David. 1998. Another fine mess at UBS. *Euromoney* 11:41–43.

————. 2000. Lessons from the collapse of hedge fund, Long-Term Capital Management. http://risk.ifci.ch/146480.htm.

Sifakis, Carl. 1982. *Encyclopedia of American Crime*. New York: Facts on File.

Smithson, Charles. 2000. What's new in the options markets? *Risk* 5:54–55.

Standard & Poor's. 1996. April 1 credit week.

Stigum, Marcia. 1989. *The Repo and Reverse Markets*. Homewood, IL: Dow Jones-Irwin.

Taleb, Nassim. 1997. *Dynamic Hedging*. Hoboken, NJ: Wiley.

Thaler, Richard. 1992. *The Winner's Curse*. New York: Free Press.

————. 1993. *Advances in Behavioral Finance*. New York: Russell Sage Foundation.

Tuckman, Bruce. 1996. *Fixed Income Securities*. 1st ed. Hoboken, NJ: Wiley.

————. 2002. *Fixed Income Securities*. 2nd ed. Hoboken, NJ: Wiley.

Varian, Hal. 1987. The arbitrage principle in financial economics. *The Journal of Economic Perspectives* 1, no. 2:55–72.

Weiss, Gary. 1994. What Lynch left out. *Business Week* (August 22).

Whaley, Elizabeth, and Paul Wilmott. 1994. Hedge with an edge. *Risk* 10:82–85.

Williams, Jeffrey. 1986. *The Economic Function of Futures Markets*. Cambridge: Cambridge University Press.

Wilson, Charles. 1989. Adverse selection. In *The New Palgrave: Allocation, Information, and Markets*, edited by John Eatwell, Murray Milgate, and Peter Newman. New York: Norton.

Wilson, Thomas. 1998. Value at risk. In *Risk Management and Analysis*. Vol. 1, edited by Carol Alexander. Hoboken, NJ: Wiley, 61–124.

Winters, Bill. 1999. Wrong-way exposure. *Risk* 7:52–55.

about the CD-ROM

INTRODUCTION

The files on the enclosed CD-ROM are saved in Microsoft Excel 97, Microsoft Word for Windows 97, and Adobe Acrobat Reader. In order to use the files, you will need to have spreadsheet software capable of reading Microsoft Excel 97 files, word processing software capable of reading Microsoft Word 97 files, and Adobe Acrobat Reader 5.0.

SYSTEM REQUIREMENTS

- IBM PC or compatible computer
- CD-ROM drive
- Windows 95 or later
- *Microsoft Word for Windows 97 or later or other word processing software capable of reading Microsoft Word for Windows 97 files.
- **Microsoft Excel 97 or later or other spreadsheet software capable of reading Microsoft Excel 97 files.
- ***Adobe Acrobat Reader 5.0 or later.

*For users who do not have Microsoft Word for Windows 97 on their computers you can download the free viewer from the Microsoft web site. The URL to the viewer is:
http://office.microsoft.com/downloads/9798/wdvw9716.aspx

**For users who do not have Microsoft Excel on their computers you can download the free viewer from the Microsoft web site. The URL to the viewer is:
http://office.microsoft.com/Downloads/2000/xlviewer.aspx

Use of the program with an earlier version of Microsoft Excel or other spreadsheet software might result in some formatting and display anomalies that we cannot support.

The Microsoft Excel 97/2000 Viewer is recommended for use with a stand-alone computer that does not have Microsoft Excel installed. This product allows the user to open and view Excel 97 and Excel 2000 spreadsheet files. The viewer is not suitable for use on a server.

***The paper on Risk Management Using Quasi-static Hedging is provided in Adobe Acrobat (.PDF) format and requires Acrobat Reader 5.0 or later in order for you to open and view the file. If you do not have Acrobat Reader already installed on your computer, you can download the Acrobat Reader for free from Adobe's web site http://www.adobe.com/acrofamily/.

USING THE FILES

Loading Files

To use the files, launch your spreadsheet or word processing software. Select **File, Open** from the pull-down menu. Select the appropriate drive and directory. A list of files should appear. If you do not see a list of files in the directory, you need to select **Word Document** (*.doc) or **Microsoft Excel Files** (*.xls) under **Files of Type**. Double click on the file you want to open. Use the file according to your needs.

Printing Files

If you want to print the files, select **File, Print** from the pull-down menu.

Saving Files

When you have finished editing a file, you should save it in a new directory on your C:/ drive by selecting **File, Save As** from the pull-down menu.

USER ASSISTANCE

If you need assistance with installation or if you have a damaged disk, please contact Wiley Technical Support at:
Phone: 201-748-6753
Fax: 201-748-6450 (Attention: Wiley Technical Support)
URL: www.wiley.com/techsupport

To place additional orders or to request information about other Wiley products, please call (800) 225-5945.

index

Note: Boldface numbers indicate definitions; italic numbers indicate illustrations; italic *t* indicates a table.